BUILDING KNOWLEDGE

NICK HAYNES · CLIVE B. FENTON

BUILDING
KNOWLEDGE

An Architectural History
of the University of Edinburgh

Historic Environment Scotland
in association with the University of Edinburgh
EDINBURGH · MMXVII

Historic Environment Scotland
Longmore House, Salisbury Place, Edinburgh EH9 1SH
Telephone + 44 (0) 131 668 8600
Scottish Charity SC045925

British Library Cataloguing-in-Publication Data.
A catalogue record for this book is available
from the British Library.

ISBN 978 1 84917 246 2

Designed and typeset in Fleischman by Dalrymple
Printed in Wales on Perigord 150gsm by Gomer Press

Front jacket illustration: Old College quad, University of
Edinburgh, photographed by Neale Smith

Frontispiece: Atrium of the Scottish Centre for
Regenerative Medicine, photographed by Andrew Lee

Back jacket illustration: Entrance Hall of the
Royal (Dick) School of Veterinary Studies,
photographed by Paul Zanre

THE UNIVERSITY *of* EDINBURGH

A NOTE ON THE STRUCTURE OF THE BOOK

The book is arranged largely in chronological order,
focusing on the main teaching and residential
buildings, rather than providing comprehensive
coverage of all buildings.

The first three chapters chart the development of
the Tounis Colledge and the construction of what
we now know as Old College.

The remaining chapters cover key periods in the
development of the rest of the estate beyond Old
College. They start with an introductory essay and
then proceed to more detailed consideration of sites
and significant buildings. The sites and buildings
are generally ordered from the city centre outwards.

Where historic buildings have been purchased
or acquired through merger, they are described in
the chapter covering the period when they entered
the University estate. For example, the 17th-century
Old Moray House is included in Chapter Nine,
which deals with the period 1985 to the present day,
because it became part of the University estate in
1998 on the merger of Moray House Institute of
Education with the University of Edinburgh.

When capitalised, City refers to the local
authority, town council, Edinburgh Corporation
(until 1975) and Edinburgh District Council
(1976–1996), or the present day City of
Edinburgh Council.

Contents

THE UNIVERSITY · OF EDINBURGH

Forewords

I get tremendous pleasure from contemplating most of our University buildings. Many are very beautiful. They tell us about the aspirations and values of the University at the time they were acquired or constructed. Entering the Old College quad in the early morning is an uplifting experience. That experience is enriched by historical knowledge. I know what the earlier buildings looked like. I now know about the iconography of the external classical decoration with the Playfair Library subtly signalling its importance relative to the apparently identical opposite façade of the Law School. I know that the magnificent iron gates were not added to keep the students in but instead to keep the Edinburgh police out. The controversial 1960s redevelopment of George Square can still divide opinion today. If I had a time machine I would certainly go back and plead with the University leadership of the time to find other routes to providing a modern library and smart new lecture theatres. However, if fifty years ago the University had quit the George Square area and moved in its entirety to the King's Buildings site then the city and the University community would have lost a great deal.

We have been working hard to be good custodians of our heritage. The condition and appearance of the Edinburgh Centre for Carbon Innovation, Moray House, New College and the Old College quad are a legitimate source of pride. I am very enthusiastic about the enhancements to the McEwan Hall and St Cecilia's Hall. We are treating these two treasures with the respect and love they deserve. We also know much more about the history of our older sites and I am very appreciative of the leadership Mary Bownes has shown in this area. I enjoy imagining medical professors scurrying between the Royal Infirmary and the anatomy lecture theatre in the Old College. In the last few years we have put up some really wonderful new buildings and I find excuses to go to and admire again the Informatics Forum and the Royal (Dick) Veterinary School at Easter Bush.

Attractive, well-designed and carefully stewarded buildings make our students, staff and the public happy. This book will add to the general understanding of our buildings and should add further to the pleasure that they offer. I encourage you to buy and read this book. Then climb to the top of Arthur's Seat and admire our University buildings scattered across the city.

PROFESSOR SIR TIMOTHY O'SHEA
*Principal and Vice-Chancellor of the
University of Edinburgh*

1 The University of Edinburgh crest
carved in stone outside the Informatics Building
Paul Zanre Photography

DONOR'S FOREWORD

In the late 18th century, the then Principal of the University, the great Enlightenment historian William Robertson, was ashamed to show his famous visitor from London, Dr Johnson, the 'mean buildings' of the College. He was referring to what is now Old College before the transformation wrought by two of the finest architects of the period, Robert Adam and latterly, William Henry Playfair. Thanks to the leadership and vision shown by successive Principals and University governors since Robertson's time, it is fair to say that today's Principal feels no such shame when he welcomes visitors to the magnificent surroundings of classical Old College or indeed to one of the more distinguished modern buildings elsewhere on the campus. This concern and care for the conservation and improvement of the University's physical estate has culminated in Principal Sir Timothy O'Shea's own benign and highly effective time in office, during which he and his colleague Professor Mary Bownes have reasserted the importance of the historical buildings not only to the University's tradition and identity as an ancient seat of learning but also in contributing a vital sense of pride and confidence in the institution as an academic powerhouse playing on a world stage.

As a history undergraduate in the mid-1970s I witnessed the final stages of what architectural historian and critic Gavin Stamp has called the 'wilful destruction' of the historical mid-18th century classical buildings of George Square to make way for the purpose-built tower blocks and library in the 1960s,

which still remain. While the 1960s buildings in George Square may be lauded by some today, it is my personal regret that I did not have the courage then to lie down in front of the bulldozers, although I, and many others at the time were conscious that a part of the University's history was being irretrievably lost. Happily we now live in more enlightened times and I am delighted to have this opportunity to atone for the passive acquiescence of my student days by supporting the University in its efforts to both document and conserve its architectural history and heritage. It is hoped that this book and wider sponsorship will contribute to a better appreciation of that past while also fostering a spirit of optimism about the future which will help shape the expansion and modernisation of the University's buildings to accommodate an aesthetically attractive, thriving and globally competitive organisation fit for the 21st century.

HUGH LANGMUIR
Alumnus and Benefactor of the University of Edinburgh

THE BUILDING KNOWLEDGE PROJECT

Since the University of Edinburgh was established as the Tounis Colledge, our key asset has been our community of staff and students. However, educating each generation of students from around the world and undertaking internationally groundbreaking research requires places to study and work. Our estate and buildings are a key part of our story.

Our buildings and their environment make a huge difference to how our staff and students feel, their quality of life and what they can achieve. As part of a thriving city we also have an impact on residents and visitors alike and part of our aim is to maintain that positive relationship between town and gown.

We have expanded beyond the confines of the city to reflect our growing numbers of students and disciplines. Each discipline has its own needs and this is reflected in the buildings. While some were built for us, others came as a result of mergers or were acquired and modified for our purposes.

This book reflects and traces these stories. We love our historical buildings and we are responsible for some of the city's most iconic landmarks. Taking good care of them and making them fit for purpose today requires sensitivity and vision.

It has been a huge privilege to work at the University for a short window in its history and to have worked alongside the authors and Historic Environment Scotland as well as all the other colleagues and organisations who have helped to deliver this book. We hope you will find it as fascinating as we have.

MARY BOWNES
Building Knowledge Project Leader

CHLOE KIPPEN
Building Knowledge Project Manager

HISTORIC ENVIRONMENT SCOTLAND

Our historic environment gives our communities a sense of place and a strong cultural identity. For international organisations like the University of Edinburgh it also promotes a positive image of Scotland across the world. The University has an impressive heritage and a significant part of that heritage is in its magnificent historical buildings. Under careful and sensitive stewardship the University has shown that some of our most important listed buildings can be adapted to meet new and changing needs and have a long and positive future ahead of them.

While this book was being written, Historic Environment Scotland worked with the University's Estates Department to review the listed and unlisted buildings across the estate. The University now has up-to-date listed building records, which provide comprehensive information about the special interest of its buildings.

By focusing on quality and innovation in recent commissions the University is also constructing what may well be the listed buildings of the future. The commitment to continuing the great tradition for exceptional architecture, begun when the University first employed the architect Robert Adam in the 18th century, is inspiring.

It has been a great pleasure to work in partnership with the University of Edinburgh, the authors and the many other people who have worked together to produce this beautiful and meticulously researched publication.

ELIZABETH MCCRONE
Head of Designations
Historic Environment Scotland

Chapter One

The First College Buildings 1582–1785

NICK HAYNES

When students began studying at the College of Edinburgh on 14 October 1583, they were entering the precincts of Scotland's fourth university, and the first to be established here after the upheavals of the Reformation in 1560. Although in many ways the University owed its existence to the fallout from these great religious tumults, it was emphatically not an ecclesiastical foundation. Unlike the 15th-century universities of St Andrews (1413), Glasgow (1451) and Aberdeen (1495), which were all founded by papal bulls (charters) promoted by bishops or archbishops, the University of Edinburgh derived its status from a secular charter, promoted by the town council and granted by King James VI in 1582.[1] There was to be no special jurisdiction for the staff and students at Edinburgh, as there was in the ecclesiastical foundations.

The patronage of the town council was critical to the nature and character of the early institution, from its funding and the appointment of staff, to the regulation of the students, the method of teaching, the curriculum, and the location and physical environment of the College. For the best part of 200 years the University was commonly known as the 'tounis colledge'. The town's influence was both a blessing and a curse. The council took a pride in the College, but decision-making, particularly on expenditure for buildings, was slow, subject to political in-fighting, and depended greatly on the interest and advocacy of an annually elected bailie (the magistrate who chaired the College committee). Private philanthropy was an early and necessary element in the development of the University's estate. It was not until the Universities (Scotland) Act of 1858 that the University of Edinburgh finally emerged as a completely self-governing institution.

The modern university has developed on the same site selected in the 16th century. Like many of the city's other great projects, the foundation of a university took a considerable length of time to come to fruition and attracted significant controversy.

By the second half of the 18th century, the University's decrepit estate had become something of an embarrassment. James Boswell recorded Principal William Robertson's standard joke about the buildings: 'The Principal said to Dr Johnson [Samuel Johnson] that he must give them the same epithet that a Jesuit did when showing a poor college abroad: "Hae miseriae nostrae" [These are our miseries].'[2] It was not always so. A number of the early buildings were structures of significance and prestige in their day, reflecting the practical requirements and ambitions of the University and the generosity of its benefactors.

2 Portrait of John Mylne (1611–1667), master mason, possibly by L. Schuneman. John Mylne came from a famous family of architects, stone masons and engineers. John himself was principal master mason to the Crown in Scotland by 1636.

National Galleries of Scotland, Edinburgh

TOWARDS THE FOUNDATION OF A UNIVERSITY 1556–1582

The circumstances leading up to the foundation of the University are complicated and obscure. Although the full facts of the matter are debated, there is some agreement amongst historians on two key issues: firstly that the origins of the University project lie in the mid-1550s; and secondly that throughout a quarter of a century of false starts, many of the principal supporters appear to have been Protestant lawyers from the circle of Robert Reid, Bishop of Orkney.[3] Although the pre-history of the University has been much rehearsed, it is worth repeating here in brief for the bearing it has on the story of the Old College site and buildings.

Edinburgh was well-established as the legislative, judicial and administrative capital of Scotland by the mid-16th century, but in ecclesiastical matters the parish kirk of St Giles in Edinburgh submitted to the higher authority of the archdiocese of St Andrews. In spite of the need for convenient local training for the capital's clergymen, lawyers and bureaucrats, there was little incentive for the bishops and archbishops (from 1472) of St Andrews to dilute their patronage, influence and resources by founding a rival academic institution in Edinburgh. In any case, the University of St Andrews, like those of Glasgow and Aberdeen, was on the point of collapse and in urgent need of resuscitation by the 1560s. As a result, many of Edinburgh's flourishing merchant and professional classes sent their sons abroad to finish their education at universities including Paris, Orléans, Poitiers, Bourges, Cologne, Leuven, Bologna, Padua and Oxford.

The Register of the Privy Seal of Scotland for 1556 records the first serious attempts by the French-influenced regency government of Mary, Queen of Scots, to address the problem of higher education in Edinburgh, granting a generous annual pension of £100 from the Treasurer to Master Alexander Sym to be the 'lectoure and reidar in the lawis or ony utheris sciences' to the Queen-Regent, Mary of Guise, and 'all other young men of fresche and queik ingynis'.[4] A similar instruction to the treasurer followed in June 1556 in respect of payments to Master Edward Henryson, who was to 'profess, teiche and reid within oure burgh of Edinburgh ane publict lessoun in the Lawis and ane uthir in Greik thrice in the week except the vacance fra Lammes to Martymes [from Lammas on 28 August to Martinmas on 28 November, which coincided with the recess of the Court of Session]'.[5] Like Sym, Henryson was not only a scholar, but also a practising lawyer and prominent Protestant, who had amassed a considerable fortune of £6,700 by the time of his death in 1585.[6] Henryson and Sym, along with Clement Litill and other early promoters of the University project, went on to become Commissaries of Edinburgh in the new civil courts established after the Reformation.[7] The Queen-Regent's public lectures were held in the recently built Magdalen Chapel in the Cowgate, for which the town treasurer made payments 'for making of an pulpet to Maister Alexander Sym' in 1556.[8]

Although there is no evidence of any intention to expand the public lectures into a more structured establishment, there was a French precedent for a royal secular foundation, discreetly sidestepping the vested interests of the church and the existing universities.

3 Plan of the first College buildings

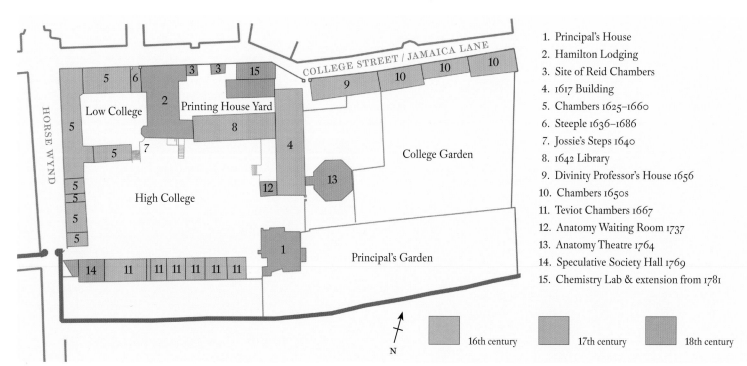

1. Principal's House
2. Hamilton Lodging
3. Site of Reid Chambers
4. 1617 Building
5. Chambers 1625–1660
6. Steeple 1636–1686
7. Jossie's Steps 1640
8. 1642 Library
9. Divinity Professor's House 1656
10. Chambers 1650s
11. Teviot Chambers 1667
12. Anatomy Waiting Room 1737
13. Anatomy Theatre 1764
14. Speculative Society Hall 1769
15. Chemistry Lab & extension from 1781

COLLEGE STREET / JAMAICA LANE

HORSE WYND

Low College

Printing House Yard

High College

College Garden

Principal's Garden

N

16th century   17th century   18th century

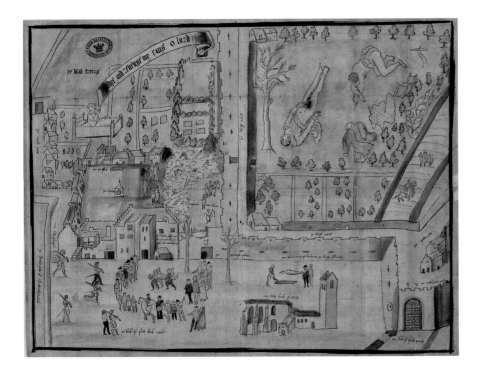

4 Kirk o'Field after the murder of Henry Stuart, Lord Darnley, 1567. This extraordinary 'crime scene' record was made for William Cecil, 1st Baron Burghley, Secretary of State to Queen Elizabeth I of England. It is the first known depiction of the site on which the University was to develop.
National Archives, Kew

The Collège de France in Paris had begun life without dedicated buildings for the 'lecteurs royaux', the five teachers of Greek, Hebrew and mathematics appointed personally by Francis I in 1530.[9] The Queen-Regent would certainly have known of the development of the Collège from her visit to France in 1550–1, and from her brother, Charles, Cardinal of Lorraine, who secured the services of the famed educational reformer, Peter Ramus, at the Collège in 1551.[10]

Robert Reid, Bishop of Orkney, was a further major player in the pre-Reformation attempts to improve the higher education opportunities in Edinburgh. Reid, a former Abbot of Kinloss, founding senator of the College of Justice in 1532 and Lord President of the Court of Session from 1543, was a significant patron of scholarship and supporter of the Catholic Queen-Regent.[11] He was responsible for the recruitment of the Piedmontese humanist scholar Giovanni Ferrerio to lecture on philosophy, classical literature and theology at Kinloss, and he also established a grammar school and a song school at Kirkwall. Ferrerio recommended Edward Henryson to Reid as a Latin and Greek scholar in 1555.[12] Nothing is known of Reid's intentions towards the foundation of a college in Edinburgh during his lifetime, but under his will of 1557 Reid bequeathed 8,000 merks to buy the Cowgate tenement of Sir John Ramsay 'for to big ane college, in the quhilk wes appontit to be thre scolis, ane thereof for the bairnis in grammar, ane uther for thame that leirnis poetre and oratore, and chalmeris to the Regentis, with ane hall and utheris houssis necessar; the thrid scole for the techeing of the civile and canon lawis […]' [to build a college, in which there were to be three schools, a grammar school

for children another school for those learning poetry and oratory, and rooms for the regents, with a hall and other necessary houses; and a third school for teaching civil and canon law].[13]

Reid died unexpectedly in 1558 on an ambassadorial visit to France in preparation for the marriage of the Dauphin Francis to Mary, Queen of Scots, leaving his executors and procurators to attempt to recover a 'wadset', or mortgage, of 4,000 merks granted by Reid over disputed lands in Strathnaver, Sutherland. The difficulties of recovering the money and the turmoil of the Reformation in 1559–60 buried Reid's worthy scheme for nearly two decades. However, only 4,000 merks of the money were eventually released when the town council took action against Reid's nephew, Walter, through an Act of the Privy Council in 1582.[14] This was to form the first private benefaction to the fledgling University of Edinburgh.

In spite of the intention of the *First Book of Discipline*, the first tract of the reformed church in Scotland, to renew the universities and establish liberal arts colleges in the principal towns, it had little practical effect on education. As Michael Lynch has shown convincingly, the complex factional politics of the church, town council and royal court in the 1560s placed the Protestant Reformation in Edinburgh on a knife edge: it was not inevitable that Protestantism would succeed.[15] The new Protestant order took firm hold only in the 1570s. Although there was general support for a college project from the various factions, the nature of the proposed institution, its siting and personnel became caught up in the national and local controversies and power struggles.

SEARCH FOR A SITE

The familiar double-sided comb pattern [fig.5] of Edinburgh's Old Town, with its broad High Street and narrow closes leading off at right angles, was laid out in about 1130. A parallel street, the Cowgate, developed to the south of the old King's Wall in the 15th century. By the mid-1500s the town had once again expanded to fill the land within the boundaries of a new town wall, known today as the Flodden Wall, to the south, east and west. The separate burgh of the Canongate prevented eastward development, the Nor' Loch and steep slopes of the High Street ridge hindered northern expansion, and the town council had no feudal superiority over the adjacent lands to the south and west. Even some lands within the walls belonged to the parish of St Cuthbert's. The main open spaces within the town walls were those along the southern stretch of the Flodden Wall belonging to the monastic houses of the Grey Friars and Black Friars and the collegiate church of St Mary-in-the-Fields, or 'Kirk o'Field'. The buildings of these suburban

sites had been damaged substantially by the Earl of Hertford's English forces in 1544 and 1547 during the 'Rough Wooing', and remained in a ruinous condition through lack of money for repairs. Further destruction of altars and images occurred under the Protestant Lords of the Congregation in 1558. In the last quarter of the 16th century and into the 17th century the pressures on lateral expansion of the town led to the extraordinary upward development of residential accommodation in towering tenements along the High Street and the steep closes leading off it.

It was only natural that the search for a site for the new university should seek to exploit the larger open spaces. Bishop Reid's will had envisaged the use of a tenement and yard in the Cowgate, but the availability of secularised land at the Kirk o'Field after the Reformation and the town's grant from Regent Moray of the old collegiate foundation of Trinity Kirk and Hospital (just outside the burgh on the site of what is now Waverley Station) in 1567 opened up further possibilities. The first attempt to acquire a site appears to have been in August 1562, when the town council appealed to Queen Mary to 'haue the place, kirk, chalmeris and houssis of the Kirk of Field to big ane scule' along with the annual revenues of the chaplainries and friaries to support the running costs.[16] In view of the construction of a new building for the High School to the east of the Kirk o'Field in 1555, it seems likely that the 'scule' refers to the proposed college. Mary's response was to require the council to make their own provisions for the building before she would grant a site. Determined to pursue the Kirk o'Field site [fig.4], the

town council then tried to purchase it for £1,000 from the titular provost of St Mary-in-the-Fields, William Pennycuik.[17] The negotiations dragged on into 1564. In order to pressurise the town council to conclude the purchase, Pennycuik started to sell the stonework of the old kirk.[18] Although a deal was ratified by the council, it failed to gain possession of the site and the university scheme seems to have fallen into abeyance. Certainly by the time of the infamous murder of the queen's husband, Henry Stuart, Lord Darnley, at the Kirk o'Field on 9 February 1567, the new provost in possession of the site was Robert Balfour. Balfour continued in the post until 1579, when parliament forfeited the lands for his alleged part in the murder of Darnley.

From 1568 to 1573 Edinburgh took centre stage in the Marian civil war that raged between the supporters of the deposed Queen Mary and the men who ruled in the name of her infant son James VI. The university scheme made no further progress in this troubled period. By 1578, when the king's party had triumphed and revived discussions centred on the establishment of a university, the site under consideration was that of the collegiate kirk and hospital of the Holy Trinity: '[T]he prouest, bailies and counsell ordanis Alexander Clerk, William Litle and Johne Johnestoun to convene vpon Setterday aftir none nixt with Mr Robert Pont and entir forther ressonyng with him tuiching the erectioun and fundatioun of the vniuerseteis in the Trinite College and report thair answer the nixt counsall day.'[19] The report of the negotiations does not survive, but discussions with Robert Pont continued throughout 1579 towards the foundation of 'ane college of theologe'.[20] Pont was

5 Bird's-eye view of Edinburgh by James Gordon of Rothiemay, 1647

National Library of Scotland, Edinburgh

the provost of Trinity College, minister of St Cuthbert's and a senator of the College of Justice. He was also one of the four talented reforming ministers who lived in an informal collegiate manner in the manse of St Giles. The others were James Lawson, John Durie and Walter Balanquhal. These men had a strong interest in improving higher education and were long recognised as influential in the founding of the University.[21] They also had close links with Andrew Melville, the theologian, reformer, outstanding scholar of his age and Principal of the University of Glasgow.

Mary of Gueldres had founded Trinity Hospital 'for the reception of poor and needy persons' in 1460, then further endowed a church of some magnificence in memory of her husband, James II[22] [fig.6]. The construction of the church and associated accommodation for the college of clergy proceeded under the master of works, John Halkerston. The collegiate buildings stood to the south of the kirk, and the hospital lay to the east, across the lane known as Leith Wynd.[23] Attempts to complete the church continued well into the 16th century, but work never progressed further than the choir and the transepts. The church was damaged during the Reformation riots in 1559 and by Mary of Guise's French auxiliaries in 1560. In the end, financial and political wrangling ended consideration of the Trinity site, and it was abandoned as a potential home for the new college. However, Trinity Kirk was to become the official place of worship for the scholars and regents between the 1590s and 1620 after they outgrew the accommodation set aside for them in the High Kirk of St Giles. A magnificent graduation ceremony, attended by the queen, Anne of Denmark, was held in the church in 1594, and a year later a dedicated college loft was

constructed at the east end.[24] This loft was expensively finished with a stone stair, two supporting columns and decorative paintwork in oils by Jon Warkman.[25]

William Litill, one of the town council's negotiators for the Trinity site and later provost of Edinburgh, was also the executor for his brother, Clement Litill.[26] Clement, who died in 1580, was a noted bibliophile and lawyer.[27] Under Clement's will, his collection of precious theological books was to be gifted to the 'kirk of Edinburgh to be usit and kepit be the said kirk to the use of the ministeris, elderis and decanes thairof'.[28] However, when William finally handed over the gift, it was to the town council for use by the kirk. The 268 books and a catalogue were sent to the manse of St Giles, where James Lawson had charge of them in a specially converted part of the attic.[29] All the books were stamped with the words: 'I AM GEVIN TO EDINBURGH & KIRK OF GOD BE MAISTER CLEMENT LITTIL, THAIR TO REMAN. 1580.' These books were to form the nucleus of the University library when they were transferred to the keeping of Robert Rollock [fig.7] in Hamilton Lodging in 1584.[30] The brothers' role in the establishment of the library is celebrated on the monument erected by their great-grandson in Greyfriars Kirkyard.

William Litill also proved instrumental in the final push to establish the University. A loan of 10,000 merks to James VI in 1681, to which Littil had contributed, appears to have been crucial in obtaining royal confirmation of Mary's gift of the chaplainries and friaries for the burgh to support the ministry, schools, and new ambitions of repairing schools and promoting letters and science. The royal charter expressly confirmed the Kirk o'Field site as a possession of the burgh and allowed the town council to found colleges. On 14 April 1582 a large

6 Trinity College Chapel and Hospital with Calton Hill in the background by David Octavius Hill and Robert Adamson, about 1843–8

University of Edinburgh [EU 1073]

7 Robert Rollock, first Principal of the University by unknown artist

University of Edinburgh Art Collections [EU 0011]

deputation from the town council travelled to Stirling to obtain the king's signature on the College charter of confirmation.[31]

At the insistence of James Lawson, minister of St Giles, the town council courted Robert Rollock, a philosopher at St Andrews, as their first regent.[32] The appointment was a great success, drawing in students and establishing a sound basis on which to grow. The council promoted Rollock to be the first Principal of the College in 1585, a position that he was to hold for life.

KIRK O'FIELD BEFORE THE COLLEGE

Kirk o'Field was renowned as 'a place of good Air'.[33] The official name of the kirk, St Mary-in-the-Fields, derived from its location outside the old town wall, although subsequent rebuilding of the wall in the 15th century, and its refortification as the Flodden Wall in the early 16th century, brought the site within the protection of the town. The kirk was reputedly founded in the 13th century by the Austin Friars of Holyrood under the patronage of Alexander II and later became a prestigious collegiate institution. The college comprised a non-monastic, self-regulating community of clergy. As the college expanded in the early 16th century, new accommodation was provided for the provost, precentor (ceremonial officer), prebendaries (a type of canon whose stipend was funded by specific revenues attached to the church) and other priests.[34] The Augustinian friars who founded the college were associated with teaching, and there was certainly a strong connection between the Kirk o'Field and the High School.[35] The 1567 depiction of the Darnley murder scene [figs 4, 8, 12] shows the church in an incomplete and ruinous state and a quadrangle of houses to the east, the largest of which belonged to the provost.[36] Several of the prebendaries' houses appear to have been lost in the explosion that preceded Darnley's death.

The old steeple was taken down by Michael Hunter in 1616, and in about 1628 or 1629 the last remnants of the old kirk were removed when the upper court of the College was 'cast into three level walks' (terraced), and some quarrying of the site also took place.[37] The 2010 excavations in Old College quad revealed numerous graves from the surrounding kirkyard, but no remnants of the kirk itself were discovered.[38] A fragment of what is thought to be one of the prebendaries' houses was uncovered in the south-east corner of the quad.[39]

Some sense of the buildings inherited on the Kirk o'Field site and the work undertaken to make them fit for the purposes of the College can be gained from several sources including the town council minutes, the town treasurer's accounts, the extraordinary 'crime scene' depiction of the site following Darnley's murder in 1567 and an early description of about 1646 by Thomas Craufurd, Professor of Philosophy and Mathematics:

It consisted then of two parts, divided by ane narrow lane goeing from the Cowgate, on the west syde of Mr Alexander Guthrie's yards; thorow the place where the common-hall now stands; and from thence towards the west, where now the back gate of the Colledge leadeth to the Potter-row Port. On the north-west of this lane was the great lodging where now are the schools of the private classes. This was the lodging of the Duke of Chatteleraut, Earle of Aron, and, by the forfeiture of the Hamiltons, disponed to some Courtiers, and by them to the Magistrats of Edinburgh. On the east and south side of this land, was the yarde, chambers, and lodging, and kirk, belonging to the collegial provestry and prebendaries of the Kirk-a-field, commonly called Templum et Praefectura Sanctae Mariae in Campis, *because that, when the Cowgate was an logch, it was in stead of the wall of the town. But afterwards, the religious houses of the Blackfryars, Kirk-a-field, and Greyfriars, thought it more safe for them to have the town-wall drawn about without them; and so, drying the Cowgate logch, they enlarged the town on the south syde. This Kirk-a-field stood along towards the east from the Potter-row Port, having ane garden on the south, betwixt it and the present town-wall. On the east end thereof was the lodging of the Provest, where now the Principal of the Colledge hath his rooms; and to the east from thence, (within the present Colledge yeard), were the prebendaries chambers, blown up with fire at the murther of King Henry; and to this religious convent belonged all the Colledge yards.*[40]

Preparations for opening the new university centred on works to Hamilton Lodging. The earliest new buildings were fourteen 'chambers', known as the Reid Chambers, which were built adjoining the north 'jamb' of Hamilton Lodging along the north wall of the site in 1583. The town council ordained that students from outside the city should be charged 40 shillings each and sleep two to a bed unless they paid extra.[41] Clearly these were intended as residential accommodation,

8 Detail of the ruined Kirk o'Field from the murder scene of Lord Darnley

National Archives, Kew

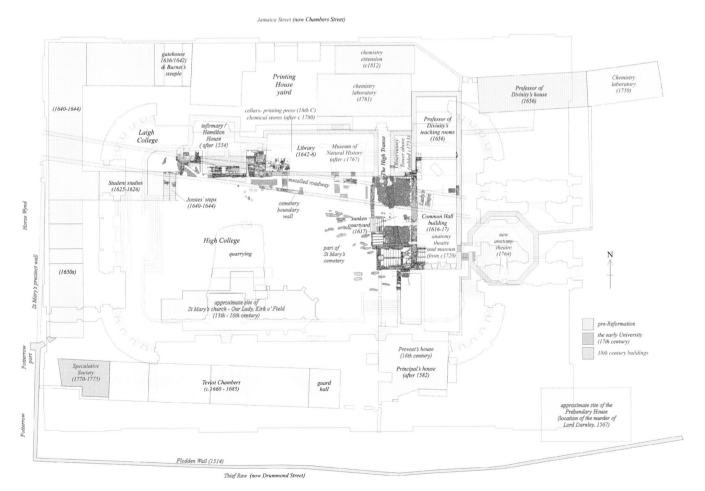

the College, but the number of students had increased to somewhere between 150 and 170 students. It seems clear that the residential aspect of the College started to dwindle at an early date and was not revived.

HAMILTON LODGING

Hamilton Lodging, also known as 'the great lodging' or 'the Duke's Lodging', was the former townhouse of James Hamilton, duc de Châtellerault and 2nd Earl of Arran, who was the half-brother and first regent to Mary, Queen of Scots. It appears to have been a Renaissance mansion of some significance. The grounds stood to the north of the Kirk o'Field, where the Chambers Street range of Old College is now, and were separated from the kirk and its kirkyard by a narrow lane.[44]

In about 1551, at the height of his power as 'ane noble and mychtie prince', Hamilton had acquired the old hospital, or almshouse, of the Kirk o'Field on account of its ruinous condition in the wake of the Earl of Hertford's 'Rough Wooing'.[45] He may also have purchased an adjacent early site of the High School.[46] Hamilton and his wife, Margaret Douglas, immediately set about laying out a garden and building the new house. As there are no known reliable depictions of the building, evidence for its appearance and arrangement are to be found in documentary sources and discoveries made by Addyman Archaeology during excavations in Old College quad in

9 Elevated view of Old College from the west during archaeology dig, 2010

HES [DP 086333]

10 Plan of the main archaeological finds, 2010

Addyman Archaeology

but quite quickly they were appropriated for other purposes, including a classroom for the humanity regent and living quarters for the College porter and even external tenants.[42] Further properties were purchased in 1587, possibly for the purpose of teaching Divinity postgraduates, including houses belonging to the lawyer James Richie in the Kirk o'Field and Wynd.[43] By the 1590s the Reid Chambers were still the only lodgings in

2010.[47] These archaeological investigations uncovered the basement level of the south-west and south-east corners of the house and the footings of a turnpike stair. Post-excavation analysis is ongoing, and undoubtedly will provide a better understanding of the evolution of the building.

The designer of Hamilton Lodging is not known, but he was almost certainly a figure of high capability working in royal circles. Beneath an entry of £2,333 for 'the furnising of my lorde governoures [Hamilton's] hous' the Lord High Treasurer's accounts for 1552–3 reveal £2,303 was paid to John Scrymgeour of the Myres (Fife), 'Maister of Warke to my lorde governoure to be spendit upoun the warkis to be the space of this compte'.[48] These sums may relate to Hamilton's new house in Edinburgh, but could equally refer to other Hamilton properties. Scrymgeour was Master of Works to the Crown of Scotland, in charge of royal building works under James V and Mary of Guise, including Holyroodhouse and Falkland Palace. A laird by birth, Scrymgeour possibly acted as architect for the royal works, but it is more likely he was the 'devyser', or administrator, overseeing the contracts and managing a master mason and teams of craftsmen.

It is not clear how much of the old hospital buildings survived when James and Margaret Hamilton began their new house. The archaeological evidence suggests that at least two major phases of construction are represented in the south-west and south-east corners of the house.[49] The earlier phase probably belongs to the medieval hospital, while the later work may belong to Hamilton, or, less likely, to the University. The house consisted of a 75 foot long by 40 foot wide north–south gabled range with two semi-octagonal stair-towers projecting from the western elevation and two short

wings, or 'jambs' projecting at either end of the east front.[50] The northern stair appears to have been known as the 'Bell-stair'.[51]

The earliest phase of construction in the south-west room included a large arched chimney opening and a stone slop-sink, suggesting that it was built as a kitchen for the hospital.[52] These features were covered up by the insertion of a stone-vaulted room within the earlier kitchen, probably as part of Hamilton's scheme. Other contemporary archaeological remains show the base of a turnpike stair and a passage that ran along the west side of the building.[53] Documentary evidence of the occupation by the College reveals that the house had three student chambers and lower and upper halls, which were used for teaching, exams and graduations.[54] In 1589 a further turnpike stair was proposed to provide access to the 'galry'.[55] Galleries were typical features of high-status houses in the 17th century. They were often located at the top of the house to command the best views, and could serve a number of purposes including communication, space for exercise, and a place to hang family portraits. Writing in the 1640s Craufurd referred to both a lower and an upper gallery, which seem to have been located at the southern end of the building.[56]

Taking into account the magnificence of at least one of Hamilton's other architectural creations, the surviving part of the palace at Kinneil in West Lothian, the Kirk o'Field lodging is likely to have been decorated and finished in sumptuous style [fig.11].[57] Hamilton also embellished several other properties, including Hamilton Palace and Brodick Castle on Arran. Hamilton's works to his lodging were completed in 1552, when four locks were ordered for the yard yetts (gates) and the doors to two turnpike stairs.[58]

11 Arbour Room, Kinneil House, Bo'ness, decorated for James Hamilton, duc de Châtellerault and 2nd Earl of Arran
Nick Haynes

12 Detail of the Provost of the Kirk o'Field's House (later converted as the Principal's House) shown in the Darnley murder scene of 1567
National Archives, Kew

Remains were also discovered relating to the external staircase, which was added by John Jossie in about 1640.[59] John Mylne was responsible for a major reordering of the building in 1647–8.[60] At this time, 'ane old hinging stair hinging out on the north syde of the old hous', was to be removed.

On Hamilton's fall from power and the forfeiture of his properties to the crown in August 1571, the house was given to the king's valet, Sir John Gib of Knock, and sold by him to the town council for £1,000. The town's claim was disputed by Hamilton's descendants, and was to cost the town a further £3,000 in settlement in 1613.[61]

PRINCIPAL'S HOUSE

Writing in 1727, the English trader, writer, journalist, pamphleteer and spy, Daniel Defoe, described the Principal's 'handsome Dwelling-house and Garden in the College'.[62] The west-facing building was located at the south-eastern corner of the College buildings (under the east end of what is now the Playfair Library), and had a long, narrow garden stretching eastwards along the inside of the Flodden Wall.

Before its demolition in the 1790s the Principal's house comprised some of the oldest fabric in the College precincts. Craufurd's 1646 history of the College placed the Principal's chambers in the old lodging of the provost of the Kirk o'Field, which is depicted as the main intact building in the 1567 image of the Darnley murder scene [fig.12]. From this image, the crowstepped L-plan lodging appears to have been a building of some size and significance, comprising two storeys and attic / gallery with a rectangular stairtower in the angle of the two wings. It was built in about 1512 to replace an earlier structure on a different site.[63] The last provost, John Gib, feued the house to James VI's comptroller clerk, John Fenton, who continued to live in the house well after the College's formal acquisition of the property in 1583.

As late as the 1640s the building was still known as 'Fenton's House', even though it had long been occupied as student chambers and then by the College Principals.[64] Principal John Adamson had to vacate the house in 1648 on account of its ruinous condition.[65] At the very least, substantial repairs, if not complete reconstruction, took place in that year.[66] In 1664 the town council tasked John Mylne with converting an existing room to a kitchen and adding a new two-chamber wing.[67] A further north-east jamb was constructed for Principal Gilbert Rule in 1698.

BUILDING THE COLLEGE 1583–1620

One of the earliest tasks of the town council in respect of the 'colledge laitlie founded' was to pursue through the Privy Council the sum bequeathed by Bishop Reid. More finance was required, and this was eventually to come from several sources including the grant of the lands and revenues of the parsonage and vicarage of Currie.

The town council minutes of 26 April 1583 record the appointment of Bailie Andrew Sclater, merchant, and David Kinloch, baxter (baker), as masters of work for the 'bigging of wallis' at the new College, supervising the workmen and paying their weekly wages.[68] Sclater and Kinloch were both prominent Protestant radicals and rebels against Queen Mary.[69] Their principal tasks appear to have been the conversion of Hamilton Lodging, the addition of a range containing fourteen 'chambers' or 'studeis', and construction of an enclosing wall around the whole site. The town council minutes of 3 January 1583 record that Bailie Andrew Sclater, 'maister of the colledge wark', had overspent on the slating of the 'studeis nocht complet'.[70] Later that year, he was instructed to 'caus sett up the students beds in the chambers quhilk payis maill, and siclyke to by the skellett bell to the said College [...]'.[71]

After the Union of the Crowns in 1603 the Scottish court followed James VI to London for his coronation as James I of England and Ireland. Both king and court stayed on in England permanently, leaving a lord high commissioner, the remaining nobility and gentry, and

13 Sketch of Principal Robertson's house, Old College by unknown artist, about 1840

HES [Revd John Sime Collection: DP 026589]

14 King James VI and I (1566–1625). This engraved equestrian portrait of King James VI and I is an illustration in William Drummond's *Forth Feasting: A Panegyricke to the King's Most Excellent Majestie* (1617), a poem written to celebrate the king's visit to Scotland in that year.

University of Edinburgh [EU 0022493]

the civic and church authorities to jostle for influence in the government of Scotland and the dispersal of all-important patronage. Perhaps surprisingly, in the absence of the court, the early years of the 17th century were relatively stable and prosperous for Edinburgh. The year 1617 was significant in the city as James VI's 'salmonlyke instinct' brought him on his sole return to the country and town of his birth [fig.14].[72] For more than a year before the visit a series of warrants, directions and proclamations directed the repair of the royal palaces and the sprucing up of Edinburgh's streets and accommodation for the enormous royal retinue of 5,000 men.[73]

The College was extremely keen to use the occasion of the royal visit to promote itself and particularly the teaching of divinity, which was under threat from the rival St Mary's College in St Andrews. There may have been some hope of attracting funding or gifts of books from the king, who had founded and promised money for the St Mary's library in 1612. On James VI's arrival in Edinburgh on 16 May 1617 the College dispatched the lawyer Patrick Nisbet to make a speech of welcome and to present him with a sumptuously bound volume of verses in Latin and Greek by various staff and supporters. The speeches, theses and poems from the entire Scottish visit were gathered together by Principal John Adamson and published under the title *The Muses Welcome*.[74] From Craufurd's account, the College of Edinburgh clearly intended to encourage the king to attend a public philosophy disputation in the new common hall.[75] In the end, the king summoned the masters of the College to Stirling, where the disputation eventually took place on 29 July. Such was the success of the event that the king formally granted the name 'King James his Colledge' and promised a 'godbairne [god-father's] gift'.[76] Although the king's gift was never made, his endorsement of the College does seem to have encouraged generosity in others, such as Isabele Alan and Hugh Wight, who contributed towards the

teaching of divinity and the College fabric. The new name, King James' College, had some currency over the next century and a half, but the institution was known more commonly as the College of Edinburgh or the Tounis Colledge.

In the year of the king's visit to Edinburgh the College produced forty-six graduates, a record number for any of the Scottish universities at that period. The College was proving popular with the professionals and merchants of the town for its provision of cheap and local higher education for their sons. Before 1640 there were four regents of philosophy, one professor of humanity and a Professor of Divinity in addition to the Principal.[77] Students could live at home and there was no need for expensive travel and accommodation. The non-residential aspect of the College shaped the extent and nature of its estate until the great expansion of the University in the 20th century.

1617 BUILDING

Although this building was variously called the 'greit school and hous', Common Hall, Bibliothek, Librarie, High Library or Old Library, the term '1617 Building' is used throughout this text to distinguish it from later library buildings. The northern end of the building was demolished in about 1818 and the rest propped up as a temporary measure before it was finally flattened in 1827. Wall footings and fragments of the building were discovered during the archaeological investigation of the Old College quad in 2010.[78] Rubble from the demolition was used to infill the remaining wall footings.

Craufurd records that in May 1614 sixteen members of the town council, the town's five ministers and three advocate-assessors carried out a visitation of the College. The visitors found the Magistrand (final-year students for the Master of Arts degree) and Bajan (first-year students) halls too cramped for the whole College to assemble, so they resolved on 'amplifieing of the fabrick'.[79] The following year the town council received

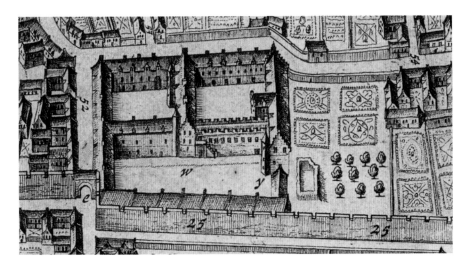

17 Detail of the College from bird's-eye view of Edinburgh by James Gordon of Rothiemay, 1647

National Library of Scotland, Edinburgh

18 Detail of *Edinburgh from the South East* by Thomas Sandby, about 1748–64, coloured to indicate the College buildings.
Orange: Principal's house
Brown: chambers
Blue: 1617 Building
Purple: Hamilton Lodging
Green: steeple

National Galleries of Scotland, Edinburgh

3,000 merks in church land leases from Walter Scott, 2nd Baron Scott of Buccleuch, which they dedicated to the repair of the halls in Hamilton Lodging and to the construction of a 'commoune schoole and librarie' for the College.[80]

The new structure was probably designed by the master mason John Taillefer (Telfer), who led teams of eight to eleven masons on the project. He was likely the same mason responsible for the 'Telfer Wall', an extension of the Flodden Wall around the city in 1628–36. The 1617 Building was to be the first purpose-built communal building of the University, 30 feet wide by 120 feet long and two and a half storeys in height, containing a common hall on the lower floor, a dining hall on the upper floor and an attic above. By the time of construction the residential dining facilities had been abandoned and a library substituted for the dining hall. The reasons for the change of plan are not recorded, but may relate

partly to hostility of the town's burgesses towards a more expensive residential system and partly to rivalry for facilities with St Mary's College in St Andrews. Building began in 1616 and continued until 1619, by which time it had cost over £16,000.[81] It is likely that stones from the old Kirk o'Field, which was demolished in about 1616, were reused in the construction of the 1617 Building. Preparations for the king's visit to Edinburgh occupied many of the town's craftsmen and workmen, delaying work on the College building in 1616–17.[82] The town council minutes show that timber was brought from Copenhagen, presumably for the roof.[83]

The precise appearance and arrangement of the original edifice is now difficult to reconstruct, as there are few visual records of the building before a major remodelling of the upper floor in 1753–5 (see below). What can be said with certainty is that the building was oriented north–south and lay parallel with, and about 115 feet east of, Hamilton Lodging. Whether by design or accident, the east-facing alignment of the building and first-floor location of the library corresponded with the continental practice of library construction, codified by Gabriel Naudé in 1627.[84] The northern end of the new building aligned with the centre of the garden front of Hamilton Lodging. It was constructed of red sandstone rubble with squared facing masonry and lime pointing and had a heavy grey slate roof on a steeply pitched roof.[85]

Gordon of Rothiemay's 1647 bird's-eye view of the College from the south [figs 5, 17], which is unreliable in many respects, shows an external three-storey turnpike stair at the south-west corner of the building, a string course above the principal storey, a crowstepped south gable, a number of dormers, a range connecting to Hamilton Lodging, and a short jamb projecting from the west side of the building. This short jamb is described as a stairtower in later accounts.[86] Parts of the building can also be glimpsed behind the Royal Infirmary in Thomas Sandby's mid-18th-century view [fig.18], before the heightening and the addition of an anatomy theatre. This depiction from the east shows a tall window with a dormer above it projecting into a steep roof with substantial chimneys. Later records of the west front of the building [figs 16, 86] show a string course above the ground floor, three large windows at the first floor and a corbelled projecting circular stairtower at the join with the west jamb. The public latrines were located against the north gable of the 1617 Building until 1628, when much to the dismay of the Bristo neighbours they were moved to the west wall and created a 'filthie puddell' that leaked under the town wall.[87] The archaeological evidence suggests that the north-west jamb (stairtower) was added after the construction of the 1617 Building, but before the addition of the 1642 Library.[88] A pend

through the base of the jamb was known as the 'High Transe' (high passage), and connected the lower Printing House Yard with the sunken yard in front of the 1617 Building and the High College Yard.

A number of high-quality carved stones from the 1617 Building are still preserved in the Court Room vestibule of Old College [fig.19]. The stones are all assembled together, and it is not now clear where they were located originally on the 1617 Building. A further stone is built into the exterior of Sir Walter Scott's house at Abbotsford in the Scottish Borders. Some decorative stones are now untraceable, but the inscriptions were published in 1834.[89] Of particular interest is the stone that was purported to read: 'r. m. f. robertus milne fundavit' ('Robert Milne laid the foundation'), from the foot of the back entry to the library.

A graduation thesis of 1620 praised the *speciosas et spatiosas aedes* ('beautiful and spacious apartment'), but foreign admiration from the Englishman Christopher Lowther was more muted: '[T]here is one part of the college built by the Senate and the people of Edinburgh, which is better than any other part of the college beside.'[90] The master wright John Scott constructed benches at either end of the Common Hall in 1657, creating a central space for ceremonies and a means of keeping out 'the common people quho make confusioun at such solemnities'.[91]

For some time in its later life the ground floor of the 1617 Building was divided into at least three rooms: the divinity hall and theology library to the north; the common hall for public assemblies and exams in the middle; and the anatomy classroom and museum to the south. The plan of the anatomy classroom can be seen in the plans drawn up for the new anatomy theatre in 1764 [fig.28] and archaeological evidence for this area of the building, including 17th-century decorative plasterwork, was uncovered in 2010.[92] The library itself was on the floor above, but probably did not occupy the full 120-foot length of the building. Volumes were housed in thirteen tall and narrow presses, or 'repositaria', of between nine and twelve shelves, which probably stood between the windows. The conditions were not ideal for the books, as is clear from the town council's order of 1626 requiring the keeper to hire a servant to prevent further damage by heating the room and airing the books as necessary.[93] The newfound attention to the library may have been brought about by the gift of more than 360 books and manuscripts by the famous poet William Drummond of Hawthornden in the same year.[94] The library collections expanded rapidly during the 1620s and 1630s through gifts, legacies and informal levies at matriculation and graduation.

Agnes Campbell, indomitable widow of the King's Printer for Scotland, used the attic of the 1617 Building

for drying printed papers for over thirty years from 1687.[95] The printing presses themselves were kept in the lower storey of the 1642 Library. The business continued after Campbell's death until the mid-18th century. Although the College gained rental and free printing, the noise and smell of the printing business was not conducive to academic study, and the vibrations of the presses and bulk deliveries of paper and ink were thought to be causing damage to the buildings.

By 1753 the roof of the 1617 Building was in a perilous state. The initial plan was to simply repair the roof, but sensing an opportunity to consolidate all the printing activity in one place in the 1642 Library and recover the whole 1617 Building for its own use, the College proposed raising the walls by over 13 feet to create a new galleried library. It is likely that the first floor windows were enlarged and adorned with cornices at the same time as new windows were provided for the gallery of the library.[96] The new library was not only intended to deal with the condition of the 1617 Building, but also to relieve pressure on the now inadequate accommodation of the 1642 Library.[97] The Copyright Act of 1710 had marked a major change in the pace of acquisition in the

19 Sculpted stones from the 1617 Building in the former Court Room vestibule, Old College

HES

library, granting the University the right to acquire a copy of every book registered at Stationers' Hall.

Work started on the scheme to heighten the 1617 Building in 1753, but the interior was still incomplete in February 1755 when the Principal reminded the town council that the 1642 Library had been let to new printers and the books needed to be moved to the new library as a matter of urgency. At the request of John Stewart, Professor of Natural Philosophy, and Matthew Stewart, Professor of Mathematics, the roof of the old stairtower was to be replaced with a flat roof so that it could be used for astronomical observations. Work was nearly finished by July 1755, when the old library presses (cupboards) were moved from the 1642 Library, eight large balusters had been provided for the rail around the gallery, and only a new floor, a few gallery seats and grates for the two chimneys were missing.[98] The proposal for raising the roof and creating the new library conformed to 'Mr Adam's plan', presumably that of the architect John Adam, who had inherited his father's properties next door to the College in 1748.[99] George Stevenson, Deacon of the Incorporation of Wrights, and collaborator with Adam on the completion of Arniston House, Midlothian, was responsible for the timberwork. The interior of the new Edinburgh library, with its three-sided gallery, was probably similar in dimensions and character to that of the University of Glasgow library, designed by William Adam in 1732. Writing in 1774, Principal William Robertson noted the 'good appearance' of the room.[100] Patrick Bowie, manufacturer of gold and silver lace, retained a garret in the building, which was accessed from the turnpike stair off the main staircase jamb.[101] Another extension of the library gallery to four sides of the room was planned in 1775.[102] The 1617 Building was finally demolished in autumn 1827 [fig.87].

EXPANSION AND RENEWAL 1620–1640

Thomas Craufurd recorded the construction of a 'house built of timber' near to the College well in 1620.[103] It was designed to contain the great astronomical quadrant sent by Henry Briggs of Gresham College, London, to the famous mathematician John Napier of Merchiston. Before his death in 1616 Napier had sent the quadrant on to Andrew Young, Professor of Mathematics, with the wish that it be housed in the College. Although the appearance of the wooden house is unknown, and the purpose of the quadrant is not stated in the contemporary sources, the instrument must have been of some size and was therefore likely to be intended for astronomical measurements. In spite of its ephemeral materials, the structure was possibly Scotland's first purpose-built observatory.[104]

A new means of developing the College estate was tried in 1625. The town council allowed Sir Thomas Hope of Craighall to construct two student chambers, one above the other, along the west wall of the High College for free use by his children. William Rig of Atherny, a merchant, built another two chambers next door in the following year. The council stipulated that the buildings should not be used as sleeping accommodation, rather as 'convenient plaices quherunto young students may for thair better exercise reteir, thame selffis the more easilie to applye thair mynd to thair buikes'.[105] The two benefactors agreed to add their names and arms to the buildings as an encouragement to others to build chambers. In spite of this encouragement no other chambers were built until the late 1630s.

In 1628 the rules of the College were set down in the town council's minute books.[106] These rules are interesting for the light that they shed on the curriculum, the content of exams, the requirements of staff and students and the day-to-day life of the College: all students must promise on matriculation to be obedient to the masters; no absence from the kirk; only Latin to be used and 'none be fund speiking scottes'; no daggers or swords; no swearing, blaspheming or fornication; 'none weare long haire'; no unlawful games, such as dice or cards; students to go home directly after classes, and not gather at the College gate; 'none goe to taverns or any uther unseemlie plaices for scollers to be fund in'. The rules also reveal the key role of the College porter in the maintenance of the buildings. He was responsible for guarding the gate, ringing the bell, locking the doors of the schools, lighting strategic candles in winter, sweeping the classrooms, and 'attending to the fabrick of the worke'. The College porter was paid extra for maintaining the security of the various building sites.

In 1634 the town council purchased a range of 'baggage-thatched' houses to the west of Hamilton Lodging from John Charteris, demolished them, and in 1637–8 constructed a substantial enclosing wall beside the main entrance to the College.[107] The formation of Low Court started in 1636 with a new L-plan range of student chambers within the corner of Jamaica Lane and Horse Wynd. These were funded before 1647 by legacies from (in order of chambers moving west and south away from the gateway) Bailie John Trotter, Robert Elise, the lawyer Dr Robert Johnston and Bailie John Fleming, and by gifts from Bailie Laurence Henderson, Dean of Guild George Suttie, Town Clerk William Thomson and James Murray.[108] The tidying of the main entrance continued in 1636–7 with the construction of a 'new great gate of the College' (see 'The College Gate and Steeple' section below).[109] John Mylne oversaw the construction of a southwards extension to the 1637–8 wall in 1647, with the intention of continuing to build student chambers against it. The first new set of chambers was funded by a bequest of £1,000 by Thomas Dods, 'ordinarie plumber to the Toun'.[110] Dods's arms can now be found in the Court Room vestibule of Old College.

It is perhaps no surprise that a key figure in the new developments of the 1630s and 1640s was the master mason John Mylne [fig.2]. As master mason to the crown, the town council and Heriot's Hospital, Mylne had an involvement in almost every major building project in the city from the mid-1630s to the mid-1660s. Mylne's omnipresence in the building world was not without its critics. The lawyer John Nicoll's diary entries for 1655 accused John Mylne and the wright John Scott of misleading the town council and fleecing the citizens of Edinburgh through constant changes of plan and exorbitant charges.[111]

Charles I's attempt to reimpose episcopal authority in the church in 1633 required major reordering of St Giles to convert it into a cathedral, and the construction of two new churches (an unfinished church on Castlehill and the Tron Kirk in the High Street, of 1637–47) to accommodate the Presbyterian congregations evicted from St Giles. In addition to his royal and civic projects, Mylne succeeded William Aytoun at Heriot's Hospital in 1643 and seems to have played a part in the construction of Lady Yester's Chapel next to the College in 1647. As Colonel Mylne, he and Scott also played a significant role in preparations for defence of the city against Cromwell in the autumn of 1650.[112]

THE COLLEGE GATE AND STEEPLE, 1636–1686

The College steeple, or gate-tower, is one of the city's lost landmarks. The arrangement paralleled that of the tower at Heriot's Hospital, which stood in alignment with the sharply sloping northern approach up from the Grassmarket via Heriot's Bridge. The College steeple also advertised the College's presence in the townscape, and was placed prominently at the head of College Wynd, the steep route up from the Cowgate to the College. The steeple and gateway had a long period of development. There appears to have been a simple gate from an early date, but it first began to take a more substantial form in 1636 when the merchant John Jossie built 'a fabric of great strength, and not inelegant' including a student chamber above.[113] There is a strong likelihood that John Mylne was involved, at least with the initial gateway. According to the *Scots Magazine* of April 1790, the steeple itself took another fifty years to reach a completed state in 1686:

From the inscription which it bears, it seems to have been erected at the expense of a person of the name of Thomas Burnet. It was a tall tower, about 12 feet square, and 6 stories high, or about 80 feet from the ground on the top

of the wall; upon which was a pavilion roof, terminating with a vane. The different small chambers of which it consisted, and which were entered from a turnpike-stair, made part of the house inhabited by the Professor of Greek. The front to the north was of polished ashlar work, with rustic corners. Immediately over the gate were the city arms, but wanting the supporters; and higher up, betwixt two of the windows, were the arms, as is supposed, of the above-mentioned Thomas Burnet.[114]

In fact the steeple remained incomplete into the 18th century, as is demonstrated by the town council minutes of 1705, which record instructions to the College treasurer to get it finished.[115] The celebrated master mason of Heriot's Hospital, William Aytoun, supplied an expensive painted sundial to the College in 1638.[116] This is thought to have been located on the gatehouse.

EXPANSION 1640–1700

The year 1640 saw two new and dynamic appointments to the supervision of the College: Alexander Henderson, one of the principal draftsmen of the National Covenant in 1638, as Rector and 'eye of the council'; and John Jossie as the College's first 'thesaurer', or treasurer.[117] From this date the College accounts were separated from the general financial accounts of the town council, making expenditure on the College estate easier to identify. As can be seen from his activities in the 1630s, Jossie had already taken a strong interest in developing the College estate through private legacies and gifts of fellow burgesses and bailies, and was a generous benefactor himself. Despite the extremely volatile political situation in the aftermath of the 1639 and 1640 Bishops' Wars and the turmoil of the civil wars of the three kingdoms from 1644 to 1651, Henderson and Jossie managed to secure a number of major benefactions and further building projects were undertaken. In an

20 View of the College steeple from the south in *Edinburgh in Olden Time, 1717–1828* by George Thomas Stevenson
HES [SC 390268]

21 Bust of Bartholomew
Somervell, private house,
Perthshire

HES [SC 390268]

of Dunbar in 1650. Nicoll recorded in his diary entry for November 1650 that a great part of the College was 'wasted' by Cromwell's New Model Army.[122] As a result, the College transferred to Kirkcaldy for much of 1651, and significant resources were expended on repairing the damage in the following decade.

In 1639 Bartholomew Somervell of Saughtonhall, the son of Peter Somervell, a rich burgess and bailie of Edinburgh, had left 40,000 merks to establish a Professor of Divinity and a further 6,000 merks to purchase a house for him. The town council finally purchased Curriehill House, the Edinburgh lodging of Sir James Skene, which stood in a large garden just to the east of the College site in what is now High School Yards.[123] The Professor of Divinity occupied the house for a period, and the Principal stayed there while repairs were carried out to his own house, but Curriehill was becoming increasingly ruinous. In 1656 the town council sold Curriehill to the Incorporation of Surgeons and commissioned John Mylne to construct a new house for the Professor of Divinity against the Jamaica Lane boundary to the east of the 1617 Building.[124] This is the building shown in the process of demolition in the famous engraving of the laying of the foundation stone for Robert Adam's Old College [fig.30], and it was over the doorway that a stone bust of Somervell was placed [fig.21]. Mylne may well have carved the bust himself, but it appears to be based on an earlier plaster bust recorded in the 1647 College accounts: 'Item – to James Turke for plaistering of umquhil [the late] Mr Bartholmew Somevell his portraitor in the professor's house.'[125]

A final round of chamber building began in 1667 and lasted until 1671. Andrew Rutherford, Earl of Teviot, a mercenary soldier in the French army, returned to Edinburgh in 1660 to spend his last years living in the College. On his death in 1664 he left the substantial sum of 8,000 merks, which with interest was used to construct four double chambers along the south wall of the High College in 1667 [fig.15]. Bailie George Drummond, Deacon Thomas Sandilands, Bailie David Boyd and John Bonar of Bonitoun contributed further sums to complete the row, which was named in Rutherford's honour as 'Teviot Chambers'.[126] This was the last major building programme of the 17th century. As the College grew, it became increasingly difficult to defend the new buildings from encroachments by professors and regents seeking study, teaching and even living spaces. Gifts and legacies were directed towards academic purposes, and the small sums requested from the town council were spent on repairs.

interview with Charles I in London in 1641 Henderson sought reallocation of money from the former bishoprics to the Scottish universities. Later that year, Henderson acted as chaplain to the king on his visit to Edinburgh and managed to secure funds for the College building projects from the abolished bishopric of Edinburgh. The most notable of these schemes was the new College library (see below).

The earliest of Jossie's projects as College treasurer was the building of a stone staircase linking the new Low College Court to the High College Court. This was known as 'Jossie's Steps'. Archaeological evidence of its location and construction came to light in the 2010 excavations in Old College.[118] Jossie clearly had an interest in improving circulation within the precincts and buildings of the College, as he also commissioned Mylne to provide three generous entrances to Hamilton Lodging. One of these was the 'great stair on the south of the great lodging leading into the higher gallery', remnants of which also emerged in the 2010 excavations.[119]

Craufurd records the intention to 'continue the work of building along the west wall, as far almost as the latrines, and thence eastward to the provost's lodging [Principal's house]'.[120] More student chambers were built along the west wall at this time and in 1658 a new gate onto Potterrow. The ubiquitous John Mylne seems to have been responsible.[121] Whatever the extent of plans for redevelopment of the College, they were reduced by rising building costs from 1645 and then dashed by the Cromwellian occupation of the city after the Battle

1642 LIBRARY

South of the Cow-Gate, and on a rising stands the College, consisting of one small quadrangle, and some other lodgings without uniformity or order, built at several times, and by

divers benefactors, who thought probably to be better distinguished by this variety of forms and situations in those buildings. In the midst hereof is the library, a large and convenient room made about 60 years ago for that purpose. The roof is covered with lead, and is neatly kept within; well furnish'd with books, and those put in very good order, and cloister'd with doors made of wire which none can open but the keeper, and which is thought a better way than our multitudes of chains incumbering a library, and are equally troublesome and chargeable to us. It has (as all other publick libraries) many benefactors, whose books are distinguish'd by their several apartments, and the donors names set over 'em in golden letters. A device, grateful and honourable enough for the parties concern'd, encourages others to follow their examples; such especially who may be charmed to the doing of a good work, tho' not always upon a principle of goodness. Over the books are hung the pictures of divers Princes, and most of the reformers, as Luther, Melancthon, Zuinglius, Calvin, &c., and near them Buchanan's scull, very intire, and so thin that we may see the light through it, and that it is really his appears from hence, because one, Mr Adamson, principal of the College, being a young man of 24 years of age, when Buchanan was buried, either out of curiosity or respect to the dead, brib'd the sexton sometime after to procure him the skull, which being brought he fastened these verses to it, and at his death left it and them to the College. (Thomas Morer, description of the 1642 Library in 1689)[127]

A new library was built between 1642 and 1646 running east–west between the south jamb of Hamilton Lodging and the stairtower of the 1617 Building [fig.24]. Like the 1617 Building, the new construction was known by various names, including the 'Low Library' and 'New Library', but for purposes of clarity this text will use '1642 Library'. The reasons for building a new library just twenty-five years after the construction of a spacious library in the 1617 Building are not clear. Although the old library contained 3,054 books by 1641, it can hardly have been bursting at the seams.[128] If James Gordon of Rothiemay's 'view' of the College [fig.5] in 1647 is read as a proposal scheme for marshalling the haphazard buildings into ordered quadrangles, like Heriot's Hospital or Glasgow's Old College, then the 1642 Library can be seen as the first step towards this grand unifying plan. Undoubtedly the new library was intended to be a symbol of prestige at the heart of a rejuvenated complex, and to house a collection that had been greatly augmented by gifts in the 1630s. As Thomas Morer pointed out rather disapprovingly, the names of benefactors were added in gold above the books as an encouragement to others. The library was a key building, not just for the storage of books, but for the reputation of the institution and the city and as a means of encouraging philanthropy.

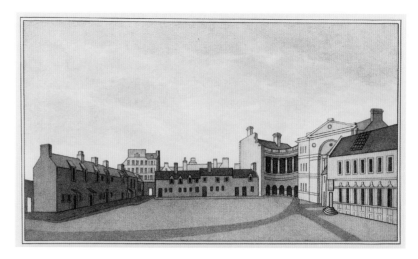

22 View of High College from the east in *Edinburgh in Olden Time, 1717–1828* by George Thomas Stevenson
University of Edinburgh

23 Exterior view of the 17th-century student chambers from the corner of Horse Wynd / Potterrow and Jamaica Lane in *Edinburgh in Olden Time, 1717–1828* by George Thomas Stevenson
University of Edinburgh

24 View of the 1642 Library from the south in *Edinburgh in Olden Time, 1717–1828* by George Thomas Stevenson
University of Edinburgh

The rector, Principal and College committee of the town council determined the location of the new library in April 1642.[129] Funding was secured from a number of benefactors including: a legacy of £2,666 from one of the city's richest merchants, Bailie John Fleming, who had a monopoly on the timber trade from Norway; a gift of £1,466 from Margaret Shoner, Lady Forret; and a donation of 2,000 merks from the Covenanting General Sir Alexander Hamilton, friend of John Mylne and inventor of a light artillery armament known as a 'frame gun'.[130]

Detailed accounts for the building survive in the College treasurer's account books, which are held in the Edinburgh City Archives.[131] The great bulk of the money was paid on account to John Mylne for the work of the masons and the barrowmen and for the purchase and carriage of lime for mortar and stone from the city's Ravelston quarry. Mylne was certainly the main contractor, and is likely to have been the overall designer too. The roof was constructed, and perhaps designed in detail, by John Scott, the wright who was responsible for the magnificent roof of Parliament House and the roof of the Tron Kirk.[132]

Laurie's plan of the College of 1767 shows the dimensions as approximately 80 feet long by 30 feet wide [fig.27]. Constructed into a slope, the building originally had a single storey facing south towards the High College Yard and two storeys facing north. The library itself was on the principal upper floor over 'an arched sunk storey'.[133] The arcaded lower storey

presumably served as a covered access between Hamilton Lodging and the 1617 Building. There are no known images of the north side of the building, but it can probably be imagined as a less ornate and lower version of the north range of Heriot's Hospital (without the tower). On the south front the range had ten pedimented windows and a doorway with a decorative stone panel above. Perhaps the most extraordinary feature of the library in its first state was the almost flat roof set behind crenellated parapets. This feature is shown clearly in Gordon's 1647 'view' [fig.17]. Local precedents for this type of high-status roof could be found in the north range of Heriot's Hospital and at Parliament House, and the flat roof that had been proposed at the Tron Kirk. Further afield, Inigo Jones's Banqueting House (1619–22) in London and the Seldon End of the University of Oxford's famous Bodleian Library (1640) had similar 'hidden' roof arrangements.

John Scott's team used more than 9,400 flooring nails in constructing the timberwork of the roof. The town council arranged for custom-free lead to be sent from London in 1643 for the city's three big projects: the Tron Kirk, Heriot's Hospital and the College library.[134] Whether the design, materials or workmanship of the College roof were defective is not known, but it proved problematic from an early date:

Taking to consideratioun the defectis and faultiness of the roofe of the great hall in the Colledge quhairby the buikes in the bibliotheck are much indangered and the haill hous

25 Panorama of Edinburgh from Calton Hill by Robert Barker, 1792. The College buildings are shown on the edge of the town, in front of the Pentland Hills to the centre-right of the image.
University of Edinburgh Art Collections [EU 0492]

much indammaged quhilk they find to be occasioned be the beating of the weather on the lairge flait roff thairof. Thairfoir they have thought fitt that the said hall be thicked or covered with lead [...]
(town council minutes, 14 June 1648)[135]

The finishing touches to the interior were carried out in 1649 when the town council instructed work:

to put a laiche [low] *chimney in the new liberarie with ane yrone grate befoir it to hold up the coallis from falling upon the floor and to put knocks* [clocks] *upon the twa dooris of the liberarie and to line some presses with buckrome and such lyke and to make the liberarie watertight quhair is necessarie and to plaster the entrie and the names and soumes of benefactours dotted* [endowed] *to the Colledge be put upoune some pairt of the liberarie.*[136]

The fireplace is possibly represented on the bare gable wall shown in Lizar's engraving of 1817 [fig.86]. No later visitors thought to remark on the internal structure or appearance of the roof, which suggests that it was finished plainly, perhaps simply with joists (like the underside of a floor).

Although the lower level of the building was used as a printing house from 1686, the library room above retained its original use until the removal of the books to the new library in the remodelled 1617 Building in 1755. At this date, Gavin Hamilton and John Balfour, noted Edinburgh booksellers and publishers, were appointed as the College printers and took over the 1642 Library in its entirety. The old library was used for printing and the lower level for storing lumber. This arrangement

continued under the firm's new partner, Patrick Neil, until 1764, when Principal Robertson resumed the building for College use. Initially the proposal was to use the old library as a museum for 'natural curiosities', but for a relatively small sum the building could be heightened by a storey and two new rooms provided for natural philosophy and an additional room for the library.[137] Much of the cost was to be recouped through sale of the lead from the old roof, which was removed under the supervision of soldiers.[138] Old casement windows were to be replaced with new sash and case windows. The mason / architect responsible for the project appears to have been William Mylne, the great-great-great-nephew of John Mylne, the original contractor for the building.[139]

In 1800 the new Professor of Chemistry, Thomas Charles Hope, removed the equipment of his eminent predecessor, Joseph Black, to the basement of the 1642 Building.[140] It is thought that the chemical compounds and apparatus recovered by Addyman Archaeology from the site in the Old College quad in 2010 belonged to Black, and that they were simply abandoned in the building when it was demolished.[141]

QUIESCENCE, REPAIRS AND REMODELLING 1700–1785

The early years of the 18th century were quiet in terms of development within the College precincts. The traveller Edmund Calamy described the scene in 1709:

The College is a good building, with three courts. There is a high tower over the great gate, which looks to the city. The public schools are large and convenient. There are also accommodations in the College for a number of students to lodge, though they are seldom made use of, but by those in meaner circumstances. There are also handsome dwellings for the Professors and Principal, with good gardens.[142]

A nearby development that was closely associated with the College and the teaching of medicine was the foundation of the Royal Infirmary. Initially known as the Hospital for the Sick Poor, the Physicians' Hospital, or Little House, it was established at the head of Robertson's Close in 1729. The venture flourished and gained a royal charter in 1736. William Adam designed a purpose-built hospital, which was built on a site just to the east of the College in 1741.

A scheme for an observatory in the College was almost agreed in 1736, when the Porteous Riots broke out over the shooting of innocent civilians by the city guard, and the subsequent unrest put an end to the proposal.[143] Colin MacLaurin, the renowned Professor of Mathematics, revived the scheme in 1741, commissioning a design for a gothick tower to stand in the middle of

26 Portrait of William Robertson by Sir Henry Raeburn, 1792
University of Edinburgh Art Collections [EU 0011]

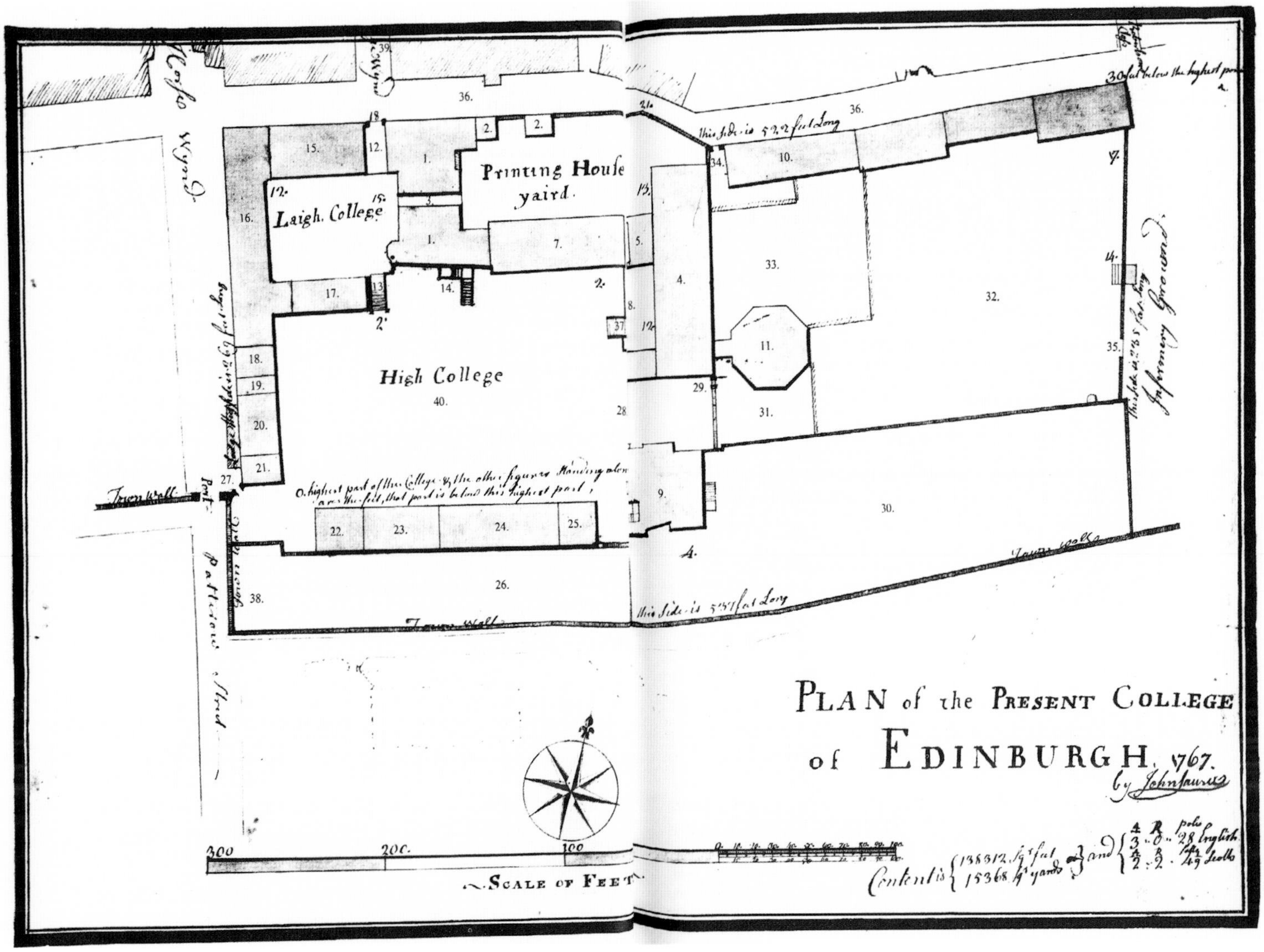

27 Plan of the College of Edinburgh by John Laurie, 1767. This plan shows the new octagonal anatomy theatre projecting from the southern end of the 1617 Building, with the waiting room of 1737 on the west side.
Sir Robert Clerk of Penicuik

the range of 17th-century buildings along the southern boundary of the College. The unrest surrounding the Jacobite Rising of 1745 and MacLaurin's death in 1746 ended the proposal for good. MacLaurin also 'projected a suitable place for performing experiments', which was supported by Sir John Clerk of Penicuik and the Earls of Morton and Hopetoun, but this specialist laboratory too came to nothing after the 'Forty-Five'.[144]

After more than half a century of stasis and 'make do and mend', a wind of change swept through the College with the appointment of the celebrated historian and churchman William Robertson as Principal. Robertson brought a new energy and dynamism to the position, leading the University for thirty years through a golden age, the period of the 'Enlightenment', when human reason and empirical evidence advanced many fields of study. He nurtured an extraordinary number of stellar academics, including the anatomist Alexander Monro secundus, chemists Joseph Black and William Cullen, natural historian John Walker, philosopher Adam Ferguson, mathematician John Playfair [fig.70], and philosopher and mathematician Dugald Stewart. The poor condition of the College's outmoded estate did not escape Robertson's attention. At first he sought to relieve the most acute problems through small construction projects, but eventually through managerial skill and persistence he persuaded the town council to back a radical plan to rebuild the whole campus (see Chapter Two). The smaller projects included heightening the 1617 Building and the 1642 Library, and the construction of the new anatomy theatre and chemistry classroom.

As early as 1767 Robertson began his long campaign to rebuild the College. Firstly the surveyor John Laurie was commissioned to produce a survey of the existing buildings [fig.27]. With the support of a joint committee of the town council and the College, Robertson put forward a proposal to the town council to 'provide a Library-room, a Museum, a Hall, and proper school or teaching-rooms for the several classes, as well as houses for the Principal and Professors'.[145] Accepting Robertson's proposal, the town council paid the mason / architect David Henderson for a plan 'of the new intended College'.[146] Several newspapers, including the *Caledonian Mercury*, published Robertson's 'Memorial Relating to the University of Edinburgh' in February 1768.[147] He outlined the 'mean, irregular, and contemptible appearance' of the old buildings and the enormous growth of the University and its reputation, particularly in medicine.[148] There were now some 600–700 students studying a whole range of subjects taught by twenty-one professors.[149]

The proposal was to form a board of trustees to raise public subscriptions of £6,500 and to 'rebuild the fabric of the University according to a regular plan, and in a decent manner, on the ground where it stands at present. The situation is in every respect commodious; the area, containing above three acres, is sufficiently extensive, and would afford one large, free, and open square, around which all the buildings could be placed to advantage.'[150]

Lack of money thwarted the 1768 scheme. The aftershock of the collapse of the Ayr Bank in 1772 and the general instability surrounding the wars in America prevented a serious opportunity to revive the proposal until 1785.[151] Then the rebuilding of the College was to be tied to the development of the city's new South Bridge, and the University's most famous architect, Robert Adam, entered the story (see Chapter Two).

ANATOMY THEATRE 1764

The Monro family dominated medical education in Edinburgh for much of the 18th and early 19th centuries, providing three distinguished professors to the College, all Alexanders: Monro primus (1697–1767); Monro secundus (1733–1817); and Monro tertius (1773–1859).

On his appointment as Professor of Anatomy in 1720, in common with his predecessors, Monro primus taught his students both anatomy and surgery at the nearby College of Surgeons. The syllabus was based on that of the celebrated University of Leyden. However, in the face of accusations of complicity in grave-robbing and popular demonstrations against the practice, the town council allocated Monro a classroom within the more secure confines of the College in 1725.[152] This is thought to have been the classroom at the southern end of the ground floor of the 1617 Building, which was in use as an anatomy theatre by the early 1750s. Neither the lighting nor the seating was suited to the demonstration of dissections, there were far too many students for the space, and the presence of unrefrigerated bodies must have been decidedly unpleasant for other users of the building.

In September 1758 Monro primus and his son, Monro secundus, wrote jointly to the Lord Provost and the town council seeking a remodelling of the existing anatomy theatre.[153] Whatever measures were taken proved insufficient, as just six years later Monro secundus wrote again, this time offering to loan £300 for the construction of a completely new anatomy theatre.[154] Although the plans of the building appear to be drawn by Monro secundus himself in a very amateur hand, the mason / architect William Mylne was the contractor.[155]

The new theatre was to connect to the existing anatomy classroom at the southern end of the 1617 Building via a short corridor and vestibule. Bodies for dissection could now be brought into the theatre discreetly through an external door in the vestibule. The floor level of the existing classroom was raised.[156] The new theatre was octagonal in form, 36 feet wide, with a capacity for 300 students [figs 28, 29].[157] A large south-facing window and a huge 12 foot roof-light allowed plenty of light to fall on the dissection table that was placed in the centre of the room. Although modest in scale, the Edinburgh anatomy theatre was in the European tradition of specialist dissection rooms. Some of the earliest anatomy theatres were built at the universities of Padua in 1594 (surviving) and Leyden in 1596 (reconstructed). The octagonal form was not uncommon, but other examples were of higher architectural quality. Olof Rudbeck designed and built a top-lit octagonal theatre of similar capacity at Uppsala in 1662–3, the Cutlerian Theatre at the Royal College of Physicians was designed by Robert Hooke in 1674, and the rector of the University of Leuven, Henri Rega, commissioned a small octagonal theatre in 1744.

28 Amateur design of 1764 for the anatomy theatre of Alexander Monro secundus
Edinburgh City Archives

29 John Guest's class ticket of 26 October 1785 for lectures in anatomy and surgery by Alexander Monro secundus. In the background is the octagonal Anatomy Theatre designed and financed by Monro in 1764.
University of Edinburgh [0022285]

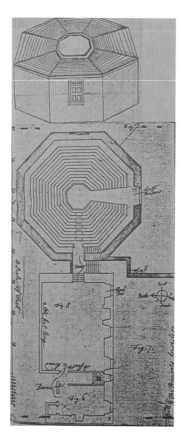

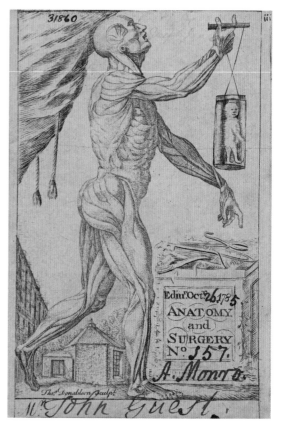

30 A print of *Laying the Foundation Stone of the University of Edinburgh* by David Allan, 1789. A drawing of the planned building is attached to a wooden pole above a block of stone. The building shown in the course of demolition was the house of the Professor of Divinity, designed by John Mylne in 1656.

Capital Collections, Edinburgh [11074]

Monro's lectures continued to attract large numbers of students, reaching 436 in 1783, well over the 300-person capacity of the little theatre. Again Monro used his own funds to add a gallery.[158] Overcrowding of the anatomy theatre was one of the arguments deployed to secure the comprehensive rebuilding programme in the late 1780s. The anatomy theatre was demolished in 1793 on completion of a new theatre in the north-west corner of Robert Adam's new building.[159]

SPECULATIVE SOCIETY HALL 1769

Six students, William Creech, Allan Maconochie, Alexander Belsches, John Bruce, John Bonar and John Mackie, founded the Speculative Society on 17 November 1764 for 'improvement in Literary Composition and Public Speaking'.[160] The society's name was derived from the nature of its papers and debates, which were 'confined to academical exercise and speculation'.[161] In 1769 the society raised £164 and applied to the town council to construct a new hall 28 feet long by 19 feet wide on a plot of vacant land adjacent to the south-west gate of the College.[162] The town council accepted the College committee's recommendation that the hall would not injure the College,

rather 'beautify the same'. It had a 'coach roof' and arched windows facing High College.[163] Internally there was a raised platform at the west end for the president's chair and table and a desk at the east end for the speaker. A green baize bench ran round the room. A lobby was added in 1775.[164] The old hall was demolished in 1817 to make way for William Henry Playfair's new buildings, where a replacement room was provided for the society in 1819 (see Chapter 3).[165]

CHEMISTRY LABORATORY 1781–1782

In 1724 three professors of medicine and chemistry, Andrew Plummer, John Innes and John Rutherford, purchased a house adjoining the College garden for use as a chemistry laboratory.[166] On inheriting this makeshift arrangement in 1766, Black began to press for a new laboratory. Eventually this was built in Printing House Yard to the north of, and parallel to, the 1642 Library at a cost of £300, in 1781–2.[167] The appearance of the building is not recorded and it was demolished in 1820. Footings were discovered by Addyman Archaeology in the continuing excavations in 2017.

Chapter Two

Robert Adam's Old College 1785–1800

NICK HAYNES

31 Plan of the principal storey
of the University by Robert Adam
Sir John Soane's Museum, London [vol.28 / 35]

This chapter describes the first phase in the development of Old College, from the initial designs of Robert Adam in 1785, through partial construction and financial disaster in the 1790s, to 1800, when the stalled scheme awaited a redesign and a new building campaign.

THE ARCHITECT: ROBERT ADAM 1728–1792

I have lived long and much with many of the most distinguished men in my own times, but for genius, for worth, and for agreeable manners, I know none whom I should rank above the friend we have lost. (Principal William Robertson on the death of Robert Adam in 1792)[1]

Such was the distinctiveness of his designs that Robert Adam [figs 32, 33], like his later compatriot, Charles Rennie Mackintosh, acquired the honour of an architectural style in his name. The term 'Adam Style' is synonymous with the form of intricate neoclassical decoration devised by Robert Adam to integrate and harmonise the treatment of walls, ceilings, fireplaces, furniture, fixtures, fittings and carpets in town and country houses. In his lifetime, and indeed after his death, the style was both admired for its ingenuity and reviled for its extravagance.[2] The reconstruction of the University of Edinburgh was Robert Adam's largest and most ambitious public project. Here he was concerned less with the intricacies of an architectural style than with the creation of a practical, beautiful and appropriately monumental public building within a planned urban setting – the second stop after Lady Nicholson's column on what has been termed a 'great *Via Triumphalis*', or Roman triumphal route, into the city.[3]

ROBERT ADAM AND URBAN PLANNING IN EDINBURGH

Robert Adam conceived many of his individual urban buildings in the context of monumental town planning schemes. Some schemes, such as the Adelphi project, Portland Place and Fitzroy Square in London and Charlotte Square in Edinburgh, were partly realised during Robert's lifetime, but others, including the rebuilding of Lisbon after the 1755 earthquake, the design of Bathwick (Bath), and plans for great 'megastructure' bridges of shops and tenements in Edinburgh remained on the drawing board.[4] These looked to bring about unity, harmony, rationality and above all 'public virtue' and 'improvement' of the mind, taste, society, economy and environment through architectural design. Even when no large scheme was in the offing, Robert thought about individual buildings in terms of their broader physical contexts (actual and potential) of street patterns, viewpoints, skyline profiles, relationships with other landmarks, open spaces, connecting routes and the movement of people in and between spaces. In an urban context individual projects were treated almost as stepping-stones towards a greater whole. Robert made proposals for the streets surrounding the new University buildings, but these were largely unrealised.[5] Throughout his life, Robert retained an interest in the theatre and scenography (performance design), and many of his designs incorporate dramatic or theatrical devices, spatial and visual illusions, screening, lighting and sculptural effects to engage the minds and emotions of the spectator. Practicality was also a major consideration, including the enhancement of communications and economic stimulation.

Robert's early passion for the 'beautiful spirit of antiquity' remained a lifelong influence on his work.[6] In urban settings it was the rationalising, ordering and monumental qualities of Roman antiquity that drove his designs. In rural and suburban locations a more generic antiquity of battlemented medieval castles often cloaked a neoclassical plan. Another influence at work on Adam's designs was his interest in 'picturesque' composition, the organisation of buildings and their settings to simulate the effects of a carefully arranged picture.[7] Something of Robert's intentions in picturesque design can be gleaned from the brothers' preface to *The Works in Architecture of Robert and James Adam*, the sumptuous and influential books of engravings of their buildings:

Movement is meant to express, the rise and fall, the advance and recess, with other diversity of form, in the different parts of a building, so as to add greatly to the picturesque of the composition. For the rising and falling, advancing and receding, with the convexity and concavity, and other forms of the great parts, have the same effect in architecture, that hill and dale, fore-ground and distance, swelling and sinking have in landscape: That is, they serve to produce an agreeable and diversified contour, that groups and contrasts like a picture and creates a variety of light and shade, which gives great spirit, beauty and effect to the composition.

It is not always that such variety can be introduced into the design of any building, but where it can be attained without encroaching upon its useful purposes, it adds much to its merit, as an object of beauty and grandeur.

The effect of the height and convexity of the dome of St Peter's [Rome], contrasted with the lower square front, and the concavity of its court, is a striking instance of this sort of composition [...] and with us, we really do not recollect any example of so much movement and contrast, as in the south front of Kedleston House in Derbyshire, one of the seats of the right Honourable Lord Scarsdale [...][8]

St Peter's in Rome was the product of more than a century of architects, including principally Donato

Bramante, Raphael, Antonio da Sangallo the Younger, Michelangelo and Gian Lorenzo Bernini. The description of movement in the exterior design of St Peter's in Rome continued to have a resonance throughout Robert's career, and is clearly visible in his designs for the University, particularly the dome and the planned crescent in front of the entrance. Robert noted the powerful impression of the basilica in a letter of July 1755 to his financial agents in London, William Innes, Thomas Clerk & Company:

I have now been witness to the Illuminations & fireworks exhibited here on St Peters day, & do own they exceed any thing I ever saw or had any Idea of, Particularly the Dome of St Peters which to the very top of the Cross is stuck as full of Lamps & Flambeaus as it can stick & forms a most glorious prospect both near & at a Distance.[9]

The interior of St Peter's possibly also excited the imagination of the young Robert, with its complex flowing spaces of differing geometric forms and volumes. This complexity is evident in Robert's abstract plan studies of the 1750s, and in the original plans for the University.

Throughout his life Robert produced thousands of architectural 'capriccios' – watercolours of imaginary buildings and dramatic mountainous landscapes based on memory, fantasy and invention.[10] Many of the fantasy landscapes included mountains in the form of Arthur's Seat and Salisbury Crags in Edinburgh, and most contained rivers, lochs, distant settlements and wiry figures with horses and carts wending their way towards austere castles. These capriccios were often produced for pleasure or for sale as art works, but in some instances it is difficult to tell whether they are imagined scenes or designs for real buildings. Certainly in later years they appear to have played a part in the design process of real buildings, almost as testbeds for their picturesque qualities.[11] In a similar way to his architect father, Robert drew on a wide range of sources, never slavishly copying, but reworking and integrating buildings and landscapes through his fertile imagination. Harnessing the spectacular topography of Edinburgh to the practical needs of the city and heightening the visual effects of his buildings were clearly Robert's concerns, as can be seen in early sketches for the University and Calton Bridge [figs 40, 41].

THE SOUTH BRIDGE PROJECT

From 1785 the proposals for new University buildings became bound up in a larger civic project, the construction of the South Bridge over the Cowgate. This ambitious scheme was a southwards extension of the North Bridge scheme of 1763–72, providing a link and a grand entrance to the New Town from the Old Town and the main route south. Effectively the new access bridge and road also opened up the south side of the city for further development. The South Bridge project was to have both physical and financial impacts on the University. The approach road to the bridge from the south would cut through the College lands, separating off the College gardens and revealing the decrepit state of the old buildings. Therefore, the 1785 Private Act of Parliament for 'Opening a Commodious Communication from the High Street of Edinburgh to the Country Southwards' contained provisions for 'designing, ordering, and causing to be erected such

Buildings in the said University of Edinburgh as they [the trustees for the University and South Bridge] shall think proper'.[12] As initially proposed, the money for the new University buildings was to come from subscriptions and the profits of land dealings and feu duties after the completion of the bridge and paving of the new southern approach of Nicolson Street.[13] Other funding proposals were put forward by James Gregory, Professor of the Institutes of Medicine, who appealed unsuccessfully to Henry Dundas to consider allocating a third of the profits of the state lottery, or setting up a special lottery, to raise the estimated £40,000 for rebuilding the College and Edinburgh's prison.[14] As the South Bridge scheme progressed, the funding measures for the University buildings were watered down in an Act of Parliament of 1786, and eventually abandoned in a further Act of Parliament of 1787.[15]

The origins of the projects for both the North and South Bridges lay in the 1752 *Proposals for Carrying on Certain Public Works in the City of Edinburgh*, which resulted in the building of the First New Town and other public projects.[16] The driving force behind this and earlier civic improvements, such as the construction of the Royal Infirmary in 1738, was George Drummond, long-serving magistrate and Lord Provost of the city on six occasions between 1725 and 1764. Drummond was active in his support of the University, particularly the medical faculty, fostering links with the Royal Infirmary and establishing two medical chairs under the patronage of the town council. According to the *Caledonian Mercury*, when another lottery scheme was

34 Proposed scheme for South Bridge by Robert Adam, about 1785

Sir John Soane's Museum, London [vol.34/2]

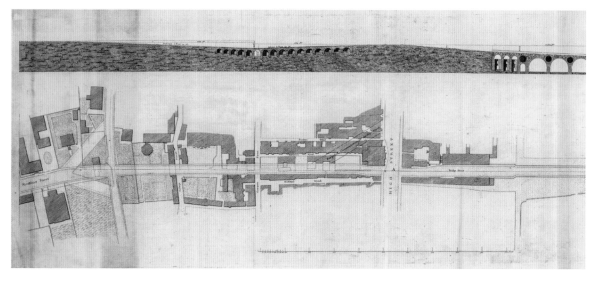

35 South Bridge proposals
by Robert Kay, 1785
National Library of Scotland,
Edinburgh

under consideration in 1768, Drummond had approved an earlier lottery proposal to fund reconstruction of the University buildings, but it had failed to secure the necessary parliamentary consent at Westminster.[17] With such large and prestigious building schemes in prospect, it is perhaps no surprise that both John and Robert Adam set out to influence and to try to secure commissions flowing from the *Proposals*: Robert appears to have provided a design for the North Bridge in 1752; John designed the new Royal Exchange in 1754 (although he lost out on the contract for its construction); Robert appears to have designed the timber triumphal arch for the Masonic foundation stone ceremony of the Exchange; John was one of the adjudicators in the competition for laying out the First New Town in 1766; and John and Robert assisted with amendments to James Craig's initial competition-winning entry in 1766–7.[18] The selected design for the North Bridge, across what is now known as the Waverley Valley, was by William Mylne. Unfortunately the bridge suffered a partial collapse in August 1769, killing five people, just before its planned opening.

Another major civic project, secured by Robert in 1771, was the construction of Register House at Multrees Hill on the axis of the North Bridge. It was built between 1774 and 1785 as a home for Scotland's public records. Robert maintained an interest in the approaches to Register House, designing a grand piazza in front of the building, a curving terrace of houses in Leith Street to the east (1785), and two bridges: South Bridge (1785), on the axis of Register House and North Bridge; and a further bridge (1791) across the Lower Calton valley to the east (eventually developed as Regent Bridge by Archibald Elliot in 1815) [figs 40, 41].

After the construction of the North Bridge, the old approach from the south through the Cowgate valley remained 'both difficult and disgusting'.[19] The first serious South Bridge proposal of 1775 sank in a

mire of controversy over finance.[20] A pamphlet by the architect / developer of George Square, James Brown, promoting the new bridge stated that '[a] new College is much talked of'.[21] There was certainly much talk amongst the professors, who fired off regular and well-founded complaints to the College Committee about leaky roofs, broken windows, overcrowded classrooms, lack of space and poor equipment throughout the 1770s and 1780s. A third lottery proposal for rebuilding the University got as far as a draft Bill in 1777, but again failed to reach the statute books.[22]

It was another half a dozen years before the banker and newly elected Lord Provost, James Hunter Blair, championed a revised bridge project in his *Proposals for Erecting a Bridge across the Cowgate and for Establishing an Effectual Fund for the Support of the Poor in Edinburgh*. The new proposals were to be self-financing through speculative residential and commercial development along the sides of the bridge. This was intended to neutralise much of the criticism aimed at the 1775 scheme. This scheme would also rationalise various levies and taxes in the town, removing the need to maintain the old city walls and gates. The *Proposals* went on to detail the benefits to the University:

The mean and unworthy appearance of the buildings allotted for the use of the university, which are not merely incommodious, but hardly sufficient for the accommodation of the Professors and their students, has long been a subject of common observation and just regret; and plans have at different times been suggested for building a new college, more worthy of the city and of the university. By the proposed plan for a south bridge, there will be left, in the most public part, and almost in the centre of the city, an ample area of 230 feet long, and 80 feet deep, for the front of a college, that shall be at once a public ornament to Edinburgh, and in every respect worthy of that university, which has done so much to honour this country, and been of such essential service to this city.[23]

The 1785 Act specified eleven 'Trustees for the University and South Bridge'. These represented a range of powerful interests in the city, and included influential figures from the Lord Provost and Dean of Guild to Henry Dundas of Melville, 'The Uncrowned King of Scotland', and James Brown, the architect of George Square. The trustees also provided personal security for the project. With the exception of the College lands, which were already owned by the town council, all other necessary land identified in the Act was to be acquired by compulsory purchase.[24]

Robert Kay was variously described as surveyor, draughtsman or inspector to the South Bridge Trustees. He drafted the published plan [fig.35], probably in the second half of 1785, and seems to have acted as the Lord Provost's professional advisor and agent throughout the protracted planning and construction process. However, as Andrew Fraser has pointed out, it is probably a mistake to consider Kay as the sole author and architect of the scheme.[25] On occasion Kay drew amendments to the plans from instructions by developer / architects James Brown and John Baxter, and Hunter Blair is described as the 'author' on the foundation stone. Notable features of this first plan were the absence of any new buildings for the University and a proposed kink in the bridge around the Tron Kirk. In its original five-bay form, the Tron Kirk intruded on a direct axial alignment of the South Bridge with the North Bridge and centre of Register House. This aspect of the proposal attracted complaints from a number of quarters.

It is not known exactly how Robert Adam became involved in the South Bridge / University scheme. However, given his connections and his interest in the town planning of the city, it was perhaps no surprise to find Robert in consultation with Lord Provost Hunter Blair in London in early 1785.[26] Hunter Blair was there

to promote the Act of Parliament for the South Bridge and University, which moved swiftly from a petition in February to receiving royal assent in May 1785. On the instruction of impatient fellow trustees, Hunter Blair pressed Robert for delivery of the proposals in the same month.[27] Robert replied apologising for the delays in sending plans, which he attributed to the illness of one of his draughtsmen.[28] Impatient to proceed, the trustees invited price estimates for construction of the bridge element of the scheme in June 1785. Naturally the lack of plans made estimating very difficult, as the contractor Alexander Laing noted on his submission.[29] Robert finally delivered his proposals in July 1785, accompanied by a long note to Hunter Blair. The accompanying drawings and later invoices detail the ambitious extent of Robert's proposals:

To a plan of that part of the City of Edinburgh which is situated between the high street and Lady Nicholson's Obelisk with the different wynds, Closes etc. tinted in yellow & on which plan is drawn a design for the new Square by the Tron Church containing nine private Houses & a Public Building, the new Street leading from the high Street to the new Bridge over the Cowgate containing plans of 17 houses on both sides with Shops & a Collonade the whole length & the Street continued also from the other end of the Bridge with plans for 9 houses, a plan for a Circus opposite the University containing nine Houses, a design for the front of the University with a House for the Principal & another for one of the Professors, a plan of a large & Commodious Inn, & a plan for a Coffee House & Assembly Room, which terminates the new intended street.[30]

Undoubtedly this enormous scheme, unified by a continuous colonnade along the great axial vista from Register House to Lady Nicolson's Column and

36   Robert Adam's South Bridge scheme on plan, showing a screen of classical buildings in front of the old College buildings and a crescent opposite

Sir John Soane's Museum, London [vol.34 / 11]

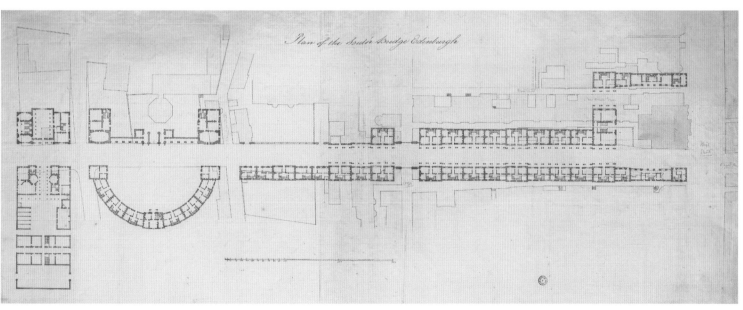

Plan of the South Bridge Edinburgh

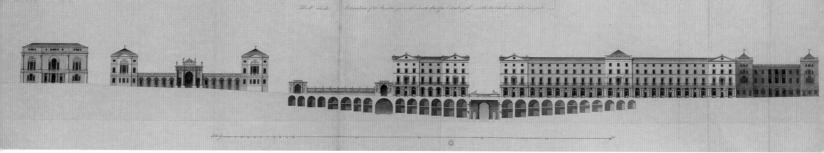

strategically punctuated with public buildings, would have formed one of the most significant pieces of European architecture and town planning of the age if it had left the drawing board [figs 34, 36, 37, 38].

The note accompanying the drawings also identifies the state of proposals for the University element of the South Bridge scheme in July 1785: 'I have also sent the Elevation of [...] a new front for the College with two Houses, one for the Principal & another for the Professor of Divinity. I did intend to have formed an entire new plan for the whole University, but found if I was to have attempted that it would have taken more time than your Lordship would have thought proper. I therefore propose that for future study.'

Robert's first proposals for the University are interesting in the context of the scheme that was adopted eventually in 1789. Essentially the design was to provide a unified neoclassical screen to hide the ramshackle collection of existing University buildings to the west of the new South Bridge street [fig.38]. At the centre of the screen was a single-storey triumphal entrance arch linked by a colonnade to three-storey symmetrical pavilions (houses for the Principal and the Professor of Divinity).[31] The scheme shows a slope at the northern end of the site, requiring an unusually deep basement level in the north pavilion. This was brought about by the insistence of the influential Lord President of the Court of Session, Robert Dundas Jr of Arniston, that the new road should not obscure the windows of his John Adam-designed house in Adam Square. Instead of a gentle slope rising from north to south through the whole South Bridge scheme, Dundas's demands created a sharp incline at the end of the bridge as it met the University site. This characteristic of the road is visible to the present day. Opposite the screen, on the east side of the new street, Robert proposed a crescent or 'circus' of speculative houses, aimed at the University's professors.

Even without a new plan for the whole University, the heroic scale and magnificence of Robert's South Bridge proposals appear to have alarmed the trustees. They made no communication with Robert between July 1785 and February 1786. It is clear from later correspondence that during this critical period the trustees rejected Robert's plans outright, mainly on grounds of cost, risk and concerns about the scheme extending beyond the land permitted by the parliamentary Act. Without informing Robert, the trustees instructed work to begin on a more modest scheme for the bridge and associated shops and tenements, drawn up by Robert Kay. The foundation stone ceremony took place on 1 August 1785 and John Beugo engraved the scheme for publication in August–September 1785 [fig.35].[32]

The winner of the architectural competition for the New Town, James Craig, also drew up a plan for the South Bridge in the second half of 1785, perhaps at the invitation of the trustees or a faction within the trustee group.[33] Again, it is not clear how Craig's involvement

37 A section through Robert Adam's South Bridge proposals, showing the elevation of a classical screen in front of the old College buildings
Sir John Soane's Museum, London [vol.34 / 3]

38 A detail of Robert Adam's proposed classical screen in front of the old College buildings
Sir John Soane's Museum, London [vol.34 / 3]

came about. He also published his proposals in the following year, along with a set of explanatory notes. The notes state that Craig was unaware of Robert Adam's proposals, but there are some similarities in the scale and ambition of both architects' plans. Craig certainly identified a site for rebuilding the whole University, and suggested acquisition of further land to the south and west to allow for a more generous layout. However, only the site boundaries are shown on Craig's plan, and no detailed design work is known.

39 Lord Provost Thomas Elder by Sir Henry Raeburn, 1797
University of Edinburgh Art Collections [EU 0005]

Rumours of the construction work on the piers of the bridge had reached Robert in London by December 1785. Perhaps not unreasonably, he wrote to Hunter Blair complaining about the poor design and shoddy workmanship and urged the adoption of his own plans.[34] Hunter Blair eventually responded in February 1786, setting out the reasons for the trustees' decision and firmly discouraging any further involvement in the bridge scheme: 'they [the trustees] do not wish you to be at any more trouble, until it is known whether the plan of a New College can be carried into Execution'.[35] This response clearly irked Robert, and he spent much of 1786 trying, unsuccessfully, to undermine confidence in Hunter Blair's design and to out-manoeuvre his opponents amongst the trustees. Having failed to secure the commission, Robert submitted a bill to the South Bridge trustees for his troubles amounting to a hefty £1,228, which led to a protracted dispute lasting until at least 1789 and a final arbitration by Henry Dundas. One of the trustees' responses to the bill was to suggest

that they had never sought a screen front and houses for the University.[36] The kerfuffle over the South Bridge did not bode well for Robert's further involvement in public works in the city, but the election on 30 September 1788 of the wine merchant, Thomas Elder of Forneth, as Lord Provost, appears to have reinvigorated his chances [fig.39].

ROBERT ADAM – PLANS 1789

Little documentary evidence survives about the circumstances of the renewed scheme to rebuild the University and the appointment of Robert Adam as the architect and 'surveyor' (supervising architect). Certainly the new Lord Provost, Thomas Elder, played a key role, and it seems likely that Robert exerted every possible influence to gain the commission through his contacts and patrons in the city, including Henry Dundas, Principal Robertson, Professor Andrew Dalzel, and the Lord Advocate and MP for Edinburghshire, Robert Dundas. By the time of the first public mention of the project in October 1789, Robert Adam had clearly been in discussion with the Lord Provost and magistrates for some time and had prepared designs, which were 'much-admired'.[37] A private letter from Robert to Thomas Kennedy of Dunure of the same date records the extent of his lobbying and preparations:

I have been in Scotland for some Weeks & have made out my Northern excursions. What cheiffly brought me down this Autumn was to show a plan I made for a new College & brought with me from London.

I have hitherto found every body, ministerial & anti-ministerial, High & low, rich & poor & all the Professors pleased with the design & eager to have it carried into execution under my direction. They seem also most willing to subscribe for that purpose, & the subscriptions are to be from one Guinea to what greater sum each person shall feell disposed to bestow.

What I wish is to get the foundation stone laid, & the building sett a going; I have very little doubt of the success of it. But till it is begun no body will subscribe or take any concern about it. We are assured of having a very liberal aid from Government next year But private exertions will be the best spur to public aid as it will shew that we do not entirely depend on their assistance for our University.[38]

A second letter to Kennedy of 20 October 1789 records Robert's financial expectations of the project:

I did intend to have returned an Answer by course of post to your very obliging letter of the 12th, had not the multiplicity of things I had to consert about the new College prevented me – I think that business is now nearly settled, & I hope in such a way as will turn out both creditable & profitable, at least there will be no risk as the 5% on the

Expenditure will secure me against loss at all events, and may put something in my pocket.[39]

John Adam, who had fallen out with his brother over financial matters, recorded a sad chance meeting with Robert in autumn 1789:

We were both surpris'd, but behaved with Civility to each other as one Gentleman should do to another. The short Conversation we had turn'd upon the Visits he had paid and was to pay to different people in the Countrey, in the way of his profession; And he said a good deal about his plan of the College.[40]

Robert was not the only architect to seek the prestigious and valuable job. Robert Morison also produced plans, but seemingly far too late in the day to topple his former master from the design of the project.[41]

On 20 October 1789 a meeting of the city magistrates and a committee of the University professors in Goldsmiths' Hall resolved that 'New Buildings for the University within the City of Edinburgh, shall be begun to be erected with all convenient speed, conformably to a Plan and Elevation prepared by the said Robert Adam, which has met with general approbation.'[42] The same meeting determined the date of the foundation stone ceremony and arranged for subscription papers to be issued. Three days later, Henry Dundas joined the continued meeting to draw up a list of commissioners, who were to include the Lord Provost and office-holders of the council, all the great officers of the legal and medical professions, the Principal of the University and two professors, two MPs, and three others, elected by subscribers over £100.[43] Any seven or more of the commissioners could make decisions with full authority. It is notable that some two centuries after the University's foundation, the legal establishment still took a very prominent role in the development of its estate.

Although Robert's designs were met with 'general approbation', his position as supervising architect was less secure. Oversight of the project carried with it a large degree of patronage and control over the award of contracts for the work, which the powerful interests of the trades on the town council were reluctant to cede to a London-based outsider. Similar concerns had thwarted Robert's designs and oversight intentions for the South Bridge in 1785. Keen to avoid any ambiguity from the outset, Robert persuaded Henry Dundas to bind the trustees to maintaining his position as surveyor by identifying him specifically in the subscription papers. Even so, the award of contracts continued to cause trouble, particularly with Alexander Reid, Deacon of the Masons, who did not gain work on the building and consequently tried to undermine Robert at every opportunity.[44]

The few surviving original drawings for the project have a complicated history, and a great many other drawings for various purposes are now buried, missing

40 Pen and ink proposal for Calton Viaduct by Robert Adam, about 1789. The sketch includes a number of Adam's other proposals including the Bridewell, South Bridge and an enormous baroque-domed scheme for the University.
Sir John Soane's Museum, London [vol.2/50]

41 Sketch for a Calton Viaduct by Robert Adam, about 1789. The inked townscape appears to be by a local contact, perhaps John Clerk of Eldin, and from his London office Adam has drawn in pencil his proposals for the viaduct and the University on the horizon.
Sir John Soane's Museum, London [vol.2/52]

or destroyed. An important part of Robert's design process was sketching. Two early sketches including the University buildings survive in the Soane Museum [figs 40, 41]. One set of 'Plans, Sections and Elevations' is buried inside one of the bottles beneath the foundation stone.[45] A large drawing of the east front was hoisted on a pole and processed through the streets as part of the foundation stone ceremony [fig.30]. It is not clear what became of that drawing. Another incomplete set of eleven undated presentation drawings is now in the Soane Museum in London, one of which is labelled 'College drawings from Edinr. Duplicates – 22 July 1796'.[46] It seems likely that at least some of these Soane Museum drawings are original Edinburgh office copies of the presentation drawings of 1789.[47] There was in all likelihood a client copy of the presentation drawings too.[48] The College Trust minutes record that Robert Adam was to produce 'such drawings as will be required for conducting the work by, & to make out every particular part at full size of outside & inside mouldings, dressings, cornices, strings and all the drawings for forming the Carpenters work in Roofs & floors – and for all the different branches of the building'. All these working drawings are now lost or destroyed. Finally, a set of three engravings of two elevations and the principal storey plan were made in 1791 for fundraising purposes. These engravings demonstrate differences from the original drawings, mainly reductions in carved detail and rearrangement of the professors' houses,

which indicates that revisions to the plans were made after the approval of the initial scheme. The set of drawings from which the engravings were taken is now lost.

The double-quadrangle plan and design proposed by Robert Adam represented a sophisticated and elegant resolution of physical constraints and practical considerations [fig.31]. The physical constraints on the site were those of the boundaries of the ancient College and the new South Bridge street and the awkward slopes upwards from east to west and north to south. In spite of various proposals to move the University to a new, and unconstrained, location, there was significant support for retaining the existing site from within both the town council and the University itself. There was potential to expand the existing site to the north, west and south, but none of these had materialised by the time Robert was planning the new building, and various opportunities slipped away during its construction. The ground levels within the site between the Low College and High College Courts of the old buildings had long been problematic. Robert's design included a stone plinth of varying depth, which absorbed the different ground levels around the site. Within the complex, the quadrangles, or 'courts', were at two different levels with pedestrian steps and coach ramps on the axial entrance route from east to west. In order to provide a suitable viewing space for the main east front, Robert maintained the proposal, first set out in his South Bridge scheme, to build a crescent opposite:

42 An engraving of the east elevation, used to promote the fundraising scheme for Robert Adam's new building
Author's Collection

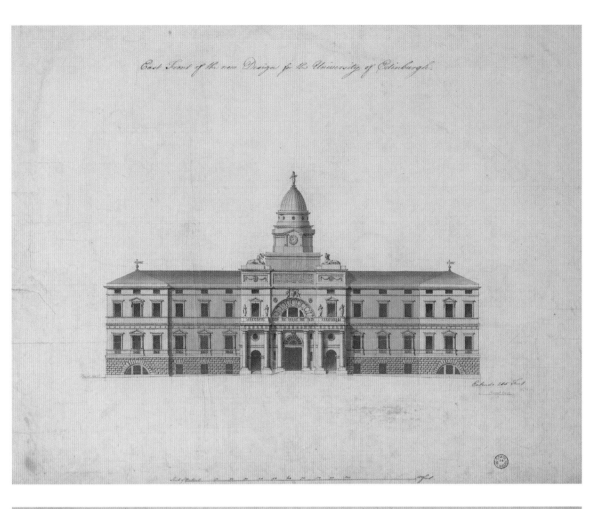

East Front of the new Design for the University of Edinburgh.

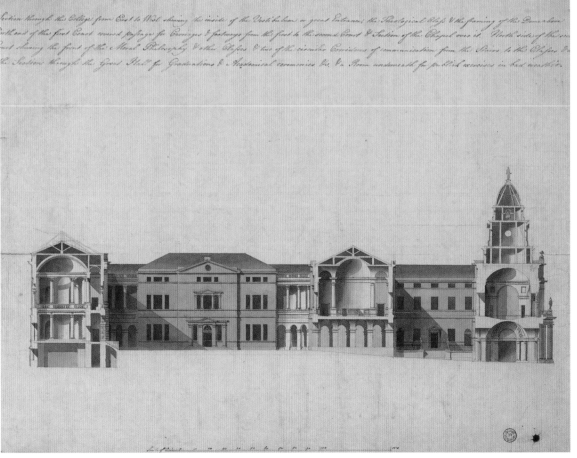

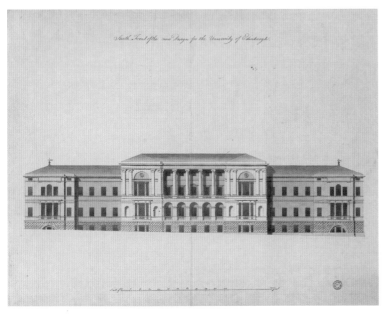

South Front of the new Design for the University of Edinburgh.

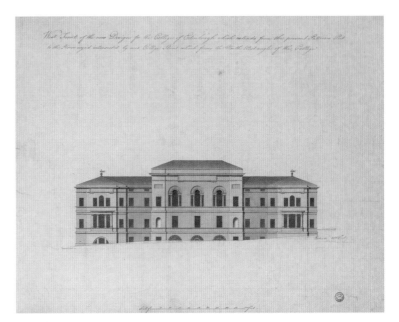

West Front of the new Design for the College of Edinburgh which extends from the present Return Plot to the New rejected intersected by new College Street extended from the North West angle of the College.

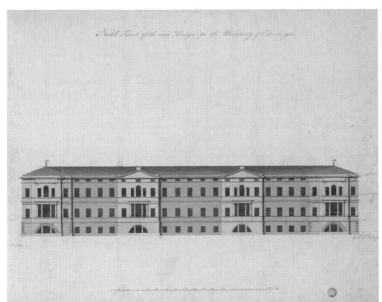

North Front of the new Design for the University of Edinburgh.

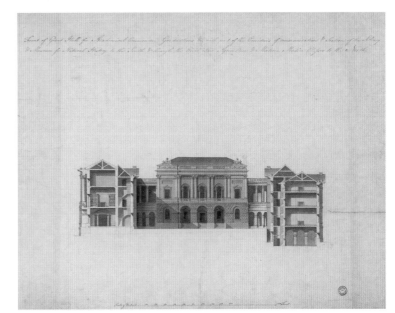

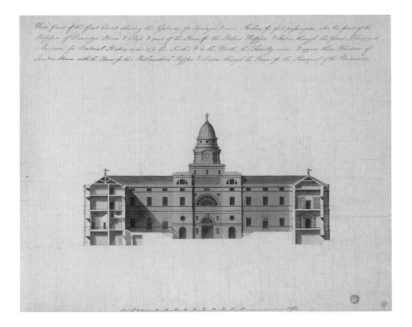

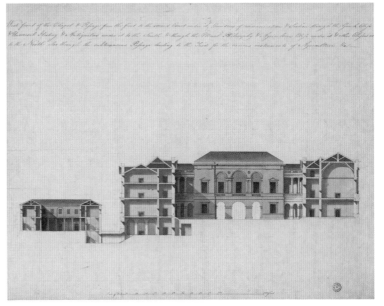

*In order to remedy the want of a proper point of view,
He was exceedingly anxious, that the Street opposite the
East front in Nicolson's street should be thrown quite back
to the Infirmary & formed into a Crescent, which would
have enabled the spectator, standing in the centre of the
Crescent, to have a tolerable view of the East front. And
to prevent Objection from the Managers of the Infirmary,
that throwing back the street on it would confine it &
prevent a proper circulation of air, he proposed, that the
Crescent should consist only of a Range of Shops of one
Story high. Why this part of his Plan was not executed,
I do not remember – probably the Trustees for the South
Bridge could not afford to sacrifice so much feu duty, as
would be lost by building nothing but Shops of one story
on that ground.*[49]

The physical constraints were challenging enough, but
the practical considerations were almost impossible to
reconcile fully. James Gregory, Professor of the Institutes
of Medicine, had set out the general requirements
during the preparation of the South Bridge scheme
in 1785:

*It surely, therefore, cannot be thought superfluous or
unreasonable to have at least as many halls for teaching
in, as there are professorships at present established. These
halls must be of different dimensions, and differently
constructed; and some of the classes, besides the teaching-
room, will require several other apartments. This is
especially the case with the classes of Natural History,
Natural Philosophy, Chemistry, and Anatomy: and the
Divinity class should be accommodated with a proper
place for a theological Library, which is distinct from the
general library of the College. Many of the teaching rooms
should be of such dimensions as to accommodate between
200 and 300 students, and some still larger. The Chemical
Theatre should be fit to contain at least 300 and the
Anatomical 500, or more properly 600.*[50]

Gregory had also argued that the existing site was the
best, as it would be conveniently located next to the new
South Bridge for easy access from the city, close to the
Royal Infirmary for the medical departments, and on
hand for the existing student lodgings. By 1789 student
numbers stood at 1,090 and the number of library books
was increasing by 600–700 volumes per year.[51] There
were twenty-four professorships. Botany was taught
outdoors in summer only in botanical gardens. Teaching
and research were changing, particularly in medicine
and the sciences, towards more empirical methods and
practical experimentation, which required more space
for preparation, equipment, stores, demonstrations etc.[52]

Robert appears to have discussed the professors'
requirements in detail before his appointment as
surveyor to the University in October 1789. These ranged

from the specialist demands of individual professors
for their classrooms to the requirements for communal
spaces (such as the library, great hall and chapel),
circulation spaces (stairs, vestibules and corridors),
service spaces, heating and lighting. Most intractable of
all were the professors' houses, which formed the subject
of endless argument and bickering amongst the staff.
Correspondence between Robert and two of the key
academics, Joseph Black and Andrew Dalzel, sheds some
light on the protracted negotiations over the academic and
residential accommodation required in the new building.

Robert's quadrangular plan filled the entire site to the
old boundaries of the College, and created new unified
neoclassical frontages to each of the surrounding streets

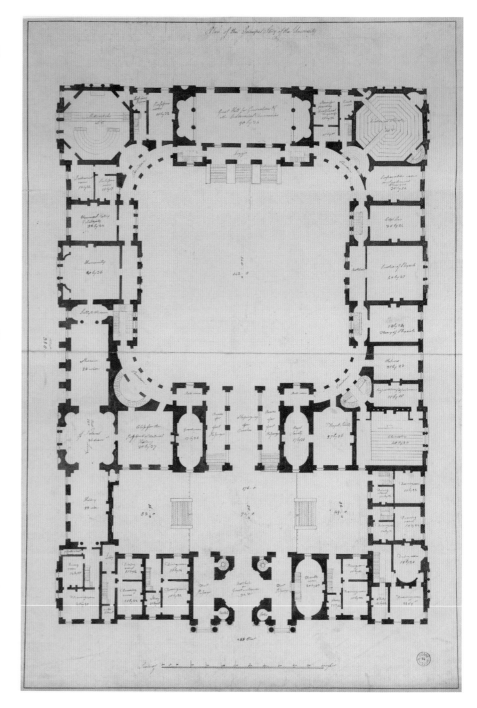

51 Plan of the ground
floor of the University by
Robert Adam

Sir John Soane's Museum, London
[vol.28/34]

52 Detail of the east elevation
of Robert Adam's College
design, 1789

Sir John Soane's Museum, London
[vol.28/26]

53 Elevated view of Old College quad from the west, showing the dome by Robert Rowand Anderson
Neale Smith

like a great Italian Renaissance palazzo occupying an entire city block, or like Diocletian's monumental palace in Split. The nearest precedent in Scotland was the 17th-century double-courtyard complex at the University of Glasgow, which occupied a site in the dense urban landscape of Glasgow's High Street. George Heriot's Hospital, nearby at Lauriston in Edinburgh, another magnificent 17th-century courtyard structure, offered a more local precedent, but here the building stood in its own spacious grounds like a prodigy house. Certainly from the evidence of his sketch designs [figs 40, 41], Robert envisaged the building would stand out from its low-rise suburban context like Heriot's, but the rapid expansion of the city around the site never allowed such views.

At 225 feet by 355 feet, with two internal courts, the design was enormous, representing the largest civic building project of the 18th century in Scotland. The irregular rectangle of the plan was laid out from east to west, with the main entrance occupying the short east-facing elevation to South Bridge. At the corners and centres of each elevation were 'pavilions', taller, advanced blocks with more elaborate architectural treatment. As befitted the entrance, the central block of the east elevation was the most elaborate of all, taking the form of a Roman triumphal arch with a dome set above it [fig.52]. In the early designs, Robert planned sculpted classical figures along the parapet of the upper storey, a carved plaque containing the city arms, and a sculpted sphinx and unicorn flanking the base of the dome. These decorative elements were dropped as the costs of the project rose.

The organisation of the plan is ingenious, particularly when it is considered that there were no contemporary examples of a complete university built from scratch on which Robert could draw.[53] The requirement to provide housing for a number of the professors resulted in a need for a cross-range to form two courts within the overall quadrangular plan. Robert regretted the cross-range because it resulted in a narrow and dark court to the east, but it was simply not possible to accommodate the University's requirements within a single large quadrangle. Some sense of Robert Adam's concerns about the first court can be found in a much later letter from Charles Hope, Lord President of the Court of Session, to Samuel Shepherd, Lord Chief Baron of the Court of Exchequer:

Yesterday I received yours of the 15th on the subject of the College plans & lose no time to possess you with my Ideas, as far as I can convey in the compass of a letter – I am the more desirous & bound to do so, because I believe that I know more of Robert Adam's own views of the subject, than any Man now alive – Probably you know that He and my Grandfather travelled all over Italy together, & that a constant friendship subsisted between them to the last. On this account, when Bob Adam came down to Edinburgh with his Plans, & to set the subscription agoing, He was in our house in St Andrew Square almost every day – & as he knew my Grandfather's correct taste, they had much communication on the subject, at which I was often present. I remember distinctly that Mr Adam was much dissatisfied with the ground & situation of the College, both as too small & confined, & as being so surrounded with other buildings, as not to afford a proper point of view for any of the fronts. The smallness of the space, & the necessity which he had been told there was to provide Houses for the Principal, Librarian, and several Professors, drove him to adopt the cross building, forming the area in the two Courts. This he deeply lamented because the space was not large enough to admit of two Courts of proper size, & in order to procure one of a tolerable size, he was forced to reduce the other so much, that I remember He himself called it a Well.[54]

The east–west axis through the main South Bridge entrance forms a key processional route to the communal spaces of the chapel (in the cross-range) and the great hall (in the west range). The east range of the complex was effectively formed from a terrace of professorial houses and also contained the divinity classroom beneath the dome. At the time the houses would have enjoyed a relatively unobscured easterly aspect towards Arthur's Seat. The houses also allowed the professors to monitor the only entrance to the building and control activities in the first court. The processional route continued underneath the chapel in the cross-range and through the great court to the steps of the great hall [fig.54].

Perhaps influenced by his own experience of the ancient College buildings, which were not all connected and had few places to shelter between classes, Robert proposed a semi-open circulation space surrounding the great court: curved open arcades and colonnades in the corners linked through vestibules and stair-halls on both the main floors. The other main communal spaces, the natural history museum and the library, were to form a T-plan on the south side of the complex, with the library projecting into the cross-range. The remainder of the great court was to be dedicated to teaching spaces. Although externally neoclassical in appearance, the building was far from symmetrical internally. The south range was to be slightly narrower than the north range, and there were all sorts of differences in room sizes and shapes between the north and south ranges. The internal arrangement did not necessarily reflect the external hierarchy: for example the library occupied only part of the central pavilion of the south range, but also spilled over into the less-embellished linking range to the east. A significant feature of the projected plan was the variety of room shapes, from square to rectangular, oval, circular and octagonal. Like its predecessor, the anatomy theatre was to be octagonal [fig.58]. In terms of arrangement, the classrooms seem to have been allocated in accordance with their space requirements, rather than in logical subject groups (for example the medical classrooms were interspersed with civil law, Hebrew and rhetoric classrooms). The plans indicate open hearths in each room.

A number of the professors took a strong and continuing interest in the design of their facilities, notably Alexander Monro secundus, Professor of Anatomy, Joseph Black, Professor of Chemistry, and Andrew Dalzel, Professor of Greek and Keeper of the Library. Before the advent of mechanical refrigeration in the last quarter of the 19th century, the handling of corpses for dissection was a particularly noxious activity. Robert's design placed the new anatomy theatre in a discrete unit as far away from the public face of the University as possible in the north-west corner of the complex. It was lit and ventilated by a cupola over a complicated domed roof, for which a special model was made.[55] A separate service court was built to the north of North College Street (sometimes known as Jamaica Street) for the handling and preparation of corpses, with a connecting tunnel to the basement of the main building. In order to complete the service court plan, it was necessary to purchase additional properties around the old College, including the tenement at the head of College Wynd in

54 Elevation of the great hall for academical ceremonies by Robert Adam

Sir John Soane's Museum, London [vol.28/36]

Large Elevation of the Great Hall for Academical Ceremonies

which the author Walter Scott was born, and land owned by the Incorporation of Bakers.[56] The service court was destroyed when Chambers Street was constructed in the 1870s, but the tunnel survives [fig.57]. Although the facilities for Joseph Black and Andrew Dalzel were not built in their lifetimes, both men had strong views about what was required and how the rooms should be arranged. From correspondence with Robert Adam, it is clear that Black's teaching placed an emphasis on empirical methods, with a requirement for preparation room and facilities for practical demonstrations. In anticipation of rearranging the College books when they transferred to Robert's proposed library, Dalzel toured George III's library, then housed in the Queen's House (later remodelled as Buckingham Palace), and unspecified college libraries at Cambridge, in the company of George Nicol, the king's bookseller.[57]

Such was the success of Robert's design for the University that when James Stirling, the Lord Provost, was looking for harmonious designs for the proposed Charlotte Square, he suggested modelling them on the 'Elegant Simplicity' of the north front of the College.[58] The *Scots Magazine* stated that the architecture of the new building would 'not only do honour to the city, but to the nation, and to Europe'.[59]

FINANCE 1789–1800

In June of 1784 the town council had urged the city's MP, James Hunter Blair, to push the Pitt government for funds from the Forfeited Estates for two great civic improvement projects: construction of the South Bridge; and rebuilding of the University, 'which is in so flourishing a condition with regard to its professors and stands so much in need of improvements with regard to the buildings'.[60] James Gregory led the funding drive of 1785 in respect of the University.[61] At first the two projects were intertwined, but at an early stage the rebuilding of the University was dropped. The precise date and reasons for this decision are not clear, but presumably it was taken to simplify the South Bridge project and contain the costs and risks.

The financial foundations for the new University scheme were somewhat shaky from the start. Estimates must have been provided, but the projected cost of the whole building was never revealed publicly in any of the subscription papers or newspaper articles, and no indication of a figure is given in any of the surviving trustee documents or private correspondence. The earliest reference to the proposed funding is in the minutes of the Senatus for 19 October 1789, which reveals that the town council 'had been encouraged by the prospect of a liberal contribution from the public and of aid from Government, which the Right Hon. Henry Dundas, Treasurer to the Navy, had undertaken

to use his utmost influence to obtain'.[62] Essentially the whole project appears to have been founded on hopes and promises, rather than on a secure funding stream and realistic budgeting.

Recognising that the town council was unable to fund the rebuilding, subscriptions were sought from the general public. Subscription papers could be collected from Goldsmiths' Hall, the College, the Royal Bank of Scotland, the Bank of Scotland, a number of booksellers in Edinburgh, several private banks in Edinburgh and London, and from Robert Adam's office at 13 Albemarle Street, London. Completed papers committed subscribers to paying their contributions into the Royal Bank of Scotland or Bank of Scotland and private banks in Edinburgh and London. The masonry price contract between Robert Adam and James Crichton specified that Crichton could only claim for payment against the Bank of Scotland account containing the subscription, and that he could not pursue claims against individual subscribers.[63]

Subscription lists were published from time to time in the newspapers to encourage further giving. Heading the list at the outset were the town council (£400 per annum for five years); the Writers to the Signet (200 guineas for three years); the Faculty of Advocates; the Royal Society and the 3rd Earl of Hopetoun (100 guineas for five years); and the 7th Earl of Wemyss, who promised the same amount for three years. In 1794 Sir Ralph Abercromby contributed the largest single subscription of £1,845. Some subscribers offered materials in kind, such as Sir John Dalrymple, who supplied 500 bags of lime from his estate at Oxenfoord in Midlothian.[64] Others offered more esoteric gifts, such as the anonymous farmer, who praised the 'noble undertaking' and gave two bullocks, which were sold for nearly £35.[65] However, not all the subscribers made good their promises, and it was necessary to chase up the outstanding amounts through the macer (court officer) of the Court of Session.

Andrew Dalzel, Professor of Greek, University Librarian, Secretary to the Senatus and husband of Robert Adam's niece, was closely involved in the building project, and reported news of the subscriptions to his friend Sir Robert Liston in February 1790:

The subscriptions have gone on far beyond my expectations, though they were abundantly sanguine. They are now up at £15,000, though they have not yet been set foot in London. This was delayed until Parliament should meet and the town should be full, and till Mr. Dundas should go up, which he proposes to do in a few days. I have put your name down for ten guineas as you desired me, which is a very genteel sum. We expect £8000 or £10,000 from India. Mr. R. Adam has the conduct of the building, and it will be the prettiest thing in the island.[66]

By November of the following year, the subscriptions stood at £20,000 and the rumoured sums from India had still not arrived.[67]

Robert Adam continued to be heavily involved in the fundraising campaign. The plans were available for viewing in his London house at 13 Albemarle Street.[68] In January 1791 he agreed with Francis Jukes the sum of fifty guineas for engraving the elevations of the east and south fronts of the University buildings. Jukes recommended James Dickson as the printer for 1,000 copies, which along with two plans and a section would sell for one guinea. The calls for subscriptions were published widely, including in the London newspapers.[69] Notices of subscriptions from around the world were also inserted in the newspapers as exemplars, such as the news of Dr George Caley of the Russian army dispatching his second subscription and the formation of a society of 'respectable Gentlemen' in Calcutta for the specific purpose of collecting subscriptions.[70] Before leaving London for Edinburgh in May 1791, Robert met with Provost Stirling to discuss the production of further engravings of the University plans to send to Jamaica [fig.42].[71] In May 1791, Robert travelled to Hopetoun to collect the Earl of Hopetoun's subscription of 100 guineas a year for five years.[72]

By the time of the meeting of the trustees on 2 July 1791, the project was in severe financial difficulty, and John Paterson, the clerk of works, was ordered to employ fewer hands and make slower progress.[73] Efforts to collect unpaid subscriptions and instalment subscriptions were redoubled and new subscribers sought. The trustees sent circular letters and subscription papers to the magistrates of each royal burgh and copies of the engravings to the convenor of each county in Scotland. In spite of all the publicity, many prominent citizens of Edinburgh had still not subscribed. The trustees formed a special sub-committee to make individual approaches.[74] The financial problems continued into 1792 with the trustees struggling to find enough money to pay the contractors.[75] In November 1792 the trustees applied successfully to the Treasury in London for £5,000 to continue the work.[76] This was the last government aid for the project until after Napoleon's defeat in 1815, as resources became stretched by the wars with France.

The day-to-day management of the expenditure was delegated to the clerk of works, John Paterson, with approval and oversight by the clerk to the trustees, John Grey, and the preses (chairman) of the trustees, Thomas Elder, Lord Provost. Paterson and his assistant were paid annual salaries of £100 and £25 respectively.[77] Workers' wages were paid weekly. Adam charged his customary 5 per cent of expenditure per annum on the project.[78] From the outset it was understood by the trustees that Adam would visit the site only once a year.

PROGRESS

Francis, Lord Napier, Grand Master Mason of Scotland, laid the foundation stone of the new University buildings with great pomp and ceremony on Monday 16 November 1789. Lord Cockburn recalled that the boys of the High School were given a half-day's holiday to witness the occasion.[79] Like many such events, it was partly a celebration at the outset of a great project, partly a Masonic ceremony, and partly a publicity and fundraising effort. The proceedings were described in great detail in the *Scots Magazine* and other newspapers and recorded by David Allan in his famous engraving of the occasion [fig.30].[80] In advance of the festivities the *Caledonian Mercury* advertised that 'A triumphal arch is to be erected, designed by Mr Robert Adam, under which the procession is to pass', but this feature is not described or depicted in the accounts after the event.[81] The military and city guard lined the streets, and an astonishingly large crowd of 30,000 assembled. At 12.30pm a long and splendid procession of dignitaries of the town council, University and freemasons set out for the site from Parliament House in the High Street, accompanied by a band of musicians and singers. The foundation stone itself is not now identifiable, but it is described in the town council minutes as located 'on the east side of the College, being the corner stone of the north side of the entry to the College'.[82] It had been intended to place the stone at the north-east corner of the complex, but difficulty making a suitable foundation led to a location further south.[83] The Glasshouse of Leith cast two glass bottles to be buried with the foundation stone.[84] These contained copies of the plans, a series of coins, a short account of the foundation of the College, and a miscellany of papers including newspaper articles, subscription forms and a list of the attending dignitaries.

The construction of the great palace of learning was to be phased to match the available funding and planned to minimise disruption to teaching.[85] The old buildings were to remain in use until the replacement accommodation for each class was ready. This planning skewed the construction to areas of the site that were relatively clear of classrooms, but contained antiquated housing for professors. Perhaps unsurprisingly top priority was placed on construction of the showpiece east range, which would also disguise the guddle of old buildings and construction mess behind. However, as much of the new east range was to be dedicated to professorial housing, it would do little to alleviate the crisis in teaching accommodation. The decision was taken to proceed in two areas almost simultaneously with separate teams of contractors: the east range, beginning at the Principal's house in the north-east corner of the site; and the anatomy theatre and classrooms in the north-west corner. The intention was to link the two corners by gradual construction of the north range, working from both ends towards the centre. The west and south ranges would follow as funds allowed.

Land on the east side of the new street was obtained from the South Bridge trustees for storage of materials; 'shades' or shelters / workshops, were erected for James Crichton's masons and carpenters; and work started on the massive foundations of the east range. The only significant demolition required here immediately was the Professor of Divinity's house. Rather more substantial demolitions were required for operations in the north-west corner of the site in March 1790, including the College gate and steeple, the houses of the Professors of Greek and Hebrew and also those of the janitors.[86] More shades were built in the upper court, and a separate team of masons, led by Robert Thomson, began work on the new anatomy theatre on 1 April.[87] It proved problematic immediately: the foundations and subterranean passages (required for the delivery and removal of corpses to the theatre) hit hard whinstone.

The stone for the building was to be obtained from different local quarries according to its purpose: Craigleith Quarry stone for the best polished, droved and broached ashlar in prominent areas; slightly cheaper Redhall Quarry stone for less prominent areas; and strong Hailes Quarry stone for door and window jambs, hearths, 'hanging stairs' and floors.[88] The roof slates came from the Easdale Slate Company in the Firth of Lorn, Inner Hebrides.[89]

In July 1790 Robert reported optimistically to the trustees that he hoped to roof the anatomy theatre, construct the east range to window height on the principal storey, and lay the foundations of the north wall (joining the constructed north-east and north-west corners) during that building season.[90] In fact the anatomy theatre was not completed until late 1792.

The issue of development opposite the University on land owned by the South Bridge trustees on the east side of Nicolson Street raised its head again in October 1790, when Lord Provost Stirling asked Robert to revisit his 1785 proposals for the trustees and draw up detailed designs.[91] By now the ambitions for the site were more civic, incorporating a concert hall, retiring rooms, a tea room, a stationer's shop, offices for the Highland Society, a coffee room or eating house and ten 'front and back shops'. Robert duly produced a couple of alternative single-storey schemes for Stirling's consideration [figs 55, 56].[92] Although beautiful in themselves, the crescent proposals were really Robert's attempt to create a civic space and 'proper point of view' as a setting for the University. The proposals probably foundered again because the single-storey crescent design failed to maximise the development potential of the site and in consequence the feu duty payable to the South Bridge trustees.

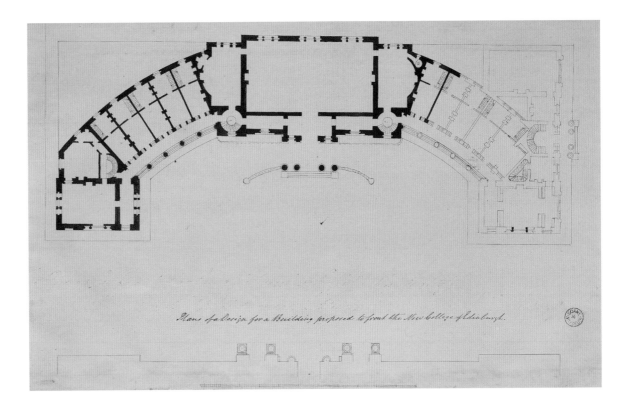

55 One of the alternative plans of a crescent opposite the College of Edinburgh by Robert Adam, 1791

Sir John Soane's Museum, London [vol.34/14]

56 Robert Adam's elevation of a proposed crescent opposite the old College buildings, 1791

Sir John Soane's Museum, London [vol.34/12]

John Paterson, the first clerk of works, was an architect/builder in his own right. He described his position as the director of the executive part of Robert Adam's business in Scotland.[93] Paterson set aside time every Monday to write a report on the business of the week to Robert Adam in London.[94] The relationship between Paterson and Adam as revealed in the surviving correspondence is interesting. At times Adam appeared to distrust Paterson for no obvious reason and asserted his authority over decisions but Paterson seems to have had a high degree of regard and loyalty towards Adam, acting attentively on his own initiative to secure Adam's best interests and then meticulously recording the reasons for his actions. As late as 1790 Paterson referred

57 Tunnel under Chambers Street to allow discreet transportation of corpses to the anatomy theatre. Initially, the tunnel was planned to link the agriculture classroom to a 'Yard for various instruments of Agriculture' (see fig.48).
HES

58 Robert Adam's anatomy theatre, divided horizontally by Playfair in 1824
HES

diplomatically to the South Bridge as 'your bridge' in the context of discussions about a new approach road (later Lothian Street), even though the modified design and construction bore little resemblance to Robert's spectacular proposals.[95] There are signs in the correspondence that Adam had lost some of his knowledge of the Edinburgh building trades during his time in London.[96] One sign of this was the controversy that arose over the masonry contract, which was awarded to Alexander Reid on the basis of price alone. Having won the contract, Reid then attempted to renegotiate a higher price, using his influence with the trustees. Paterson urged Adam to appoint tradesmen that could be trusted.

On 19 March 1791 Paterson reported the successful erection without incident of the first of the six enormous monolithic columns at the entrance.[97] These were a real Roman extravagance, particularly in view of the shaky finances of the project. Four days later the remaining columns had been carefully lifted into place, observed by Thomas Elder and James Stirling, the new Lord Provost. The columns, which measured 22 feet 4 inches in height by 3 feet 2 inches diameter and weighed 16 tons, were drawn from Craigleith Quarry on purpose-built carriages. By April 1791 Paterson was reporting that the north-west corner of the College was 'fare advanced' and that he hoped the roofing would take place in May.[98]

When the financial difficulties began to bite in July 1791, twenty masons were dismissed overnight, mainly those working on the anatomy theatre, which was nearly complete anyway. The relationship between Robert Adam and John Paterson also deteriorated to the point that the clerk of works was dismissed and replaced by Hugh Cairncross (Adam's clerk of works at Culzean and Dalquharran Castles in Ayrshire) in November 1791.[99]

59 Plan of the work completed to Robert Adam's plan by 1800
Crown copyright 2017 Ordnance Survey [Licence Number 100021521]

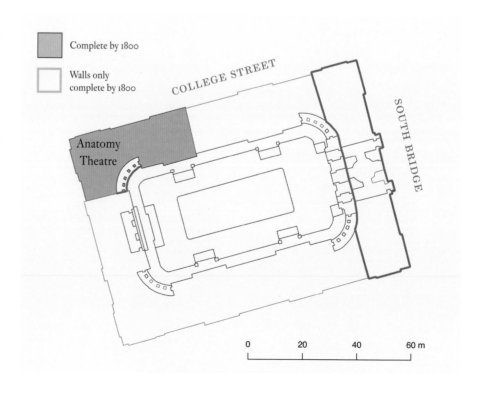

Complete by 1800

Walls only complete by 1800

COLLEGE STREET

SOUTH BRIDGE

Anatomy Theatre

0   20   40   60 m

Although relations between Robert and his brother, John, had soured in the aftermath of the financial problems of William Adam & Co., and there was a slightly stiff and formal accidental meeting between the pair in the street, Robert promised to show John his plans of the College, and John got in touch about a request by a plasterer, Gilchrist, for a share of the work on the University.[100]

The death of Robert Adam on 3 March 1792 brought further difficulties to the troubled project. James and William Adam wrote to the trustees on 16 March excusing their delay in making contact on account of the 'multiplicity of concerns' left behind by Robert and offering to complete their brother's scheme as 'better qualified than any body to fall in with our late Brother's ideas'.[101] The trustees accepted James and William's offer and appointed them surveyors of the new buildings on the same terms as Robert. James visited the site and recommended completion of the new anatomy theatre so that the old theatre could be demolished and the ground raised to prevent unequal settlement of the new east range.[102] A further recommendation was the demolition of Hamilton Lodging and construction of new classrooms to the east of the anatomy theatre (in the north range).[103]

Just the day before the death of Principal Robertson on 11 June 1793, James reported to the trustees that Dr Monro had taken possession of the new anatomy theatre and that the adjoining section would soon be ready for roofing.[104] However, the funding crisis worsened to the point where the trustees ordered a stop to all new work in September 1793, with only the roofing

and completion of the existing classrooms continuing. By December, they were forced to call a halt to all work because there was not enough money to cover the outstanding debts to tradesmen.[105] Completed work included three classrooms adjacent to the anatomy theatre, the 'offices' in the yard at the north-west corner for receiving corpses, and the Principal's house and two professors' houses at the north-east corner.[106] The removal of the old anatomy theatre had allowed work to start on the staircases and great piers beneath the intended dome at the centre of the east front. The tradesmen offered to continue working on the basis that they would charge interest on overdue bills. Little further work proceeded in 1794 and 1795, with the exception of the foot pavement and parapet wall on the east front, which were deemed essential for the purpose of public presentation and preventing deterioration of the incomplete east range.[107] James Adam died in London on 20 October 1794. The youngest of the Adam brothers, William, and his clerk, John Robertson, appear to have assumed responsibility for the minor works that followed James's death. With the termination of Hugh Cairncross's salary as clerk of works on 31 December 1795, the building work ground to a complete halt. It was not until 1809, when several tradesmen took their claim against the town council to the Court of Session, that accounts for the first phase of work were finally paid from the profits of the South Bridge.[108]

For four years the project lay in abeyance, with only the north-west and north-eastern corners complete and large parts of the half-completed east range open to the elements. An emergency government grant in 1799 allowed the College to secure the parts of the new building that were in danger of ruin. Further progress was hampered by the financial and manpower impact of the Napoleonic Wars, and it was 1816 before a new programme of works to finish the building was contemplated.

60 Plan of the City of Edinburgh dedicated to Thomas Elder by Thomas Brown and James Watson, 1793. The plan shows the intended double courtyard.
National Library of Scotland, Edinburgh

61 Halfpenny minted to celebrate the new University, 1797
SCRAN [000-100-083-198-c]

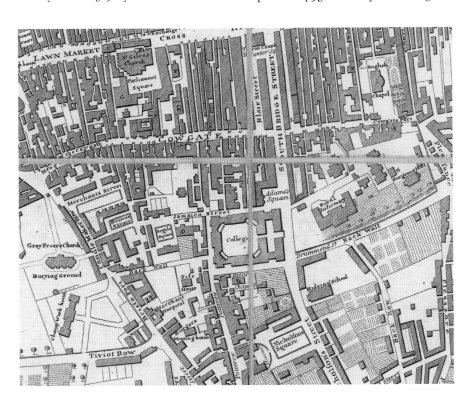

Chapter Three

Old College 1800 to the Present Day

NICK HAYNES

This chapter relates the various plans and proposals for completing Robert Adam's University buildings between 1800 and 1815, the architectural competition of 1815–16, the development of the site under William Henry Playfair between 1817 and 1840, Robert Rowand Anderson's dome, and 20th- and 21st-century alterations.

HIATUS 1800–1815

The greatest irony of the Adam building was that for more than twenty years it remained in an indeterminate state of construction, less of an impressive new home for the University and more of an imperial Roman ruin, like those depicted by Piranesi and admired by Adam. In many ways the University estate was in a far worse condition in 1800 than it had been before Adam's new building began in 1789: students and staff picked their way around a building site, frozen in time since 1795; only six rooms in the north-west corner of the new complex were occupied and three houses at the north-east corner were roofed; the roofless shells of the new east range and parts of the north range were open to the elements and already decaying; useful teaching and living accommodation in the old complex had been removed and not replaced; and the remaining dilapidated 17th-century buildings, housing only five classrooms and the library, continued to crumble.[1] Not only were the building funds exhausted, but also some £3,000 remained outstanding to contractors, and another £90,000 was required to complete the scheme.[2] Although there were twenty-seven professors and the Principal, two professors received no salary at all and the average for the remaining staff was a derisory £85 per annum.[3] Drawn to the University for its academic reputation, numerous visitors recorded their surprise and disappointment at the state of the accommodation. Joseph Frank, a German doctor visiting Edinburgh in 1803, was typical:

As the building, in which the lectures were given, partly had fallen into decay, and partly was found too small, they began to rebuild the same a few years ago. The lack of the necessary funds, however, has prevented the completion of this creation according to a grand plan. The façade is magnificent. It is a shame that this building is not in the new city. The library [in the 1617 Building] is handsome and of great utility.[4]

The Professor of Materia Medica, for instance, has no Laboratory, and in consequence is deprived of the opportunity of preparing and exhibiting to his students those practical processes that it is a leading object of his chair to explain. The Professors of Mathematics, of Natural Philosophy, and of Agriculture have no apartments for the reception and presentation of their instruments and models, while those of Divinity and Oriental Languages are under

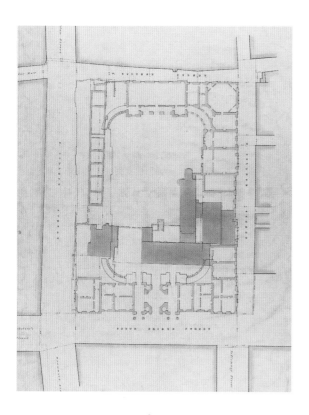

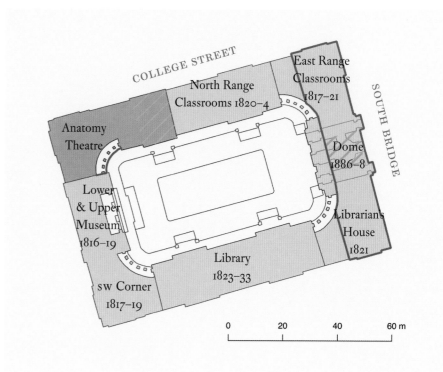

the necessity of teaching by the light of candles, although their classes meet in the forenoon. Others again are obliged to read their lectures in rooms not capable of containing the number of their Students, and some can obtain no accommodation at all either in the new or old Buildings.[5]

If the physical and financial condition of the University was fragile, this was in stark contrast to its thriving intellectual state. Matriculated student numbers rose from 1,193 to 1,332 in the decade between 1790 and 1800.[6] Nine regius professorships were established under George III, but the crown paid only for their salaries, not for their accommodation or equipment. Some of the greatest minds of the late phase of the Scottish Enlightenment continued to teach at the University including John Playfair, John Leslie, John Walker, Dugald Stewart and Thomas Brown. Societies flourished, including The Academical, which Henry Cockburn recalled in his *Memorials of His Time*: 'It met in Playfair's class-room, which was then the great receptacle of youthful philosophers and orators. There were more essays read, and more speeches delivered, by ambitious lads, in that little shabby place [Teviot Chambers], than in all Scotland.'[7]

It was clear that substantial sums of money would be required to finish the building, and that only the government could find the necessary amounts with any degree of reliability and continuity.[8] The trustees prepared a memorandum to Henry Dundas in 1799 requesting government funds to pay off their debts and to at least secure the incomplete parts of the building

from the weather.[9] This request was repeated in 1800 and £5,000 was finally granted in 1801.[10] The Crown Agent, Hugh Warrender, administered the money, and a new ad hoc committee oversaw the partial spending of the grant. The southern houses in the east front were roofed, but no windows were installed, the central block, intended for the divinity classroom and theology library remained roofless and the walls facing the courtyard incomplete, leaving the range still exposed to the elements and largely unusable. Friends of the University continued to push for funds to complete the building, but new suggestions for a lottery failed to galvanise the magistrates.[11]

The new Lord Provost, William Coulter, made a fresh attempt to restart the building project in December 1808, when he asked the former clerk of works, Hugh Cairncross, to prepare an estimate to complete Robert Adam's scheme. The resulting figure of £148,684 was dauntingly high.[12] Unsurprisingly, Coulter turned to Robert Reid, newly appointed King's Architect and Surveyor in Scotland, to revise Adam's plans on a smaller and more economical scale. Reid had inherited and redesigned another of Adam's schemes for the College of Justice in Parliament Square in 1803.[13] The royal appointment, for which Reid had lobbied through his clients, the Barons of the Court of Exchequer, was widely regarded as a reward for his work in Parliament Square.[14] With the notable exception of his early Greek Revival Leith Customs House (1810), Reid worked largely in Adam's neoclassical style throughout his career. His designs for the remodelling of Parliament Square

63 Plan of the Old College site in June 1818 by W.H. Playfair. The grey outlines show the old College buildings and the pink outlines show the walls completed to Robert Adam's design by 1816. University of Edinburgh [0057339]

64 Plan of Old College, as completed by W.H. Playfair and Robert Rowand Anderson
Crown copyright 2017 Ordnance Survey [Licence Number 100021521]

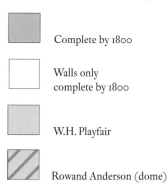

Complete by 1800

Walls only complete by 1800

W.H. Playfair

Rowand Anderson (dome)

and extension of Parliament House drew heavily on Adam's designs for the University, which undoubtedly stood him in good stead with the Lord Provost for advising on the completion of the University, as did his warm relationship with the Barons of the Exchequer (who effectively controlled the London Treasury's public spending in Scotland).

Reid drew up plans and a report on the University buildings in 1810, estimating that he could complete the job on a reduced scale, omitting the southern range and cross-range, converting the professors' houses for teaching use and relocating the dome as an observatory on the north range, for a bargain £61,850.[15] Robert Morison, the former assistant to Robert Adam, who had submitted rival plans to those of his master in 1789, also appears to have drawn up an unofficial three-sided quadrangular scheme in 1810.

The Barons of the Exchequer added their support for Treasury funding of Reid's scheme to petitions by the University Senatus, the Lord Provost and magistrates and the politically influential Convention of the Royal Burghs of Scotland, even quoting recent government grants to the University of Glasgow, the Royal College of Surgeons in London and Trinity College, Dublin. The Lords of the Treasury, occupied with the pressing concerns of the war with France, appear to have forgotten the submission quickly and lost the papers, including Reid's plans.[16]

The dilapidated University buildings remained a live issue in Edinburgh, however. The problems were now chronic. Even the parts of the new building that had been completed were in a shocking state. Amongst the numerous effects of passing time and lack of maintenance, the most alarming were the large panes of glass crashing to the floor of the anatomy theatre from the unpainted and heavily rusted iron-framed cupola above.[17] Architect Richard Crichton prepared further unofficial plans for the completion of the buildings in 1812.[18] By the following year there was increasing public clamour:

Permit a well-wisher to his native city, through your Miscellany, to address himself to the Magistracy on the old and oft-repeated subject of the deplorable situation of our University, which has been standing for many years in one of our most public streets, in a half-finished state, serving no purpose, but to remind us how usefully the elegant pile ought now to have been employed. We have often been tantalized by being told that steps were immediately to be taken to get it finished, yet we never hear of any such being taken. I can scarcely suppose, if either the town-council, or a meeting of the inhabitants, were to petition Parliament for a grant of £50,000, or even £100,000 Sterling for such a National purpose, that it would be refused, particularly after stating the worse than useless and unemployed state in which it is at present, and the slender prospect there is of its being finished.[19]

The outgoing magistrates washed their hands of the problem: '[W]e have resolved that no new work of any magnitude shall be begun until these great and unprecedented advances shall be paid off, and we would also beg leave most earnestly to entreat our successors in office to pursue the same plans of economy as the only means by which the funds of the city can be relieved from the heavy burdens into which they have unavoidably been involved.'[20]

In this dark hour for the University's building project, a new champion came to the fore in the person of William Dundas, Tory MP for Edinburgh, Lord Commissioner of the Admiralty, and younger brother of Chief Baron Robert Dundas. In April 1813 William Dundas renewed the approach to the government, this time through the Prime Minister, the 2nd Earl of Liverpool, for another £5,000 to deal with the immediate crisis.[21] Although unsuccessful in the first instance, Dundas maintained pressure in Westminster for grant-aid throughout 1814 and into 1815.[22]

The formal grant approval followed what appears to modern eyes as a topsy-turvey parliamentary process: the Lord Provost was informed of the success of the town council's application for public funding in March 1815; the town council were then invited to submit a formal petition for the money, which was scrutinised and approved by a select committee, chaired by William Dundas; finally on 21 June 1815 the Chancellor of the Exchequer, Nicholas Vansittart, proposed a vote in the House of Commons for £10,000 for the 'extension and improvement of the public buildings of the University of Edinburgh'.[23] At the request of the Lord President and the Chief Baron, Robert Reid had travelled to London to discuss his plans with William Dundas and other members of the select committee.[24] The Lord Provost, Sir John Marjoribanks, had also requested the opinion of the noted civil engineer, Robert Stevenson, on the siting of the new university buildings. Stevenson, who had been a student at the University, argued unsuccessfully that the fragmentary Adam building should be moved stone-by-stone for completion in a new spacious setting on Calton Hill.[25]

Interestingly, and perhaps reflecting the promotion of the grant by Dundas, the Chancellor described the vote

as a mark of gratitude of the country for the benefit derived from that establishment [the University] *by the numerous medical gentlemen whom the army and navy had received from it; and an additional claim was given on account of the want of room, principally for the library, which had greatly increased in extent.*

Francis Horner, MP for St Mawes in Cornwall, alumnus of the University and friend, acolyte and fellow member of the Edinburgh literati's Friday Club with Professor John Playfair, suggested that 'Not only architects should be consulted, but also the professors of the several branches of science, whose accommodation ought to be particularly consulted.' Horner continued to take a strong interest in the building project until his emigration to Italy on health grounds in late 1816, and may well have been a key ally of Professor Playfair in promoting the views of the academics in the procurement process.[26] Technically, the money was granted to the king, who then dispersed it to the Lord Provost and town council under a royal warrant. At this stage the government gave no further commitment than £10,000, although Dundas's report suggested a figure of 'between Seventy and Eighty Thousand Pounds' and there seems to have been a general understanding that a further six annual instalments of £10,000 would follow, but it was enough to initiate a flurry of activity in Edinburgh.

COMPETITION 1815–1816

As the money was to be vested in the Lord Provost and town council, Sir John Marjoribanks, the Lord Provost, took the lead back in Edinburgh. Perhaps partly through desperation to get started before his term of office expired in October 1815, partly through enthusiasm, and partly underestimating the influence and patronage of the legal profession in the city, Marjoribanks set off a somewhat chaotic procurement process. Firstly he met with William and Robert Dundas and other political and legal worthies.[27] The discussions are not recorded in detail, but the outcome of the meeting was that on 9 July 1815 the town council issued an advertisement for an architectural competition 'for finishing the College of Edinburgh on a reduced scale' with a prize or premium of 100 guineas.[28] Initially the closing date for competition entries was set for 1 September 1815, and the advertisement stipulated sticking as closely as practicable to the Adam design, but omitting the south range and cross-range.

Recognising that the competition would take some time to complete, and being keen 'to set the work agoing as a claim for getting the money voted by Parliament', Marjoribanks instructed the architect Archibald Elliot and George Cairncross, son of Adam's clerk of works, to start work on Adam's original plans for the graduation hall in the west range using the contractors Scott & Lorimer.[29] By November the old chambers along the west wall had been demolished and construction of the walls of the intended graduation hall had reached the top of the ground floor arcade [fig.65].[30] However, there were well-founded concerns about the construction proceeding before the official selection of an architect

and adoption of a revised plan, and building stopped only a third complete in early 1816 when Elliot began suggesting amendments to the design.

The decision to advertise for plans reflected the parliamentary advice to consult architects (in the plural) and the professors for their latest requirements, however, it represented something of a snub to Robert Reid, whose designs of 1810 had formed the basis of the approach to parliament. Clearly piqued, Reid declined to enter the competition, and with the experience of the Signet Library in mind, refused to be considered as executant to another architect's designs, but nevertheless requested that his proposals should be considered as an alternative to the eventual competition-winning design.[31] Archibald Elliot also refused to submit to the competition on the grounds of his senior standing as an architect. However, at the insistence of the Lord Advocate, Sir William Rae, Sir John Marjoribanks offered Elliot eighty guineas to submit a plan separately.[32] A further 100 guineas was authorised by Marjoribanks as a fee to another special case, William Adam, who promised to supply a more suitable scheme than any other person on the basis of his elder brother's plans, in spite of the fact that he was a businessman and not an architect.

It was certainly sensible to determine the up-to-date requirements of the professors, as Reid's 1810 proposals had been based on a straightforward reorganisation of the Adam plan without the domestic accommodation. Circumstances had changed significantly since work had

65 Ascent of John Sadler's hydrogen balloon from the College on 3 November 1815, taken from James Millar's *Encyclopaedia Edinensis* (volume 1, plate 1) published in 1827. The north-west corner of the quadrangle, as constructed by Robert Adam, is visible, as is the lower floor of the museum, built by Archibald Elliot in 1815, and the western end of the old 1642 Library (on the right of the image).

Private Collection

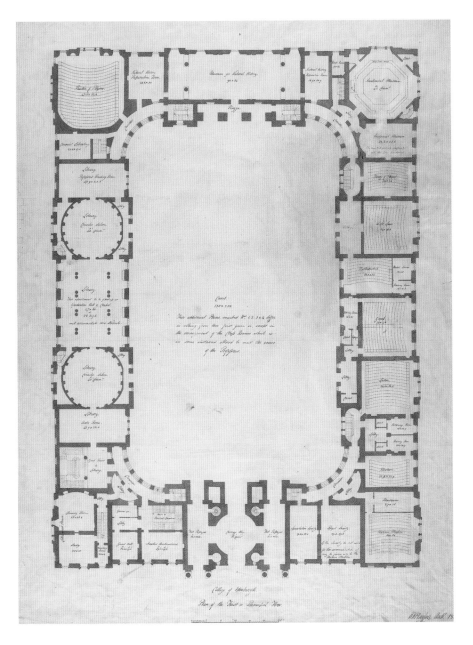

66 Proposed plan of principal floor by W.H. Playfair, 1816

University of Edinburgh [0013913]

library, reading rooms, museums, chapel, a concert room, meeting rooms, examination hall and graduation hall. As more of the influential Edinburgh legal fraternity became re-engaged with the project, it quickly became clear that the competition deadline was too tight and the design instructions were too restrictive. Just a month after the opening of the competition, a new advertisement was published in the newspapers, extending the deadline for submissions to 1 January 1816 and removing the stipulation that the south range and cross-range should be omitted, simply leaving it to architects to decide for themselves how best to reduce costs and preserve Adam's design.[34] The deadline was later extended again to 15 February 1816. The reasons for the delay in judging the competition are not entirely clear from the documentation, but the change in composition of the town council, the jostling of powerful patrons for influence in the selection of a scheme, and the determination of the professors to have their say, undoubtedly played a part.

Some months after the launch of the competition, in October 1815, Duncan gathered the requirements of the professors, along with some general thoughts of his own, into a single printed document as guidance to the architects. The professors' responses and Duncan's comments provide an interesting insight into practical concerns about the existing Adam buildings and with regard to contemporary teaching methods and equipment. Duncan made a number of practical recommendations including: removal or reduction of Adam's court-side circulation spaces, which created significant noise and restricted light from the south to the classrooms; placing of the junior classes on the ground floor to reduce the noise and disruption between classes at the upper levels; placing late afternoon classes on the upper floor to maximise light; allowing for fast filling and emptying of the classrooms by careful attention to the design of the access; ensuring that professors had their own separate entrances near their chairs; classrooms were to be long, rather than square or broad, for optimal sight and sound; professors' chairs should be raised and central, lit from behind or the side; and heating should be designed to serve the room evenly, rather than roasting the professor and freezing the students. Most professors specified 'boards' (panels of slate assembled to form a blackboard) or two sliding boards, and some specified the ability to darken the room for demonstrating experiments.

Anatomy, chemistry, materia medica, natural history, midwifery, humanity, Greek, mathematics and natural philosophy were to have specially designed classrooms. Chemistry, which had expanded into the most popular course under the inspirational leadership of professors Joseph Black and Thomas Charles Hope, had the greatest demands for space and facilities, totalling seven rooms in all. In recognition of the dangerous

ceased on Adam's plan: the city had grown up around the University and noise and distracting onlookers from the streets were now issues; a number of new subjects had been added to the University's teaching responsibilities, and class sizes had grown.[33]

A very thorough consultation with the professors was organised through Andrew Duncan Jr, Professor of Medical Jurisprudence and Medical Police and secretary to the Senatus. He provided a detailed questionnaire to each professor requesting their input on: the size of their classes; any particular location, lighting, heating (fireplace, furnace or stove) or seating requirements; special teaching equipment (e.g. 'a board for the exhibition of figures'); the need for a dedicated classroom or a willingness to share facilities; the need for private reading rooms, class libraries or museums and apparatus, laboratory, preparation or dissection rooms; and comments on the communal requirements including a

67 Presentation drawing
of the quadrangle by
W.H. Playfair, 1816

University of Edinburgh
[coll-13/55/4881]

nature of the experiments, the demonstration area in
the classroom for over 500 students was to have a floor
of stone and an enclosing railing, a dedicated water
pipe and cistern, a hood over the fireplace to carry
away noxious vapours and separate flues for the two
additional furnaces.

In addition to the teaching rooms, a number of requirements for public and administrative rooms emerged from
the consultation with the professors. Naturally the library
headed the list of specifications, requiring: space for at
least 100,000 volumes (double the existing number of
books); a means of securing valuable manuscripts and
rare books; reading rooms or recesses for professors and
students; dry, bright and uniformly heated space or spaces
with minimal causes of dust; easy access; precautions
against fire; and an entrance arrangement that made
the librarians accessible, but protected the books and
catalogues from the students. The largest of the University
museums, the natural history museum, was to be
allocated two or more rooms of 90 to 100 feet in length,
with similar heating and lighting requirements to the
library, and a lumber room for 'containing boxes &c. and
coarse things' nearby. Two rooms were to be allocated for
meetings of the Senatus and committees. If no residential
accommodation was to be provided for the Principal, he
should be allotted official chambers. A chapel, graduation
hall and concert room were also included in the list of
public room provision.

The newspaper advertisements provoked a strong
interest in the University's architectural competition.

Seven architects submitted proposals: William Burn;
William Henry Playfair; John Paterson; James Milne;
Thomas Hamilton Jr; Robert Morison; and Richard
Crichton re-sent his previous scheme after the
competition deadline. William Adam submitted his
scheme in October 1815, presumably drawn up by one
of his firm's draughtsmen in London or possibly by his
cousin Daniel Robertson.[35] Archibald Elliot followed
suit in March 1816, after the deadline, to ensure that
his commissioned design was not mistaken for a
competition entry.

The plans differed quite fundamentally in respect of
the omission of the south range and cross-range. Milne
and Hamilton adhered to Adam's two-court plan, which
was not favoured by the professors. Paterson's scheme
appears to have retained the stubs of Adam's cross-range,
but removed the central chapel, also ruled out by the
professors. Crichton resubmitted his three-range, U-plan
scheme, open to the south and the dome relocated to the
north elevation, again rejected by the professors. Reid's
1810 scheme, submitted as part of the parliamentary
grant application, was similarly three-sided, and was
not reconsidered by the professors. Morison submitted
both a new quadrangular scheme and his old three-sided
scheme. By April 1816 the professors had narrowed
down the favoured proposals to those that retained all
four external elevations of Adam's design, but opened
the internal space into a single, unified courtyard or
quadrangle. These schemes were by William Adam,
William Burn, Archibald Elliot and William Henry

Playfair. However, the decision-making responsibility lay with the town council at this point, and the professors could only comment and lobby behind the scenes.

With no council-approved plan in place by June 1816, there were clearly concerns in London about the conduct of the project. In approving the second tranche of £10,000, the Lords of the Treasury instructed that the selection of an architect should be overseen by 'a Committee of Gentlemen' including the Lord Provost, the Lord President, the Lord Justice Clerk, the Lord Chief Baron, the Lord Chief Commissioner of the Jury Court, the Principal of the University (George Husband Baird, who was in place until 1840), William Dundas, Sir John Marjoribanks (by now the MP for Berwickshire) and Hugh Warrender, the Crown Agent.[36] The selected committee members then sought a wider remit to 'direct & control the issue and expenditure of the whole money voted for that purpose [execution of the plan]'.[37] The committee members formed the new College commissioners (or trustees, as they were known originally). A much more methodical approach to the project took hold from the first meeting on 12 September 1816. Further members were appointed in October 1816: Lord

Advocate, Alexander Maconochie; Secretary of the Senatus, Andrew Duncan; and First Bailie of the town council, Alexander Henderson.

In view of the widely differing approaches to the architectural competition, the commissioners' first decision was to establish the overall form of the building and invite the competing architects to refine or resubmit their proposals. The trustees honed the brief yet again to stipulate that 'the exterior of the original design of the late Mr Adam should as far as possible be adhered to, leaving out the cross-building, provided it can be made to suit the accommodation required', and a new deadline of 3 October 1816 was set.[38] The architects duly amended their proposals, and the professors considered the revised plans over the course of October and November 1816. Once again, Andrew Duncan sent a very thorough questionnaire to each of the professors, asking for an overall preference and comments on detailed issues including the method of dealing with the differences in the levels of the site, the design of the public rooms, the design of individual professors' rooms, the general arrangement of the internal spaces, any defects in designs, and any completely objectionable designs.

68   Presentation cross-section of the quadrangle by W.H. Playfair, 1816. The drawing shows Playfair's first design for the north range, which he altered at a later stage.
University of Edinburgh [coll-13/55/4886]

-COLLEGE-OF-EDINBVRGH-

-ELEVATION-OF-THE-BVILDING-ON-THE-NORTH-SIDE-OF-THE-COVRT-WITH-SECTIONS-OF-THE-BVILDINGS-AT-THE-EAST-AND-WEST-ENDS-

Perhaps to clarify the professorial recommendation to the commissioners, a vote on various aspects of the plans was staged on 23 November. By this time the choice had narrowed to Playfair and Burn, with Playfair attracting by far the majority of votes on his overall scheme and detailed planning.

Like most of the other competitors, Playfair used the lengthy deliberation period to refine and amend his original submission. Although the drawings submitted at the outset in February 1815 have been identified, it is not entirely clear which drawings were on the table when the decision was finally made almost a year later.[39] Playfair adopted three principles in his design: economy; adherence to the spirit of Adam's existing buildings; and attention to 'the present and the probable wants of the University'.[40] Playfair's scheme retained much of Adam's exterior elevations and the internal elevation of the great hall (museum under Playfair's scheme), but reorganised the three remaining internal elevations around a single courtyard, repeating Adam's corner colonnades and reconfiguring the articulation of the longer elevations [figs 67, 68]. He relocated the accommodation from Adam's proposed cross-range into the east range, omitting all the proposed domestic residences there with the exception of the librarian's house. Playfair dismissed use of the basements (street noise) and attics (lack of light and height) for anything other than minor ancillary use. The library took up the entire south range in Playfair's plan, allowing for a tripling in book storage (from 50,000 to 150,000 volumes) and reading spaces [fig.66]. Playfair substituted the natural history museum for Adam's great hall. The lecture theatres and professors' rooms were to be arranged on the two main floors of the north range and in the south-west corner, between the library and the museum. Other miscellaneous rooms, including the librarian's house, the Senate room, the Principal's chambers and the Speculative Society rooms were to be placed in the east range.

The secretary and clerk to the commissioners, Carlyle Bell, drew together the mass of correspondence, opinions, explanatory reports and minutes into a single printed document for the commissioners' consideration.[41] Although individual professors' views were printed as an appendix, the professors' report contained just two paragraphs, clearly and succinctly announcing their preferred scheme and architect. All the architects' plans, few of which can now be traced, and also models by Burn and Playfair, were laid before the commissioners at their meeting in the City Chambers on 4 December 1816. It was on this date that the commissioners finally determined to award the competition premium of 100 guineas to the professors' choice, William Henry Playfair.[42]

THE ARCHITECT: WILLIAM HENRY PLAYFAIR (1790–1857)

To modern eyes the appointment by the College commissioners of a rookie twenty-six-year-old architect, William Henry Playfair, to complete the huge and complicated University building, was an act of astonishing faith, verging on foolhardiness. Even the commissioners recognised the appointment was something of a gamble:

[I]t *would be desirable that he* [Playfair] *should devote himself mainly to this work – that at his early age, the Report alone of carrying such a work into execution, would attach to him that permanent eminence in his profession, which the superiority of his plan, and the genius displayed in it, gives every reason to prognosticate – That this no doubt would constitute an important part of his reward* […][43]

Apart from the design difficulties of reconfiguring Robert Adam's work elegantly to meet new circumstances, the task involved a mind-boggling array of financial, administrative, technical and logistical

69 Portrait of William Henry Playfair (1790–1857), possibly by William Nicholson, about 1815
Royal Institute of British Architects, London

challenges. Facts about Playfair's early life and training are relatively few and far between, but it is worth examining what is known for clues to his meteoric success as an independent architect in the long and arduous University competition of 1815–16.

William Henry's father, James Playfair, was a son of the manse, born in Benvie in Angus to the Revd James Playfair and Margaret Young. The young James was an extremely talented architect, designing extraordinary neoclassical buildings after the manner of the French architects Boullée and Ledoux, such as the Lynedoch mausoleum (to the 'Beautiful Mrs Graham') at Methven in Perthshire and Cairness House, near Fraserburgh in Aberdeenshire. James's elder brother, John, went on to become one of the outstanding academics of his age as joint Professor of Mathematics, then Professor of Natural Philosophy (with a particular interest in the emerging science of geology), at the University of Edinburgh [fig.70]. His youngest brother William was a colourful character and equally talented in his various fields of interest, becoming an apprentice to the engineer James Watt, an inventor and 'manufacturer of hardware', a noted writer on political economy, the inventor of pie charts and bar graphs, a participant in various dubious business enterprises and eventually a notorious fraud.[44]

By 1783 James Playfair and his wife, Rachel Barclay, had left Scotland for London, to join his brother William. In that year James published his pamphlet on *A Method of Constructing Vapour Baths*. He continued to cultivate Scottish clients in London, and travelled to Scotland once a year.[45] In London he

70 Portrait of Professor John Playfair (1748–1819) by Sir Henry Raeburn, 1814. This portrait was given to the University of Edinburgh by William Henry Playfair's trustees following his death in 1857.

University of Edinburgh Art Collections [EU0013]

exhibited architectural designs regularly at the Royal Academy annual exhibition.[46] It was from the circle of the Academy that many of his closest friends were drawn, including the artist and professional gossip Joseph Farington, and the architects George Dance the Younger and John Soane. James also cultivated influential patrons, including Henry Dundas, for whom he designed Melville Castle (1786–91) in Midlothian. With the proceeds of a reasonably successful business, James travelled to France (1787) and Italy (1792–3), and purchased two properties in Russell Place (now Fitzroy Street), a stone's-throw from the Adam brothers' Fitzroy Square development.[47] The Playfairs' fifth child, William Henry, was born in the house at 13 Russell Place in July 1790.[48] James died in Edinburgh at the age of thirty-eight in 1794, 'from a broken heart in consequence of the death of his eldest Boy' according to Farington.[49]

James's unexpected death left his family in London in turmoil and financial difficulty. Farington, Dance and Soane rallied round Rachel Playfair, providing practical help in resolving business matters, selling drawings and artworks, and trying to obtain funds to support the family from the Royal Academy.[50] Soane purchased many of the drawings for inclusion in his museum, where they remain to this day.[51] The eldest surviving son, James George, was sent to Edinburgh to live with his Uncle John, aunts and grandmother to complete his education, first at the High School from 1797, then as a medic at the University.[52] The other children remained in Russell Place with their mother. Eliza Soane offered to take in one of the Playfair children, Jesse, Graham, or Emma, but Rachel refused to contemplate such a move. Unable to let out the Russell Place houses, and in the face of continuing financial distress, Rachel contemplated a return to Scotland in 1797, but ended up instead in Berkhamsted by November 1799.[53]

Rachel was still in difficult circumstances in May 1801 and suffering from rheumatism. Farington recorded that 'Mr Mills will take her Son [William Henry] when He is proper age into his Counting House – I [Farington] told her I wd. speak at the proper time to Members of the Academy to endeavour to obtain the £10 a year which she solicits, while Her Son is educating. He is now 10 years of age [...].'[54] Thankfully John Playfair seems to have intervened again, adding William Henry to his bulging household at 6 Buccleuch Place in Edinburgh. The professor had taken in several other young university scholars, including Lord John Russell (later Whig politician and Prime Minister), Charles Brownlow (later Lord Lurgan, politician and client of William Henry) and Basil Hall (later naval officer and author) and the house served as an astonishing intellectual hub, attracting some of the most brilliant minds of the Scottish Enlightenment. Here William

Henry met many of his close friends and later clients, drawn from the Whig political circles of his uncle. He appears to have attended the class of the noted classical scholar, Alexander Christison, at the nearby High School between 1801 and 1804, alongside one of his closest friends and patrons, Andrew Rutherfurd, later Lord Advocate.[55] In 1805 and 1806 William Henry matriculated in the mathematics class of the faculty of arts at the University, and in 1807 and 1808 he matriculated in both the faculty of arts and the Faculty of medicine.[56] Like Robert Adam before him, William Henry does not appear to have graduated formally from the University.

On completing his university career, Playfair returned to London in 1809, where, probably through the influence of Dance or Farington, he obtained an apprenticeship in the office of the rising young architect Robert Smirke.[57] Normal architectural apprenticeships of this period lasted between five and six years, and were paid for by the apprentice's family. The project on which Playfair is said to have cut his architectural teeth was the rebuilding of Covent Garden theatre, where the site architect was his compatriot and fellow High School alumnus, William Burn. To replace the old theatre, which had been completely destroyed by fire in September 1808, Smirke designed one of the earliest Greek Revival buildings in London, incorporating a giant pure Doric portico modelled on the Parthenon.[58] The building was extremely influential. In spite of strong criticism of the building by Smirke's former master, John Soane, both Burn and Playfair were to return to Edinburgh enthused with the purity and rationality of Greek architecture. Here they were to make physical the intellectual distinction of the city, which had gained it the epithet 'the Athens of the North'.[59]

Following a stint in Benjamin Dean Wyatt's London office, Playfair joined the office of William Stark in Edinburgh in about 1811.[60] The talented Stark, who had moved from Glasgow to Edinburgh on medical advice in early 1811, died at the age of forty-three in 1813, earning Sir Walter Scott's lament that 'more genius died than is left behind among the collected universality of Scottish architects'.[61] Playfair too held Stark in high regard, writing of his Hunterian Museum for the University of Glasgow that 'I would rather be the author of that sweet little bit of good proportion than all the other ostentatious Glasgow buildings put together and most of those in London.' It is not known exactly how Playfair was employed in Stark's office, but it is likely that he continued in an apprenticeship role.

Projects that were in progress between 1811 and Stark's death included: Glasgow Royal Asylum; Glasgow Justiciary Court Houses; alterations to Bowhill House, Selkirkshire; Dundee Royal Lunatic Asylum; Muirkirk

Parish Church, Ayrshire; the interior of the Signet Library, Edinburgh; the interior of the Advocates' Library (now Upper Signet Library), Edinburgh; Cornwall Lunatic Asylum; Gloucester Lunatic Asylum; Edinburgh City Observatory; and a new parish church at Dunfermline Abbey, Fife.[62] In addition, Stark was working on a *Report to the Lord Provost, Magistrates and Council of Edinburgh on the Plans for Laying out the Grounds for Buildings between Edinburgh and Leith*, which was published posthumously in 1814.

Playfair may well have had a hand in the production of drawings and probably also in the supervision of the contracts on site in some cases. Certainly Playfair seems to have honed his technical drawing skills during this period, producing everything from pencil sketches of a crane at the Bell Rock Lighthouse to beautiful presentation drawings of the Hunterian Museum in Glasgow.[63] Of the projects in progress in 1813, Playfair was later to return as executant architect for works to the Signet and Advocates' Libraries, the City Observatory and the plan for the lands between Edinburgh and Leith. Although there is no direct evidence of Playfair's involvement in the schemes under Stark, it seems plausible that he was sufficiently involved with the projects at that stage to establish his credentials and merit his later appointment as architect in 1818–19.

In 1816, just before the University competition, Playfair went with his uncle to France. He never made it to Greece, but later in life, he travelled to see his brother in Naples, taking in Florence, but not Rome.[64] Whilst admiring the picturesque qualities of the Scottish Highlands in the 1830s, Playfair described 'the most frightful mountains'.[65] His travels seemed to have disappointed on every occasion, suggesting that his evident interest in the picturesque and admiration for the antique world was cerebral, gained from books and filtered through his imagination.

It should be noted that Playfair seems to have had more than a passing interest in Robert Adam's work. He owned copies of both Robert's *Ruins of the Emperor Diocletian at Spalatro* and Robert and James's *Works in Architecture*.[66] Although he was not in the market for purchasing the whole Adam drawing collection when he advised John Clerk of Eldin's heirs on its disposal in 1833, Playfair nevertheless acquired Adam's office drawings at some point, including elevations of Gosford House in East Lothian.[67] In 1819 Playfair was paid £40 for work at Dalquharran in Ayrshire, a house designed by Adam in 1782.[68]

During the twenty-four years that Playfair was working on the University buildings, he collected an impressive range of other prestigious public and private projects, mainly in Edinburgh, including the development of the area to the north of Calton

Hill (1818–19), the City Observatory and John Playfair Monument on Calton Hill (1818, 1825), a staircase for the Advocates' Library (now Signet Library, 1818–19), houses in Royal Circus (1820–3), the Royal Institution building at the foot of the Mound (now Royal Scottish Academy, 1822–6, extended 1832–5), the National Monument on Calton Hill (with Cockerell, 1824–9), St Stephen's Church in St Vincent Street (1827–8), the current Advocates' Library (1829–33), and Surgeons' Hall (1829–33).[69] Although Playfair's reputation favours his Greek Revival legacy, in fact he worked in a wide range of historicist styles, from Italianate and Gothic to Tudor and Scottish Baronial. With the University project under his belt, Playfair was able to pick and choose his projects, which he did with careful avoidance of anything that smacked of commerce. Of the post-University commissions, the most important were Donaldson's Hospital (1842–54), the National Gallery of Scotland (1850–7) and the Free Church College ('New College', 1845–50).[70]

Playfair's will was not specific about the fate of his office drawings, but his trustees determined to offer the collection to the University on the condition that they should be catalogued and placed on exhibition in the library.[71] Some weeding of the collection took place, but the surviving drawings, Playfair's incomplete journal and letterbooks, and some of the project correspondence, provide a fascinating insight into Playfair the architect and Playfair the man.[72] The University drawings form the earliest part of the collection, and from these it is immediately apparent that he was meticulous and controlling of quality to the point of obsession. Every detail of the building was drawn from numerous angles and at various scales to ensure that there was no room for error in its execution. Stonework, plasterwork, timberwork and ironwork were all painstakingly hand-drawn, from whole elevations to nuts and bolts and door handles [figs 71, 74]. The specifications supplied to the University contractors have not survived, but a hint of the level of detail is given in some of the notes on the drawings, for example: 'N.B. The Queen Bolts to be screwed up until the Beam is cambered 2 inches. All the Iron Work about the Roof, except the Braces & straining Pieces to be of the best Scottish Iron.'[73]

Such was the primacy of presentation and meticulous design that drawing materials represented more than a quarter of the total annual office bill for the University project, including the salaries of the Principal and temporary clerks.[74] Playfair himself admitted that 'Nothing good in Architecture can be affected without a monstrous expenditure of patience and India Rubber.' He maintained an office on site at the University for almost twenty years, enabling him to keep a close eye on the quality of the works throughout its construction. He was a hard taskmaster, quickly remonstrating or issuing letters of dismay to contractors who failed to meet his exacting standards. His assistant in the late 1820s, David Cousin, told 'with great glee many stories of the strictness and vigour of Mr. Playfair's rule, and the devices to which his assistants had to resort to escape detection if at fault'.[75] At times Playfair was ill or busy with other projects, but he refused to compromise on quality, so to the evident annoyance of the commissioners on occasion, the lack of working drawings slowed the University project to a halt.

Work dominated Playfair's life. He had a small circle of intimate friends based around the Rutherfurd family in the New Town of Edinburgh, he never married, and told his fellow architect Charles Cockerell that he was too busy to woo.[76] Indeed Playfair blamed his dedication to his art for the ill health and loneliness that afflicted him frequently.[77] Like his mother, he suffered from debilitating bouts of rheumatism. Perhaps conditioned by his illnesses and loneliness, Playfair was a difficult and contradictory character. At times he was remote, spiky, fragile, autocratic, aloof and sensitive to criticism, and at other times energetic, robust, practical, brave, loyal, kind, thoughtful and generous. However, his intelligence, professionalism and ethic of hard work always shone through in his day-to-day dealings with his clients and contractors. One illustration of the brave and practical Playfair can be found in his response to a fire in the Anatomy Department of the University in 1817:

71 Playfair's attention to detail even extended to designs for the museum doorhandles
University of Edinburgh [0025063]

Mr Playfair, the engineer, was distinguished by his anxiety and intrepidity on the occasion. Hurrying from some distance on the first alarm, he was soon on the roof, directing the operations of the firemen: and when part of the roof was broken in, he descended into the part on fire with a rope fastened to his body, and the pipe of one of the engines in his hand; and this intrepid example being followed by several of the firemen and others, the water was soon made to play with more powerful effect upon the part of the building which was in flames.[78]

Thomas Telford, the great engineer, attached such great esteem to Playfair that he bequeathed him £200 in 1834.[79] Playfair himself left generous legacies to his family, friends and servants.[80] Although not generally regarded as clubbable, from 1842 Playfair maintained his links with London through membership of the Athenaeum, an exclusive invitation-only club for 'individuals known for their Scientific or Literary attainments, Artists of eminence in any class of the Fine Arts [...]'.[81] After a protracted illness and a probable stroke, Playfair died at home in Great Stuart Street on 19 March 1857, and is buried in the Dean Cemetery beneath a memorial stone of his own design.

FIRST PHASE OF PLAYFAIR'S OLD COLLEGE 1816–1823

Following Playfair's appointment the first tasks were to develop management and project plans and organise the contracts. Recognising that the full complement of commissioners was an unwieldy body for regular and effective decision-making and oversight, a standing committee of five commissioners, with a quorum of three, was established.[82] Playfair himself was to receive 5 per cent on the total outlay of £10,000 per annum. Unlike Adam, who paid the contractors by measurement of completed work at pre-agreed prices, Playfair proposed competitive tenders for fixed packages of work based on the architect's working drawings and written specifications. Contractors could tender for a whole work package under a single master mason, or each trade could tender separately for different elements of the package (wrightwork, plasterwork etc.). In practice the competition for the tenders was restricted by Playfair's oversight of the selection process, which favoured the contractors that he knew could deliver to his high standards.

Another means of ensuring quality was Playfair's recommendation of James Scott to the commissioners as the new clerk of works.[83] Scott had been a partner with Lorimer & Inglis in the construction of the ground floor of the museum under Archibald Elliot's direction, and prior to that a foreman on the University job under Robert Adam and also a clerk of works at Culzean Castle

in Ayrshire and Gosford House in East Lothian. The contracts were to be drawn up and administered by the clerk to the commissioners, Carlyle Bell, and approved sums drawn from the government grant banked in the cash account of Sir William Forbes & Co. The Treasury added two new commissioners with recent experience of a major building project (Calton Hill) and who had enough time to devote to the standing committee: James Clerk-Rattray of Craighall Rattray in Perthshire, one of the barons of the Exchequer; and Robert Johnston, former Dean of Guild of Edinburgh. Along with Johnston, Andrew Duncan, Carlyle Bell and Playfair, Clerk-Rattray effectively ran the project until his death in 1831.

Playfair drew up a new report on how the project should progress.[84] The work was to be divided up into small lots that would fit within the annual budget allocation, meet with the University's priorities and allow teaching to continue with minimal disruption. The first phase of the work was to include completion of the natural history museum in the west range and construction of the practice of physic, chemistry and natural history departments in the south-west corner.[85] This would release the large complex of old laboratories on the north side of the site for demolition and redevelopment. Inglis and Lorimer were to finish the masonry of the museum on the same terms as their previous contract, but all the other work would need to be opened to competitive tender. On 25 March 1817 Playfair recorded the start of work at the University in his new journal:

March 25. The first stone of the College of Edinburgh laid – being the commencement of the Execution of my Design for the completion of that Building. This stone is in the Wall at the back of the Piazza of the Museum of Natural History – the Piazza Wall which had been begun by Mr. Elliott's directions, before my Design was adopted, having been pulled down by me, and the present one built, leaving a broader Piazza than Elliott had intended.[86]

In May 1817 Playfair took possession of the old mathematics classroom as his office. The weight of history attached to the room was not lost on the young architect, who recorded that it was here that Colin MacLaurin first taught the *Principia* of Isaac Newton and that his Uncle John had also presided over the mathematics class.[87] Having recommended competitive tendering as the best way to commission the works, Playfair almost immediately sought to back-track by commissioning workmen directly under James Scott on weekly contracts for the divinity hall and foundations of the south-west corner.[88] With these two elements of the scheme begun, Playfair received an urgent request from the Professor of Divinity, William Ritchie, to begin work on the divinity hall, as his existing classroom was so damp that it affected his health.[89]

Once the project was securely under way, Playfair faced a number of new pressures from various academics. Some were straightforward requests to complete their classroom accommodation, but others were more difficult: accommodation for newly appointed staff; alteration of existing rooms; incorporation of gas lighting; provision of specialist equipment. The commissioners had no authority to provide movable apparatus and handed over responsibility for each element of the building to the town council as it was completed. Alterations to completed rooms were therefore outside Playfair's remit, as were any pieces of equipment that were not built in. The town council's lack of funds made maintenance of the completed structure difficult, and requests for subsequent alterations or specialist equipment went largely unheeded.

LOWER AND UPPER MUSEUM HALLS

The earliest collections of the University derived from the bequests in the 1690s of Robert Sibbald and his fellow doctor and founder of Edinburgh's Botanic Garden, Sir Andrew Balfour. Unfortunately the bequests did not contain funds to house the 'Museaum Balfourianum', and they mouldered for six decades in the hall of the 1617 Building before being largely discarded.[90] In 1765 the town council procured a room adjacent to the College for the museum, which enjoyed a revival under the Professors of Natural History, Robert Ramsay and Revd John Walker. On Walker's death in

1804, his trustees removed most of the collection, which included items from Captain James Cook's voyages to the Pacific, leaving the new professor, Robert Jameson, to start again in the 1642 Building almost from scratch. Using donated specimens, bequests and some of his own money, Jameson quickly amassed an enormous collection of 2,290 animal specimens and 19,000 minerals and rocks. In 1812 Jameson appealed successfully to the crown for £100 annual funding to preserve and augment the collection, acquiring for it the title 'Royal Museum of the University'.

By the time Playfair was preparing his plans in 1815–17, Jameson's influence in the University was strong and his voracious collecting habits were hindered only by the lack of display area in the 1642 Building and poor, damp, storage space in the cellars and attics of the old College. Jameson stressed the urgency of new housing for the collections and Playfair paid careful heed, detailing the needs for copious light, steady heat, damp-proofing, fireproofing, and plenty of space for expansion.[91] He allocated the whole of Adam's great hall and chapel in the west range to the museum. In order to protect the light for the museum, reduce the risk of fire spreading, and preserve the amenity of the University building more generally from encroaching taller buildings, the commissioners began to acquire surrounding properties on the west and north sides of the complex. The old houses on the west of the College behind the museum were demolished in 1820, leaving only Aikman's Chapel.[92]

72 Longitudinal section of the lower museum by W.H. Playfair, 1817

University of Edinburgh [coll-13-1-1-16]

Ostensibly Playfair retained most of Adam's exterior design for the west range, but a detailed comparison with Adam's early design shows a number of differences. Expensive decorative carved work, such as the reeded and Vitruvian-scrolled band courses and the festoons and royal busts on the parapet were omitted. Playfair deepened the modelling of the east elevation by increasing the projection of the outer stair bays and by adding pilasters and balustrades to the windows here. It is impossible to know Adam's plans for the construction of the columns from his drawings, but it is likely that he intended them to be of single monolithic blocks of stone, like the entrance columns, rather than the cost-saving jointed columns provided by Playfair. Perhaps the most significant alteration to the exterior was the substitution of Adam's tall piended (hipped) roof with a flat lead roof that disappears behind the wallhead balustrade. If the design is blockish and less refined than Adam's proposal, the quality of the workmanship is more than equal. Such was Playfair's attention to detail that he made full-size scale elevations and sections of the Corinthian capitals, and also commissioned James Berrie of Leith Walk to make plaster models of them. The carver, gilder and dealer in prints, John Steele, made timber models of the Venetian window capitals.[93]

Although Playfair was bound by the commitment of the commissioners to the general appearance of Adam's designs for the exterior of the University, he was completely free to redesign the interiors. Playfair took full advantage of this freedom, and in many respects the interiors are far more confident and successful than the external elevations with their necessary compromises. The museum was Playfair's first chance to demonstrate his skill and ingenuity at interior design on a major scale. He abandoned Adam's single full-height great hall in favour of two museum halls separated by a fireproof cast-iron floor.[94] The lower hall was built over shallow vaults to allow air circulation and avoid damp. Work on the walls progressed rapidly during the summer of 1817 and drawings for the interior finishing of the museum were ready by September 1817.[95] Lorimer & Inglis succeeded in their tender for the interior fitting out, which was largely complete by October 1819.[96] However, it was another year before the display cabinets and heating system were completed and the halls were ready to receive students and the paying public.[97]

One of the most advanced features of the museum was the fireproof floor of the upper hall, which Playfair researched in London and detailed very carefully in his designs.[98] It was formed of cast-iron joists and 8-foot by 3-foot iron plates, supplied by John Anderson's Leith Walk Foundry. The finishing of the iron floor caused much debate, but eventually it seems to have been painted and covered with an oil-cloth and a grey

drugget (coarse fabric carpet).[99] In order to accommodate the weight of the iron floor and the lead roof it was necessary to demolish and rebuild the back wall of the 'piazza', or arcaded open loggia, already constructed to Adam's design under Elliot in 1815.[100] The roof too incorporated 'best Swedish iron' girders and ties to support the massive weight of the lead covering.[101] A large cockle stove in an excavated room below the lower hall supplied hot air via a network of iron ducts that threaded through the floors of the building and the free-standing columns of the lower hall, avoiding the need for open fires that had plagued the old College with dust and the risk of damage. The initial system, installed by John Paterson of the Edinburgh Foundry, failed and was replaced.

Significantly, the lower museum hall was designed in a severe Greek Doric temple style with fluted timber columns, engaged around the walls and free-standing to form screens at either end of the room, and a deep frieze decorated with laurel wreaths [fig.72]. The use of the Greek style probably reflected a number of influences including Playfair's early masters Smirke and Stark, his friend, the artist Hugh 'Grecian' Williams, and also the growing conception within the city of Edinburgh as the 'Modern Athens'.[102] Here at the intellectual heart of the capital was a new μουσεῖον (mouseion, or museum), a temple to the muses of literature, science and the arts,

73 Watercolour presentation drawing of the upper museum by W.H. Playfair, 1816
University of Edinburgh
[coll-13/55/4880]

built in a modern manner with a cast-iron fireproof floor and piped hot air heating. As befitted the lower of the two halls, the Doric order represented strength and stability below the lighter Ionic order of the upper hall. The lower hall was intended to be open display space for free-standing objects including the collection of stuffed animals. Splendid though the effect of the room was, Jameson complained in 1820 that the columns blocked useful wall space for further display cabinets.[103] When Playfair's friend and fellow architect, Charles Robert Cockerell, viewed the completed building in 1822, he criticised the unacademic use of the Greek order in his private diary:

Saw Mr Playfair's Museum 90 × 30 22 high, below a doric room [...] nonsense to put doric entablature wh. is the outside representation of beam ends, inside Ro[om]:, never done by ancients I believe – as usual the example is folowed as far as it leads & then blank we can go no further. I would have shown the beams & so made an ornamental & reasoned cieling as did the ancts [...] 80,000£ has built whole of North side (not NW angle) Museum the apartments towards the street which had got the dry rot Mr Playfair judiciously adopted a style which had the greatest affinity to Adams.[104]

Of the two halls, the real architectural fireworks were reserved for the upper hall [figs 73–7]. The Venetian windows of Adam's design and the practical requirement for museum cabinets made the creation of a pure Grecian interior in the galleried upper hall impossible. Instead, Playfair resorted to a more Roman form after the manner of Sir John Soane or William Stark at the Signet Library, with shallow domes top-lit by glazed cupolas. Playfair went to considerable trouble to design the cabinets for the museum.[105] He was particularly keen to obtain expensive plate glass to avoid the manufacturing blemishes of crown glass that would distort views of the objects on display. In his

enthusiasm to have the cabinets built by William Trotter, who had designed the existing museum cabinets in the 1642 Building, Playfair attempted to bypass his own competitive tendering rules by simply commissioning the eminent Edinburgh cabinetmaker directly. The commissioners queried the lack of tendering and appealed to Professor Jameson for his advice. Conveniently for Playfair, Jameson argued strongly that Trotter was the 'only person' for the job and that the museum would be 'ruined' if the cabinets were put out to tender.[106] Playfair and Jameson got their way, and eventually in 1820 Trotter was commissioned to provide further sumptuous furnishings including an 'elegant Octagon table', a 'Mahogany ottoman with carved vase ends nicely stuffed', '6 Large Mahogany Tables with astragal ends on richly carved massive legs, the tops framed, and inlaid with fine crimson Cloth', carpeting and blinds [fig.75].[107] Robert Buchan painted the interior of the museum, and was to complete a number of contracts for painting the new buildings.[108]

Having secured a substantial increase in space in the museum, Jameson went on a spree of acquisitions, including the purchase of the famed Paris collection of Louis Dufresne in 1819 and parts of the William Bullock collection in London. He also encouraged the donation of various international specimens from explorers and travellers, which duly arrived in copious quantities on a daily basis. The minute book of the commissioners contains frequent memos from the autocratic Jameson requesting incursions into other professors' territory, more display space, further cabinets, and repairs to the cupolas of the upper hall and staircases, which leaked prodigiously. Once the museum was complete to the original specification, there are signs that Playfair dragged his feet in meeting Jameson's constant demands, on one occasion earning him a sharp rebuke from the commissioners.[109] Jameson took on an assistant and curator for the museum in 1823, William MacGillivray,

74 Design for the plasterwork of the upper museum arches by W.H. Playfair, 1818

University of Edinburgh [coll-13/1/1/69]

75 Engraving of the upper museum as fitted out with William Trotter's furniture. Three large dogs lurk under the cabinets.

University of Edinburgh [0012943]

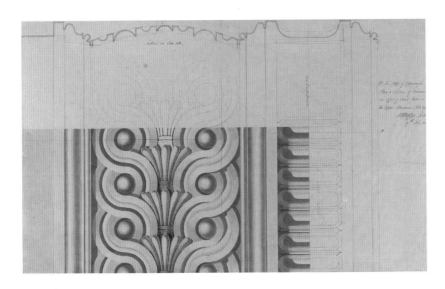

who provided order to the collections and gave encouragement to the students, notably Charles Darwin.[110] The collections now covered zoology, palaeontology, geology and ethnography. By 1826 the collections had doubled in size since the opening of the new museum in 1820, and the attics of the east range were pressed into use. Jameson continued to build the natural history collections until they were considered 'second only to those of the British Museum'.[111]

The success of the Great Exhibition at Crystal Palace in 1851 and the subsequent foundation of the South Kensington Museum in London, prompted the possibility of a similar institution in Scotland. Keen to increase space in Old College and reduce the financial burden of caring for the University's enormous collections, the Senatus began negotiations with the Treasury to endow the new national museum with its collections. The new national Museum of Science and Art (now the National Museum of Scotland) was built on the adjoining site to the west from 1861. In 1865 the collections transferred to the east pavilion of the new museum across the Italianate 'Bridge of Sighs', designed by the engineer and architect to the Department of Science and Art, Francis Fowke, to link the University museum to the Museum of Science and Art. The newly released space in the University museum became a natural history laboratory. The removal of the collections began a fractious relationship between the University and the museum, which eventually led to closure of the bridge and the start of a new University natural history collection.

The Natural History Department finally moved from Old College to King's Buildings in 1929, leaving the old museum spaces free for expansion of the University library in the upper hall and an exam hall below. The upper hall of the museum was converted to the New Reading Room in 1932.[112] In the 1950s the lower hall became a student common room.

The completion of the new University library in George Square in August 1967 again released the upper hall for a new use, this time as a student art centre. The architectural practice of Ian G. Lindsay & Partners undertook the conversion with funding from the Gulbenkian Foundation in 1969–70 and 1973–4.[113] The upper hall remains in use as Gallery 2 of the University's public gallery of contemporary visual art, the Talbot Rice Gallery. Raked seating was introduced to the lower hall in 1973 when it was converted for use as the Senate Hall, also by Ian G. Lindsay & Partners. Later the seating was removed and the hall used as open plan offices.

The most recent reincarnation of the lower hall is in progress at the time of writing, as part of a 2013 scheme by LDN Architects to restore the space as a magnificent new reading room for the relocated law library.

76 The Talbot Rice Gallery (upper museum)
HES

SOUTH-WEST CORNER

Although work began on the foundations of the south-west corner in June 1817, the detailed working drawings for the exterior were not ready until September.[114] Playfair stuck fairly rigidly to the external design by Adam with the exception of additional balustrades below the ground floor windows. The corner block was intended to house the scientific departments then lodged in a rag-tag of buildings along the northern boundary of the College. The release of the old buildings for demolition would allow work to begin on Playfair's new north range. The natural history classroom was not large, but it needed to be located adjacent to the natural history museum that was taking shape simultaneously in the west range. Next door, at first floor level, was the chemistry classroom, which seated over 500 of Professor Hope's students, and was by far the largest classroom in the whole complex.

77 The Talbot Rice Gallery, detail of the ceiling (upper museum)

HES

This room, stripped of its raked seating, is now part of the Talbot Rice Gallery. Below, on the ground floor, was a practical laboratory for chemistry, fitted up by Sibbald, Smith & Co., and a large classroom for the practice of physic. This area is now much altered. The masonry was complete by December 1818 and the block was ready for the first students a year later.[115]

EAST RANGE

The east entrance range as Playfair inherited it was a ruin: the front wall was complete to the wallhead and the blocks either side of the central block were roofed, but the internal walls and the wall facing the courtyard were incomplete and there was no glazing; much of the range had been open to the elements for a number of years and dry rot was rampant in the original timberwork; the existing internal walls had been planned for the professors' housing, and were not in the correct locations

for the revised use as teaching accommodation and offices. Playfair faced a complicated and delicate task of replacing the timbers damaged by dry rot, unpicking some of the work that had been done, and completing the rest to the new plans without damaging the structural integrity of Adam's frontage. The scheme involved deepening the range and reconfiguring the courtyard elevation to align with the new colonnades that were being introduced to match Adam's designs for the west range. All this needed to be accomplished with restricted access on the courtyard side, caused by the need to keep the old 1617 Building in use as the library.

The commissioners approved Playfair's scheme in three stages: firstly the divinity classroom in June 1817; then the Speculative Society and the Oriental languages and church history classroom in May 1818; and finally the remainder of the east range in December 1818. Lorimer & Inglis were awarded the first two contracts,

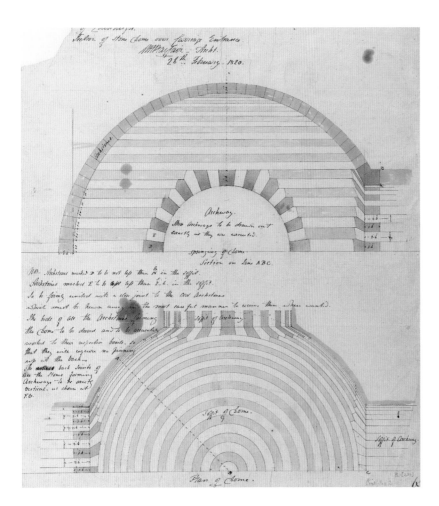

but a new team, Henderson & Currer, won the major contract. The old janitor's house and the northern end of the 1617 Building were demolished in late 1818, and the old Principal's house followed to make way for Playfair's scheme. Henderson & Currer made rapid progress in building the new elevation facing the courtyard and the quadrant colonnades during 1819 and 1820.[116] The janitor's house in the basement below the Speculative Society rooms, the materia medica classroom in the north-eastern corner of the ground floor, and the classrooms for rhetoric and civil and public law on the ground and first floors of the stub of the north range, were completed and occupied by the end of 1819.[117] Playfair reported the whole east range, except the dome, complete in October 1821.[118]

He provided copious working drawings, including a very detailed explanation of how the vaults over the entrance arches should be constructed and tie into Adam's work [fig.78].[119] In the location where the dome should have been constructed, which had remained open to the elements since Adam's day, Playfair needed to provide a temporary pyramidal roof to cover the proposed theological library. The central room of the library was intended to be domed to reflect the vaulting of the main entrance below. However, there was never enough money to fit out the theological library, and it remained on the

to-do list long after Playfair's departure. Its immediate use was for temporary storage of books from the attics above the old museum and other overflow from the old library in the 1617 Building.[120] When the dome was finally constructed in the 1880s, the newly created Watson-Gordon Professor of Fine Art, Gerald Baldwin Brown, occupied the space.

The constant discovery of dry rot in the old timbers of the range and other 'unavoidable extras' increased the cost of the east range by some £12,000, more than a year's worth of the government grant, which contributed significantly to some of the later financial problems.[121]

DIVINITY HALL

The first of the academic staff to press his case for new accommodation directly with Playfair was the Professor of Divinity, Dr William Ritchie. The divinity hall, or classroom, was planned to occupy the first floor to the right of the entrance in the east range. The space had been partially built as housing and needed to be reconfigured.[122] In many ways this classroom was typical of the new teaching rooms with its steeply raked and gently curving benches and book boards. The windows were surrounded by reeded architraves and the upper windows had scrolled brackets. The distinguishing features of the room were the professor's pulpit and a

78 Design for the masonry of the entrance arch in the east range by W.H. Playfair, 1820
University of Edinburgh [coll-13/1/6/287]

79 Masonry vaults over the entrance
Nick Haynes

smaller octagonal pulpit for the students to practise their preaching skills. Lighting was still by candle and heating by means of a stove. The classroom and accompanying lobby and professor's room were completed by November 1817. At the time of writing, the room, long stripped of its original benches and reconfigured several times, is being converted by LDN Architects as the moot court room for the Law School.

SPECULATIVE SOCIETY ROOMS

The old Speculative Society rooms, which had been privately funded by the society members, were demolished in 1817 to make way for the south-west corner, leaving the society homeless. In May 1818 Playfair allocated a large debating hall, library and lobby to the society on the ground floor adjacent to the northern pedestrian entrance arch. Although the rooms are within the University complex, they remain in the private ownership of the society [fig.80]. Lorimer & Inglis, who were also working on the west range, won the tender, and work proceeded quickly.

The rooms have been little altered since Playfair's time, but they have been redecorated at least twice: once in 1929, when the oak floor and mantelpiece of the lobby were installed; and again in 1967–8 under Ian Carnegie, architect.[123] The lobby was also painted in 1954 in preparation for the admission of the Duke of Edinburgh as an honorary member. The rooms retain much of their character and many of their original fine furnishings, designed by William Trotter for the society. When gas was provided to the lobby and library in 1838, the society decided to maintain the candlelight provided by the beautiful wooden chandelier in the debating hall. The hall remains without gas or electric light to this day.

ORIENTAL LANGUAGES AND CHURCH HISTORY

This classroom was located on the first floor in the north-east corner of the east range, and progressed alongside the contract for the Speculative Society in 1818–20.[124] The priority for fitting out this room was that it enabled the repair of the roof and the completion of the rooms below. Like the divinity classroom, it contained two pulpits and rows of gently curving raked seating, and a stove in the south wall.

SENATE HALL

The Senate Hall was located on the ground floor to the south of the main entrance. It comprised three rooms: the lobby, the hall itself and the Guard Hall. The last two rooms could be joined together by opening a large set of double folding doors. The first Senatus meeting was held in the room on 26 August 1822. For a long period the rooms were divided up as offices, but they were restored to Playfair's scheme in 1989 to celebrate the 200th anniversary of the laying of the foundation stone of Old College.

PRINCIPAL'S CHAMBERS

As only the librarian was to be provided with housing in the College, it was considered appropriate to provide offices for the Principal. The grand stair beside the Senate Hall led up to the Principal's chambers. Trotter again provided furniture, some of which is still identifiable in the University's collections.

80 Old College, Speculative Society debating hall
HES [Crown copyright: SC 904841]

81 View of the old Senate Hall (now Elder and Lee Rooms), photographed by Alexander Adam Inglis after Robert Morham's reconfiguration of the librarian's house in 1880
HES [Scottish Colorfoto Collection: SC 1119836]

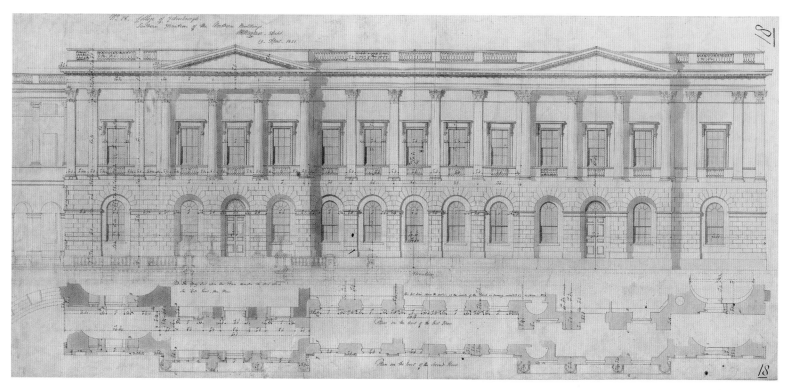

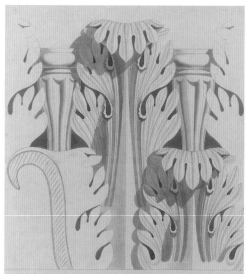

LIBRARIAN'S HOUSE

The only, and much-coveted, house in the College was set aside for the use of the librarian. It occupied the same position as Adam's proposed librarian's house, but Playfair reorganised the accommodation to provide a dining room and study on the ground floor and a drawing room and bedroom above. The ground floor rooms were completely reconfigured as the Senate Hall in the 1880s by the city architect, Robert Morham. They are now known as the Raeburn Room and the Carstares Room after the University's fine collection of Henry Raeburn portraits and the portrait of the early 18th-century Principal, William Carstares. Above, the rooms were reconfigured as the Principal's office.

NORTH RANGE

Attention turned to the completion of the north range in 1820. Playfair estimated the cost of the north range at £12,000, with £25,000 yet to go on the south range and library and £3,000 on the dome over the entrance, making a total of £100,000.[125] Two stubs of the north range built by Adam were in place, and it was a question of removing the old chemistry and 1642 Buildings. Dr Monro tertius also requested the subdivision of Adam's huge two-storey anatomy theatre into two rooms: the upper room to be a new, smaller theatre; the lower to be a new anatomy museum. Now that the natural history museum and south-west corner of the new buildings were occupied, the old buildings were largely emptied of overflow books

82 Longitudinal section of the north range by W.H. Playfair, 1821. This shows the classrooms of mathematics, Latin and Greek on the ground floor, natural philosophy and logic on the first floor and midwifery in the attic.
University of Edinburgh
[coll-13/1/7/343]

83 Design for a capital on the north range by W.H. Playfair, 1821
University of Edinburgh
[coll-13-1-7-369]

84 North range of the Old College quad
Nick Haynes

85 Professor J. D. Forbes
teaching in the natural
philosophy classroom on the
first floor of the north range,
about 1855

University of St Andrews
Photographic Collection
[Group-1855-1]

from the library and demolished.[126] Playfair prepared new drawings for the range, which were approved by the commissioners in February 1821.[127] At this stage the proposals were very similar to the competition proposals, retaining Adam's arrangement of tripartite windows in the projecting pavilions of the courtyard elevation. However, Playfair and the sub-committee of the commissioners were clearly troubled that simply removing the cross-building from Adam's plan left the long elevations facing the courtyard too weak visually to tie in with the bold modelling of the colonnaded short elevations. After receiving tenders, the commissioners requested amendments to the original plan at the end of March 1821, and Playfair redrew the elevation, spacing the windows evenly throughout the whole elevation, introducing round-headed windows at the ground floor and enlivening the modelling with a colonnade of pilasters and engaged columns at the first floor and a balustrade along the wallhead.[128] This proposal required refacing of part of the western stub of the north range already built by Adam [see fig.65]. Playfair also made amendments for the experimental and teaching requirements of Professor John Leslie (natural philosophy) and a small rooftop observatory for Professor William Wallace (mathematics). Alexander Armstrong was finally appointed as the contractor on the lowest tender of £15,845 in October 1821.[129]

The basic construction of the north range proceeded smoothly, and Playfair reported its completion on 21 February 1824.[130] However, by then Playfair was struggling with the various demands of the professors. The commissioners recorded a number of frustrations

with Playfair in the mid-1820s, particularly in respect of the work requested by Dr Monro for his Anatomy Department.[131] Eventually Playfair reported that the two-storey anatomy classroom had been divided in two, as requested, and the new theatre on the top floor was 'much warmer, much lighter, and better adapted for hearing'.[132] The new room below was to become the anatomy museum after further wrangling about the cupboards and display cases.

SECOND PHASE OF PLAYFAIR'S OLD COLLEGE 1823–1840

After eight years and £80,000 of grants, the original government support came to an end in 1822. The north, east and west sides of the courtyard were complete, but the south side was unstarted. It remained occupied by the old Teviot Chambers, and the rump of the 1617 Building still served as the University library. On Playfair's advice, the commissioners reckoned that at least a further £37,000 was needed to finish the library, the courtyard terrace and the dome. Once again the commissioners turned to William Dundas MP to pursue their case for additional funding with the Lords of the Treasury. The commissioners needed to explain why the building was costing more than the original estimate. They identified four principal causes: the additional fitting up of the 'great national object', the museum, to an appropriate standard; the purchase of old houses around the College to control the light to the museum, protect the College buildings from fire, and ensure an appropriate setting for the building (although not stated to the Treasury, the site to the west of the College was being increasingly considered for expansion of the museum); the necessary alterations to the north range to meet the teaching and experimental requirements of Professors Leslie and Wallace; and unforeseen repairs and alterations to the completed parts of the Adam building.[133] The commissioners also confessed to having previously omitted from their calculations the expense of drawing up plans, the architect's 5 per cent commission, the costs of the clerk of works, the clerk to the commissioners and the cashier, and the normal 10 per cent contingency.

In support of their application to the Treasury, the commissioners supplied a set of four engravings [figs 15, 86, 87] by William Home Lizars showing the dramatic juxtaposition of the three sides of the elegant neoclassical courtyard with the ramshackle appearance of the old Teviot Chambers and the propped-up 1617 Building. The visual shock tactics worked and the Treasury granted a further four years of funding at the same rate of £10,000 per annum.[134] In 1826 the commissioners requested a further £6,000 for the following year.

86 The position in 1823, as depicted by William Home Lizars. The 1617 Building was still in use as the library while Adam and Playfair's buildings were constructed around it.
Edinburgh City Archives

87 An engraving of the 1617 Building by W.H. Lizars, 1823, showing it propped up against the east range of the new College buildings. It was demolished in 1827 on completion of the new library.
Edinburgh City Archives

The commissioners approved Playfair's revised plans for the library and south range on 21 February 1824, and instructed him to prepare working drawings and specifications for a tender and contract.[135] In June 1824 they awarded the contract to the builder / architect, Adam Ogilvie Turnbull, who submitted the lowest offer at £23,000, with a completion deadline of 31 December 1826.[136] However, the inflationary pressures of the late 1820s took a heavy toll on Turnbull, who faced rapidly rising wage bills and difficulty obtaining credit on materials. On numerous occasions he approached the commissioners for advances. Although Playfair did his best to improve the contractor's fees for a number of other small jobs outside the main contract for the south range, Turnbull continued to struggle until the commissioners finally lost patience in September 1829 and appointed other builders to finish off the library.

The last instalment of the renewed four-year government grant was paid in 1826, but when Playfair totted up the estimates the commissioners found themselves short of £16,889 to complete the library, courtyard terrace, dome and other miscellaneous items including fitting up the divinity hall and library, railings, lamps and water supply.[137] This was almost £11,000 more than had been advised to the Treasury the previous year. Again, Playfair was required to account for the new estimate, and the commissioners sent another plea to the Treasury. This time Playfair attributed the additional costs to extra demands from the professors (mainly those of natural history and anatomy), more accurate estimates, extra requirements for the library, the purchase of old houses around the College, and increases in the price of labour and materials. The Treasury took a harder line, refusing to extend the grants any further than the £6,000 that had been requested the previous year, and then only after the Royal Commission on the Universities and Colleges of Scotland had reported.

By 1824 relations between the University and the town council had reached boiling point over which body had the power to make regulations for degrees. After an unsuccessful legal appeal, the Senatus petitioned the Home Secretary, Sir Robert Peel, to appoint a commission to settle the issue. The resulting Royal Commission on the Universities and Colleges of Scotland took on a much wider remit than the Senatus had expected, including the establishment of a code of rules, statutes and ordinances for every university and college in Scotland. When it finally reported in 1830, the commission also recommended the establishment of a University Court with powers to inquire into and regulate revenues and expenditure. Eventually the recommendations were embodied in the fundamental Universities (Scotland) Act 1858, which gave the University its independence from the town council. As part of the commission's evidence-gathering in Edinburgh, Playfair was quizzed on the University's building project. Playfair's evidence probably had very little impact on the commission's report, but the Treasury used the commission to delay payment of the promised final £6,000.

From 1827 Playfair's project lurched from one financial crisis to the next. The death of Clerk-Rattray in 1831 prompted the disbandment of the sub-committee that had steered the project since 1816, and the Lord Provost set up a new working group. The payment of the government's £6,000 in 1832 allowed the completion of the courtyard terrace and steps, but the commissioners had no more money, and the town council's financial position was even worse. A long list of items still needed attention, of which the dome was the closest to Playfair's heart. Sadly, it was not to be. His final contributions to the design of the University buildings were the great iron entrance gates, which were erected in 1840.

THE SOUTH RANGE AND LIBRARY (PLAYFAIR LIBRARY)

From the outset of the University project, Adam had always intended the library to be the great showpiece of the whole complex. Playfair too lavished a great deal of thought and attention on the library in his competition submission of 1816. By the time he returned to the

opposite

88 Early design for the library by W.H. Playfair, about 1816
University of Edinburgh
[coll-13/55/4898]

89 Presentation longitudinal section of the library by W.H. Playfair, about 1823
University of Edinburgh
[coll-13/55/4887]

90 Library longitudinal section by W.H. Playfair, 1824
University of Edinburgh [0001845]

91 Library ceiling design by W.H. Playfair, 1824
University of Edinburgh [0001844]

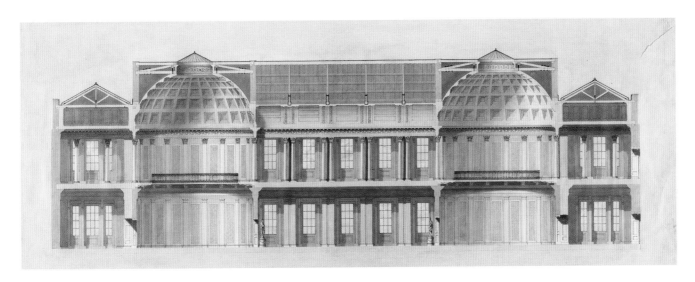

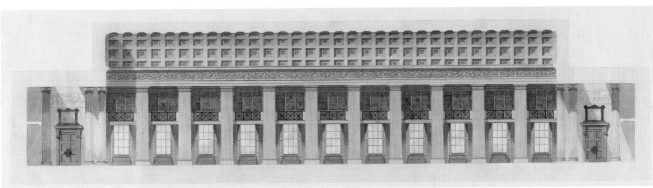

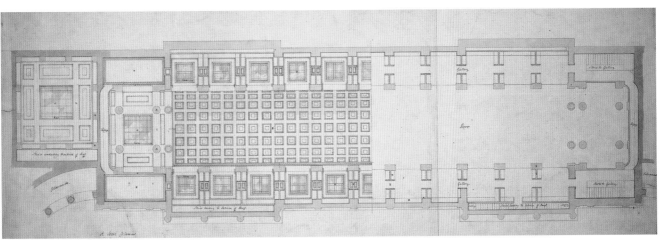

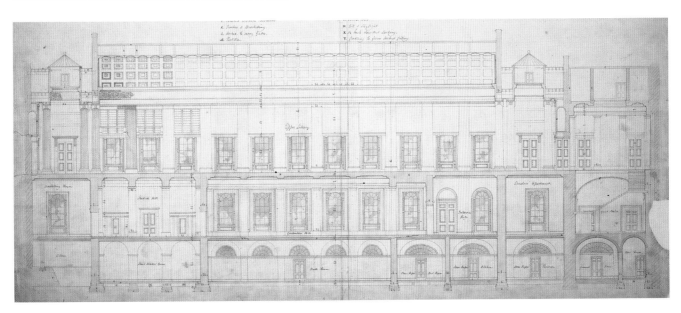

design of the library in 1823 and 1824, circumstances had changed significantly and a radical rethink was necessary:

It will no doubt be recollected that according to my original design, The College Library was divided in its length into five compartments – an arrangement which was induced by the External architecture [Adam's original design]. Since the time however at which that Design was adopted, an alteration has been made upon the front of the Buildings towards the Court, by which there is introduced a repetition of similar windows at equal distances along the whole line of the Building. This enables me to form the upper Library into one large apartment – 190 feet in length, 50 feet in breadth, and 40 feet in height – an opportunity rarely to be met with, and not to be neglected. There are but few Columns introduced, each Book-case serving as a kind of Buttress or Pier, projecting into the room and supporting the Entablature, the whole of the ornament being displayed upon the Roof, so as not to obscure or interfere with the effect of the Books, which must surely ever be considered as the fittest decoration for a Library.

Below this great room are the Graduation Hall and Chapel, & what may be termed the Working part of the Library, where the students will receive and return those Books they are in the daily habit of using.[138]

Playfair had been considering the redesign of the library and south range for a number of years while the courtyard elevation of the mirroring north range was being altered. In the spring of 1823 Playfair also visited London, Oxford and Cambridge to study a number of libraries. He noted sniffily that 'although I may not have observed any thing highly worthy of imitation, I have yet seen much to be avoided, & have acquired useful information on several points'.[139] When Adam had drawn up his proposals for an ornamental colonnade on the south elevation in 1789, the lands to the south of the College were largely undeveloped, and there was some chance that the College would be widely visible from that direction. When Playfair submitted his competition design in 1816, South College Street was already developed with tall tenements, but he still felt constrained to follow the commissioners' instructions to maintain Adam's decorative external elevation. By 1823, Playfair was securely entrenched in his employment at the University, and now proposed a much simpler and cheaper treatment for the overshadowed south elevation. The north-facing courtyard elevation almost mirrored the north range opposite, but the subtle addition of pedimented first-floor windows in the pavilions marked the special nature of the room within.

Essentially the new plan was to do away with all the internal divisions and rotundas of the upper library on the 1816 competition plan and create a single, long, double-height, barrel-vaulted hall across the full width of the first floor of the south range, accessed by its own ceremonial staircase at the east end. The spectacular appearance was to depend on the sheer size of the room, the perspective effect achieved by the repetitive arrangement of bookcase bays and decorative fluted columns, and the soaring Roman-style arched coffered ceiling. On showing off his great library, Playfair used to relate an anecdote about one impressed visitor:

The late Admiral Duckworth once came to visit this fine interior. On being told that it was one hundred and ninety feet in length, he struck his foot on the floor, and exclaimed, 'By God! Just the length of the entire deck of my ship.'[140]

To some degree Playfair drew on the layout of Edinburgh's two great law libraries in Parliament Square, the upper and lower Signet libraries, designed internally by his master, William Stark, in 1812. However, the arrangement of the books was to be largely in accordance with modern library principles, set out by Leopoldo della Santa in his seminal *Della Construzione e del Regolamenta di una Pubblica Universale Biblioteca* of 1816, which recommended the creation of secure closed stacks for the books and separate reading rooms for the users.[141] The reference collection and rare books were to be stored in locked cabinets in the great public hall of Playfair's upper library, but it was not intended for daily access by the students. The ground floor below was to contain the entrance hall, reading rooms, a supervised 'consulting room' (now the Reid Room) for rare books, offices for the library staff, the working collections of books (guarded by the under-librarians) for the students, and a graduation hall / chapel. Internal access stairs allowed the librarians to move between the two floors of the library. By 1833 the graduation hall was already converted to a student reading room. Further significant alterations to the ground floor rooms followed in the 20th century. Omission of the internal divisions on the first floor and ornamental exterior from his original plan allowed Playfair to save on some structural costs and plough the savings into the decoration and fitting out of the upper library.

The first job was the removal of the old Teviot Chambers, where Playfair had maintained his office since 1816, and the sale of the demolition materials with the exception of any carved stones or other 'curiosities'.[142] The structural work proceeded quickly initially, but the contractor's financial difficulties soon kicked in, and by the contract deadline at the end of 1826, the

92 The Playfair Library
Nick Haynes

interior remained only a shell ready for plastering.[143] Under the aegis of the noted antiquarian David Laing, the Senatus had spent more than £2,000 in repairing, rebinding, reordering by subject and recataloguing the books in preparation for the promised move to the new library, and were becoming concerned that the money would be wasted if the books remained in the damp conditions of the old library for much longer.[144] The commissioners therefore agreed to push Playfair and Turnbull to complete the lower library and all its ancillary rooms for the beginning of August 1827. The decanting of the books took place in three stages: first to piles on the floor in adjacent classrooms; then to the new graduation hall where the old library shelves had been relocated as a temporary measure; and finally into the upper library when it was ready towards the end of 1828.

Having emptied the old library, the materials of the 1617 Building were sold at auction to Turnbull for £112.[145] Playfair was ordered to remove all the carved stones, particularly those of the Rutherford family, and incorporate them into the entrance hall of the mathematics classroom (what is now known as the Court Room Vestibule) in the north range. The 1617 Building, the last surviving remnant of the old College and the 'unsafe and unsightly pile which at present blocks up the entrance of the College', was finally demolished at the beginning of September 1827.[146]

Although Playfair's competition entry had promised iron floors and iron doors to provide fireproofing, he quietly abandoned these proposals in his final design, possibly on the grounds of cost and in the light of the difficulties created by the iron floor in the museum. Iron shutters were provided on the South College Street side only, presumably to maintain security rather than for fireproofing. The library roof contained iron ties, braces and shoes, but no 'fireproof' iron joists. The heating was designed as originally promised, by means of hot air ducts leading from a large stove room in the basement, but eventually cost-cutting led to a much simpler arrangement of individual cockle stoves.[147] By 1828 Turnbull's credit problems were really beginning to impact on progress, and it was necessary for the clerk of works, William Gowans, to travel to London to pay for and release the supply of oak flooring that had been ordered.[148] The following year the commissioners sacked Turnbull, which led to a legal wrangle.

Robert Buchan carried out the painting of the upper library in 1831. His account reveals that the ceiling, frieze and columns were painted a cream colour, with the ornaments of the coffers and the capitals picked out in gold. The bookshelves themselves were 'grained' to look like oak. The upper library was redecorated in 1898 and again in the 1950s.[149] Although the books were finally transferred to the library in 1831, the building funds were exhausted. Frustratingly it was impossible to open the upper library properly until the end of 1833, as for the sake of £40 and 'the dilatory proceeding of the founder, Mr. Patterson' the ironwork for the great stair remained unfinished.[150]

Initially there was no plan for statuary in the upper library, but in 1828 the commissioners were offered a statue of Robert Burns by the sculptor John Flaxman.[151] In the end, the statue went to a specially designed monument by Thomas Hamilton on Calton Hill, but the idea of decorating the upper library with sculpture had begun to form. A decade later, when the upper library was complete, the great bibliophile Thomas Frognall Dibdin suggested a series of marble busts of 'a few of the great men of Scotland' against the pilasters.[152] Playfair 'did not put his veto upon the proposition', and so the familiar collection began.

93 The lending library underneath the Playfair Library, photographed by Alexander Adam Inglis, about 1905
University of Edinburgh
[EUA GD63]

94 The professors' reading room beneath the Playfair Library, photographed by Alexander Adam Inglis, about 1905
University of Edinburgh
[EUA GD63]

95 Old College, photographed by George Washington Wilson, 1880

Capital Collections, Edinburgh [7777]

96 *Snowballing Outside Edinburgh University* by Sam Bough, 1853

National Galleries of Scotland, Edinburgh

COURTYARD (OR QUADRANGLE) 1832

Playfair's original design of 1816 to level out the courtyard and provide access to the buildings had been a terrace and continuous steps in front of the buildings. When the money to carry out the terrace finally arrived from the government in 1832, Playfair took the opportunity to revise the design to incorporate a balustraded terrace with nine flights of steps linking it to the lower courtyard. The commissioners approved the design and accepted a tender from Lewis A. Wallace in November 1832.[153] The terrace was built in a mixture of Craigleith and cheaper Humbie sandstone to reduce costs. The corner steps were never much admired, and were removed in 1950.

There was not enough funding to finish the courtyard itself. It remained with a rough temporary finish from the 1840s onwards, and was in use as a car park until 2005. With generous funding from an anonymous donor, the University appointed Simpson & Brown Architects to draw up a scheme to complete the courtyard in a manner sympathetic to Playfair's terrace and steps. Playfair's intentions for the surfacing of the courtyard were not clear from the documentary evidence. A lawn was introduced to soften the space and make it flexible for a number of uses, and the surrounding paving and balustrading was designed with reference to Playfair's completed work at the College and also at Donaldson's Hospital, New College, the National Gallery, and Heriot's Hospital courtyard. The archaeological survey described earlier was undertaken prior to the works, The Chancellor, HRH the Princess Royal, opened the completed courtyard in 2011.

PLAYFAIR'S GATES 1840

The magnificent iron gates at the carriage and pedestrian entrances from the South Bridge were Playfair's last contribution to the architecture of the University in 1840. Alone amongst all Playfair's work on the College, these were funded by the University's patrons, the town council. They were commissioned from the Shotts Iron Company for £184 17s 6d in response to the 'Snowball Riot' of 1838, a Town and Gown snowball fight that got out of hand and resulted in an army regiment from Edinburgh Castle being called to calm the situation. The temporary wooden gates had not been sufficient to keep the brawling out of the courtyard. Playfair's gates have stood the test of time in providing more substantial security.

LATER 19TH-CENTURY ADDITIONS
THE DOME AND OTHER WORKS

On his death in 1872, the lawyer, Robert Cox, left £2,000 to his alma mater for the specific purpose of completing the dome over the entrance.[154] The sum was insufficient, and in order to meet the costs fully it was allowed to accumulate interest for fourteen years. The Senatus established a dome committee comprising Professors Sir William Turner (anatomy), George Armstrong (engineering) and Gerald Baldwin Brown (fine arts). On the basis of his work for the University at the new medical buildings, Robert Rowand Anderson was by now regarded as the 'University architect'. He was appointed without competition, and plans were submitted to the Dean of Guild for approval on 5 August 1886.[155] It is not known how far Anderson studied the original Adam plans and sketches, but he opted for a broad and tall neo-baroque design akin to Adam's initial sketches [figs 97, 98]. The substantial stone base and drum below the timber and lead dome allowed the incorporation of an additional room, a museum of comparative sculpture for Baldwin Brown. The wilful asymmetry of the protruding drum of the staircase on the north-west side marks the dome as a pragmatic later 19th-century addition rather than an original neoclassical design. Although the city skyline had changed immeasurably since Adam's day, the dome still had a substantial picturesque impact on the skyline of the city, particularly in views from approaches along the bridges from the north and along Nicolson Street / Clerk Street / South Clerk Street / Newington Road from the south.

Contractors W. & J. Kirkwood began work immediately, but were delayed by poor weather in the winter of 1886 to 1887.[156] On completion in April 1887 the new stone contrasted strongly with the older Craigleith sandstone below.[157] Only at this stage was John Hutchinson commissioned for 400 guineas to sculpt the 6-foot gilded bronze figure of 'Aspiring Youth bearing the Torch of Knowledge' that commands the top of the lantern.[158] The sculpture was placed on display in Old College quad before being hoisted into position in the autumn of 1888.[159] The 'Golden Boy' is modelled on the Edinburgh boxer, Anthony Hall. The plaster model for

the bronze was exhibited at the Royal Scottish Academy in 1889 and now forms part of the University's sculpture collection.[160]

Careful husbanding of Cox's legacy allowed £444 for the University to commission Anderson for some further improvements to the exterior of Old College.[161] The opening of Chambers Street in 1870 had left the north elevation of the College looking rather austere, so Anderson proposed the removal of the iron railing and parapet and redressing the basement level of the three western pavilions to match the rustication of the easternmost pavilion. The decorative string course above the principal floor of the eastern pavilion was also matched on the remaining pavilions.

BREWSTER STATUE

On 1 August 1870 Lord Neaves unveiled at the west end of Old College quad, a Sicilian marble statue by William Brodie to Sir David Brewster, the polymath and Principal of the University from 1859 to 1868. Along with the Cumming Fountain it survived the triennial traumas of rectorial election-day battles in the quad by being boarded up, until it was removed to the relative safety of King's Buildings in the early 1920s.

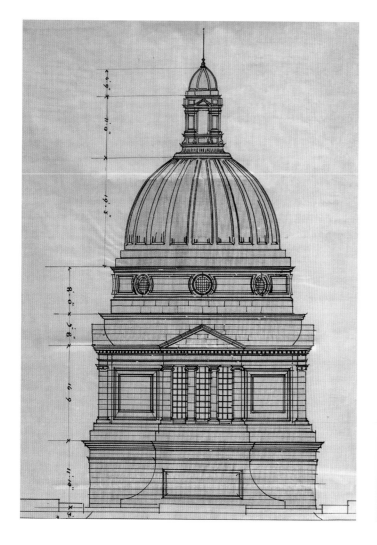

opposite

97 Design for the dome by Robert Rowand Anderson, 1886

Edinburgh City Archives, Dean of Guild Collection

98 Old College not long after the completion of the dome, about 1890

HES [Scottish Colofoto Collection: SC 1119786]

above

99 Old College quad, which was laid out to designs by Simpson & Brown Architects in 2007–11

Neale Smith

THE CUMMING DRINKING FOUNTAIN 1886

Two drinking fountains had been donated to the University by John Hope and set up in the quadrangle in 1866.[162] However, these must have proved inadequate, as a much more splendid affair, gifted by Dr William F. Cumming and designed by Sydney Mitchell & Wilson was erected in the quad in 1886.[163] The 13-feet high structure was formed from Binny stone with bronze dolphins at each corner, which spouted water into bowls with chained cups for drinking. The fountain is rumoured now to form part of the foundations of one of the King's Buildings after a disastrous attempt to relocate it in the 1920s.[164] The foundations of the fountain were uncovered during the 2010 excavations.

20TH- AND 21ST-CENTURY CENTURY ALTERATIONS

Throughout the 20th century and into the present century, minor works and the commissioning of major works at Old College have fallen to a division of the Estates Department of the University, known variously as: the Clerk of Works Office (until the 1940s); Works Department (1940s–1995); and Works Division (1996–present). The myriad of minor works is too numerous and complicated to chart here, but the major schemes have had a significant impact on the appearance and character of the complex. Only outlines of the major works are considered here.

In 1923 Sir Robert Lorimer designed a memorial in the arcade of the lower museum commemorating the University dead of the First World War. The bronze sculptural elements were executed by Charles d'Orville Pilkington Jackson. Lorimer & Matthew Architects expanded the memorial in 1947 to include the dead of the Second World War.

The University's ambitious expansion plans of the 1950s and 1960s, and the subsequent decanting of the library and other departments, led to a re-evaluation of the purpose and function of Old College. Ian G. Lindsay & Partners prepared a report on its history and future use in 1964.[165] Following on from the report, Lindsay submitted renovations and alterations proposals including the Court Room (1966), the Principal's Room (1966), the Raeburn Room (1966), the Centre for European Studies (in the old library, 1967), a Student Art Centre and Picture Gallery (Talbot Rice Gallery) for south-west corner (1968–74), renovation of the south side and south-east corner (1968–72), renovation of the north range for the law faculty (1969–73), renovation of the Senate Hall (1972), and renovation for the Department of Criminology (1977).[166]

Simpson & Brown Architects designed the 2007–11 quad, and LDN Architects are currently responsible for the major refurbishment and reconfiguration of the north range and parts of the east and west ranges for the Law School, 2013–18. Further works are planned, including refurbishment of the Playfair Library.

Chapter Four

Beginnings of the Modern University 1840–1900

NICK HAYNES

100 View of the exhibition hall in the Medical School anatomy museum with skeletons of large mammals and a bust of Dr Monro secundus, photographed by Bedford Lemere, 1895
HES [Bedford Lemere Collection: SC 694690]

The period 1840 to 1900 was to see the introduction of far-reaching changes in the size, constitution, administration, finances, curriculum and facilities of the University. At the outset, the University operated under the patronage of the town council; it was required to appoint a religious minister as Principal and all professors had to swear obedience to the established Church of Scotland. It numbered some 1,600 male undergraduate students under thirty-two professors, there were no social or residential facilities for students, and all teaching took place within Old College. By the end of the century the University had its autonomy under a University Court and independence from the established church, There were 2,914 students including a small number of female students, forty subjects taught by their relevant professors and assisted by thirty-four lecturers and fifty-six assistants (still all male), two students' unions, private halls of residence, a ceremonial hall, and new sporting facilities and teaching and research accommodation outside Old College.[1] Money, as always, remained an issue, but the acute problems of the 1840s and 1850s had eased.

CONSTITUTION AND ADMINISTRATION

If what is usually called the 'University of Edinburgh' be in fact just 'the College of the town', then let the Town Council be left to find the means for its support, while national endowments are reserved for national institutions.[2] (Lord Advocate's Bill 1858)

The year 1858 saw the final settlement of what Sir Alexander Grant called the 'Thirty Years' War' between the University and the town council.[3] In that year the Lord Advocate introduced 'A Bill to make Provision for the better Government and Discipline of the Universities of Scotland and improving and regulating the Course of Study therein; and for the Union of the Two Universities and Colleges of Aberdeen'.[4] The resulting 1858 Act completely remodelled the constitutional structures of the universities and invigorated the whole higher education system.[5] New courts, presided over by rectors (elected by the matriculated students), were to review all decisions of the Senatus and act as courts of appeal from the Senatus. General Councils, comprising all professors and graduates of the universities, led by elected chancellors, were also established 'to take into their consideration all questions affecting the well-being and prosperity of the University and to make representations from time to time on such questions to the University Court, who shall consider the same, and return to the council their deliverance thereon'. The Act had other important implications including a provision for regular government grants, removal of the requirement for the Principal to be a minister of the Church of Scotland, an increase in stipends for professors, provision of pensions to retired professors, creation of new chairs, and appointment of professors' assistants, or lecturers. Arising from the Disruption of 1843, the University (Scotland) Act of 1853 had already removed the requirement for professors to swear obedience to the established Church of Scotland.

The impact of the 1858 Act was strongest in Edinburgh, where the University was finally released from the control of its founding patrons, the town council, and from the politics of the church in the appointment of its Principal. The Act also removed the town council's direct power to appoint the Principal and professors, instead instituting seven 'curators of patronage', drawn from the town council (four curators) and University Court appointees (three curators). The Senatus remained responsible for academic and disciplinary matters, and administration of property and revenues, but answered to the University Court.

More radical reforms were discussed in the 1860s and 1870s, leading to the appointment of another Royal Commission on the Universities of Scotland in 1876, their report in 1878, and a controversial parliamentary Bill in 1883. The most alarming proposal in the Bill related to the abolition of the modest Treasury grants, which amounted to about £9,000 per annum in the case of Edinburgh.[6] The universities opposed the Bill of 1883 and those that followed each year until 1888. The final result of all the discussions and failed Bills was the Universities (Scotland) Act of 1889, 'An Act for the Better Administration and Endowment of the Universities of Scotland', which was to have far-reaching effects on Edinburgh and the three other ancient universities. These included: the five-year appointment of a new and powerful regulatory body of Scottish University Commissioners, whose responsibilities covered the

preservation and maintenance of all the fabrics and buildings of, or connected with, the Universities and Colleges, and the better custody and management of any libraries, museums, and laboratories thereto belonging, or the contents thereof, and of any collections, furniture, apparatus, or objects acquired, or to be acquired for the use of the Universities [...]

The Court increased in size from eight to sixteen members, and was given the power to alter, revoke and make new ordinances with the approval of a new Scottish Universities Committee of the Privy Council; the Students' Representative Council was formally recognised; women students were to attend classes and graduate on terms of equality with the men; and the professors were finally allocated salaries, rather than collecting class fees directly from their students.[7] The

new Finance Committee of the Court was established to deal with the financial responsibilities that passed from the Senatus.

Two important ordinances of the Scottish University Commissioners were made in 1895 for the encouragement of special study and research and the appointment of research fellows (Ordinance 61), and for higher degrees in arts and sciences (Ordinance 62). The expansion of postgraduate research was to have a particularly significant effect on the accommodation requirements of the sciences (see Chapter Five).

FINANCES

The town council's bankruptcy in 1833, as the result of the disastrously over-ambitious Leith Docks scheme, continued to cast a shadow over the University's finances into the 1840s and 1850s. The release of the University from the grip of the town council in 1858 did little to improve its financial situation in the second half of the 19th century. The Edinburgh University Property Arrangement Act of 1861 transferred to the Senatus the 'Site of the Buildings of the University of Edinburgh, with the whole Buildings thereon, Parts and Pertinents thereof, and Furniture and Museums therein, so far as now belonging to or vested in the city', along with city revenues allocated to the University including £2,170 per annum from the harbour and docks of Leith.[8]

It was clear that the existing revenues were barely sufficient for maintaining the current staff and buildings, let alone any expansion or improvement of facilities. In the light of this gloomy financial outlook, the founder of the Sanskrit chair, John Muir, established the Association for the Better Endowment of the University of Edinburgh in 1864.[9] The association

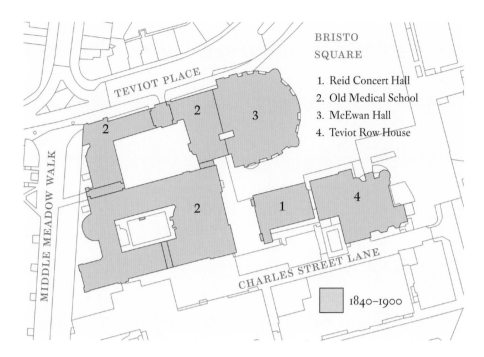

BRISTO SQUARE

1. Reid Concert Hall
2. Old Medical School
3. McEwan Hall
4. Teviot Row House

1840–1900

101 Plan showing development of the main University buildings outside Old College, 1840–1900

Crown copyright 2017 Ordnance Survey [Licence Number 100021521]

provided relatively modest contributions, but its annual report drew attention to the needs of the University. Later that year twenty-one graduates of the University came together to form the Edinburgh University Club of London. Although the club was founded for social purposes, the University was quick to realise the potential for fundraising, accepting a contribution of ten guineas in 1866, and seeking to create a network of clubs throughout the world.[10] By 1910 similar clubs had been established in Manchester, Birmingham, Liverpool, Newcastle and Sheffield.

In spite of various Treasury threats to reduce annual grants to the Scottish universities, the trend throughout the period 1840 to 1900 was a gradual increase in the government's contribution. By 1893–4 annual government grants almost matched the class fees.[11] Endowments represented 11 per cent of the annual income, and matriculation, exam and other fees brought in a further 16 per cent. Almost 70 per cent of expenditure went on teaching salaries, while some 9 per cent was on upkeep of the buildings. The spending on building maintenance remained relatively stable in percentage terms into the next century.

As previously in its history, personal benefactors provided the catalyst for renewed private and public investment in the University's estate. After a very pro-tracted battle, the legacy of General John Reid provided the first building outside Old College in 1859, the music classroom in Park Place (now Teviot Row). In 1873 Sir David Baxter of Kilmaron bequeathed £20,000 to the University towards a new Medical School. This generous sum purchased part of the site at Park Place / Teviot Row, and triggered a series of successful public appeals and a further £80,000 of capital from the government. Perhaps the most spectacular gift of all came from the brewer, William McEwan, who offered to pay for the construction of a ceremonial hall if the University would purchase the site. McEwan's pet project ended up costing over £115,000, three times the original budget.

WOMEN STUDENTS

Sophia Jex-Blake's 1872 essay, 'Medical Education of Women', records the traumatic and then continuing struggle by the 'Edinburgh Seven' to secure a medical education for women at the University, typified by a riot at Surgeons' Hall when the women arrived to sit an anatomy exam [fig.102].[12] In 1876 Jex-Blake's campaign finally resulted in the amendment of the regulating Medical Act 1858 to allow women to study medicine in separate classes, sit the prescribed exams and be duly registered as doctors. Mary Crudelius led other efforts to obtain a university education for women through the lectures of the Edinburgh Ladies Educational Association, which she helped to establish in 1868. This later became the Edinburgh Association for the University Education of Women (EAUEW), whose influence on the Universities (Scotland) Act of 1889 led to the formal admission of women. The first women students matriculated at Edinburgh in 1892. The associa-tion's previous classes were accepted as counting towards degree requirements, and the first eight women duly graduated in 1893. Eleanor Anne Ormerod, a self-taught

102 Sophia Jex-Blake, pioneering campaigner for female medical education at the University of Edinburgh
University of Edinburgh [0041836]

103 Women's Students' Union, 53 Lothian Street, Edinburgh, photographed by Alexander Adam Inglis, about 1905
University of Edinburgh [EUA GD63]

entomologist, received the first honorary doctorate awarded by the University to a woman in 1900.[13] By 1903 women comprised 10 per cent of the student population, but there were no female professors.[14]

David Mather Masson, Professor of Rhetoric and Belles Lettres, championed the cause of women's education at the University. When a new hall of residence and library for women opened at 31 George Square in 1897, after a fundraising campaign by the EAUEW, it was named in his honour.

The Students' Representative Council was mixed-gender from the admission of women to the University in 1892. The first female senior president was elected in 1915. However, the union was a different affair, jealously guarding its gentlemen's club atmosphere. Relations between the Students' Representative Council and its offspring, the Edinburgh University Union, were fractious throughout much of the 20th century, particularly over the union's refusal to admit women (finally overturned in 1971). Recognising that the prospects of sharing accommodation with the union were remote, Elizabeth Baldwin Brown and Elsie Inglis became the driving forces for a separate women's union, which opened at 53 Lothian Street in 1905 [fig.103].[15]

HALLS OF RESIDENCE AND PATRICK GEDDES

One of the most significant changes in the last quarter of the 19th century was the provision of student accommodation, not by the University itself, but through a pioneering independent initiative under the energetic and inspirational leadership of the demonstrator in botany, Patrick Geddes. From the 17th century, students had lived at home, with relatives or in lodgings around the city. By the middle of the 19th century many of these lodgings were to be found in the nearby slums of the Old Town. The Principal, Alexander Grant, and the Senatus were sympathetic to the problems of decent student accommodation and improving social interaction. In 1863 they established the Edinburgh University College Hall Company Limited with the aim of providing 'board and lodging [...] and an opportunity of associating together under suitable superintendence'.[16] The necessary finance failed to materialise, and the company was soon wound up. Apart from the costs, there was an entrenched suspicion of the proposal as a threat to the independent spirit of the Scottish student. Still, Grant continued to hope for a financial backer:

And yet, if some pious millionaire were desirous to immortalise his name by improving the social life of the Edinburgh University Students, we should recommend him (for anything done on a small scale would be a drop in the bucket and comparatively useless) to buy up the whole of George Square and turn it into a set of chambers for Students. With suitable restaurants within the bounds, and with the centre of the square for a place of recreation, this plan might afford great convenience to some 500 Students. Perhaps this idea may be carried out before the 400th birthday of the University, if not by a Benefactor, by a Company (limited)!
(Sir Alexander Grant writing in 1884)[17]

The exit of the middle and upper classes to the expanding New Town from 1767, a massive increase in industry and the working-class population, and a stagnation in house-building for workers had contributed to the overcrowding and insanitary conditions of the Old Town with its associated public health, economic and social crises.[18] The problems were similar in many other rapidly expanding cities, and recognised at national and local government levels. In Edinburgh, the town council, led by Lord Provost William Chambers, used new powers under the Edinburgh Improvements Act 1867 to carry out large-scale demolitions of thirty-four 'unhealthy areas' and create new or widened streets including Jeffrey, East Market, Cranston, Blackfriars, St Mary's, Guthrie and Chambers Streets. In spite of the loss of 2,700 dwellings, almost a third of the housing stock of the Old Town, and the displacement of 8 per cent of the city's entire population, this expensive scheme focused on new non-residential buildings and did relatively little to provide decent replacement housing. The new housing that was built was largely at the instigation of the City Improvement Trust, and designed by their architects, David Cousin and John Lessels.

Patrick Geddes was appointed as a demonstrator in botany at the University in 1879 at the age of 26 (the only University assistant without a degree).[19] He had a wide range of interests beyond the field of botany, including zoology, biology, evolution, ecology, economics, statistics, geography, 'civics' (applied sociology) and urban history. Geddes had witnessed the cruel disruption of the grand Haussmann scheme in Paris to the lives of the displaced and the negative impact on the historic character of the city. Like members of the newly formed Cockburn Association, Geddes saw a similar effect in Chambers' 'improvement' schemes in Edinburgh. He became an advocate for what he termed 'conservative surgery', an incremental and pragmatic approach to regeneration and physical improvement of the city that avoided unnecessary destruction of old buildings, minimised cost and disruption to residents, and respected the local social and cultural traditions.[20] Geddes played a part in activist groups including the Edinburgh Social Union, the Edinburgh Health Society and the Social and Sanitary Society of Edinburgh, led largely by middle-class women volunteers. The housing work of Edinburgh Social Union

opposite

104 As student organisations and halls of residence developed in the late 19th century, more events to encourage social interaction took place, such as this summer gathering at Ramsay Garden in 1897
HES [DP 052685]

105 Edinburgh University Cycling Club, Scottish cycling meet, George Street, 1884
Capital Collections, Edinburgh [13856]

drew on Octavia Hill's work in London, where volunteer groups took over the management of existing buildings, carrying out modest physical improvements from surplus funds from rents. Making use of his position within the University, Geddes supported Edinburgh's part in the universities extension movement of the 1880s, taking teaching beyond the limits of the university.[21]

Geddes and his new wife, Anna Morton, moved to the then crumbling Lawnmarket in April 1887, and set about encouraging sanitary and other improvements in

the area. Separately from the Edinburgh Social Union, Patrick and Anna Geddes turned their attention to student accommodation 'to supply the long and widely felt need in Scottish universities of college life as understood in England, with its obvious social advantages and avoidance of the isolation and other drawbacks of solitary life in lodgings'.[22] Officially opened in June 1887, Mound House (later expanded and named Lister House), part of a tenement at 2 Mound Place, was the first of a series of halls of residence that were to become known collectively as 'University Hall'.[23]

The initial intention was that the hall should follow the model of Toynbee Hall in London, established as a 'settlement house' in which students from Oxford and Cambridge universities could undertake social work in the deprived East End of London. University Hall adopted the motto *Vivendo Discimus*, or 'by living we learn', and aimed to provide social contact both within and beyond the University. Students from the hall conducted 'classes for working lads living in the neighbourhood'.[24] Overall responsibility for the hall lay with a committee of students, graduates and teachers at the University, but day-to-day management rested with the house committee, elected monthly from amongst the residents. The building was rented from a private landlord, and fees charged to cover the housekeeping costs without generating a profit. Further men's residences followed under Geddes's initiative as part of the Municipal Sanitary Improvement Scheme of 1893. Geddes allocated three out of twenty-four flats at his Burns Land development as the first residence for women students, which opened as Crudelius University Hall in 1894. Friends of Geddes established the Town and Gown Association to rescue the various schemes that had been halted by his financial difficulties in 1896. The Town and Gown Association continued to own many of the residences into the middle of the next century.

SOCIAL WELFARE AND SPORT

The sedentary life of the students, poor diet and lack of social spaces in Old College, or even shelter between classes, was acknowledged and debated by the Senatus at an early date, but the cramped conditions for basic teaching pushed these wants to the bottom of the priority list. The removal of the enormous natural history and agriculture collections to the neighbouring Museum of Science and Art finally released enough space to set up a refreshment room in the old upper museum, a drill hall in the lower museum and a gymnasium in the agricultural museum, in 1866.[25] It is clear from the Senatus's discussions that it was not just the physical comfort of the students that motivated the new arrangements, but also their moral wellbeing, which could only be ensured within the protective environment of the College. It is perhaps for this reason that the social facilities were not well used, and the space demands of the teaching staff soon took precedence again. The gymnasium was driven downstairs into the basement in the north-west corner of the quad.[26] There was also a fencing room.[27]

The Senatus delayed the University's tercentenary celebrations from 1883 to coincide with the opening of the new Medical School in April 1884.[28] One of the major concerns of the University authorities was the potential for rowdy behaviour by the students at the festivities. They therefore welcomed a proposal from two students, Robert Fitzroy Bell (grandson of the founder of Bell's Whisky) and David Orme Masson (postgraduate in chemistry), to establish a Students' Representative Council, which promised to promote order, a 'wholesome esprit de corps' and a sense of loyalty to the University. In 1883 Bell had visited Strasbourg, then part of the German Empire, and been impressed by the Studentenausschuss, a students' committee that acted as a liaison between the students, the university and the civic authorities.[29]

The first meeting of the Edinburgh council took place on 17 January 1884 and the three principal aims were set out: '(1) To represent the students in matters affecting their interests; (2) To afford a recognised means of communication between the students and the University authorities; and (3) To promote the social life and academic unity among the students'.[30] The first test for the new council was to maintain order at the inaugural address of the Rector, Stafford Henry Northcote, 1st Earl of Iddesleigh. The success of this and the subsequent week of tercentenary celebrations encouraged the Senatus to support the council in broader social and welfare initiatives, such as the construction of a union building. The Edinburgh model soon took root at Aberdeen (1884), St Andrews (1885) and Glasgow (1886). In 1889 the Universities (Scotland) Act gave formal recognition to Students' Councils in all four Scottish universities.

Although students had played various organised sports since the foundation of the University in the 16th century, it was not until 1866 that a more formal association took place with the advent of the Edinburgh University Athletic Club. Sports held under the auspices of the club in the late 19th century included gymnastics, cricket, rugby, football, lawn tennis, boxing, fencing, rowing, swimming, field events, single stick, shinty, hare and hounds, fishing, golf, and cycling [fig.105]. With the support of the Senatus, which increasingly recognised the benefits of Juvenal's maxim *Mens sana in corpore sano* ('A sound mind in a sound body'), the club leased a level field (now Union Park) near the railway station in Corstorphine from 1873. In 1879 they added a small

pavilion to designs by James McLellan Fairley.[31] The distance of Corstorphine from the College and the slow pace of transport there led to the purchase of a new and more convenient field at Myreside, Craiglockhart, in 1896. Two years later the club constructed a half-timbered pavilion with a balcony, designed by the civil engineer, W. Allan Carter, at a cost of £2,000.[32] The renowned architect Robert Lorimer designed a very plain and functional boathouse at Meggetland on the Union Canal for the rowing section of the Athletic Club in 1897.[33] The University's support for these relatively modest facilities marked the first tentative steps outside its narrow teaching responsibilities and into the broader concerns of student welfare.

EXPANSION

With the exception of music, all the University's teaching still took place in Old College until the late 1860s. The removal of the natural history and museum collections and the construction of the music classroom had released some space in Old College, but this was quickly compensated for by new subjects, increasing student numbers, and new requirements for dedicated scientific demonstration and laboratory spaces with all their associated preparatory rooms and staff.

The space restrictions were felt particularly in the medical departments, where the professors struggled with rooms that had been designed almost eighty years earlier and built nearly fifty years previously, and equipment that was similarly outdated. Medicine and medical teaching were advancing rapidly, and up-to-the-minute facilities opening in competing institutions around the world. A particular urgency was brought to the situation by the opening of a purpose-built, state-of-the-art medical building at the University of Glasgow in 1870.[34] A further lack was felt in respect of a common, or graduation, hall, in which the whole University could assemble for ceremonial occasions. Again, this was something that had been designed into Glasgow's new Gilmorehill campus, and took shape in the form of the magnificent Bute Hall from the late 1870s.

Revd George Baird, the longstanding Principal, who had presided over the University throughout the period of Playfair's works, died in 1840. His successor John Lee, also a moderate Church of Scotland cleric, was much involved in the religious tumult surrounding the Disruption of 1843, but was unable to make any headway with the University's financial difficulties. Although the polymath Sir David Brewster was one of the outstanding academics of the period, he only became Principal at the age of seventy-seven and then needed to devote his energies to the constitutional issues of the 1858 Act rather than dealing with the University's estate. The appointment of Sir Alexander Grant as Principal

in 1868 finally galvanised the University into action
on the inadequacies of its buildings and facilities. The
University Court began to discuss expansion beyond
Old College and kept a careful eye on potential sites,
for example by asserting their interests in lands in
North College Street during discussions about the
formation of Chambers Street in 1868, and by talking
to the managers of the Royal Infirmary in 1869 as they
developed their plans to vacate the old Royal Infirmary
site in Infirmary Street and High School Yards for the
new David Bryce-designed buildings in Lauriston
Place.[35] Grant formalised the expansion proposals in
1871, when he set up a small provisional committee to
explore the possibilities. The committee's initial finding
was that Old College should be devoted to the faculties
of arts, divinity and law, and that a new building should
be constructed for the nine professors and 900 students
of the Medical School. The University of Edinburgh
Buildings Extension Scheme should include refurbishment and reorganisation of Old College to meet its
revised functions and expansion of the library.

THE BUILDINGS 1840–1900
REID CONCERT HALL

John Reid [fig.106] passed the 'pleasantest part of
his youth' at the University and went on to a sixty-
year military career, serving in the Seven Years' War
(1756–63) against France and then on other missions
in North America. Eventually in 1798 he was promoted
to general. He had a keen interest in music, both as a
flautist and a composer. Reid's tune, 'The Garb of Old
Gaul', composed for the 42nd Regiment (Black Watch)
in around 1756, is still the regular slow march of the
Scots Guards and other Scottish regiments. He acquired
a fortune of more than £50,000 from his cousin and
fellow army officer, John Small, in 1796.

In 1807 John Reid left £52,000 in trust

*to be life-rented by an only daughter, who married
without his consent, a Mr [Stark] Robertson; whom
failing, to her children; whom failing to the College of
Edinburgh. When it takes that destination, he desires
his executors to apply it to the College, imprimis, to
institute a Professor of Music, with a salary not less than
300l. [£300] a-year; in other respects to be applied to the
purchase of a library, or to be laid out in such a manner
as the Principal and Professors may think proper.*[36]

A codicil left his music books to the Professor of Music
and stipulated that he

*will cause a concert of Music to be performed on the
13th of February being my birth-day, in which shall be
introduced one Solo for the German Flute, Hautbois,
or Clarionet, also one March and one Minuet with*

*accompaniments by a select Band, in order to shew the
taste of music about the middle of last Century, when they
were by me composed and with a view also to keeping my
memory in remembrance [...].*

Reid's daughter, Susanna, died childless in Paris in
1838. Instead of administering the bequest themselves,
Reid's trustees determined to hand over the whole sum,
now standing at £68,876, to the Senatus as trustees.[37]
Unable on their own account to create the new chair,
the Senatus requested the town council, as patrons, to
establish the professorship of the theory of music. The
town council obliged and Reid's trustees' nomination,
John Thomson, was appointed in January 1839. He
organised the first Reid Concert in 1841, which is
staged annually on or about 13 February to this day. No
classroom was set aside for teaching music and neither
Thomson nor his two successors, Sir Henry Bishop and
Hugh Pearson, delivered any lectures in six years. The
legacy accrued interest at about £3,000 per annum, as
the only music-related expenses were the £300 salary to
the professors and the annual expense of the concert.

From the appointment of the advocate John
Donaldson as Professor of the Theory of Music in
May 1845, the Reid bequest became tangled up in the
more general squabbles between the Senatus and the
town council over the running of the University's affairs
and in a personal dispute between Donaldson and his
colleagues in the Senatus. Donaldson was interested in
the science of music, particularly in the 'Logier Method'
taught by Johann Bernhard Logier in Dublin and 'the

elucidation of the phenomena of sound, and the general theory of acoustics'. He acquired a considerable quantity of experimental apparatus for teaching and research purposes.[38] After reluctantly allocating a classroom to Donaldson, the Senatus refused to reimburse the town council from the Reid bequest for the necessary alterations to the room and made no provision for instruments or an assistant to help with the 150 regular students and the equipment.[39]

In November 1847 the town council began legal action, broadening the case to challenge the implementation of Reid's will both by the original trustees and by the Senatus. The result was a long and acrimonious battle in the Court of Session, which eventually found in favour of the town council in July 1855. The judgement obliged the Senatus to use the trust funds to endow the music chair effectively before spending the residue on anything else. Amongst other purposes, the court ordered that £8,000 should be spent on acquiring a site and a purpose-built classroom and £2,000 should be allocated to the purchase of an organ.

Both the Senatus and the town council's College committee established sub-committees to determine a site for the new building in June 1856. The powers of these sub-committees were eventually extended to cover the design and construction of the building. Firstly they investigated a site immediately to the west of the College, but it was considered likely to interfere with the new industrial museum, so attention shifted to the purchase of another site to the west of the Southern Academy (formerly Ross House, then the lying-in hospital, or maternity hospital) at Park House in Park Place for £340.[40]

If the fractious relationship of the two sub-committees had been tested by the purchase of the site, the design and construction of the building took matters to a new level of pettiness and skulduggery. Chastened by the Court of Session decision, but determined to get something that they really wanted out of the Reid fund, the Senatus sub-committee proposed that the new music classroom should be combined with a 1,000-seat common hall for the University. Donaldson, backed by the town council's sub-committee, devised a set of specifications for the music classroom that made the combined usage very difficult and expensive to achieve. In order to test the possibilities more thoroughly, the sub-committees appointed the city's architect, or Superintendent of Public Works, David Cousin, to produce a report and drawings. Perhaps unsurprisingly, Cousin's report backed up the assertions of Donaldson and the town council: the ground floor dimensions could not be adjusted because it was required to accommodate a 'great string, called a Monochord'; galleries for a common hall would interfere with the teaching of the music class; and no windows could be provided at the lower level because Donaldson needed to hang his diagrams on the walls.[41]

The Professor of the Institutes of Medicine, John Hughes Bennett, objected strongly to the consultation with only one architect and to Cousin's conclusions and his proposals for a 'highly ornate and beautiful exterior, with statues etc.'. Bennett was not entirely without justification in demanding a wider field of architectural input. As most of his predecessors had done, Cousin

107 Interior view of the Reid Music School showing the extraordinary original organ and some of the experimental acoustic equipment. This engraving after a photograph by John Moffat is taken from Grant's *Old & New Edinburgh*, vol.4, p.345.

108 Reid Music School, now the Reid Concert Hall, photographed by Alexander Adam Inglis, about 1905
University of Edinburgh [EUA GD63]

maintained a substantial private architectural practice in addition to the Superintendent of Public Works position, acting as architect to the new Free Church and the British Linen Bank amongst other clients.[42] Although Cousin supervised minor alterations to the Adam / Playfair building in his official capacity as superintendent, and letters regarding the music classroom were addressed to him at his office in the City Chambers, the project was a new private commission from the funds of the Reid trustees and not subject to the superintendent's authority.[43] However, the town council's sub-committee prevailed and in April 1857 Cousin was instructed to draw up detailed plans for the music classroom, a museum, a library, a ladies' room and a retiring room for the professor.[44]

David Cousin understood the politics of the situation extremely well. He had been an assistant to Playfair on the University and other projects until 1831. Like Donaldson, and a number of other professors, Cousin was a founding member of the Aesthetic Club of Edinburgh in 1851. The purpose of the club was to establish a science of beauty through a mathematical analysis of harmonic proportion in art and architecture (including colour and spatial relationships), the human form, and music. Cousin believed that the key to harmonic proportion in buildings lay in the ability of the human eye to perceive perspective through the ratios of angles formed by diagonals in rectangles, rather than strict mathematical measurement of the sides of the rectangle.[45] He applied his principles to his own buildings and observed them in operation in those of Inigo Jones, Christopher Wren and Charles Barry.

Cousin delivered his plans on 17 July 1857 with an estimate of £6,206 excluding his fee, the salary of the clerk of works, the furniture and contingencies.[46] The design was Italianate in style, with a heavy bracketed cornice, architraved windows and round-headed niches. The designs were exhibited in the following year at the Royal Scottish Academy.[47] Cousin's assistant, John McLachlan, remembered the development of the Italianate music classroom design:

The latter design is a remarkably harmonious and pleasing one. I have a vivid recollection of seeing the drawings, on the groundwork of which he prepared his design. Music and architecture, he held, were similar arts in producing harmony and discord. In the one the effect was produced on the mind by sounds, in the other by lines. Fully possessed of this idea at the time of the Music Classroom, what may be called the foundation drawing of this fine structure, – and the same principles were applied internally and externally, – was a complicated series of circles, and arcs, and curves, proportions and ratios.[48]

George Wilson, Regius Professor of Technology and first director of the industrial museum, representing the

Senatus, objected to the scale of the estimates, which looked like totalling more than the court-specified £8,000. Cousin revisited the estimates with the lowest tendering tradesmen and reduced the scheme to exactly £8,000 in total by cutting some of the masonry work by George Paterson & Son.[49] The Senatus then intended to approach the architect David Bryce to advise them if the estimates were realistic, but finding him away for several days appointed John Henderson instead.[50] Cousin willingly shared his designs and the specifications with Henderson, who promptly confirmed their accuracy. Having exhausted every obstructive tactic, the Senatus were then obliged to approve the scheme.

Preparation of the site finally began in January 1858. In the absence of Principal Lee, Lord Provost Sir John Melville laid the foundation stone 'with as little ceremony as possible' on the anniversary of General Reid's birthday.[51] A small lead box containing newspapers and coins of the day, a copy of General Reid's march, his will and the Edinburgh Almanac was inserted with the foundation stone. The specially commissioned silver trowel had a handle in the shape of a guitar and was 'chastely ornamented' with inlaid pebbles. Not long into the construction of the foundations a problem came to light with one of the servitudes, or rights, of nearby owners.[52] In order to remove any possible difficulty and avoid the land affected by the alleged servitude, Cousin proposed to rotate the building through 90 degrees clockwise. The entrance elevation therefore moved from facing north to facing west. By November 1858 the building was far advanced and the decision to omit the cornice from the south side of the building was looking like a mistake.[53] Cousin pleaded successfully with the clients to reinstate it. Criticism continued to dog the project: 'the final erection of a new and costly music hall in a city which can scarcely support those it possesses already, can only be regarded as an act of wanton extravagance'.[54]

Although the shell of the building was complete by early 1859, fitting out of the classroom to Professor Donaldson's exacting standards continued for several years. Donaldson's experimental apparatus was transferred to the new classroom in November 1859, but he refused to lecture until the organ was finished in July 1861 [fig.107].[55] William Hill & Son of London 'took more than their usual pains and interest' in the installation of the magnificent pipe organ, which was augmented and improved by Donaldson up to his death in 1865.[56] However, the completion of the music classroom was not the end of Professor Donaldson's problems. A student riot erupted over the allocation of tickets to the first Reid Concert held in the new hall in February 1862, which favoured the great and the good of the city over the students.[57]

Music teaching transferred to Alison House in nearby Nicolson Square in 1964, but the Reid building remained in use as a concert hall and museum for the University's collection of historical instruments. The organ was completely replaced in 1977–8. James Ian Haig Marshall of Ian G. Lindsay & Partners designed the new case, and Jürgen Ahrend of Leer constructed the twenty-one-stop, two-manual instrument in consultation with Peter Williams.[58] When the hall was redecorated in 1993, the architects E. & F. McLachlan applied the colour principles of Donaldson's fellow Aesthetic Club member, D.R. Hay, as set out in his book *The Laws of Harmonious Colouring*. Hay suggested that the seven colours of the spectrum were analogous to the seven notes of a musical scale, and that colour, like music, could be arranged in 'keys'. The 'key' of purple-blues in the hall is set off by a contrasting and slightly discordant red at the lower level.[59]

UNIVERSITY HALL: MOUND HOUSE; MARY CRUDELIUS HOUSE; BLACKIE HOUSE; RAMSAY LODGE; ST GILES HOUSE; MASSON HALL; MUIR HALL

University Hall is the name originally allocated to a collection of buildings converted or designed as student residences under the auspices of Patrick Geddes. Mound House (later expanded and named Lister House), a rented part of a tenement at 2 Mound Place, was the first of the buildings to open in June 1887.[60] Initially twelve students were accommodated in bedrooms and studies on the first and third floors with a dining hall and drawing room on the floor in between. The other two floors of the tenement remained in private occupation. The new hall was tastefully decorated by William Welsh MacFarlane.

Geddes continued his mission to establish more student residences as part of the Municipal Sanitary Improvement Scheme of 1893, through which he was allocated responsibility for the sanitary improvement of two major sites off the Lawnmarket: Wardrop's Court and Riddle's Close. In pursuit of his improvement schemes, Geddes gathered a number of sympathetic architects including Stewart Henbest Capper, Arthur George Sydney Mitchell and George Shaw Aitken.

As part of the Wardrop's Court site facing the Lawnmarket, Henbest Capper designed a large new tenement in 1892 named Burns Land after the connection of the site with Robert Burns's first visit to Edinburgh in 1786.[61] Capper divided the frontage into three units, each with an overhanging gable and oriel window to reflect the character of the previous buildings on the site. Geddes's son, Arthur, carved the dragon brackets over the pend, which led to a new open space created from demolitions in Wardrop's and Paterson's Courts. Geddes allocated three rooms in Burns Land to the first women's hall, named in honour of Mary Crudelius (the founder

of the Edinburgh Ladies Educational Association). Gladstone's Land and Lady Stair's House were largely retained and repaired as part of the scheme. Sydney Mitchell reconstructed a late 17th-century tenement on the north side of Wardrop's Court in a similar style to Burns Land to form Blackie House in 1894.[62]

The development at Riddle's Close involved a much more constrained site and retained all the buildings around two small courtyards, including the late 16th-century Bailie McMorran's House, an early 18th-century tenement facing the Lawnmarket (where David Hume first lived in Edinburgh), and parts of Victoria Terrace converted for use as the Edinburgh Mechanics' Subscription Library in about 1840. Sydney Mitchell made some early internal alterations to Bailie McMorran's House in 1890 and Capper carried out a more thoroughgoing restoration and conversion to a hall of residence with help from Aitken in 1893–5.[63]

Outside the Lawnmarket improvement areas, Aitken converted the David Bryce-designed offices of the *Edinburgh Daily Review* in St Giles Street into a further hall of residence, St Giles House, in 1895–8.[64] Perhaps the most extraordinary of Old Town developments in the 1890s was that of Ramsay Garden [fig.104], which contained flats for University staff and other professionals sympathetic to Geddes's social experiments and a student hall of residence called Ramsay Lodge. This large and prominent scheme on the castle esplanade was designed by Capper and Sydney Mitchell in the spirit of an organic extension of the Old Town, and funded by a syndicate in three phases from west to east between 1892 and 1894.[65] Capper designed the western end before one of his frequent illnesses set in. Sydney Mitchell completed the northern and eastern portions.[66] Ramsay Lodge or 'Allan's Luggy' (wooden basin used for porridge), the house designed by the poet Allan Ramsay for himself in about 1740, formed the main part of the student residence.[67] Further east, timber-framed gables and oriel windows were added facing Princes Street to incorporate three mid-18th-century properties into the picturesque and colourful jumble of gables, towers, turrets, oriels and chimney-stacks of the new flats. Inside, John Duncan, Helen Hay and Helen Baxter carried out a series of murals of scenes from Celtic and Scottish history in the common room of Ramsay Lodge. Patrick and Anna Geddes took a flat in the new development, which was a short distance from the Outlook Tower, the 'world's first sociological laboratory', purchased and established by Geddes as a regional museum in 1892.[68] Ramsay Lodge was sold to the Commercial Bank of Scotland by the Town and Gown Association in 1945.

Closer to the new Medical School, two women's halls, Masson Hall and Muir Hall, were established in existing

109 Ramsay Garden photo-
graphed by James Valentine
of Dundee, 1893. This was
one of a number of build-
ings commissioned by the
Town and Gown University
Settlement (founded by
Professor Patrick Geddes)
providing staff and student
accommodation within the
Old Town of Edinburgh.

Royal Institute of British
Architects, London

townhouses at nos 12 and 31 George Square respectively,
in 1898. These residences were funded and constituted
separately from University Hall.

OLD MEDICAL SCHOOL, TEVIOT PLACE

Discussions about new buildings for the Medical
School began in 1869, but it was felt that the recent
appeal for a new Royal Infirmary had exhausted the
public appetite for charitable giving.[69] Sir David Baxter's
legacy of £20,000 in 1872 encouraged the University
to start looking for possible sites. Apart from North
College Street and the old infirmary site, the main
contenders were sites in South College Street and at
Park Place / Teviot Row (now known as Teviot Place).
The University favoured the old infirmary site, but it
was fortunate that negotiations fell through, as the site
would only have become available for work to commence in 1880. The College Extension Site Committee
enlisted the help of the architects David Cousin, Robert
Matheson (Chief Architect for Scotland in the Office
of Works and executant architect of the western part
of the arts and science museum) and John Paterson
in advising on the suitability of each of the remaining
sites.[70] Although the Park Place / Teviot Row site was
further from Old College than the other sites, the

architects plumped for it very firmly because it would
house the Medical School conveniently close to the
new Edinburgh Royal Infirmary and it would also allow
plenty of room for future expansion. The 80,000ft²
L-plan site was bounded by Teviot Row on the north,
Park Street and Park Place on the east, George's Mews
(now Charles Street Lane) on the south, and Middle
Meadow Walk on the west. It contained a number of
late-18th-century tenements, houses, stables and gardens.
Existing tenancies were transferred to the University
on purchase, and continued until the building work
began.[71] The University also acquired the Edinburgh
Road Trust's interests in the roadways of Park Place
and Park Place Lane.[72] As with the music classroom,
servitudes turned out to be an expensive problem on
the site.

Negotiations for the Park Place / Teviot Row site
began immediately in November 1871, and an initial
tranche of buildings and land was purchased, using
£14,820 of Sir David Baxter's legacy, in 1873. Further
purchases amounting to a total of £50,000 were
eventually required for the whole site, as the first
purchase included only the stables in Park Place and
four of the nine buildings in Teviot Row. Funding for
the project was a key issue. The initial target for a public

appeal was for £100,000. It was also hoped to persuade the government to provide an additional contribution. The appeal was launched officially at a public meeting on 6 April 1874, but some £39,896 had already been promised through discreet private canvassing.[73] The appeal prioritised funding for the new medical buildings over the other aspirations, including the ceremonial hall.

Sir Alexander Grant became chairman of a new acting committee to carry out the project. This comprised the Principal, the Lord Provost, the MP for Edinburgh and a number of professors, lawyers, professionals and businessmen.[74] Honorary local secretaries were appointed throughout Scotland and in selected cities in England, India and the British colonies to help with the fundraising. A public meeting in London, hosted by the Duke of Edinburgh, attracted considerable attention. The acting committee sent out 1,600 circulars and pamphlets, and issued regularly updated subscription lists to the newspapers. By August 1874 the amount paid or promised was over £69,000.[75]

The professors of anatomy, chemistry, physiology, pathology, materia medica, surgery, practice of medicine, midwifery and medical jurisprudence became the principal consultees for the design work and were to

110 Portrait of Robert Rowand Anderson by John Aiken, 1927
Royal Incorporation of Architects in Scotland, Edinburgh

111 Design for the Medical School and McEwan Hall by Robert Rowand Anderson
University of Edinburgh [018134]

provide a list of requirements. The acting committee first considered the appointment of an architect in May 1874 and determined to hold a limited, invitation-only, competition.[76] Six of Edinburgh's most respected architects were invited to submit sketch plans for the medical buildings and the ceremonial hall by 1 December 1874: Robert Rowand Anderson; David Bryce; David Cousin; John Lessels; Peddie & Kinnear; and Wardrop & Reid. Bryce declined the invitation and David Cousin and John Lessels decided to submit a joint proposal. On learning of the competition through the newspapers, 'certain gentlemen in England' had written expressing a desire to send in entries, but the acting committee refused to open the competition further.[77] A ground plan, printed instructions and a schedule of the professors' requirements were supplied to each competitor.

After an extension of a month, a sub-committee of professors considered the plans in relation to both the ceremonial hall and the 'arrangements for the Scientific requirements of the Medical Faculty' in January 1875.[78] The sub-committee requested written opinions from the relevant professors on the merit of each architect's interior plans and also considered general issues such as heating and ventilation, access, domestic accommodation for the janitor, corridors and toilet provision. Cousin and Lessels fared badly in the exercise, while Anderson vied with Wardrop & Reid for first place. There was no favoured plan for the ceremonial hall, but the sub-committee recommended Anderson's plan for the medical buildings as the clear winner on the grounds of its arrangement, lighting and overall design. Accordingly, Anderson was appointed as architect for the project on 29 January 1875 [fig.111].[79]

Anderson's Italianate scheme envisaged a double courtyard, divided by the great anatomical museum, with the ceremonial hall adjoining on a connected limb. Anderson spoke of his design in 1884, describing the popular Palladian style as too rigid and the Gothic unsuited to the scientific spirit of the age: 'I have made use of that phase of art which arose in Italy during the second half of the fifteenth century when the great minds of that country began to burst the bonds of dogma and ecclesiastical authority and were determined to inquire into the nature of all things.'

A grand campanile clocktower, loosely modelled on that of San Marco in Venice, was intended to mark the new complex on the skyline of Edinburgh and in views along Lothian Street and Lauriston Place. The

112 Design for the Teviot Place elevation of the Medical School

University of Edinburgh [0009635]

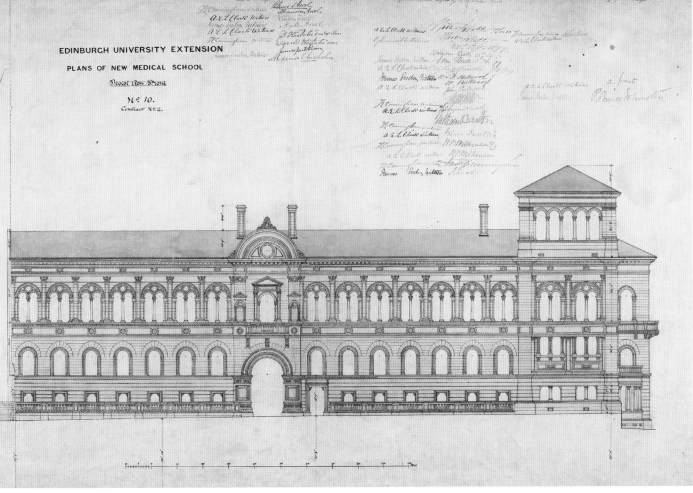

campanile was also justified on the grounds that it would serve as a useful space for 'secular experiments' in the Department of Natural Philosophy. The private southern quadrangle, away from the bustle and prying eyes of Teviot Row, was to house anatomy, pathology, surgery, practice of physic, physiology and midwifery. The public northern quadrangle, at the main entrance from Teviot Row, was reserved for chemistry, materia medica and medical jurisprudence. Anderson's design was exhibited at the Royal Scottish Academy in 1877.

In drawing up his plans Anderson consulted the published plans of all the latest European scientific buildings and visited an astonishingly wide range of British and Continental sites including those at Glasgow, Liverpool, Manchester, Oxford, London, Berlin, Leipzig, Bonn, Aix-la-Chapelle, Utrecht and Amsterdam.[80] He met most of the professors working

113 The Medical School under construction, about 1889
HES [DP 074901]

114 The entrance to the Medical School, Teviot Place, about 1890
HES [Scottish Colorfoto Collection: SC 1235432]

opposite

115 The crania collection room, photographed by Alexander Adam Inglis, about 1905
University of Edinburgh [EUA GD63]

116 The physiology laboratory, photographed by Alexander Adam Inglis, about 1905
University of Edinburgh [EUA GD63]

117 The dissecting room, photographed by Alexander Adam Inglis, about 1905
University of Edinburgh [EUA GD63]

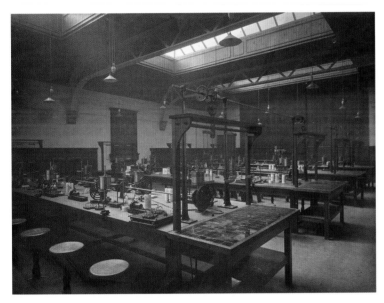

in the buildings and a number of eminent architects. Anderson held that classrooms were best planned in semi-circular form, like Greek theatres, to make the most of natural acoustics. The anatomy, pathology and midwifery classrooms were all planned in this way, but where long rectangular demonstration tables were required, he adopted rectangular-planned rooms, for example materia medica and medical jurisprudence.

Anderson started to revise and cost his proposals in preparation for working and contract drawings. A sum of £261,500 was thought necessary for the medical buildings, ceremonial hall and refurbishment of Old College.[81] Benjamin Disraeli, the Prime Minister, received a University deputation who had gone to London to make their case for government grants in June 1876. Further negotiations with the Treasury removed the ceremonial hall and campanile from the proposals, removed the external works to Old College, and reduced the estimate to £187,500 in return for £80,000 in public money over four years.[82] Anderson divided up the construction into phases, starting with the south block.[83] The acting committee raised the issue of ownership of the plans. Anderson replied that the ownership remained with the architect, but that he would be happy to provide a complete set to the committee.[84]

In September 1877 Anderson appointed Allan Clark as clerk of works and obtained a site office for him in the old house at 1 Park Street. Clark had been the clerk of works to the architect William Burges during construction of the Speech Room at Harrow School in 1871–7.[85] The tender documents were sent to different tradesmen, rather than to a general contractor, and the lowest offers accepted. The stone was to be supplied from Polmaise, Dunmore and Plean Quarries in Stirlingshire to the masons, J. & D. Meikle of Ayr.[86] The carpentry work was offered on the condition of 'War not taking place between this Country and Russia'. The noted heating and ventilation engineer, W.W. Phipson of London, who had fitted out Glasgow University's Gilmorehill buildings in the late 1860s and Anderson's Mount Stuart House for the 3rd Marquess of Bute in 1877, won the contract for the new medical buildings in 1878.[87] One of the more controversial features of the design was the 170-foot ventilation shaft, which provoked much local criticism and a defence of its functional design by Anderson in the pages of *The Scotsman*.[88]

By December 1877 the tenants had left the houses in Park Place and demolition had begun.[89] Although the back greens and gardens were required, the tenants of the late-18th-century houses and tenements in Teviot Row were given a further year. Anderson, founder of both the Edinburgh School of Applied Art and the National Art Survey (as a library of the best examples of Scottish architecture from which students could take inspiration), set his students to work recording the interior details of fireplaces in the houses in 1879. The drawings are now housed in the National Record of the Historic Environment.[90]

Construction of the south block (now the William Robertson Wing) began in earnest in 1878. However, the rapidly increasing number of medical students and the additional facilities demanded by newly appointed professors entailed extra costs and some reworking of the plans as the building was under construction. Some classrooms were even taken down and reconstructed to house the larger numbers. By June 1879 Anderson was able to invite tenders for the second phase of works on the block facing Teviot Row.[91] The official opening of the anatomical department on 27 October 1880 marked the completion of the first phase. Physiology, practice of physic, pathology, surgery and midwifery followed, but the additional expenses of the first phase put pressure on the fitting out of the second phase, and still there were no funds for the tower or the ceremonial hall. The foundations and lowest stage of the tower were built so that when the rest was constructed any differential settlement would be minimised. The tower remains incomplete to this day. Another round of fundraising for a further £100,000 was started in the tercentenary year, 1883.

Anderson also designed the monument to Archbishop Archibald Campbell Tait (1811–1882) on the east side of the complex, which was erected by public subscription. Tait was born in a house on the site, then in Park Place, on 21 December 1811. He studied at the High School, Edinburgh Academy, Glasgow University and Oxford, before succeeding Thomas Arnold as headmaster of Rugby School. From there he went on to become Dean of Carlisle, Bishop of London, and eventually in 1868, Archbishop of Canterbury. The bust was sculpted by Mario Raggi and cast by Young & Co. of Pimlico, London.

Chemistry, materia medica, medical jurisprudence and the magnificent anatomy museum were duly fitted out in 1883–4. The completed teaching buildings opened as the centrepiece of the University's tercentenary celebrations in April 1884. It was barely more than fifteen years before extensions to the new Medical School were required. These extensions and the accompanying alterations to the Anderson building are considered later in this book as part of the broader reorganisation of buildings for the science faculty in the early 20th century.

With the 2002 opening of the new medical teaching facilities in the Chancellor's Building, adjacent to the relocated Edinburgh Royal Infirmary at Little France, large parts of the old Medical School at Teviot were released for other purposes. The school of History,

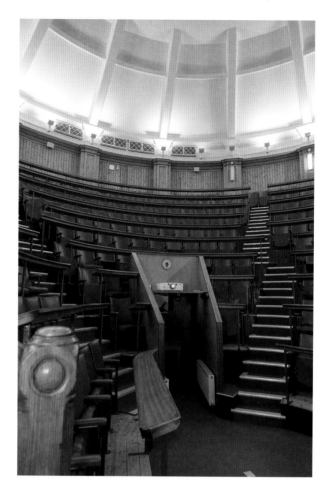

118 Medical School anatomy lecture theatre, room 425
Nick Haynes

119 Old Medical School, Teviot Place, Edinburgh. The former pathology classroom was refurbished by McLaren Murdoch & Hamilton in 2012 as the library of the School of History, Classics and Archaeology.
Nick Haynes

Classics and Archaeology moved into the West Wing, which was completely refurbished at a cost of £14m between March 2009 and August 2010 to designs by McLaren, Murdoch & Hamilton. The large bright rooms overlooking Middle Meadow Walk now house postgraduate study rooms and the Jim McMillan Room, a common room for staff and postgraduate students named in honour of a previous head of the school. Other new facilities include several archaeology laboratories, high-tech lecture theatres and dedicated study areas with fold-away workstations.

MCEWAN HALL

Funding for the construction of the ceremonial hall in Anderson's initial designs had long been a problem. In 1886 William McEwan, the brewing magnate and Liberal MP for Edinburgh Central, made a generous offer of £40,000 to construct the hall if the University could find the money for the site. Having struggled to find the resources to complete the teaching buildings, the University decided to approach the Treasury for the £12,000 needed to purchase and clear the site. A high-powered deputation went to London to make the case and the money was secured. As the construction and decorative scheme progressed, Sir William encouraged and funded an increasingly lavish fitting out, which eventually brought the total cost to £115,000, nearly three times his original donation.

In order to build the ceremonial hall it was necessary to purchase three old tenements on Park Street. Negotiations with the proprietors proved fruitless, so the University took the radical step of promoting a Bill in Parliament to purchase the site compulsorily under the Edinburgh University Buildings Extension Act 1886. Trustees were appointed under the Act to implement its provisions. The town council also purchased and demolished the old tenements in Bristo Street to provide an open setting to the east of the hall, now Bristo Square. McEwan funded the elaborate electric street lamp pillar of Portland stone that stands in the square, which was designed by Anderson in 1896–7 and presented to Edinburgh Corporation.[92] The architectural practice of Professor Percy Johnson-Marshall redesigned the square as an amphitheatre to mark the quatercentenary of the University in 1983. The scheme incorporated old bailie lamps (lamps used to mark the homes of the city's bailies). The current landscaping is designed by LDN Architects.

The *Buildings of Scotland* volume for Edinburgh famously described the McEwan Hall as a 'magnificent petrified blancmange'.[93] Anderson himself explained the D-plan arrangement of his building as 'that of a Greek Theatre', which he had laid out to achieve the best possible natural acoustics.[94] Externally, the hall presents

120 'Dr William McEwan's Christmas Gift to the Varsity', from *The Student*, vol.11, December 1897
University of Edinburgh [0002395]

121 Portrait of William McEwan by Walter William Ouless, 1901
National Trust, Polesden Lacey, Surrey

an undulating mass of masonry with very few openings, capped with a shallow lead-covered dome and lantern. Prudham Quarry at Hexham in Northumberland supplied the stone. The decorative details are Italianate, including a polychromatic blind arcade and a frieze of Renaissance swags. The carving in the tympanum over the principal doorway depicting a graduation ceremony is by Farner and Brindlay of London. Not all the external carving was completed, and the niches remain empty. Internally, two levels of galleries with fixed seating are arranged behind an arcade. They surround a flat flexible space in front of the ceremonial platform and the organ. A low level of natural lighting is achieved by circular windows just below the dome. From the outset the dramatic interior was lit by electric lamps.

The trustees for the hall approached the South Kensington Museum (Victoria and Albert Museum) in London for advice on an artist for work on the interior. They recommended William Mainwaring Palin, who devised and executed the lavish scheme of mural decoration from 1892 to 1897.[95] The Italian Renaissance-style decorations were painted on canvas, which was then attached to the walls.

The magnificent organ, which was also funded by Sir William McEwan, was not part of Anderson's original design, so the four-manual, forty-six-stop instrument had to be squeezed into various parts of the hall by the ingenious organ-builder and inventor of the theatre organ, Robert Hope-Jones, in 1897.[96] It was substantially rebuilt by Willis III in 1953 and

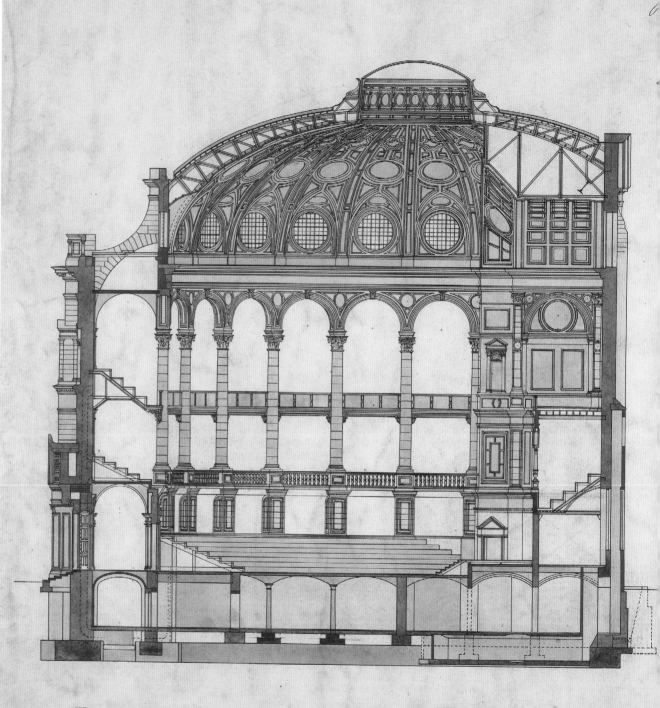

N⁰ 8.

122 Design for the
McEwan Hall by
Robert Rowand
Anderson

University of Edinburgh
[0002589]

SECTION A.B.

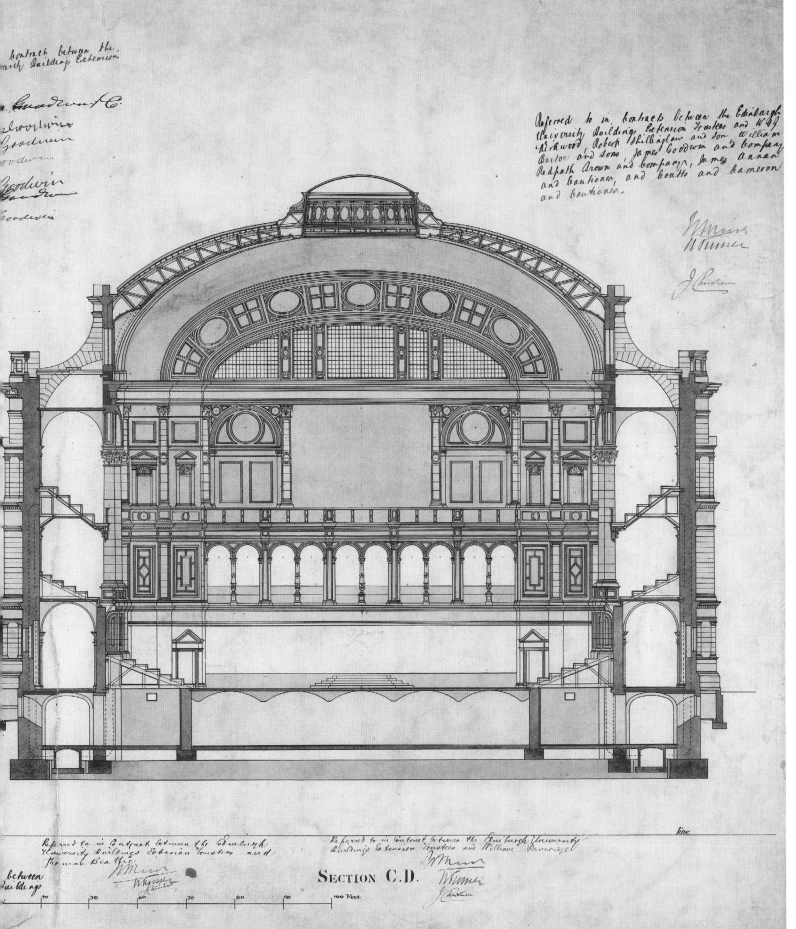

SECTION C.D.

19 St Andrew Square Edinburgh

Thos Beattie   William Beveridge

10   50   60   70   80   90   100 Feet

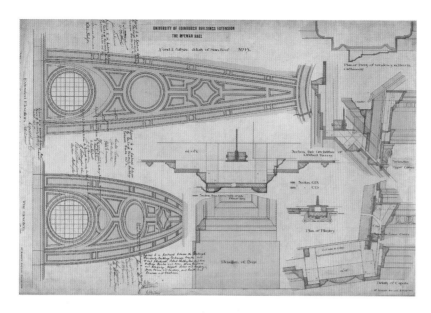

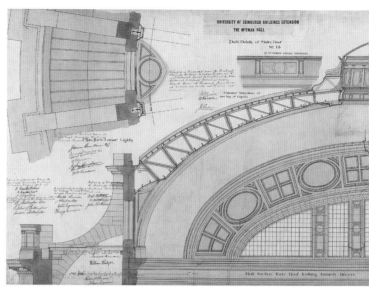

clockwise from top left

The McEwan Hall

123 Detail of a roof spandrel
University of Edinburgh [0018706]

124 Details of the dome construction
University of Edinburgh [0018708]

125 Lamp design (changed in construction)
University of Edinburgh [0018746]

126 The finished building, photographed by
Bedford Lemere, about 1897
University of Edinburgh [0007541]

127 The main staircase, photographed by
Bedford Lemere, about 1897
HES [Bedford Lemere Collection: SC 694684]

128 Interior, photographed by Bedford
Lemere, about 1897
HES [Bedford Lemere Collection: SC 694687]

129 The staircase on the first floor landing,
photographed by Bedford Lemere,
about 1897
HES [Bedford Lemere Collection: SC 694686]

130 Interior, photographed by Bedford
Lemere, about 1897
HES [Bedford Lemere Collection: SC 702090]

131 Masonry repairs at the McEwan Hall, 2016
Paul Zanre Photography

132 The McEwan Hall under scaffolding, 2016
Paul Zanre Photography

133 Carving on the McEwan Hall after conservation
Nick Haynes

134 The murals in the McEwan Hall after conservation.
They were painted on canvas by William Mainwaring Palin
between 1892 and 1897.
Nick Haynes

overhauled by Rushworth & Dreaper in 1980. A further
major restoration was undertaken by Forth Pipe Organs
in 2010–12. The room housing the swell box is known as
the coffin room because of the shape of the timber-clad
swell box housing.

The opening ceremony of the McEwan Hall took
place on 3 December 1897. Almost 3,000 people
attended, and it included the presentation of an
honorary doctorate and the freedom of the City of
Edinburgh to the donor.[97]

At the time of writing the McEwan Hall is undergoing a major £33m refurbishment project designed
by LDN Architects, the key aims of which are: to repair
and conserve the traditional building fabric; to improve
accessibility; the creation of a circular amphitheatre
featuring a contemporary glazed entrance pavilion; new
tree planting and soft landscaping to create more social
space in Bristo Square; a spectacular ceremonial hall
for graduations and events; new visitor and conference
facilities; and upgraded energy-efficient services.

TEVIOT ROW HOUSE (STUDENTS' UNION)

The first steps towards a building for 'the provision
and maintenance of means of social and academic
intercourse' for students was taken at a meeting of the
Students' Representative Council on 1 March 1884
with the formation of the Edinburgh University Union
Society.[98] The huge success of the tercentenary celebrations in April 1884 encouraged the Senatus to support
the new initiative. To some extent the new building
was to be an expansion of facilities already acquired
by the Students' Club, which had operated since 1876,
firstly at 54 South Bridge, then in converted houses at

nos 3–4 Park Street.[99] Although a number of student societies had co-operated and struggled to obtain the use of a single room for meetings in the University in 1833, there were no dedicated buildings or spaces for social or sporting activities. The Speculative Society alone had its own rooms in the University buildings, and these were not open to non-members.

Recognising that the construction of a union building would require a broad base of support and financial backing, the Students' Representative Council established the General Committee, which included a large number of representatives of the University Court, the town council, the Senatus, assistant professors, alumni and 'also a number of noblemen and gentlemen who are interested in University education in Scotland'.[100] Five sites close to the University were considered, but eventually a site occupied by Mr Turpy's livery stables off Charles Street Lane was selected.[101]

The facilities of the building were established at an early date: 'a large hall for debates and general meetings of the students; rooms for the various existing societies to meet in; reading and writing rooms for use during the day and evening; a luncheon room; and a fully equipped gymnasium'.[102] Essentially the provisions were to mirror those of a well-equipped gentlemen's club. A budget of not less than £15,000 was set for purchasing the site, constructing the building and furnishing it. Although the union was to be a male bastion, the joint honorary secretaries of the union committee recorded that

Following a classic precedent, they turned for help to the ladies of Scotland. And just as the ancient Athenians, in time of stress, were helped by their women to build the city walls, so the Students of Edinburgh will be beholden for their Union to the labour of countless fair hands which placed stone on stone.[103]

A four-day 'fancy bazaar' at Waverley Market attracted 8,000 visitors per day and raised almost £10,000. The *New Amphion*, an anthology of verse and prose published in connection with the fancy bazaar in November 1886, attracted contributions from a remarkable range of writers including Robert Louis Stevenson, Robert Browning, Andrew Lang and Margaret Oliphant. Donors to the building fund included the Senatus, the town council and the American steel magnate and philanthropist, Andrew Carnegie.[104] Further appeals to students, alumni and other well-wishers eventually achieved the target sum.

The acting committee appointed Arthur George Sydney Mitchell as architect before February 1887. He was an alumnus of the University, and had been apprenticed to Robert Rowand Anderson from 1878 to 1883, probably working on the University's new medical buildings, before setting up his own independent practice with the support of his influential father, Dr George Mitchell.

James Slater, the contractor for the building, made good progress with the construction, but by March 1888 the funding was still some £1,500 short of the £15,000 target and there were concerns about finishing and fitting out.[105] The union was papered and painted, with

135 Design for the University of Edinburgh Students' Union, Teviot Place, by Sydney Mitchell & Wilson, 1887
Royal Incorporation of Architects in Scotland, Edinburgh
[HES: DP 135997]

136 Design for the debating hall in the Students' Union by Sydney Mitchell & Wilson, 1887
Royal Incorporation of Architects in Scotland, Edinburgh
[HES: DP 135996]

opposite

137 The debating hall in the Students' Union, photographed by Alexander Adam Inglis, about 1905
University of Edinburgh
[EUA GD63]

138 The reading room of the Students' Union, photographed by Alexander Adam Inglis, about 1905
University of Edinburgh
[EUA GD63]

139 The library in the Students' Union, photographed by Alexander Adam Inglis, about 1905
University of Edinbrugh
[EUA GD630]

portraits of a series of 'worthies of the University' in the dining room, and ready for fitting out in April 1889.[106] However, it was 19 October 1889, twenty months after the opening of the Glasgow University Union, before the furniture was installed and the official opening by the Chancellor took place. To celebrate, the students held a torchlight procession from Old College through the New Town to Calton Hill, before returning to view the new building 'beautifully illuminated and shown to remarkable advantage by means of coloured lights'.[107]

The union operated on an annual subscription basis. It experienced ups and downs over the last decade of the 19th century, but by 1900 it was firmly established and increasing demands on its facilities, particularly from the nearby medical students, led to extension proposals.[108] A new acting committee was formed, and the site between the union building and the music classroom purchased. This was occupied at the time by old Park House, then in use as a synagogue, and an adjoining lecture hall. The acting committee again appointed Sydney Mitchell & Wilson as architects for the new facilities. The proposals included a new main staircase, a timber-panelled library (now the library bar) and large billiard room at ground and basement levels, a grand reading room (now the dining room), two committee rooms, a servants' hall and a small ladies' lavatory on the ground floor, and a kitchen, retiring room and furniture store on the first floor.[109] Two fives courts were to be constructed in the south-west corner of the site. Several changes to the existing building were also proposed: the entrance hall was to be enlarged by the removal of the secretary's and committee rooms; the luncheon room converted to a smoking room; a photographic room was to replace the old servery and a bicycle store formed below the photographic room in the basement; and electric light was to be introduced throughout. Andrew Carnegie again contributed towards the costs, along with another major donor, Sir Donald Currie, and the extended building opened officially on 19 October 1906.[110]

After numerous minor alterations during the course of the 20th century, a more radical addition was planned in 1962 to cater for the social requirements of a much larger student population.

Teviot Row House remains the largest provider of catering, bar and entertainment services to students in Edinburgh, acts as a meeting space for more than forty academic societies and about eighty student clubs, serves as a graduation and exam hall, and plays a major role in the annual Fringe Festival. At the time of writing, Page\ Park Architects have been appointed to develop a new student centre through a major two-phase refurbishment and extension scheme on the sites of the annexe, Wilkie Building and 1 George Square.

Chapter Five

Science and Engineering: the Centrifugal Effect 1900–1940

CLIVE B. FENTON

140 The engineering drawing office, designed by Balfour Paul in 1905. Detail of photograph by Alexander Adam Inglis.

University of Edinburgh [EUA GD63]

The first forty years of the twentieth century were to bear witness to a remarkable succession of social and political phenomena, including the crises of two world wars and serious economic depression, with which the University had to contend. None of this could have been predicted as the clock on Edinburgh's old Tron Kirk struck midnight announcing the beginning of the twentieth century to all of the citizens gathered around. The University was enjoying a period of relative stability, having achieved the structure of governance recognisable today, and the organisation of departments within faculties that was to endure until the end of the century, although it was 1908 before the three-term system replaced the six-month academic year, which had been based upon the needs of an essentially agricultural society. Sir William Muir, the Principal since 1885, served a further three years before retirement. The Medical School, for which his predecessor, Sir Alexander Grant, was largely responsible, was still known as 'the New Buildings'. Grant had also presided over the rather protracted completion of the Old College with the late addition of its crowning dome, and the building of the monumental McEwan Hall. The latter, together with the University Union, soon to be extended, were felt to have added much to the achievement of a strong 'corporate life and identity' for the University, a concept that was to have enduring currency in the succeeding years and was a strong influence on the University's evolution, and consequently its accommodation requirements.

Sir William would not have anticipated any further architectural contributions to the city in the near future. There remained an ambition to complete the ensemble of the McEwan Hall and the Medical School with its campanile, but this was not a pressing matter and, indeed, it still awaits a private donor. Capital grants for buildings from the government were few in those days and would certainly not fund such an architectural ornament. In fact, the Carnegie Trust for the Universities of Scotland, set up in 1901 by the millionaire and philanthropist, Andrew Carnegie, assumed a larger role than government in funding capital projects for university expansion, as well as maintenance grants for Scottish-born students. And this remained the case for many years, despite gradual increases in Treasury funding.

In 1900, half of Edinburgh's students were in the medical faculty and, while the new medical buildings had greatly relieved the pressure on accommodation, this was only temporary, as it happened. The number of full-time medical students grew from 2,354 to 2,911 over the next decade. Aside from the graduates going into the medical professions, a large number would follow a legal career, with most of the women expected to become school teachers. A further significant number were destined for the civil service examinations and colonial

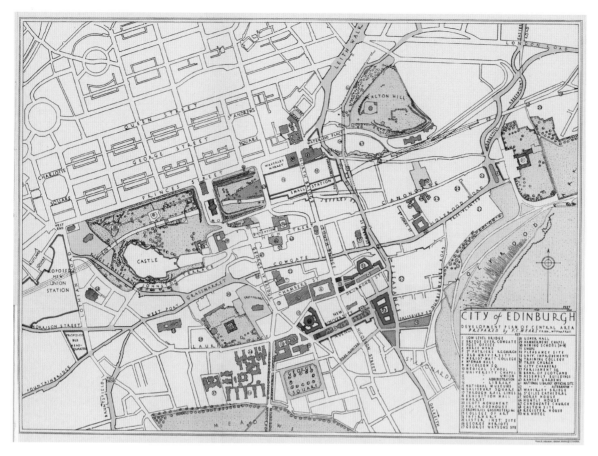

141 Proposed city plan by
Frank Mears, 1931

HES [Sir Basil Spence Archive:
DP 021585]

administration, in which Muir himself had spent much of his career. The main focus of the University remained on providing undergraduate lectures, but there was an impetus towards Oxbridge-style tutorials to supplement these. Practical work, including postgraduate research after 1919, was also becoming increasingly important, with a consequent and growing need for specialist facilities and equipment. The remarkable rise of the Department of Engineering in the first twenty years of the century was the most notable area of expansion in the period. This came under the tenure of Sir William Turner, Principal from 1903 until his death in 1916, but the driving force was undoubtably Sir Thomas Hudson Beare, who became Regius Professor of Engineering in 1901. Starting with just fifteen undergraduates, he soon moved the department out of Old College and, by 1911, there were 120 students and this growth continued steadily.

The most visible impact of the First World War was a reduction of the University population, as both student and staff undertook military service, although female student numbers increased. The war created a backlog of undergraduates in its aftermath, so that by 1920 there was serious overcrowding, as the student population reached 4,866, the highest thus far. The war, however, had highlighted the importance of the universities, especially the contributions of science and medicine, and government funding increased. But the Wall Street

Crash of 1929 triggered the world economic depression of the 1930s, which constrained both government and private funding of British universities. Inevitably, student numbers also declined because of the harsh financial situation. It was the lot of Sir Thomas Holland, Principal from 1929 to 1944, to steer the University through all this, and the Second World War. Notwithstanding such tribulations, the University was able to commission some notable buildings in the inter-war period.

The reunion of the United Free Church with the established Church of Scotland in 1929 reversed the Disruption of 1843 and resulted in the merging of the University's faculty of divinity with its former Free Church rival New College. Although it meant an immediate increase in staff and students, including six professors, there was no additional pressure on accommodation. In fact, it relieved the pressure on Old College, as the faculty was able to move into the former United Free Church college buildings at the head of the Mound in 1935. And, for the moment at least, the Kirk retained responsibility for the buildings themselves, which included the prominent college designed by William Playfair. Twenty-five years later, however, this theological marriage was to have architectural implications for the University.

The University continued to expand its range of activities, especially in science, engineering, and medicine, with a growing emphasis on research, as well as an increasing number of specialisms leading to the creation of new departments.

As the Victorian era gave way to the Edwardian, there began a steady migration of departments to other premises, at first within the vicinity of Old College, such as High School Yards, George Square, Chambers Street and other neighbouring streets. This largely involved conversion of existing buildings, institutional, commercial and residential. Then, after the First World War, Sir James Ewing, Principal from 1916 until 1929, controversially established an entirely new campus, King's Buildings, on the southern suburbs of the city to answer the needs of the science and engineering departments. The scattering out of departments from the University's original core caused some anxiety, becoming known as the 'centrifugal effect', detrimental to the effective functioning of the University as a corporate whole, and fairly inconvenient in terms of journeys required between buildings for staff and students.

By the late 1920s there were already calls for 're-integration' of the University's various parts. But the scale of the problem brought it within the field of urban design, entailing substantial redevelopment within the congested Old Town, as was seen when the City commissioned an architect to look into the various issues affecting the city centre. The proposed architectural remedies created assumptions and expectations that were to fuel a town-planning debate between City and University reaching far into the future.

THE MEARS REPORT

In March 1931, the City published 'The City of Edinburgh: Preliminary Suggestions for Consideration of the Representative Committee in Regard to the Development and Re-planning of the Central Area', which became better known as 'the Mears Report' [fig.141]. Appointed by Lord Provost Thomas B. Whitson in 1929, the committee included the Principal and Professor Sir Thomas Hudson Beare, representing the University, and representatives of other institutions occupying the city centre, including the Royal Infirmary, the Heriot Trust, Heriot-Watt College and the Merchant Company. The stated purpose of the report was to survey the situation and make suggestions to counter the 'haphazard methods of the past century'. The general opinion was that Edinburgh had been progressive in its improvement schemes from the middle of the 18th century to the early 19th century, obtaining Acts of Parliament that resulted in the creation of the New Town, and a series of new road schemes including substantial bridges between the ridges on which the city stood. Since then, it was felt, a laissez-faire approach of ill-considered private development had been tolerated.

The author of the report, (Sir) Frank Mears, was an architect and town planner, later to become head of the new town-planning course at Edinburgh College of Art. He was an influential figure in town-planning circles and in what became known as the Cities Movement of the 1920s and 1930s. This movement was inspired by the thinking of Patrick Geddes, who is regarded as the founder of modern scientific town planning. Horrified by the seeming chaos and unco-ordinated development of cities in the Victorian era, now emphasised by the advent of aerial photography, Geddes and his followers adopted a 'scientific' approach, seeing cities as living organisms in need of surgery. But this should happen only after a thoroughgoing survey, or diagnosis, and well-considered plans for treatment. Mears had been associated with Geddes for some time and had married his daughter, Nora, a landscape architect. Together they had created the master plan for the Hebrew University of Jerusalem (1919), and they looked forward to a 'Neotechnic' age, in which science and technology would be fully harnessed to the needs of humanity, as opposed to the 'Paleotechnic' era, which had immediately followed the Industrial Revolution. These ideas were adopted by the Modern Movement in architecture.

The Mears Report had two sections: Traffic and Zoning – zoning being an instrument of town planning to keep unharmonious land uses apart, such as industrial and residential, and to appropriately control future development. Mears observed that the city centre was built on three parallel ridges running from east to west: the northern ridge terminating at Calton Hill, to the east; the centre ridge terminating at the Castle Rock, in the west; and the southern ridge, which rose gradually from the Lauriston area to Arthur's Seat and Holyrood Park in the east.

He thus suggested a tripartite zoning, based on current uses and future needs. The central zone was essentially the spinal east–west route through the Old Town, from the castle to the palace of Holyrood House, already known as the Royal Mile. To the north, the First New Town had largely lost its residential status, being now mostly occupied by legal and financial institutions. So, with George Street as its east–west axis, this was designated the 'Business Mile'. The southern ridge traditionally had a concentration of educational institutions, including Old College and the Medical School, and was zoned as the 'College Mile'. There are many aspects to the Mears plan, but the only concern here is with those directly affecting the University.

Mears had adopted Geddes's notion that 'the University' was actually all of Edinburgh's educational and cultural institutions functioning together as a whole. He drew comparison with the separate, but connected, colleges at Cambridge. The educational zone itself had three sections: the Lauriston district, from the College of Art to

Park Place, including George Heriot's School, George Watson's College, the Royal Infirmary and the Medical School; McEwan Hall to the Pleasance, including the University Union and George Square; and Chambers Street to the Pleasance, including Heriot-Watt College, the Dental School, the University's Departments of Modern Languages and Mathematics, Old College and the National Museum in Chambers Street, and the University's buildings at High School Yards.

Mears's plan attempts to draw the educational elements into a coherent whole, while allocating sites for future development. This was no simple matter, for while the Old Town grew naturally around the ridge leading to the castle, and the New Town had an essentially virgin site allowing the principal street (George Street) to be located on the crest of its ridge, the College Mile consisted of a miscellaneous assortment of buildings, with different axial orientations, scattered across an undulating ridge, with no obvious crest and lacking a single east–west route. However, since all the sites were considered congested, with obsolete buildings, and the University surrounded by slums, there was the potential to clear substantial areas and reconfigure them. One such clearance area lay between Old College and the Pleasance, to the east, and included High School Yards, two primary schools, a public baths, as well as a significant quantity of tenements, which were considered unfit for habitation. This was proposed for future University development. Between the McEwan Hall and the Pleasance, Mears suggested obliterating the existing streets and buildings to create a broad 'New University Avenue', with a large library and a University chapel, at the west, terminating at the Pleasance with a large college building to replace the outdated Heriot-Watt building, at Chambers Street.

The College Mile was certainly audacious and any hope of achieving it would have required the acquisition of a large quantity of property and therefore government support, as well as a very large amount of money. However, Mears would have been aware of the recent Cité Universitaire de Paris project where the French government was persuaded to donate land formerly used by the military for international student hostels. This undertaking was intended to create an intellectual meeting place for students of all nations, in order to promote peace and harmony following the conflict of 1914–18. Many nations had subscribed, with a British hostel opening in 1927, and there had been substantial assistance from donors, including a $2m Rockefeller grant.

An additional suggestion was for a tree-lined avenue, following existing street lines, from George Square to the Pleasance. As for George Square itself, Mears proposed only the removal of the buildings on the north

side to permit future extensions to the Medical School.

The Mears Report arrived at a time of economic crisis and the City did not apply for statutory powers to implement any of its proposals. Nevertheless, the assumptions it created were that the University would extend its Medical School southwards onto north George Square, and would at some stage redevelop High School Yards, while the City would continue its efforts to remove the slums in the area.

BUILDINGS 1900–1940
GEORGE SQUARE

In 1912, something of a precedent was created when the University began erecting its first building in George Square. The increasing pressure on accommodation within Old College and the resort to ad-hoc arrangements in existing properties led to the acquisition of three houses on the north side of the square. These were demolished, together with associated stable buildings on Charles Street Lane, to facilitate a new building for three departments, forestry, agriculture and entomology, on the site of nos 8, 9 and 10. Only the mews lane separated the north side of the square from the Medical School.

George Square had been a suburban development, outside the old city wall, by James Brown, a local builder. Having acquired the land, he surveyed and laid out building plots, which were then feued out in the traditional Scottish manner, that is, those buying a feu would be responsible for erecting their own building in adherence to fairly strict regulations about height,

142 Ordnance Survey map of George Square and surrounding area, 1949
National Library of Scotland, Edinburgh

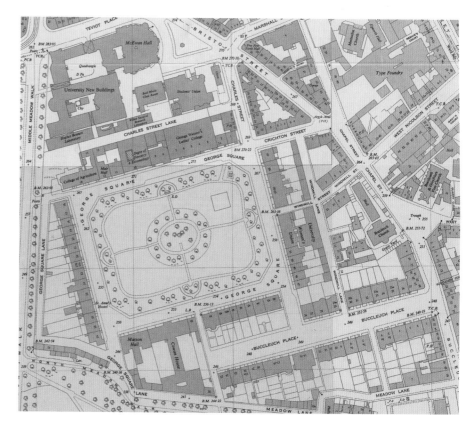

size and usage, while Brown, the feudal superior, who had laid out the roads and pavements and created the large central garden, would receive an annual feu duty, in perpetuity. The pattern he set was for two-storey houses of three bays, with the entrance to one side. These were to be built in terraced manner, and each was to have a basement below pavement level, with its own entrance, for the kitchens and so on. The corners of the square were open, and each terrace had a breach for a central lane giving access to the stables in the mews lanes behind. In Brown's original conception, only the north, east and west sides were to be built upon. Thus residents would have an open outlook to Hope Park, also known as the Meadows. Brown appears to have changed his mind at some point and developed the south side too. Here, the buildings were of three storeys above a basement, and bay width varied from three to four, in a more tenemental manner, with a mixture of main-door houses and flats accessed from common stairs. He also developed Buccleuch Place, immediately to the south, with four-storey tenements with basements. Building work on the square began on the north side in 1766, with the south completed in about 1785. Prior to the building of the New Town, George Square was the most fashionable address in Edinburgh, and it had many notable residents.

The domestic character of the square had already begun to change in the 1870s towards educational use and student residences. This was particularly noticeable on the north side (nos 1–15), where the Merchant Company built its George Watson's Ladies College, in phases between 1876 and 1910, until it occupied the sites of nos 3–7. Then there was a student hostel for women, Muir Hall, at no. 12, while the Church of Scotland had converted the house at no. 14 as a divinity students' residence, in 1897. The Edinburgh and East of Scotland College of Agriculture had occupied no. 13 since the beginning of the twentieth century, together with an additional storey and extension to the rear from 1904. With the Indian Association at no. 11, only nos 1 and 2 remained in use as dwelling houses, and relatively unaltered. Meanwhile, at no. 31, on the south side of the square, Masson Hall had been a residence for women students since 1897; it was extended into no. 32 in 1911.

The new forestry building was designed by the University's own clerk of works, Walter Clark, who appears to have been a competent architect in his own right, although he was normally engaged in fairly routine alteration work. Here he designed a well-proportioned ashlar-fronted Edwardian palazzo of six bays. In conformity with the original pattern for the square, there was a basement storey beneath pavement level, and two storeys above. The ground floor had alternating segmental and triangular pediments to the windows, and the entrance had a projecting portico with Corinthian columns.[1] The traditional appearance belied the concrete floor and steel beam construction within. Regular dormer windows, to light an attic storey above the parapet, were added in 1919. The building survived until 1977.

By 1912, the College of Agriculture had also acquired nos 14 and 15, and a strip of land to the west, in order to erect a substantial new college building. Consent to build was granted in 1913, although that project was to be shelved the following year. The design, by the architect, T.P. Marwick, was in the so-called Free Renaissance style favoured at the time, that is, an eclectic mixture of classical and baroque, here with a rather French accent. Faced with channelled ashlar, it featured a central portico sheltering steps to the entrance. Rising above the eaves, there was a pediment supported on giant pilasters, with a sculptural motif in the tympanum. The front elevation shows eight bays, symmetrically arranged, with three storeys above a basement. The roof is of the hipped variety, having four dormer windows. The west elevation to Middle Meadow Walk suggests that Marwick was attempting to continue the style of stonework established by Rowand Anderson's Medical School.[2]

While it now seemed that the future of the faculty of science was to be at King's Buildings, George Square was steadily becoming the 'University Square' of 1930s nostalgia. The gift of Dr Thomas Cowan, general manager at Leith Docks, was in gratitude to Edinburgh's students for assistance during the General Strike.[3] Balfour Paul was engaged as architect to carry out an extensive reconstruction of the buildings, which were internally reorganised, with new partitions and stairs, and extended to the rear with a brick-built bedroom wing. This provided one hundred places for male students. Stables and outbuildings onto the back lane were demolished and a kitchen block erected.[4] Although this was the first official hall of residence for the University, the previously independent Masson Hall and Muir Hall had come under the control of the University in 1919 and 1918 respectively. The former was extended by the University to accommodate fifty female students. In addition to this, the women's union, previously at Lothian Street, moved into nos 52–3, and added an extension with refectory and dance hall in 1919; it was further extended in 1927.[5]

USHER INSTITUTE OF PUBLIC HEALTH

Notwithstanding the relative newness of the Medical School, the University soon found itself responsible for yet another new medical building. Following a bequest of £5,000 by the brewer, Alexander Low Bruce, in 1893, and subsequent contributions from his family and associates, a chair in public health was endowed and established in 1898.[6] This was the first of its kind in Britain. The background to this innovation was the visit of Louis Pasteur during the University's tercentenary celebrations in 1884, his meetings with Bruce, and their discussions about brewing and microbiology.

Surprisingly, the public health laboratory, established in 1884 and extended in 1890, could find no further space for expansion, either within the new Medical School, or at the Royal Infirmary, in order to undertake its teaching and the type of research commensurate

with the new chair. The wealthy distiller, Sir John Usher, offered to pay £8,000 for a new building, should the University find a site for it. A plot identified in the residential area of Marchmont answered the needs, despite its distance from the rest of the University. Although the institute was to be administered by the University, Sir John made it clear in his deed of gift that 'the said Institute should be made useful to the Public Health Administration of the City of Edinburgh'.

Rowand Anderson & Paul might have expected to receive the commission, as they had designed the main Medical School and were effectively architects to the University at the time, whereas the selected architects, Leadbetter & Fairley, were better known for renovation and reconstruction of existing buildings, such as the Edinburgh Academy. However, Thomas Greenshields Leadbetter had married Mary Anne Usher in 1890, and Sir John was determined to appoint his son-in-law's firm to the job.[7] He instructed Leadbetter to visit and research the most important institutes in London and on the Continent, which he did, together with Professor Charles Hunter Stewart. Designs were drafted, and construction work began in 1899.[8]

In its configuration, the building contained analysis rooms for gas and water, optical and balance rooms, bacteriological and chemical laboratories, a 200-seat lecture theatre, a library and museum.[9] The building was far from utilitarian in appearance, executed in the beaux arts style popular for public buildings of the Edwardian period, with no shortage of sculptural flourishes, pilasters and pediments. It was roofed with red pantiles,

145 Photograph by Alexander Adam Inglis of the former Usher Institute of Public Health, Warrender Park Road, designed by Leadbetter & Fairlie in 1899. The building is now a student residence.

University of Edinburgh [EUA GD63]

which were felt to express affinity with the Medical School. Sir John formally opened and presented the building to the University on 11 June 1902.

The building was converted for student residences in the late 1980s, but the work of the institute continues as the Usher Institute of Population Health Sciences and Informatics at the Edinburgh BioQuarter and at Teviot Place.

OLD MEDICAL SCHOOL EXTENSIONS

Following the building of the Usher Institute, the medical faculty continued to find space a problem. As the largest such faculty in the country, student numbers alone brought accommodation pressures, but there were also changing needs, in terms of facilities. This entailed a continuing series of alterations and extensions. These included new animal houses for physiology and pathology (1904), a new lecture theatre for physiology and rearrangement of the old lecture room to form a chemical laboratory (1909), and also moving the materia medica museum to the attic to create a new laboratory in its place (1919).[10] Small spaces beside the main building were pressed into service for annexes. On the narrow strip of land between the main building and Charles Street Lane, the Hughes Bennet Laboratory was erected in 1901. This simple stone structure, originally of two storeys, but later three, was linked to the main building by a glazed timber bridge.[11]

In 1921, a small two-storey building was erected on vacant ground to the south-east of the main building. Designed by Walter Clark, it was to house an anatomy theatre for women students. As it faced onto what had been Park Place, now a small piazza, with grandiose neighbours, the Reid Concert Hall and the McEwan Hall, it was given an ashlar front and a classical doorway with a segmental pediment and carved keystone to impart some dignity.[12] It was later extended with an additional storey in 1926, and subsequently became the Wilkie Surgical Laboratory, in memory of Sir David Wilkie, the notable Edinburgh surgeon.[13]

As noted, departments that had originated as branches of medicine, such as chemistry and zoology, had been transferred to the science faculty and then moved to King's Buildings but, for as long as the Edinburgh Royal Infirmary, the main teaching hospital, remained at Lauriston Place, the medical faculty would have to remain at Teviot Place, on the opposite side of Middle Meadow Walk from the hospital. However, frustration in the faculty led to criticism of the Medical School building itself, as well as of the architect, and even those who had commissioned it. A document of 1919 claimed that had their predecessors spent a quarter of the money on land that had been spent on 'architecture' they would not be in such a predicament now. Architects seemed to have an agenda to reduce window space as far as possible, whereas 'a laboratory should be all window and skylight'. Buildings should also be constructed in such a way as to be extendable, it was asserted. These precepts explain the approach undertaken at King's Buildings.[14] Thus, the only viable long-term option for medicine appeared to be to extend to the south, that is, onto the north side of George Square.

In 1937–8, with Professor William Oliver as convenor, the University Works Committee was considering the long-term redevelopment of north George Square.[15] This was to be achieved in phases and would ultimately require the acquisition of George Watson's Ladies College, and the destruction of the University's forestry and agriculture building, which at this time was only twenty-five years old. In the meantime, however, the first phase would entail the removal of Muir Hall and the Indian Students' Union, which were owned by the University, as well as the building occupied by the Edinburgh and East of Scotland College of Agriculture, together with a narrow strip of land to the west of the square. In order to achieve this first phase of the medical extensions, another building would have to be erected at King's Buildings. This would be jointly used by the College and the University's Department of Agriculture, and ultimately, prior to the second phase, by the Department of Forestry.

This scheme promised a happy outcome for all. The College and the University's rurally-focused departments would be transferred to a more appropriate environment, with easy access to farmland for trial crops, mutual use of equipment and facilities, and plenty of space for animal houses and so on – there was already an experimental sheep-breeding unit at West Mains. Alternative accommodation would be found somewhere for the Indian Association and the lady medicals, at Muir Hall.[16]

A medical extensions special committee, chaired by Professor Oliver, was convened to report to the University Court, and the works department was charged with drafting outline schemes for both the agricultural building at King's Buildings and for the first phase of the medical extension. The medical priority was for the pathology department, which had recently taken on responsibility for all the pathology work for the Edinburgh municipal hospitals. James Cordiner, the University's clerk of works, produced sketch plans, which show the extension linked to the Medical School at its south-west corner. The plan follows the stepped boundary to Middle Meadow Walk until it reaches the building line of George Square, with a polygonal lecture theatre inserted where it turns the corner into the square, and an enclosed quadrangular court occupying the centre. This was not an ideal site in terms of lighting, as the extension is linked on the north to the existing building, which would also overshadow the internal court, while the corridors have no natural lighting. However, it was the most convenient location, in terms of access to the medical facilities and the hospital. Interestingly, there is a linking doorway through to the existing agriculture building to which it is attached on the east side, presumably so that the latter could quickly be taken over by medicine whenever agriculture and forestry moved to King's Buildings.

A site was proposed for the agriculture building at West Mains Road, to the east of the chemistry building, and a smaller site between the two for a possible new building for forestry. Cordiner's sketch plans indicate a large rectangular block, with its entrance to the north and two internal light wells. The various rooms are arranged around central corridors, with all laboratories facing north and lecture theatre, museum and library to the rear. No elevations for this proposed building are known of, but these interim plans are indicative of a rather old-fashioned Beaux Arts scheme governed by symmetry. A professional architect would, no doubt, have revised the scheme, but none was appointed at this time.[17]

Surprisingly the Rowand Anderson practice was not appointed for the medical extension – the death of Balfour Paul, senior partner in the Anderson practice, in June 1938, may have been a factor here. Neither was it to be Lorimer & Matthew, designers of most of the King's Buildings. Instead, those considered for the position were Reginald Fairlie, Leslie Grahame Thomson and J.R. McKay.[18]

McKay, whom Professor Oliver appears to have known, was ultimately selected to prepare designs. In his handling of the fenestration, McKay produced sleeker elevations than Cordiner's perspective indicated. There is little detail other than windows on the George Square façade, and the entrance is subdued, with the emphasis placed instead at the corner where there is a round tower, with a vertical band of glazing. As proposed in the Cordiner scheme, there are four storeys, plus a recessed attic, or penthouse, for the animal houses, lit by clerestory windows. The C-plan arrangement abuts the existing Medical School to create a courtyard containing a single-storey block, for human physiology and biophysics, and there is also a link, via an anatomy preparation room, to the Wilkie Building, in Charles Street Lane. The basement plan shows a proposed tunnel beneath Middle Meadow Walk to the Royal Infirmary, for the discreet transfer of cadavers.[19]

In many ways this was the most modern design produced for the University, thus far, having no blatant classical allusions and completely lacking in historicism.

Today the design would be regarded as being in the art deco idiom popular at the time, particularly in its massing of cylinder and cube, together with the railing on the parapet lending a nautical flavour. Clearly a steel-framed building, the exterior would probably have been clad in sandstone, but this level of detail had not been reached. International events intervened. By the time the special committee for the medical extensions met, Britain had declared war on Germany.

HIGH SCHOOL YARDS

The appointment of Sir William Turner, in 1903, initiated an enduring tendency at Edinburgh of choosing a scientist as Principal, which continued throughout the 20th century. Turner was an anatomist and brain surgeon, and much of his research was in the fields of physical anthropology and comparative anatomy. He had been at Edinburgh since 1854 and became Professor of Anatomy in 1867, while amassing a large collection of specimens for the medical museum. Almost immediately, he was involved in the acquisition of the High School Yards site to be used mainly for research purposes.

At the old High School, some 400m to the east of Old College, the architects, Rowand Anderson & Paul, created a series of testing laboratories, served by a lorry dock, a large workshop with a gantry crane, and a lecture theatre with drawing office above. The tower was heightened to permit a large water tank and was given an ogee lead roof. In what had been the surgery block, to the east, a lecture theatre was installed, and above this a drawing office lit by a cupola. As a direct result of the new facilities, the long-serving Regius Professor of Engineering, from 1901 to 1940, Thomas Hudson Beare, saw the lectureships in the various branches of engineering science burgeoning, with student numbers rising from fifteen in 1905 to 120 in 1915.

The two other main buildings at High School Yards were to be used by the Department of Natural Philosophy, and became known as the 'New Physical Labs'. The largest of these buildings, now entered from Drummond Street, had been designed by David Bryce, and opened in 1853. It was initially known as the 'New Surgical Hospital', since the adjacent infirmary building, designed by William Adam, survived until 1885. Immediately to the east of this, Old Surgeons' Hall was originally built for the Incorporation of Surgeons in 1697 and used as a theatre for public dissections. It was designed by James Smith, a pioneer of Palladianism in Britain, and reconstructed in the 1830s for the infirmary.[20]

Accommodation was provided at the New Physical Laboratories for an array of apparatus, including optical equipment, and there was a large lecture theatre, a new lift, a library and various rooms for professors. Anderson also created a carriageway through the old linking range

146 Aerial view of High School Yards from the south-east in 2007, before the development of the Edinburgh Centre for Carbon Innovation
HES [Crown copyright: DP 026252]

147 Plan showing development of High School Yards
Crown copyright 2017 Ordnance Survey [Licence Number 100021521]

1. Institute of Geography
2. Old Surgeons' Hall
3. Old Fever Hospital
4. Edinburgh Centre for Carbon Innovation
5. Chisholm House
6. Former University Settlement

Hatched areas re-modelled 1900–1940

Town Wall 1513

17th century

18th century

1840–1900

1900–1940

1985–present

to the former school building, allowing access through the site.[21] The new buildings were officially opened in October 1906, at a ceremony attended by A.J. Balfour, the recent Prime Minister, and Andrew Carnegie, whose Trust for the Universities of Scotland had financed the undertaking.

INSTITUTE OF GEOGRAPHY (FORMER NEW SURGICAL HOSPITAL / INFIRMARY)

Originally built for the Royal Infirmary to augment its 18th-century building in Infirmary Street, this was placed to the south-east of the old Royal Infirmary, which was subsequently demolished in 1884. Unlike its north-facing predecessor, this building is oriented to the south, thus facing, but on a lower level than, Drummond Street, which itself follows the line of the old city wall. When built, however, there was no access from Drummond Street. When the infirmary began moving to Lauriston Place, during the 1870s, the old surgical hospital was redesignated as the fever hospital, remaining in use as such until the beginning of the 20th century, when the infirmary completely vacated the site.

Frequently described as Italianate, the building would be more congruous in late-17th-century Netherlands than in any part of Italy. It is a long thirteen-bay block, with pavilions and centrepiece slightly advanced. There are two principal storeys, with mezzanine between, plus basement and attic storeys. The walls are of squared and snecked rubble, with ashlar quoins and dressings. The forceful main entrance consists of a triangular pediment borne on Doric columns, with an architrave of v-jointed ashlar forming a flat arch. The rest of the façade is fairly austere until it reaches the cornice. Here, linked chimney-stacks adorn the pavilions, and wallhead dormers are pedimented and flanked by brackets. The centrepiece is dominated by a triangular pediment, with pilasters, scrolls and ball finials. A north wing, of plain appearance, extends to the former High School, which was also part of the hospital. The various apartments were oriented to the south, and accessed by corridors running the length of the building, on the north, while vertical access was provided by means of a square stairtower, also to the north.

Bryce had a large and successful practice, operating the length and breadth of the country, undertaking all types of architectural commissions. Much of his success was due to his mastery of the many architectural styles that enjoyed popularity in the Victorian era. Country houses tended to be Scotch Baronial, while banks and insurance offices were generally in variants of Italian Renaissance. His most visually prominent

work is the neo-baroque remodelling of the Bank of Scotland on the Mound. But St Mark's Unitarian church, Castle Terrace, is neo-mannerist, while Fettes College is like a French chateau of François I's reign.

With the acquisition of the hospital by the University in 1905, Rowand Anderson & Paul were charged with its conversion. A variety of laboratories replaced wards and surgeries involving a substantial amount of structural iron. There were also rooms for professors, lecture rooms and a library, while a lift and a lecture theatre were installed in the north wing. Measures to improve access to the building and through the site, which were also undertaken at this time, are still visible today. An arched pend through the north wing was created, and a bridge was built to traverse the grass slope from Drummond

148 The entrance to the Institute of Geography in Drummond Street. Built as the New Surgical Hospital to designs by David Bryce in 1853, it was purchased by the University and converted for use by the Department of Natural Philosophy in 1905. The gatepiers are from the old infirmary, designed by William Adam in 1738.
Nick Haynes

Street to the portico, where there had previously been a horseshoe-plan staircase. Here, the gates and gatepiers from William Adam's demolished infirmary, dating from 1738, were re-erected. The piers are curiously baroque compositions of stepped pilasters clasped by bands of rustication and surmounted by urns with grotesque heads and foliation. They are remarkably similar to those forming the entrance to Old Surgeons' Hall, as depicted in the Paul Sandby drawing.

The new surgical hospital was home to the Department of Natural Philosophy, later renamed the Department of Physics, until it removed to the James Clerk Maxwell Building at King's Buildings in 1976. It was thereafter occupied by the Department of Geography, becoming the Institute of Geography, which itself became part of the School of Geosciences in 2002.

OLD SURGEONS' HALL
(CURRENTLY SCIENCE, TECHNOLOGY AND INNOVATION STUDIES)

Built for the Incorporation of Surgeons as both headquarters and public dissection theatre, the building was originally of two storeys with a hipped roof and octagonal stairtowers on both side elevations. The drawing by Paul Sandby shows it set within a walled garden with a pair of pavilions in a Palladian arrangement [fig.153]. A gateway, with banded piers, is aligned with the front door. The eastern and southern boundaries were the old Flodden Wall. The front (north) elevation, appears to be a 2–5–2 tripartite composition, with a pair of ocular windows flanking the upper central window.

James Smith, who is believed to have studied in Rome, was notable, along with Sir William Bruce,

for introducing the Palladian style to Scotland. As Surveyor of the Royal Works he was involved in the reconstruction of Holyrood Palace and he designed the Chapel Royal at Holyrood Abbey. Although known as a Palladian, as evidenced by a number of country houses, he was clearly knowledgeable about Italian Renaissance architecture more generally. His Mackenzie mausoleum, at Greyfriars' churchyard, is inspired by Bramante, while the Canongate Kirk is a baroque basilica. Old Surgeons' Hall, in its original incarnation, conforms to Smith's smaller classical country houses, but the architect was also aware of the Scottish traditions, as at Drumlanrig. Here, the octagonal towers appear to be an acknowledgement of that tradition.

In the 18th century, the building's garden was built upon and became Surgeons' Square. The hall was substantially altered during the reconstruction of about 1832 to create a fever hospital for the Royal Infirmary. Fenestration was changed and an extra storey added with a different style of roof and a square stairtower attached to the rear. It also acquired several extensions, over time, to form a range on the east side of Surgeons' Square, replacing all but one of the houses there – Chisholm House is all that remains of these. With the infirmary's removal to Lauriston Place, the new surgical hospital became the fever hospital for a time, and Old Surgeons' Hall had the status of an annexe to it.

It served a variety of purposes, sometimes simultaneously. It was partly a residence for the University Settlement, a philanthropic organisation run by staff and students as a sort of mission for the local poor. It also housed the oldest volunteer army unit in Scotland, the University's Officers' Training Corps, which took it over completely in 1915 and returned it to the University in 1929. With the removal of the Officers' Training Corps the building became part of the natural philosophy complex.

Further work was undertaken by Basil Spence & Partners in 1957. The interior was again reorganised to create a number of laboratories and a large reading room. A bridge at upper level linked it to the main physics block (the former surgical hospital) on the west. The low extension, to the east, was converted into a wind tunnel laboratory. Also, at this point, the pediment above the door was replaced and the original returned to the Royal College of Surgeons.[22]

There is little remaining today as a reminder of James Smith's original design, although one of the towers survives, partly encased within a later extension. Some of

153 Engraving by Paul Fourdrinier after a watercolour by Paul Sandby of Old Surgeons' Hall, 1753
Capital Collections, Edinburgh [8369]

154 The engineering hydraulics laboratory, photographed by Alexander Adam Inglis, about 1905
University of Edinburgh [EUA GD63]

155 Engraving of 1819 by
J. & H.S. Storer of the Old
High School, designed by
Alexander Laing in 1778
HES [SC 1244782]

the rubble masonry may date from 1797, although this is likely to have originally been concealed beneath a render. The doorway appears authentic, but the pediment is a replica, as mentioned above.

EDINBURGH CENTRE FOR CARBON INNOVATION (FORMER OLD HIGH SCHOOL)

Alexander Laing's building replaced an earlier school on this site. Laing's design is austere, but well proportioned. It has a seven-bay central portion, flanked by two-bay pavilions, and is constructed of regularly coursed ashlar. Its projecting portico is supported on four Tuscan Doric columns. The Doric order was considered both masculine and an appropriate style for educational buildings. However, there is no Doric frieze, but a simple string course between the storeys, neither are there any pediments, other than at the porch.

Laing was a successful mason, architect and surveyor based in Edinburgh, who operated widely in the east of Scotland. He designed and built Archers' Hall in Edinburgh, and was the contractor for the building of South Bridge. In Inverness, he was responsible for the eclectic Royal Academy and the formidable town steeple.[23] Shortly after the High School moved to its magnificent new premises on Calton Hill, where Thomas Hamilton had produced one of the finest works of the Greek Revival, completed in 1829, the Royal Infirmary took over the old school, converting it into a surgical hospital. At this stage a square operating theatre was added to the rear.

156 The engineering materials laboratory
University of Edinburgh [EUA GD63]

157 The engineering drawing office, photograph by Alexander Adam Inglis, about 1905
University of Edinburgh [EUA GD63]

158 Edinburgh Centre for Carbon Innovation, designed by Malcolm Fraser Architects
Graham Construction

159 Stairhall of the Edinburgh Centre for Carbon Innovation
Nick Haynes

Balfour Paul was responsible for the conversion of the building into laboratories for the Department of Engineering in 1905, which involved further substantial reconstruction. The former surgical theatre, to the rear, became a lecture theatre, with a drawing office above. A water tower was constructed, with the four floors beneath the tank housing a dark room, stores and apparatus room. This tower was given an ogee capped roof of 17th-century style. The side elevation, to the south, was given large metal doors to the gantry crane workshop.[24] Despite all this new technology, the west elevation was maintained, as it had been, as an entrance front.

When the new bespoke Department of Engineering building at Mayfield Road was completed in 1931, the engineers and their equipment vacated the old school, to be replaced by the Department of Geography. Various internal alterations were undertaken during geography's residency, from 1931 to 1984.[25] For the next ten years the Dental School used the premises, on a 'temporary basis' while awaiting their new building. The next tenant, from 1995 to 2011, was the Department of Archaeology. A further chapter in the history of the building commenced in 2011–13 when work was undertaken, by Malcolm Fraser Architects, to create the Edinburgh Centre for Carbon Innovation.

At some stage during the life of the building the courtyard solum appears to have been raised, as a drawing from 1819, by J. and H.S. Storer, shows the columns of the portico standing on tall square bases, with four steps up to the doorway; there are four courses of masonry below the cills of the ground storey [fig.155].[26] Today there are only three courses of stonework below the cills, the bases of the columns are shortened and there are only two steps up to the platt. In addition, the chimney stacks are no longer extant. Otherwise, the front of the building appears much as it did when Sir Walter Scott was a pupil.

160 The former engineering drawing office, after refurbishment in 2011–13 to become part of the Edinburgh Centre for Carbon Innovation
Nick Haynes

KING'S BUILDINGS 1900–1940

During the First World War, architectural practices went into virtual hibernation and many architects found themselves in uniform. When business resumed, they were faced with an enormous demand for war memorials, and some were asked to design cemeteries across Europe and the Middle East. Such was the loss of life incurred that every hamlet in the nation, every church congregation, every school and every university commissioned some sort of memorial, from small panels to monumental sculptural works. The great national symbolic gesture was the National War Memorial for Scotland at Edinburgh Castle, undertaken by Sir Robert Lorimer and completed in 1928. The University's own memorial, also designed by Lorimer, was installed at Old College in 1923. A sculpted stone framework with bronze panels, it records the names of 944 alumni killed in the war. This was one of the architect's many memorials, but his first job for the University, and he was soon to receive further commissions.

Of course, the war meant an instant halt to government capital funding and all current plans were shelved. The most visible impact on the University was the sudden fall in the student population, as the lecture halls began to empty of young men. Even before conscription began, students and staff began volunteering for the armed forces, although medical students were encouraged to complete their studies. Cadets in the Officers' Training Corp quickly found commissions. Student numbers fell from 3,352 in 1913 to 1,811 in 1916, and a greater proportion of these were women, who were now allowed to study medicine.

Another change during the war resulted from the death of Sir William Turner in 1916. The new Principal was Sir James Alfred Ewing, who held the post until 1929. He was to oversee a number of reforms and innovations during a difficult period for the University and the country generally. Sir James was a physicist and engineer, with an impressive career. An alumnus of Edinburgh, where he studied natural philosophy, he had been a professor at Tokyo, Cambridge and Dundee. At the time he took up the position as Principal, he was a code-breaker for the Admiralty, as supervisor of their famous 'Room 40'.

Not the least of the challenges facing Ewing was managing the post-war influx of students whose degrees had been interrupted or deferred, alongside the normal admissions. In 1919 student numbers reached 3,554, rising to 4,886 in 1921, with 1,086 of those in the faculty of science. This put enormous pressure on both staff and facilities. Ewing's response was to increase staff numbers generally, creating thirteen new chairs, and to initiate a new campus that was to be dedicated to science.

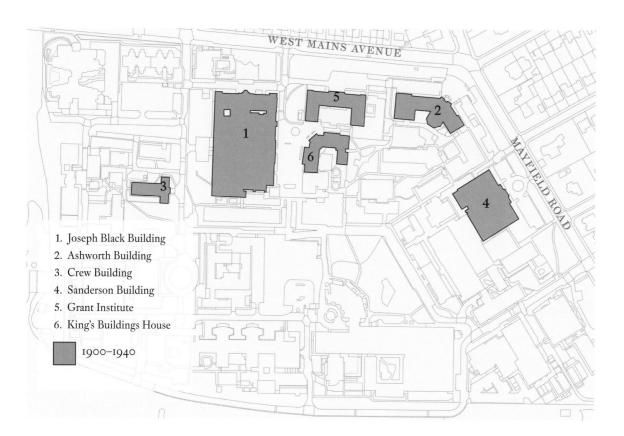

162 Plan showing main developments at King's Buildings 1900–40

Crown copyright 2017 Ordnance Survey [Licence Number 100021521]

1. Joseph Black Building
2. Ashworth Building
3. Crew Building
4. Sanderson Building
5. Grant Institute
6. King's Buildings House

■ 1900–1940

Apart from the increase in the University's population, another reason for the cramped conditions was the type of teaching now being delivered. Whereas in the 19th century the emphasis had been on lectures delivered to large numbers of students at a time, the steady growth of specialisms meant lectures for smaller departments within each faculty, together with a tendency towards group tutorials. In addition, the departments within medicine, science and engineering needed more laboratory facilities for practical demonstrations and research.

The war had taught the government how inadequate its approach to university funding had previously been, in comparison with Germany and Austria. The Department of Scientific and Industrial Research was created in 1915 to advise government on the needs of science and industry, while the allocation of funds for universities was put on a firmer footing with the creation of the University Grants Committee in 1919. Thus the total allocation for British universities rose from £149,000 in 1914 to £450,000 for the academic year 1919–20.

The faculty of science at Edinburgh had been created in 1893, with the transfer of the chairs of agriculture and rural affairs, astronomy, engineering and geology. Other departments that grew out of specialisms from the medical faculty subsequently migrated to science, although mathematics and natural philosophy (physics) were to remain with the arts faculty until 1966. At the beginning of 1918 the pressing issue of accommodation for the Departments of Chemistry, Zoology and Geology was being considered. Chemistry, for which an additional floor had been inserted in Old College in 1903, was also using the basement of the natural philosophy building and a hut at High School Yards. The other departments were at Old College, which was still overcrowded, despite the move of mathematics to a converted property at 16 Chambers Street, just before the war began. Ewing met with the heads of departments and there were proposals for these departments to be moved to the south side of George Square, because of its proximity to the Medical School, and agreement was assumed to have been reached on this.[27] However, the Principal was looking for longer-term solutions for the future of science at Edinburgh than simply further conversion of old city centre buildings with restricted sites, and he soon negotiated the purchase of West Mains Farm, to the south of the city. This provided 115 acres of land, of which part was under lease to Craigmillar Park Golf Club.

The advantages of this acquisition were patently clear. An open green field, largely flat, and adjacent to a main road, is ideal for ease of construction. Here, there was enough land for both foreseeable and for future projects as yet unknown. Of course, agricultural land cost a fraction of land in the city, and there would be no demolition costs. It was also felt that cheaper sorts of building, including temporary huts, which might not be acceptable in town, could be erected here without difficulty. For scientific experiments, the site offered an

opposite

163 Unsigned and undated design (by Lorimer & Matthew) for the Animal Breeding Research Department

University of Edinburgh Estates Department Collection (transferring to CRC)

164 Unsigned and undated design (by Lorimer & Matthew) for the Animal Breeding Research Department. Figs 163 and 164 show a larger scheme than the one executed and include a house for Professor Crew.

University of Edinburgh Estates Department Collection (transferring to CRC)

165 Design for the Geology Department

HES [DP 001852]

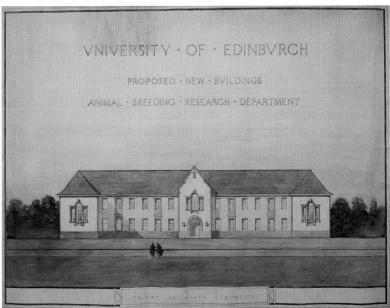

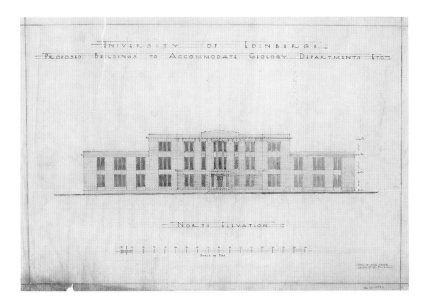

unpolluted environment, with no immediate neighbours to disturb with unusual noises and smells.

Despite the compelling nature of these advantages, some felt that the two-mile journey from existing facilities to the new site was a disadvantage. Nevertheless, when chemistry was given priority, and an appeal for funding was launched, the chemists, who had now transferred from medicine to the faculty of science, seemed enthusiastic about the prospect of purpose-built accommodation. Sir James Walker, the head of department, worked with the architect to create a brief for the new building. The aim was a truly functional construction that could be built in phases, and extended as required. Adequate lighting was an issue, thus the windows would be large, from bench height to ceiling. As Sir Robert Rowand Anderson had now retired, the architect was Arthur Foreman Balfour Paul, sole partner in the firm. In November 1919 site work began at West Mains Farm.

King George v endorsed the University's appeal for funding and gave the new campus its name 'The King's Buildings', on 6 July 1920, when he laid a foundation stone [fig.161].[28] The initial phase of construction, at £182,000 for building and equipment, proceeded unhindered, with the first classes being held in 1922. The official opening was performed by HRH The Prince of Wales on 3 December 1924.

The chemistry building was sited on the north of the new estate, set back a little from West Mains Road, in order to avoid vibrations from traffic. It had a two-storey north block, containing the entrance, with two single-storey ranges to the rear, as the first phase. The laboratory wings were constructed for ease of extension, both upwards and to the rear, when the need should arise. Notwithstanding the rigid avoidance of extravagance, the steel-framed brick structure was given the appropriate architectural manners for an institutional building of the era. For four years the chemists were alone at King's Buildings, but at least they had plenty of space for recreation on the tennis courts and football pitches.

When the time came to plan zoology, the second of the King's Buildings, Professor Ashworth appears to have been horrified by the prospect of the removal to the colony. He cited the discussion of 1918 and the idea to redevelop the south side of George Square, enlisting the support of colleagues in the faculty of science. But although the University had a policy of purchasing property in the square for ad-hoc purposes, the site was too constrained, with little prospect of expansion. The distance between King's Buildings and the medical buildings, its library and museums, and from the infirmary's facilities was a major issue for zoology. But costly demolition of Ashworth's preferred site in George

Square would have been required and there was no prospect of a suitable site in the vicinity for many years to come. Besides, student timetables could be adjusted to allow for travel.[29]

Later, when a donation enabled the University's first hall of residence, Cowan House, to be created, this was allocated nos 33–7, on the south side of George Square, and a site for zoology was selected at King's Buildings to the east of the new chemistry building, where West Mains Road joins Mayfield Road at an obtuse angle.

J.F. Matthew, partner of Sir Robert Lorimer, was soon back at King's Buildings working on four further buildings: animal genetics, engineering and geology, as well as a union with sports pavilion, within the space of a decade. The University's Institute of Animal Genetics began at High School Yards before moving temporarily to the chemistry building at West Mains.[30] Grants from the government's Department of Agriculture and the International Education Board enabled the commissioning of the new building for the institute.

While chemistry and zoology had been located to present a façade to the main road, animal genetics was more centrally placed within the new campus, with its entrance facing east. It was also a smaller building than its predecessors, and Matthew gave it a different treatment. Eschewing the monumental approach, this building is more typical of Lorimer's style, having a curvilinear Dutch gable above the entrance, harled walls with stone dressings, and Georgian-style windows of a domestic scale. With its hipped and slated roof, and entrance stairs to a recessed portico, this could have been a colonial boarding school.

The new campus was now progressing rapidly. An aerial photograph from May 1929 shows West Mains Road as a tree-lined avenue, with pastures on the north side. Chemistry and zoology address the street from a

166 Aerial photograph of the King' Buildings site in 1929. The main structures are the Ashworth Building on the left and the Joseph Black Building in the middle. The building under construction to the right is the Crew Building and the farm steading is still extant.

HES [SC 1315439]

safe distance behind a grass verge, and there is a boiler house near the centre of the site. The farm buildings are still on the west side and, beyond these, animal genetics is under construction, awaiting its roof. There are a number of timber huts that had been transported here after wartime use in St Andrew Square.[31] These now served a variety of purposes, including animal houses, the King's Buildings Union and the Department of Geology. However, plans for geology and engineering were well advanced, and building warrants were obtained later that year.[32]

The new departmental buildings joined in the monumental parade with chemistry and zoology, their façades to the main roads, but extendable to the rear. Later extensions to the engineering building were given the appropriate name of Hudson Beare, after Sir Thomas Hudson Beare. His department had grown steadily. In 1905, when engineering moved to High School Yards, seven students graduated, while in 1922 a hundred degrees were awarded. Dean of the faculty of science and engineering, Sir Thomas was also convenor of the University Works Committee for most of that period and played a key role in the development of both High School Yards and King's Buildings. The funding came from industry by means of a gift of £50,000 from R. & A. Sanderson & Co., tweed manufacturers of Galashiels, for the benefit of chemistry and engineering. The name of the main engineering building recognises this benefaction.

The classicism of the engineering building is latent, signified by the suppressed pilasters that divide the fenestration vertically. The stone façade is in a symmetrical tripartite arrangement, with an advanced centrepiece. The projecting porch is well detailed, if eclectic, having a medieval moulded architrave to the doorway, flanked by slit windows. Above this, a window is set within an arched recess behind a corbelled balcony. The ensemble is suitably truculent for what is essentially an industrial building. The stone detailing and Ballachulish slate roof, however, betray the authors as Lorimer & Matthew.

Geology's benefactor was Sir Alexander Grant, managing director of the food manufacturer McVitie & Price. He had already given £50,000 to the University's general buildings appeal, but gave a similar sum for the foundation of the Grant Institute of Geology.[33] Grant was quite a philanthropist, perhaps in emulation of Andrew Carnegie, having already given a substantial sum for the setting up of the National Library of Scotland. This was also an appropriate time to move the geology department out of the huts and into a proper building, as Sir Alfred Ewing retired as Principal in 1929, to be replaced by an eminent geologist. The new Principal, Sir Thomas Henry Holland, who had undertaken the geological survey of India, had a particular interest in mining, metallurgy and petrochemicals.

The Grant Institute was opened by Ramsay MacDonald on 28 January 1932. MacDonald was Prime Minister of a national government, formed to deal with the financial crisis that followed the Wall Street Crash of 1929. Alexander Grant's gift had come at just the right time, because benefactions to universities greatly decreased in the early 1930s, as many wealthy people saw their investments wiped out. With over two million unemployed in Britain, most were affected in some way by the crisis, and the student population dipped as a consequence.[34]

Placed between zoology and chemistry, the geology building is very similar to that of engineering, that is, a tripartite façade in Blaxter stone, with pilasters dividing the bays, a central projecting entrance and a pitched slate roof. Again, the fenestration is horizontally divided by concrete spandrel panels. The entrance is slightly less formidable than that of engineering, being recessed at the upper level and with a curvilinear gable above.

After the opening of the geology building, it was to be a considerable time before there were any further major academic buildings at the campus. However, the University Union had been lobbying for a permanent building there since 1929, having spent seven years in the timber huts behind chemistry. The suburban location was completely lacking in facilities. The Principal, Sir Thomas Holland, took a keen interest in student affairs, encouraging sporting and society activities, all in support of the corporate life of the University. It would have been a matter of concern for him that the campus common room was being described as leaking and rat-infested. King's Buildings were apparently deserted after 5pm, as well as at weekends and during vacations. The union produced sketch plans for combined social and athletic facilities but, alas, there were no funds available.[35]

Finally, Holland managed to persuade the University Grants Committee that, with five departments already relocated, a considerable number of students, staff and visitors were using the campus, and that this merited the investment in bespoke facilities. Thus a grant of £15,000, towards the estimated £22,000 required, was awarded and work commenced in the autumn of 1937 on what became known as the 'KB Union'. A less prominent site was chosen than for the departmental buildings. To the south of the geology building, conveniently adjacent to the tennis courts and the boiler house, a space was allocated. Lorimer & Matthew were appointed once more and produced a design based on an L-plan splayed out from the north-west facing entrance.

With five academic buildings, the union, and its sports pitches, the new King's Buildings campus reached the end of its pre-war development. As had been planned, there was still plenty of land for further buildings there but, as it transpired, these would have to wait for over a decade. Less than a year after the union was opened, when Professor Crew was hosting the prestigious 7th International Congress of Genetics, scheduled for the last week in August 1939, war was declared. The genetics professor soon found himself in military service, while the King's Buildings' Union found an additional use as headquarters for Home Guard and Air Raid Protection units.

JOSEPH BLACK BUILDING (CHEMISTRY)

As the University's first major new building since the beginning of the century, and the first at a new campus, its foundation stone laid by the king, the chemistry building was of great symbolic significance. Having undertaken the conversions at High School Yards, Balfour Paul could be regarded as the University's regular architect, but here had the opportunity to produce a design unfettered by existing structures, on an open site allowing ideal orientation. Paul was now sole partner in the firm, Rowand Anderson having retired, and he would have been aware that his former partner's Medical School was considered impractical and architecturally over-elaborate. Paul's career had been interrupted by the war, and he had just returned from France. Having served with distinction in the Royal

Engineers, he was doubtless eager to get the practice, and its relationship with the University, re-established.

The brief, created by the Department of Chemistry, stated that this should be a building of extreme practicality and economy, and should be seen as the first phase of an extendable project. Lighting of the laboratories was critical, and windows were to be as large as possible. Thus the plan has a main block, with the entrance to the north, and wings projecting to the south, initially of one storey, but extendable in height and length. There is no doubt about the seriousness of intent in the architect's overtly industrial statement to mark the start of the new era. Notwithstanding the sculptural embellishments, given to bestow gravitas to the dignity of the undertaking, this is clearly a steel-framed structure, with metal-framed windows and spandrel panels. The spaces between these are filled with unrendered brickwork, giving it an engineered appearance. While it lacks the industrial boldness of Gropius, Behrens and the European avant-garde, the use of facing brick on an important institutional building in Edinburgh would have been considered quite daring.

However, the façade is classicist in its symmetry and in the arrangement of the brickwork to form giant pilasters. It was also given a pediment and portico of sculpted stone, and a stone parapet and dressings, as

167 Entrance hall of the Joseph Black Building (chemistry)
Nick Haynes

168 New laboratories in the Joseph Black Building
Paul Zanre Photography

169 The Ashworth
Laboratories, photographed
soon after completion in 1928
HES [Scottish Colorfoto Collection:
SC 1208097]

the institutional tradition demanded, and befitting one
of the King's Buildings. The projecting portico is as
elaborate as the rest is austere. A monumental mason has
provided the University's crest in the pediment above
the door and the architrave has detailed foliate carving.[36]
The porch is topped with a balustrade, as it serves as a
balcony, accessed from a tall central window. The porch
appears rather diminutive, as it is dwarfed by the great
pediment rising from the cornice. In the tympanum,
an ocular window is wreathed with laurel leaves and
drapery. In 1949, the same practice was called back to
extend the building, adding a second storey for further
laboratories to the east and west wings. A.F. Balfour
Paul had died in 1938, so the principal partner, William
Kininmonth, was now in charge. In 1997–2000, a
further three-storey block was completed, with high
specification laboratories and research space for seventy
scientists, designed by architects Campbell & Arnott.

The building bears the name of Joseph Black, who
became the University's fourth Professor of Chemistry
in 1766. Previously a professor at Glasgow, Black was an
important figure in the Scottish Enlightenment.

ASHWORTH BUILDING (ZOOLOGY)

The commencement of the second of the King's
Buildings saw a change of architect. Robert Lorimer
was appointed in 1926, and soon took John F. Matthew
into partnership. The small practice was still at work
on the Scottish National War Memorial at Edinburgh
Castle and, with Lorimer in poor health, Matthew was
now in charge. Sir Robert Lorimer was to die in 1929,
having been awarded a KBE and an honorary LLD by
the University. Aside from memorials, the practice
was mainly known for country house alterations,

suburban cottages and villas, with some ecclesiastical
work, including the lavishly sculpted Thistle Chapel, at
St Giles Cathedral in Edinburgh.

The pattern of fenestration on the zoology building
followed that of chemistry, with pilaster strips forming
vertical divisions between large metal-framed windows,
in what might be termed 1930s neoclassicism. The
façade is also classical, its entrance framed within a
triumphal arch motif. The principal difference is the
outline of the plan, which has wings splayed back from
a central block, on a north-east axis. Placed at the north-
east corner of the King's Building site, the building
takes up a situation of importance, having its own gate
and driveway at the junction of two roads. The splaying
of the wings also diminishes the visual impact of the
frontage, reducing the impression of the end pavilions
and somewhat disguising the asymmetry of the façade.
Where brick represented austerity at the chemistry
building, here the entire frontage was clad in ashlar, from
the Blaxter quarry in Northumberland. Matthew also
dispensed with a portico and suppressed the pediment
to a simple stepped form. The parapet conceals a shallow
pitched roof clad in copper.

Professor Ashworth's brief was exacting. He
demanded laboratory windows from bench height to
ceiling. The depth of the building was restricted, also to
ensure good lighting. This also determined the orientation of the plan. The polygonal lecture theatre, with its
own entrance, was inserted in the re-entrant angle to
the rear. The museum was of considerable importance
too and explains the asymmetry of the plan. Situated at
the west end, it was of 25,000 ft², on the ground floor,
with a gallery above, and housed a large collection of
specimens in mahogany cabinets. A special glass with

170 The main staircase,
Ashworth Laboratories

Nick Haynes

171 *below* Cast stone oval reliefs of animals
by Phyllis Bone on the Ashworth Building

Nick Haynes

172 Detail of the staircase,
Ashworth Laboratories

Nick Haynes

173 Detail of the staircase,
Ashworth Laboratories

Nick Haynes

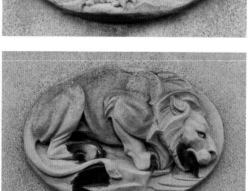

174 The former museum in the Ashworth Laboratories
Nick Haynes

175 The museum, Ashworth Laboratories
Nick Haynes

ultraviolet light filtering was developed for the museum cupola to protect the specimens. Dust was an enemy too, and efforts were made to eliminate corners where it could lurk – the terrazzo covering of the floors extends partly up the walls, seamlessly. Window blinds were to be electrically operated and enamelled steel bookshelves designed for the library. After great efforts, including a visit by Ashworth to the USA to make a presentation to the International Education Board (the Rockefeller Foundation), grants totalling £118,000 were secured.[37] Work commenced on site in the summer of 1927.[38]

Notwithstanding the rigorous utility sought in the brief, Lorimer & Matthew were noted practitioners within the Scottish Arts and Crafts idiom, and a symbolic decorative scheme was created. Sculptors Phyllis Bone and Charles d'Orville Pilkington Jackson were enlisted. Together with Alexander Carrick they were working with Lorimer on the war memorial at the castle, and were frequent collaborators. Bone, known for her animal figures, provided the models for a series of seventeen cast stone oval reliefs of animals representing the fourteen zoographic regions, which were installed in the horizontal panels between ground and first floor [fig.171]. Smaller roundels with representations of three invertebrates, scarab beetle, octopus and crab, were mounted on the lintels of the upper storey windows. Although it was not a simple matter to get animals to fit within the oval medallions – the ostrich had to be omitted – Bone's panels have their charm, and a certain whimsy. Her work continues indoors, at the main staircase, where bronze owl and monkey figures are mounted on the newels of a wrought iron balustrade [figs 172, 173]. On a more sombre note, Pilkington Jackson carved the University crest, flanked by the staff of Asclepius and the torch of learning, above the entrance, along with the date, 1928, and Zoology.

The Ashworth Building, as it was later named, was officially opened by HRH Prince George on 15 May 1929.

The most significant of the extensions to the Ashworth Laboratories was completed in 1966.[39] Interestingly, the designers were the University's own Architecture Research Unit, which had been set up by Professor Sir Robert Matthew, Head of Architecture. A substantial block of five storeys, plus basement and penthouse, the extension was placed to the south-east of the original building, and linked by a staircase at the lower two levels. Speed of construction was critical here, and it was built mainly of pre-cast concrete beams and columns, with in-situ work kept to a minimum. The eight-bay frontage is non-hierarchical, as befits an extension, consisting entirely of pre-cast window / spandrel panels with an exposed quartz aggregate, and with no special treatment to denote the entrance.[40] It was further extended in 2004.

CREW BUILDING (ANIMAL GENETICS)

The Department of Animal Genetics began its existence at High School Yards, before being temporarily transferred to the basement of the chemistry building at King's Buildings. The design of Crew Building is more typical of the Lorimer & Matthew style than the zoology building, with classical features largely suppressed. Although it is symmetrically ordered, and follows the essentially two-storey pattern, it is on a more domestic scale than the previous buildings at the site. The curvilinear gable above the entrance was a favourite Lorimer motif, and he used it for a variety of building types [fig.177]. Other Lorimerian features, such as the harled finish to the walls, the slated hipped roof, and the multi-pane timber-framed windows, help to evoke a suburban character, rather than a monumental one. The building is, however, well-detailed and appears dignified.

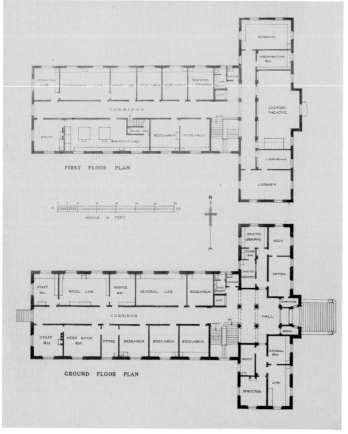

The basement storey, quoins and margins are of artificial stone, while the arched entrance is surmounted by a lancet window with a balconette. The entrance stairs, on a half arch, have side walls replicating the gable skews. Inevitably, for a Lorimer & Matthew building, the tympanum of the gable bears a relief sculpture. This depicts a nude group of man, woman and child, in a rather obscure symbolic representation of genetics [fig.177].

The building is set well away from the main road, somewhat concealed, on the west of the site, and accessed by what had been the driveway to the old farm. A T-plan layout was chosen, with the entrance front facing east, and a west wing extending to the rear [fig.178]. Here, laboratories and research rooms were arranged on each side of a spinal corridor. This could be extended to the west when required. In the entrance block, a lecture theatre, lit by the lancet window, occupies the central position on the upper floor and is flanked by a museum and library. Unusually, for the science campus, this building was not actually extended in itself, although it was augmented by various separate animal houses from its earliest days.[41]

The animal genetics building takes its name from Professor F.A.E. Crew, who was given the chair in 1928. Crew had previously been director of the Department of Research in Animal Breeding at the Board of Agriculture and Fisheries.

Many years later, after the removal of animal genetics, the building was occupied for a time by civil and environmental engineering; from 2002, the newly-formed School of Geosciences took over the Crew Building as teaching laboratories.

SANDERSON BUILDING (ENGINEERING)

Lorimer & Matthew's engineering building took up its prominent place on the perimeter of the King's Buildings site, addressing Mayfield Road. Building work commenced late in 1929, and within two years the department was able to make the move from High School Yards.[42] The Sanderson Building is similar to its predecessors in the general approach, but the classicism is less blatant, the pilaster strips having no residual bases or capitals. Its tripartite façade has an advanced centrepiece, which then projects further with a blunt pylon entrance. The front is entirely clad in ashlar and the detailing of the entrance is eclectic. The architrave around the door has roll mouldings, like a Scottish Renaissance palace, and it is flanked by curious slit windows, redolent of the Glasgow School of Art. Above the entrance is a yawning aperture for a balcony, its front wall supported on intricately carved corbels. At the wallhead, a geometric pediment is flanked by pairs of elongated scrolls. A carved sculptural panel, representing 'engineering in its earliest form', by Alexander Carrick, completes the ensemble. Despite all this detail, and the muscularity of the centrepiece, the hipped and slated roof, with its sensible overhanging eaves, entirely dominates the composition. The main two-storey block has a series of workshops and a boiler house, arranged transversely to the rear, with a tall combined water tower and chimney.

As had been anticipated, the building grew larger with numerous extensions, although not until after the Second World War. The extensions of 1958–61 are of some interest.[43] This project, costing £250,000, virtually doubled the capacity of the Sanderson Laboratories.

180 The main staircase in the Grant Institute
Nick Haynes

181 The presentation stone in the entrance hall of the Grant Institute
Nick Haynes

182 The Grant Institute (Geology), photographed about 1935
HES [Scottish Colorfoto Collection: SC 1171367]

The University generally appointed architects with a practice in Edinburgh, but the Professor of Architecture at Liverpool University also had considerable involvement at King's Buildings. Having no staff or practice, as such, Professor Robert Gardner-Medwin worked in association with Kingham Knight Associates on these occasions.[44]

Gardner-Medwin separated the functions into 'units', laboratories, lecture rooms and staff rooms, to create a group of buildings to the south of the original engineering building. These were all linked together by glazed walkways, or corridors. Each was given a different treatment. The single-storey classroom block is of load-bearing brick, with cladding, while the two-storey laboratory block has a steel frame, with lightweight cladding, and was intended to be adaptable.[45] The tallest of the blocks, now known as the Faraday Building, was the staff and library unit. This has a five-storey concrete frame, its gables clad in mosaic-faced panels, and the window spandrels have grey enamelled panels. The use of the same type of aluminium window frames throughout brought unity to the group. The most visually exciting of the ensemble was the concrete lecture theatre. Cladding was eschewed and it proudly displays the board-marked texture of the shuttering. The external cantilevered form expresses that of the raked interior, and it stands on its stem in a pond reflecting that form. Access was via a glazed steel bridge, or by an open concrete staircase. The striking interior with its exposed concrete ribs, patterned acoustic panelling, and raw concrete demonstration bench is largely intact. The water feature has been abandoned, however. Further significant extensions of the engineering building are considered in later chapters.

GRANT INSTITUTE (GEOLOGY)

Completing the formal inter-war parade of the science campus, the geology building was given a place near the north perimeter, between chemistry and zoology, and takes its name from the principal donor, Sir Alexander Grant. In its initial arrangement, it was a C-plan layout, with extendable wings to the south. The composition of the fifteen-bay façade is reminiscent of a country house, albeit one with large steel-framed windows. Each end bay projects slightly, the profile of the slated roof bestowing a somewhat tower-like appearance on these pavilions. The central three bays are similarly advanced, making the entrance seem guarded by a pair of towers, an effect emphasised by the recessed balcony above the door. The external leaf to the Grant Institute is in smooth ashlar, with concrete panels between upper and lower windows. But, interestingly, in the original submission for a building warrant, the finish to the façade was specified as harled brick, with stone dressings and synthetic stone cornice, which would have completed the impression of a country house.[46] Presumably, in the interest of uniformity with the other buildings, stone was substituted for the harling.

Alexander Carrick had the task of providing a relief sculpture to represent geology above the door. He devised a figure representing a primitive man, holding a fossil, set against a clam shell.

KING'S BUILDINGS HOUSE
(FORMERLY COMMON ROOM / UNION)

Conceived as combined sports pavilion and social club, this was John Matthew's final building at the campus and he arranged it on an L-plan around the tennis courts to the south of the geology building. Essentially a steel structure, it was given a harled brick exterior, with synthetic stone dressings and a roof of slate and copper. The entrance sheltered under a cinema canopy, the central portion having a large lounge above the hall. Tall windows in the re-entrant angle lit the staircase, and the lounge had a balcony from which to view the tennis courts. The south wing contained a dining hall to seat 150, and had reading and committee rooms above, while the east wing had showers and changing rooms, with a gymnasium above. A lower block at the end contained squash courts.

Necessarily plain in detail, the building displayed something of the then current art-deco fashion, and must have seemed relatively luxurious when it opened, having first-class facilities for athletics, a large and comfortable lounge, and being extremely well lit by the large metal-framed windows. A consciously less formal building than the Teviot Row Union, it evoked a country club atmosphere, with its white harled walls and *moderne* glazing.[47] Run by a committee of students and staff, the building was in use by the autumn term of 1938, and it was formally, though somewhat confusingly, opened as the King's Buildings Common Room, in January 1939.[48]

The last building project at the science campus before the Second World War, the common room marked an important stage in the development of King's Buildings, conferring status on an undertaking that had been often described as a colony of the University. After seventy years of alterations and refurbishment, the building has completely changed in appearance, having a frontal extension to the south wing and changes to the fenestration. The entrance is still recognisable, but a porch has been added, and the interior has been completely remodelled.

Chapter Six

Planning for the Future 1940–1960

CLIVE B. FENTON

183 Sketch perspective of George Square from the south-east by Basil Spence in 1955–6. Interlocking courtyards were to replace the 18th-century houses and tenements of George Square and Buccleuch Place.
HES [Sir Basil Spence Archive: DP 012783]

With the nation at war and emergency powers in operation, building activity was restricted to works necessary for the war effort, and materials were strictly rationed. All major architectural projects were shelved, and the University's works committee, with Professor William Oliver as convenor, was occupied with Air Raid Protection, and other measures for safety and economy. In this time of national emergency, the University faced many challenges, and the University Court appointed a standing war committee to consider these. There was an immediate 15 per cent drop in student matriculation in 1939–40, and the Military Service Act meant that third-year students and many potential students, as well as staff, were called up. The lessons of the previous war, which had been so wasteful of valuable manpower, had, however, been learned by the authorities, and there were exemptions from military duty for students of medicine and the applied sciences.[1] Nevertheless, by the summer of 1940, staff numbers were depleted by the calling away for 'special services', and student figures had decreased by 21 per cent, with a consequent loss of income from fees, although the female student population increased slightly, as it had done in the First World War.[2]

As it transpired, Edinburgh suffered comparatively little in the way of aerial bombardment and none of the University buildings was struck. However, the threat was always there and many staff and students undertook duties in the Home Guard, as Air Raid Protection wardens, or fire watching. The black-out was observed, and timetables and term dates amended. In addition, accelerated courses and special short courses for the military were organised. The extraordinary nature of the European crisis led to the medical faculty becoming host to a special Polish School of Medicine, initiated by the Polish government in exile, and marked by a ceremony attended by the Principal, Sir Thomas Holland, the Polish President, Wladyslaw Raczkiewicz, and the Lord Provost, William Darling, in March 1941.[3] The stated aim was to make provision for the future of Poland, then occupied by both the Nazis and the Soviet Union, with all its universities and higher schools closed down. The school mainly used an annexe to the rear of Lothian Street. The Polish Veterinary School also operated at Summerhall from 1943 to 1947.

During the troubling and traumatic duration of the war, however, the future provision of accommodation for the University was never forgotten. Even before the war reached its conclusion there was a general understanding that the post-war era would be very different from any preceding one. Political commitments had been made concerning social justice and equity, and there was a strong memory of the still undelivered 'Country Fit For Heroes' promised after the First World War. Change was evidently in the air, as signified by the Labour victory

Treasury, for the quinquennium 1947–52. The role of the University Grants Committee also had to change from being merely an advisor to government on the allocation of its universities budget, to a more active one involving planning the expansion of the universities and directly allocating Treasury funds. The University Grants Committee would employ its own architects and quantity surveyors to ensure that capital grants were wisely spent.

SIR DONALD POLLOCK'S GIFTS

John Donald Pollock became a figure of great importance to the University and wielded considerable influence by becoming one of its greatest benefactors. Pollock was twice elected rector by Edinburgh students, serving in this role from 1939 to 1945. He had, however, already served as rector's assessor to Viscount Allenby from 1935 to 1936 and, having failed in the rectorial election of 1936, was appointed assessor again by Sir Herbert Grierson. Thus he was closely involved in representing Edinburgh's students for over a decade. After 1945, Sir Donald continued to have a voice in the University's affairs, mainly through his Pollock Memorial Trust, so named in honour of his parents.

Pollock was a wealthy industrialist, who had studied science at Glasgow and medicine at Edinburgh. As an entrepreneur he had designed electrical x-ray apparatus, devised a method of liquid oxygen mass production, and one of his companies was hugely successful in the salvage business, including the raising of German warships scuttled at Scapa Flow. In 1938, news of Pollock's benefactions, which were still being formulated, began to emerge.[5] His trust fund had been endowed with £250,000, yielding an income of £8,000 per annum to be used for both religious work and for assistance to the University. Over and above this he had bought the redundant United Presbyterian Church at Bristo Street, to be named the Pollock Memorial Hall, for the use of students, for public lectures, religious services and meetings. He had also acquired the premises of the Edinburgh United Breweries, at the Pleasance, which he was having converted into a University gymnasium. The University had appointed a director of physical training in 1926, and by 1930 such training was taking place quite close to this brewery at the Pleasance gym, which was owned and operated by the Pleasance Trust for the benefit of the local community. Furthermore, it was announced that Pollock had acquired the Salisbury Green estate consisting of thirteen acres, plus several buildings, from the Nelson family. This he intended to be used as halls of residence. There was a topographical aspect to all this too, as Pollock pointed out. Perhaps inspired by the Mears Report, he wanted the activities of the University to be better concentrated in the central area.

in the general election of 1945, and the creation of the welfare state. There was political consensus in the drive for reconstruction, improvement, modernisation and technological progress. Following a hiatus of austerity as the country made the transition from wartime to peacetime economy, it became clear that a social revolution was taking place. As Sir Walter Moberly, of the University Grants Committee, put it: there was an intensified demand for social justice to the individual.[4]

The Butler Education Act (1944, in Scotland 1945) raised the school-leaving age and brought free secondary education for all children. This meant that school-leavers who qualified for university entry would increase in number. Added to this equation was the increasing birth rate of the 1940s, which would begin to impact upon applications for university places by 1960. Of course, had this all happened twenty years earlier this cohort of potential students might simply have been turned away, but now there was a political commitment to offer university places to all who were qualified. Architects could therefore look forward to an unprecedented programme of school, college and university building. The compelling recommendation of 'Scientific Manpower', highlighted by the report of the Barlow Committee (1946), was an important factor here. Barlow proposed that the number of science graduates should be increased from 55,000 to 90,000 by 1955, if Britain was to be industrially competitive in the post-war world. To achieve this, it was estimated that £40m for buildings and £10m for sites should be allocated by the

185 A plan of the 'island site' in 1956, bounded by Lothian Street (top left), Potterrow (right), Marshall Street (bottom right) and Bristo Street (bottom left). Areas coloured in red were owned by Sir Donald Pollock, in green by the University, and in grey by private parties. The site was eventually flattened for the Potterrow Student Centre in the late 1960s.

University of Edinburgh Estates Collection

186 Aerial view of the 'island site' and McEwan Hall from the south-east, 1951

HES [Aerofilms Collection: SC 1297651]

The Pollock Memorial Hall was actually located between Bristo Street and Potterrow and was completely surrounded by other buildings, with access through an opening in Marshall Street. The building, which no longer exists, had been erected in 1741, and could seat 1,800 worshippers. The first event in its new guise was an exhibition of modern art, in autumn 1938.

Pollock was thanked for his generosity by the students, who elected him as rector in 1939, and he was created a baronet in the same year. The Pollock Memorial Trust then allocated £5,450 for improvements to the Pollock Hall, including organ repairs, and to equip the physical training department. Lorimer & Matthew carried out the conversion of the old Bell's Brewery building, which was reported to be in full use by the summer of 1941, and it became known as the Pollock Institute of Physical Education.[6]

THE CLYDE REPORT

Notwithstanding the crisis of war and the uncertainty that it brought, Lord Reith, the Minister for Works and Buildings, had urged the nation to plan boldly for the future. One of the many responses to this exhortation was in Edinburgh, where an advisory committee was appointed to consider and make recommendations on future city development. The committee was chaired by J.L. Clyde KC, and other members were Thomas B. Whitson, and Sir Donald Pollock. Whitson had relevant experience of city development, having commissioned

the Mears Report when he was Lord Provost, and he had an additional interest as a historian of old Edinburgh. But this was a rather small and unusual committee to be considering the future development of Scotland's capital, consisting as it did of a senior advocate, a former Lord Provost and the University Rector, whose role was to represent the interests of students.[7] The absence of a standing representative of the City, of a professional town planner and, indeed, of the Principal, is notable. However, the views expressed were not unusual or unexpected.

'The Future of Edinburgh: Report of the Advisory Committee on City Development', to give it its full title, was published in October 1943. It had no drawings or plans, but consisted entirely of text, and it largely revisited the territory covered by Mears in 1931. As far as University development was concerned, the recommendation was that it should occupy one coherent area, and that steps should be taken to unite its separated parts. This is a latent reference to the existence of the King's Buildings site; the time wasted by staff and students travelling all over the city is also emphasised, and the report reiterates the aims of the Pollock Memorial Trust. It ultimately recommends that City and University should work together to redevelop the area around Old College, including High School Yards. Significantly, the report describes George Square as 'an architectural gem' worthy of preservation.[8]

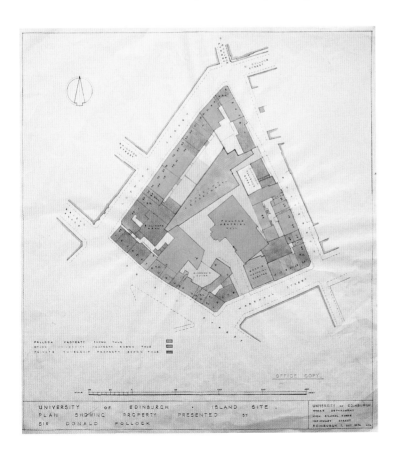

187 The south side of
Bristo Street in about 1900.
Sir Donald Pollock began
to acquire some of these
tenements on the 'island site'.
All were demolished by the
University in the late 1960s.
HES [Francis M. Chrystal
Collection: SC 1131022]

Just as the Mears Report had anticipated the new
powers of the Town and Country Planning Act 1932, the
Clyde Report anticipate the Act of 1947, and was intended
to influence the plans of both City and University.
Similarly, the catalogue for an exhibition, 'Rebuilding
Edinburgh', at the National Gallery of Scotland (July–
August 1943), commends the Mears Report, and regrets
that it had not been acted upon. The text, written by
the conservationist architect Robert Hurd, specifically
mentions George Square as a striking example of good
speculative building.[9]

In March 1943, Sir Donald Pollock announced that he
had further plans for the University, having purchased a
number of properties in the triangular city block bounded
by Lothian Street, Potterrow and Marshall Street, which
lay between Old College and George Square. This became
known as 'the island site', the centre occupied by the
Pollock Memorial Hall. The intention was that this site
would be used for student amenities, particularly a large
new student union, notwithstanding the fact that there
was already a union for men nearby at Teviot Row, and a
women's union at George Square. The terms of Pollock's
trust ensured that this land would be used exclusively for
student amenities, for all time coming. The intention was
that the existing buildings would be converted using the
income yielded by the Pollock Memorial Trust. Clearly,
Pollock had decided to direct the University's development, according to his own model.

PROFESSOR OLIVER'S MASTERPLAN

The year 1943 was certainly eventful in Edinburgh, with
the University engaged in discussions about resuming
schemes shelved in 1939, and considering how it would
deal with the anticipated post-war influx of students.
The Post-War Development Committee was convened
and all the faculties instructed to provide details about
their most urgent requirements, of which there were a
great many.

In response to a request from James Clyde's advisory
committee, the University had produced a memorandum
in which it expressed a determination not to repeat the
mistakes of the past, when no provision had been made
for expansion in the long term.[10] The long-term view
was that virtually all the land proposed by Mears for
his College Mile would ultimately be required by the
University, and that no development in the area should
be considered without first consulting the University.
The area being referred to stretched from the Royal
Infirmary in the west to Holyrood Park in the east, and
from Chambers Street in the north to Rankeillor Street
in the south. The intention was to create a precinct
around Old College, with George Square as a central
element. The properties in this large tract of land were
either condemned or likely to be, and of no historic
interest, it was claimed. Furthermore, the University was
considering whether the King's Buildings development
should be concluded, and science and engineering

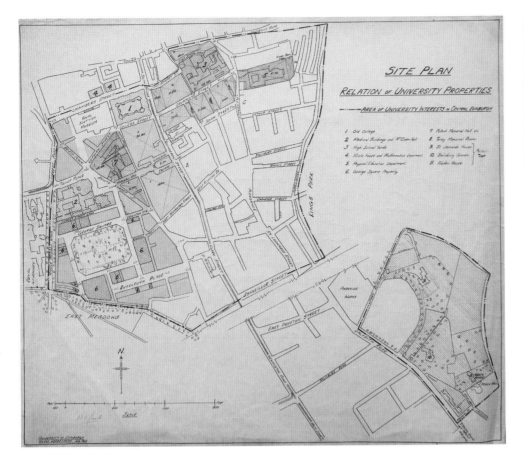

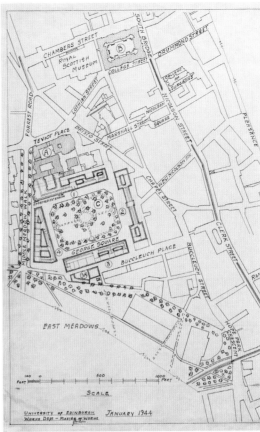

188 A plan of the University's interests in central Edinburgh in 1943
University of Edinburgh Estates Collection

189 Department of Works proposed block plan for George Square, January 1944.
University of Edinburgh Estates Collection

moved back to the city centre. It was correct that most of the 18th- and 19th-century tenements were in poor condition, but there were certainly some buildings of historical interest. Not the least of these were the buildings at High School Yards, which the University had converted in 1905.[11] Then there were two schools and a public baths at Infirmary Street and Drummond Street, but these were considered to be unnecessary because the City had begun to move most of the residents to new housing estates.[12] Nevertheless, the City had built houses at Richmond Street and East Crosscauseway in the 1930s, and these were too new to be sacrificed.

The seeds of conflict were thus sown, for while it now seemed there was agreement about extending the Medical School onto north George Square, together with University development to the east of Old College, including High School Yards, and abandonment of the King's Buildings site, the price for reintegration might mean the redevelopment of the rest of George Square, which some wanted to be preserved as 'an architectural gem'.

The first meeting of the Post-War Development Committee was in November 1943. With the Principal Sir Thomas Holland in the chair, it consisted of all the deans of faculty, as well as Professor Oliver, convenor of the works committee, and the lawyer Mr Carlyle-Gifford. Also, representing the City, there was Councillor John Falconer, who was later to become Lord

Provost.[13] Over and above resumption of the medical extensions, requirements were identified as a new library, science laboratories, administration facilities, new Departments of Agricultural Engineering and Aeronautics, and student halls of residence. But the post-war aims were not simply about providing adequate facilities and getting buildings for these, but about establishing the University as one of the major educational institutions in Britain. It was felt that the best students were now going to St Andrews: an intolerable situation.

For some time Professor Oliver had been promoting what he called 'the Master Plan', and in March 1944 the committee recommended this as the basis for future development. The scheme involved gradually replacing the buildings on east, west and south George Square with large new buildings to create 'a magnificent quad', as demonstrated in a simple block plan, drafted by the Department of Works in January 1944. Medicine, physics, mathematics, geography, engineering, astronomy and geology are allocated the south side. Chemistry (science and medicine) are on the west, while administration, a Senate Hall, examination rooms and the library occupy the east side [fig.189].

The allocation of departments to sites seems fairly arbitrary, as does the actual shape of the building footprints. The magnificence of the proposed quadrangle would, of course, depend largely on the design of its buildings, but there were clear advantages in the principle. The square had a large garden as its centrepiece, and the adjacent Meadows had plenty of space for recreation. This large open green space helped to bestow a sense of tranquillity that was rare in the city centre. The essential requirement for phased development could be met by following the block-by-block approach, and Oliver cited other practical advantages, such as shared boiler house facilities and the economical servicing of a rational layout.[14] Disadvantages seemed few. Student residences would be lost, but the land at Salisbury Green could accommodate replacements. The women's union, on the east side, could be moved to the 'island site' but, following pleas from Pollock, the University Court deferred its decision on the Oliver plan.[15]

In September of 1944, the Principal Sir Thomas Holland was forced to retire through ill health. His replacement was John Fraser, then Regius Professor of Clinical Surgery at Edinburgh. The new Principal was equally committed to bring the science departments back to the city centre when he took the chair of the Post-War Development Committee. While University reintegration was a universal desire, the means were contentious. In the dialogue between City and University, neither party spoke with a unified voice. There was some dissent within the University itself, but its executive body, the University Court, notwithstanding Sir Donald Pollock's ideas, had acquired an unwavering resolve.

Anticipating the resuscitation of the Mears scheme, Professor Oliver began compiling a convincing dossier of disadvantages inherent in development to the east of Old College, including High School Yards. His research showed that industry and domestic fires had made this the most soot-polluted part of the city, in comparison to the lighter pollution at George Square. The steep cross fall of the land to the north and east also posed architectural and construction challenges. In addition, a major traffic artery separated Old College from the site, with resultant issues of road safety, noise and vibrations, which were not ideal for lectures, study and scientific experiments. Then there was the time element. While the City was committed to slum clearance, it might be many years before the population could be rehoused. Thus, development in this area was a very long-term proposition at best.

In 1944, however, the country was still operating under emergency measures and Edinburgh was not in a position to make any decisions about future development. Nonetheless, the University pressed on with its plans. These matters were discussed under the auspices of the so-called Town and Gown meetings during 1944–5. The City was still considering the appointment of a consultant to prepare a survey and development plan at this time but, under pressure from Pollock for an alternative scheme that avoided George Square, the City Engineer, John Macartney, was instructed to look for possibilities.[16] His suggestion was for development in an area bounded by Potterrow, Middle Meadow Walk and Forrest Road. This would have entailed the acquisition and demolition of the following properties: the Victorian tenements and shops in Teviot Place and Forrest Road, including Oddfellow's Hall; Brown Square School; 18th-century tenements and warehouses at Bristo Port; the Lothian Street and Brighton Place tenements of circa 1800; St Francis's Roman Catholic Church and its Priory, the Seventh Day Adventist Church and the Royal College of Physicians laboratory in Bristo Place; and Thomas Hamilton's New North Free Church.

A further area, between Buccleuch Place and the Meadows, which conformed with Oliver's scheme, was also included. In response, Oliver considered the proposal to be a more costly alternative, because of the property that would have to be purchased, and he reckoned that it fell short of his scheme by some 328,000 square feet.[17] An important factor cited in rejecting this alternative was the spaces between buildings for, while the garden of George Square was already open space, the City Engineer's scheme would require purchase and demolition of properties to achieve open space; and it was extremely unlikely that the University Grants Committee would give grants for this. Removal of residents and purchase of commercial property was another difficulty, even with the full co-operation of the City. Acquisition of the George Square properties, not already under control of the University, would be simple by comparison as it would only involve two houses on the east side, two on the south side and eleven on the west side.[18]

There were other problems with this alternative scheme. The site at the corner of Chambers Street was already earmarked for an extension of the Royal Scottish Museum, while the block between Lothian Street and Marshall Street, the 'island site', was largely restricted in use to student amenities, under the terms of the Pollock Trust. Interestingly, the potential for student amenities was enlarged in 1945 when Pollock persuaded the University to use the bequest of the playwright, J.M. Barrie to purchase the redundant Bristo Baptist Church in Marshall Street. This was to be converted into the Barrie Memorial Theatre, to be used for student drama and the like, using funds from the Pollock Trust for its renovation. Pollock asserted that his consent had to be sought for any usage of the 'island site', which was only reluctantly given for erection of a temporary annexe, containing laboratories for the Medical School, on the backlands behind Lothian Street, and for the use of the Barrie Theatre as an examination venue, in 1947.[19] The emergence of the Pollock Trust Development

Committee, ostensibly a sub-committee of the University Court, proved to be problematic, since there was already the Post-War Development Committee, often at odds with Pollock's plans. Pollock favoured retention and conversion of existing buildings, preferably using salvaged materials. He clashed with Professor Oliver, in 1946, who declared that the Pollock Memorial Hall was structurally unsound, and therefore not viable for costly renovation.[20]

Some of the old buildings at the 'island site' were of historical interest, although Sir Donald was the only one to see this at the time. The tenements on Lothian Street, built in 1800, were certainly substantial examples of the type, as can be seen from those surviving on the north side of the street. As domestic dwellings, they could have been rehabilitated and modernised, but Pollock's idea of converting them for refectories, student health clinics, cafeterias and dance halls was unrealistic. Some of the smaller buildings in Bristo Street, with shops inserted into them, dated from the late 17th to early 18th centuries, and lent character to the area, but they had been neglected and costly rehabilitation would have yielded only small flats and shops. The most interesting building here was the large tenement known as Seceders' Land, at nos 16–19 Bristo Street, which was probably from the late 17th century. It had history and character, but the flats were already deemed unfit dwellings during the 1930s, and photographs from the early 1960s show it derelict above the ground floor level. Similarly derelict was a free-standing early-18th-century house, adjacent to the Barrie Theatre, which had served as a manse and had probably been abandoned as a dwelling before the First World War.

THE HOLDEN PLAN

With John Falconer now Lord Provost, the City of Edinburgh had decided upon Sir Patrick Abercrombie to produce its development plan.[21] Abercrombie was the most prominent city planner in Britain. He had already produced the County of London Plan (1943) and the Greater London Plan (1944), and his large practice was engaged on several other such development plans, such as those for Plymouth, Hull and Bath.

In January 1946, the Principal contacted Abercrombie for his advice, which was that the University should appoint its own professional consultant, with whom he could liaise while producing the city plan. When pressed for a recommendation, Abercrombie suggested Sir Frank Mears or Robert Matthew. Clearly Mears would not have been the best choice, as he would doubtless reiterate his previous College Mile scheme and favour development to the east of Old College. He was also a member of the conservationist group, the Cockburn Association, as was Sir Donald Pollock. At this time,

Robert Matthew was chief architect to the Department of Health (Scotland) and was currently engaged with Abercrombie on preparing the Clyde Valley Regional Plan. Abercrombie felt that Matthew would leave his government job to prepare the University's plan, but Matthew was not officially approached and instead took up the post of chief architect to London County Council that year. Instead the Principal contacted Charles Holden, with whom he was acquainted.[22]

Holden was Professor of Architecture at the University of London and had relevant experience designing that university's new buildings before the war, including the monumental Senate House, inserted amongst the leafy squares of Bloomsbury. He had also produced a post-war plan for Canterbury and, together with William Holford, was preparing a plan for the City of London, creating a new precinct around St Paul's Cathedral.

Events swiftly unfolded after Holden was appointed in March 1946, and Oliver was sent to London to brief him. By May, he had produced an interim report and reached an agreement with Abercrombie about the closure and demolition of Bristo Street. The first public indication of Holden's scheme appeared in the press in July, when it was reported that the Lord Provost's special sub-committee on post-war planning had approved it in principle, without commitment to the area selected for redevelopment.[23] In January of 1947 Holden was able to report that Abercrombie was prepared to approve his plan [figs 190, 191] and support the University in his forthcoming development plan for Edinburgh.[24]

Holden's task was to create a university zone that Abercrombie could incorporate into his development plan. If approved by the City, and then by the Secretary of State, his proposed development area would become a statutory zone reserved for educational use. He was careful to include the area proposed in the City Engineer's alternative scheme and also the area to the east of Old College, for long-term development, so that they could be eliminated as possible alternatives to the George Square scheme. As news of the scheme began to emerge, the planning dialogue exploded into a public furore.

In order to clarify the situation and put forward its case the University published a brochure in May 1947, entitled 'Proposals for the Future Development of the University of Edinburgh', which only fuelled the controversy. The brochure outlined 'the problem' as the need for reintegration of the University into the heart of the city, adjacent to Old College and the Medical School, to create a university precinct. The site for future buildings should be reasonably secluded from traffic noise and vibrations, peaceful and pleasant, and of ample size to meet future needs. It should also provide the opportunity for good architecture. The area selected was bounded by Chambers Street in the north and the Meadows in the south. From west to east, it stretched from Middle Meadow Walk to Potterrow. With George Square as the centrepiece, surrounding streets are replaced by blocks allocated to University departments. The area to the east of Forrest Road is designated for administration buildings and a chapel. And, while Bristo Street and Marshall Street have been erased, the area of Pollock's 'island site' is dedicated to student and staff amenities.

The brochure also provided answers to the objections regarding the loss of the buildings around George Square. While it is conceded that they had some architectural merit, expert opinion did not regard them as first class, and they would be replaced by better buildings. The Mears plan is included, for the sake of comparison, and Professor Oliver's arguments about the unsuitability of the area to the east of Old College are repeated. An aerial perspective shows the new George Square surrounded by large geometric blocks – a tower on the western block is not unlike Holden's Senate House at Bloomsbury. Curiously, a walled enclosure for lorries occupies a prominent central space on the east side of the square, while large piazzas have been created to the east and north of the McEwan Hall. The text of the brochure concludes that this is the best of all possible plans, pregnant with architectural opportunities. It also contains the rather rash promise that the design of the future buildings will be obtained by holding public architectural competitions. The latter pledge failed to win the public support anticipated.

Holden accompanied representatives of the University, including the Secretary and Oliver, to a meeting with the Lord Provost, to present his full scheme, which was described as 'a broad outline for long term development'.[25] Meanwhile, details of the Holden plan appeared in the press in May 1947. Leading the opposition to the scheme was the architect Robert Hurd, a conservation specialist, who was also president of the Saltire Society. He condemned the pressure being placed upon the City by the University, but Lord Provost Falconer praised the scheme for its vision.[26] Hurd also argued that the University would face insurmountable difficulties in the execution of its plans. The Earl of Selkirk, an Edinburgh alumnus, declared that 'to destroy George Square would be a crime', while Hurd admitted that George Square was not great architecture but it was human in scale.[27] The Lord Provost maintained that this was 'perhaps the greatest conception which has been submitted to the City of Edinburgh for centuries'.[28] An editorial column in *The Scotsman* described the situation as a dilemma,

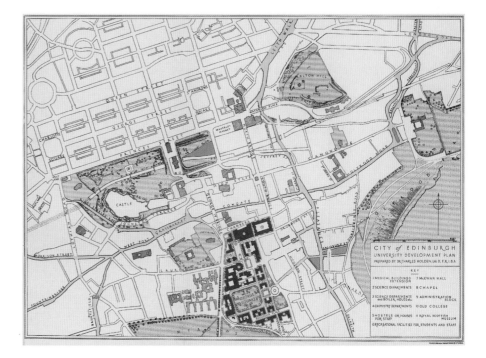

with the redevelopment of the square as tragic, yet the alternative site as extremely problematic.

Opposition had been anticipated but probably not on the scale experienced. The Cockburn Association, the Saltire Society, the Society of Scottish Artists and the Old Edinburgh Club voiced objections, and a new association, the Edinburgh Georgian Society, was created to campaign to save George Square. These groups became collectively as 'the amenity societies'. They proposed the Mears plan, or variations of it, but Holden warned the University that offering alternatives would weaken its case. Holden and Abercrombie had actually discussed development of an area to the east of Potterrow that would have provided a similar amount of space, but only if the east side of the square were included.[29] Mears himself remained silent on the matter as he believed that it was unprofessional to publicly criticise the work of another architect.

190 University development plan prepared by Charles Holden in 1946–7

HES [Sir Basil Spence Archive: DP 021583]

191 Sketch by the distinguished London architectural perspectivist, John Dean Monroe Harvey, illustrating Charles Holden's outline proposals for a university zone on the south side of the city, 1947

HES [Sir Basil Spence Archive: DP 021584]

Typically, Sir Donald Pollock had his own ideas about development and wanted the University to acquire the remaining properties and preserve them as houses for professors. He made a speech to the University Court and pleaded for delay, urging caution over any scheme that had its fruition beyond the lives of those in attendance.[30] That was unacceptable, since a crucial benefit of the George Square scheme was that it would permit early commencement, independent of progress by the City on slum clearance, house building or new transportation schemes.

While those opposing the redevelopment of George Square were very vocal, and well connected, they were actually few in number and were mostly alumni with happy memories of student days spent there. Robert Hurd was persistent in his passion for the square, where he lived in a flat rented from the University. He presented an alternative scheme for the Drummond Street area, which Holden dismissed as a last minute substitute for the Mears plan.[31]

In December 1947, the Principal, Sir John Fraser, whose health had been deteriorating throughout the previous year, collapsed and died immediately after a meeting with Pollock. Sydney Smith, Professor of Forensic Medicine and Dean of the Faculty of Medicine, became Acting Principal. While a new Principal was being sought, the cast of characters changed further in 1948, with Charles Stewart replacing Jardine Brown as University Secretary, and Sir Andrew Murray becoming the new Lord Provost.

THE ABERCROMBIE PLAN

When 'A Civic Survey & Plan for Edinburgh', commonly known as the Abercrombie Plan, was published in 1949, it gave full support to the University's plan and to Holden's scheme, as promised. The amenity societies' proposals were considered unrealistic, and the Nicolson Street/South Bridge route was judged an unavoidable obstacle. Their proposals would also conflict with his proposed south–north bypass which was to traverse the area, and with his residential zoning for the land to the east of this route.[32] Abercrombie also observed that there were rather a lot of mundane Georgian buildings in Edinburgh and questioned the architectural value of George Square. Comparing it to the monumental Charlotte Square, with façades designed by Robert Adam, it was found wanting. The amenity societies were surely right when they later said that if everything that did not bear comparison with the excellence of Charlotte Square were to be demolished, there would be very little left.[33] Abercrombie provided sketches demonstrating that the existing George Square buildings were actually too small in scale, in relation to the size of its central garden. This would be corrected when the University erected its new buildings around the square, he maintained.[34]

The Abercrombie Plan was thoroughgoing, and exceedingly Geddesian, in the breadth of both its survey and proposals. It satisfied the City's commitment to producing a development plan required by the Town and Country Planning Act (1947). Its recommendations would be subject to review and amendment, and a public inquiry, to be held in 1954, before it was accepted or rejected by the City and the Secretary of State as its official development plan. In respect of the redevelopment of George Square, however, the professional opinions of Abercrombie and Holden would be difficult to counter. There was a general moratorium on major public building until 1955, but the University was anxious to press ahead with preparations in order that the first phase of the Medical School extensions could begin then, thus ensuring the government funding that had been promised for it.

THE MEDICAL EXTENSION COMPETITION

Advice on the competition was sought from the Royal Institute of British Architects, and Sir Lancelot Keay, the recent president, assisted.[35] He came to Edinburgh to meet the Post-War Development Committee in December 1948, and recommended that a design for the entire north side of George Square should be obtained before proceeding with the first phase. This would ensure architectural continuity, but it was also tactical, since the City would be obliged to consent to subsequent phases of development, should difficulties arise here. Sir Lancelot advised against an architectural competition as a means of obtaining a suitable design. In his opinion, competitions were time-consuming affairs, and even after a winner had been chosen there would be at least eighteen months' delay before drawings could be prepared for submission to the local authority. But the Post-War Development Committee felt that the brochure of proposals it had published contained a binding commitment. Keay suggested a competition limited to invited architects, and even proposed some nominees.[36] However, an open competition had been promised and to retract would have entailed a breach of faith on the part of the University.[37]

The decision to proceed with an open competition, despite professional advice to the contrary, reflected the fact that some members of the town council were succumbing to pressure from the amenity societies. Individual councillors were less committed to the George Square scheme than Sir John Falconer's Special Committee on Post-War Development had been, although the current Lord Provost, Sir Andrew Murray, was sympathetic. The City resolved that it had no objection in principle to the medical extension, so long as no further development involving the other three sides of the square was contemplated. But, of course, it was. The imposition of such a condition was unprecedented, though, and the University obtained legal advice, before deciding to give no such commitment. Charles Stewart, the University Secretary, responded that it was unjustifiable to bind the University Court and its successors in perpetuity. He suggested that development might be restricted to the north side of the square for a number of years (until after the public inquiry), with no commitment by any party on further development. He pointed out that the City could always reject an unsuitable planning application, but it could not refuse to consider any, as yet unknown, developments being proposed.[38]

The City reconsidered the matter and imposed the following four conditions on redevelopment of the north side of the square: the scheme must be harmonious with the square, as it currently existed; the University should consider alternatives, such as retention of the façades of the other three sides of the square; if consent should be granted for the north side, neither party would be committed as a consequence to a scheme for the whole square; and the University would only seek alteration of the other three sides if it was satisfied that there was no other suitable scheme.[39]

This clearly posed an obstacle, which the amenity societies understood to be insurmountable, but in the long term it proved not to be. If the zoning proposed by Abercrombie was adopted, and should the City oppose any planning application based on conditions 2, 3 or 4, the University could appeal to the Secretary of State. In the meantime, the medical extension competition could proceed, although it would be subject to the first of these conditions. In February 1949, the City granted outline consent for the medical extension, subject to the above conditions.[40]

The Royal Incorporation of Architects in Scotland assisted in drafting the rules and overseeing the competition, which was to be formally announced in December 1949, with a decision by February 1951. The president, A.G.R. MacKenzie, acted as assessor of a design to meet detailed requirements for the Departments of Anatomy, Physiology and Pathology, together with a library and administration facilities, for the first phase. This would occupy the site of nos 12–15 George Square, plus a vacant strip of land to the east. As future medical needs were as yet uncertain, the rest had to be a series of phases, with rough estimates of the accommodation, such as a lecture theatre of 9,000ft² given. Construction might be of either steel or reinforced concrete, but the elevations had to be harmonious in form, scale and materials to the existing surroundings, as the City had requested. The University was so anxious about having a design ready for commencement during 1955 that

it was seeking a design that would harmonise with buildings that it intended to demolish. Applicants were supplied with photographs of the existing buildings, the Holden Plan, and the relevant parts of the Abercrombie Plan. Over 130 architects requested information on the competition, of which only thirty-nine actually decided to submit designs. The winner would be announced in 1951, and a new Principal would have to deal with the result.

SIR EDWARD APPLETON

In Edinburgh, both the City and the University had created their post-war schemes. But in 1949 the University still lacked a Principal, with Sir Sydney Smith steering the institution as Acting Principal since the death of Sir John Fraser. Someone exceptional was needed to meet the challenges of the new era. Perhaps the most significant challenge was the matter of national university expansion, which was about rather more than dealing with the expected post-war influx of students who were being demobilised. By 1948 Edinburgh's student roll had already increased to 6,457, against the 1938 figure of 3,826.

The candidate for Principal selected by the University of Edinburgh, at this critical stage in its development, was Sir Edward Appleton, who was uniquely qualified for the position [fig.192]. He was an eminent physicist, specialising in the ionosphere, and had received the Nobel Prize for Physics in 1947. As well as making an important contribution to Britain's radar defences, he spent the war years as Secretary of the Department of Scientific and Industrial Research. In this capacity he was the administrator in charge of the British atomic bomb project. This power over nature produced awesome results and a new threat was perceived to hang over humanity as the world moved into the Cold War era. Sir Edward was well abreast of the ethos of his age, describing the two main developments of the time as Man's recognition of his responsibility as his brother's keeper (i.e. the welfare state), and Man's increasing power over nature (i.e. the Bomb).[41] He recognised that universities had scientific, ethical and spiritual roles to play in this age of accelerating technology. Few could have commanded the respect and authority of Appleton, a proven administrator, extremely well connected in government circles, who understood the importance of scientific research. Edinburgh had the ambition to become one of the foremost universities in the country, thus Appleton was pursued and persuaded, officially taking up the post of Principal in May 1949.[42]

One of the most pressing matters for the new Principal was the issue of George Square and the future of the University's place in the city centre. Appleton clearly wanted to satisfy himself that the course being

192 Portrait of Sir Edward Victor Appleton by Sir William O. Hutchison, 1957
Copyright the artist's estate (via University of Edinburgh Art Collections: EU 0039)

followed was truly the best for all concerned when he took the chair of the Post-War Development Committee in June. He called for a fresh examination of all the possibilities, dividing the committee into four sub-groups to consider these. The alternatives were defined as: Plan A – Development to the east of Old College and South Bridge, as recommended by Frank Mears and Robert Hurd; Plan B – Development to the south of Old College, on the land between Nicolson Street and Potterrow. This was the suppressed proposal made by Charles Holden; Plan C – Abandonment of city centre schemes in favour of concentrating all new development at the King's Buildings site, on the outskirts of the city; and Plan D – the redevelopment of George Square, as proposed by Professor Oliver and Charles Holden and supported by Patrick Abercrombie, the pros and cons of which were to be re-examined. Sir Edward emphasised that this was to be a serious exercise and allowed until October 1949 for the appraisal to be concluded.[43]

Plans A and B were soon rejected. The disadvantages of Plan C, relocation to King's Buildings, included going against the avowed intent of reintegration, of which all parties were in favour. Of course, there would be a break with tradition as the University gradually moved to the outskirts, which would culminate in the unviability of Old College as the University's headquarters. For the medical faculty, the unacceptable implication was dislocation from the Royal Infirmary, surely a last resort. Total relocation would be impractical. But the King's Building's site had distinct advantages, notwithstanding the removal costs, for 112 acres of land were immediately available for development, and the golf course, owned by the University, could be repossessed when needed. Thus, with no costly purchase of land, funds could be concentrated on buildings and equipment. The site was also untrammelled by the architectural tradition of the city centre.

An appealing sketch plan indicated how the site might be laid out with proposed new buildings to replace those that would be abandoned. The money raised by selling sites in the city could be used to build bespoke new facilities, including a library and graduation hall. In the future, a University hospital might be built there too, which later proved to be very prescient, in light of the situation at the end of the 20th century. Such were the advantages that it was felt that Plan C should be held in reserve, as a contingency plan, should the City not approve the George Square development. Plans C and D were clearly not mutually exclusive. From his experience with the Department of Scientific and Industrial Research, Sir Edward knew that the long-term requirements for research were unforeseeable, but that adequate provision was essential. So, while reintegration was an aim, the King's Building's site should never be abandoned. In effect, this meant that if the City wanted reintegration, it would be based around George Square.

Appleton had convinced himself that he had satisfied one of the conditions imposed by the City, that alteration of the south, east and west sides of the square would not be sought unless there was no other satisfactory scheme for the University. The Post-War Development Committee therefore recommended the dual development of George Square plus research facilities at West Mains Farm. This was approved by the University Court in December 1949.[44]

SIR EDWARD APPLETON'S FIRST DECADE

Sir Edward had moved swiftly since arriving in Edinburgh for, although the saga of George Square was to continue, the University had a cogent development plan with which he could approach the City, and the University was moving forward on some early post-war buildings. This was not simply about providing new academic buildings to meet the needs of the proposed expansion, but also improvements to the University in terms of the immediate problems of overcrowding and, most importantly, the social and spiritual wellbeing of staff and students.

Since the University was now bulging at the seams with students, examinations posed severe accommodation problems. Every building with a large enough room had to be requisitioned, even the Pollock Memorial Hall and the Barrie Memorial Theatre, although Donald Pollock maintained that the terms of his trust limited use to student amenities. In 1948 the University had purchased the old Gaiety Theatre (previously the Operetta House), conveniently opposite Old College, and a scheme was drafted to convert the building to provide two examination halls of 300ft². But this was still not enough space and some additional property (no. 3 Chambers Street) was acquired for a new and larger building. The architect Kininmonth produced a draft scheme, approved by the University Court in May 1949, and was instructed to prepare sketch plans for an examination centre costing £175,000. The University Grants Committee approved the scheme in April 1950. At a time of rationing of building materials, being grant-aided meant that a building licence from the Ministry of Works was not required. The City quickly granted consent and the demolition of the theatre, so briefly a University building, began in April 1951.[45] Sir Edward officially opened the new building as Adam House in May 1955.

As the 1950s drew to a close, plans were in preparation for several major works at King's Buildings, including new buildings for the Animal Breeding Research Organisation, the Departments of Botany and Forestry, as well as extensions for zoology and geology, and a new refectory, with architects already appointed. Planning was also in hand for the veterinary field station at the Easter Bush estate, and for a proposed future redevelopment of High School Yards. Meanwhile, the arts faculty buildings at the new city centre campus, based around George Square, were about to commence.

With the University's full-scale expansion programme having begun, and a period of prodigious building about to commence, the committee system that had been employed to progress the many schemes was reorganised to deal with the increased volume of work. The University Development Committee remained the main steering group and advisory panel to the University Court, and the Principal was its chairman. A Major Buildings Committee, formed in 1958, took responsibility for dealing with the architects, collecting the brief from the user groups and all the detailed planning work. Robert Matthew, the Professor of Architecture, was considered the person most qualified to convene this committee. The Major Buildings Committee appointed various ad-hoc committees and advisory panels for individual buildings, and it reported to the University Development

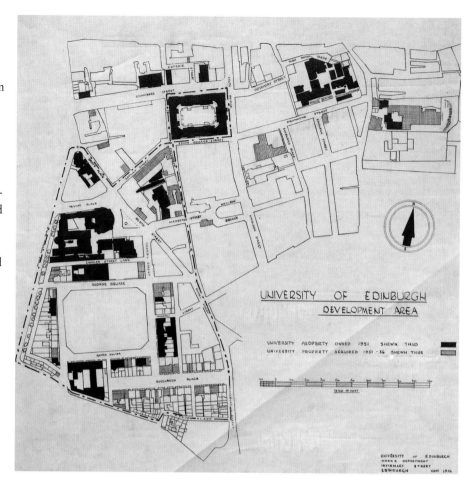

Committee in the first instance. The Works Committee now concentrated on repairs and maintenance, and some minor building work. A Minor Buildings Committee was also created to concentrate on smaller works of alteration and extension, of which there were to be a substantial number.

BUILDINGS 1940–1960
GEORGE SQUARE

In December 1950 Appleton attended a meeting of the City's Planning Committee to report on his careful re-examination of the University's redevelopment plan. He invited the City to schedule the George Square area for redevelopment, because the University would soon have a design for the north side of the square. The Planning Committee was convinced by his argument and resolved to propose to the full city council that development should proceed on that basis, although each building would require individual consent. In the following January, however, the Planning Committee heard representations from other interested parties, who stressed that they were not aiming to thwart the University's plans, but only trying to ensure that buildings of architectural and historical interest should be preserved.[46] The Planning Committee adhered to its previous recommendations.

193 Plan of proposed development area in 1956. Properties marked in black were owned by the University before 1951. The large number of purchases made between 1951 and 1956 under Sir Edward Appleton's tenure as Principal are hatched in grey.

University of Edinburgh Estates Collection

194 Competition-winning entry by Walter Ramsay of the Glasgow firm, McNair, Elder & Ridley, for the medical extension scheme on the north side of George Square, 1951

At this stage, Appleton might have been justified in thinking that the matter was drawing to a favourable conclusion. But the city council was not unanimous in its support for the redevelopment of the square, and the pressure from the amenity societies was unremitting. Therefore, in February 1951, the City agreed to the principle of redevelopment, but not unconditionally, as a motion was passed requiring that no plan entailing destruction of the façades of the other three sides of the square should be submitted unless accompanied by another design, by an architect of standing, which retained the façades. This motion was unprecedented, and legally dubious. The Provost Sir Andrew Murray described it as a compromise, but the City wanted both redevelopment *and* preservation. Aside from the expense of having to submit two schemes, there was the obvious danger that the easy option for the City would be to accept the façade retention scheme. But would a scheme of that sort actually work? There was a glimmer of hope, though, because there had been no outright demand for retention and the town clerk's letter to Appleton clarified the intention that the desire was for preservation 'unless it materially threatens the objective of a liberated and reintegrated University of proud proportions and commanding design worthy of the city and its ancient college'.[47] The objectors clearly felt that they had achieved their aim, for surely the University would either leave the rest of George Square alone or produce a scheme that retained the façades. But their complacency, resulting from the City's ambiguous ruling, was to cost them most of the square in the long run.

Against this background, the result of the competition for the medical buildings was announced in February 1951. A.G.R. Mackenzie, president of the Royal Incorporation of Architects in Scotland, awarded the first prize to the Glaswegian architect, Walter Ramsay, for a design which, although flawed, he felt best answered the University's requirements and the City's condition that it should be in harmony with the general characteristics of its surroundings.[48] It was described in the architectural press as 'a modern interpretation of the classical and Georgian style'.[49] The bird's-eye perspective of Ramsay's design certainly shows continuity of its fenestration with that of the gaunt tenements in the surrounding streets [fig.194], but the massing was clearly derived from Holden's scheme as featured in the Abercrombie Plan. In style, it was a pared-down 1930s classicism and, in truth, the façade was one of unrelieved monotony. Ramsay opted for a steel frame structure consisting of a central five-storey block, flanked by four-storey blocks. These are linked by a pair of four-storey staircase blocks, each with an entrance. At Middle Meadow Walk, outside the building line of the square, a seven-storey block, the first phase, is linked to the old Medical School. A small block bridging the entrance to a courtyard connects this to the rest of the proposed building on George Square.

The University already had outline consent from the City for the proposed medical extension. However, detailed planning applications would have to be made at each stage, and approval received from the University Grants Committee for these. So, although the design was disappointing, there was a programme for commencement of the first phase. The issue of the appearance of the façade to George Square would have to be addressed, too. Mackenzie felt that the design was in harmony with the rest of the square, as it then existed, but others may not have shared that view. He also imagined that it would fit well with a completely redesigned square. But this would be simpler when the fate of the rest of the square was certain. In the meantime Ramsay could begin preparing detailed plans for the west wing.

Further architectural authority was added to the University's cause with the appointment of Robert Matthew to the vacant Forbes chair in architecture, in 1953. There was no Department of Architecture in the University at that time, but his was a dual appointment, with the additional role of head of architecture at Edinburgh College of Art. Matthew was a public service architect, best known for the Royal Festival Hall, on London's South Bank, which he designed with Leslie Martin. His father, John, as a partner in Lorimer & Matthew, had been responsible for several of the University's King's Buildings. Upon his appointment, Matthew agreed to advise the University on how to achieve its architectural aims, joining its new University Development Committee.

The University Development Committee now required a planning consultant who could get consent for the medical buildings, provide a development plan for George Square, and also deal with the City's requirement for an alternative scheme with façade retention. Several architects were discussed, including Abercrombie, William Holford, Hugh Casson and J.L. Gleave. Matthew favoured Holford or Basil Spence, the latter especially, as he was 'local'.

THE BASIL SPENCE PLAN

Basil Spence was local in the sense that he had studied at Edinburgh College of Art and started his practice in Edinburgh, although he now lived in London and had an office there too. But he was very well known in Scotland, since his design of exhibition pavilions of the 1930s. His thriving firm, established in 1946 when he left the Rowand Anderson practice, was undertaking all manner of architectural work, including university science buildings, hospitals, schools and housing schemes. In 1951, he became internationally known for his work at the South Bank, during the Festival of Britain, and then for winning the competition to design a new Coventry Cathedral in the same year. As a result of this he was frequently featured in the media as a moderate advocate of modern architecture and design.

Spence agreed to help, and attended the meeting of the University Grants Committee in November 1954, where Appleton outlined his requirement for a campus that struck a balance between reasonable seclusion and undesirable isolation. Having considered the matter, Spence confessed that there was little he could do until certain decisions had been made about what was to be accommodated in the campus area. Appleton certainly did not want residences for professors, student halls or administration buildings in George Square. Neither did he want science buildings there, with one exception. Acceptable new uses might be: the library, mathematics, geography and commerce departments, and a University chapel. As a starting point, Spence suggested a site for the library, on the south-west side of the square, and outlined a six-step procedure for putting the University's plans into action: 1. Make a survey of existing uses. 2. Reach agreement on preferred locations for specific buildings. 3. Produce a block plan dividing the area into suitable development sites. 4. Create a model. 5. Draw detailed block plans for individual sites. 6. Commence design for individual buildings. He also advised the University to begin acquiring property in the area, both for building sites and to rehouse displaced tenants.

With some amendment to Ramsay's design, Spence was sure that he could get consent from the City for the first phase. Once that was built, there could be no

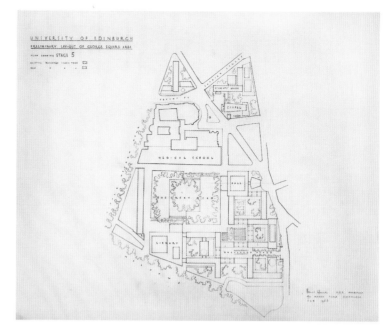

obstacle to further phases. Redevelopment of the rest of the square would follow naturally.

The architect was confident, but what of the City's desire for façade retention? Spence felt that, given the scale and layout of the medical extension, it would be impossible to retain the character of the square thereafter, contrary to what A.G.R Mackenzie thought. Strangely, no-one had argued before that the redevelopment of the north side would alter the character of the square. Spence's argument was that façade retention would therefore be pointless, as well as destructive to the scheme. On the other hand, the entire west side, which he found the most interesting, could viably be retained and restored, for the use of smaller departments.

The new development scheme was a radical departure from Abercrombie and Holden in terms of massing. The central gardens remained untouched, and the building

195 Preliminary layout of George Square by Basil Spence, 1955
HES [Sir Basil Spence Archive: DP 012577]

196 Sketch perspective of George Square from the south-east by Basil Spence in 1955–6. Interlocking courtyards were to replace the 18th-century houses and tenements of George Square and Buccleuch Place.
HES [Sir Basil Spence Archive: DP 012783]

197 A sketch by Basil Spence of the proposed arrangement and landscaping of George Square, about 1955

HES [Sir Basil Spence Archive: DP 012579]

line of the square was discernible but, instead of monolithic blocks to each side, a series of linear blocks were arranged to form semi-enclosed courtyards around the square and Buccleuch Place, much like Gropius's Graduate Centre at Harvard. The hub of the campus was to be the library, used by everyone at the University, located at the south-west corner. This was balanced by a block of similar size to the north-west. Low, linked buildings predominated, though taller blocks, on a west–east orientation, appeared towards the east side. Beyond the square, to the east, taller blocks were proposed for future projects. The massing and arrange-ment of the medical extension, with the exception of the first phase, had also been amended drastically. A taller block at the east matched the first phase on the west, low buildings lay in between and an open court was created revealing the south elevations of the music school and

the University Union. The omission of the large medical assembly hall, which Ramsay included in his scheme, would allow this open space and a rearrangement of the heights. As Spence put it: 'If we can amend the Medical School so that the students can continue on foot through successive courtyards right up to the McEwan Hall, then we will have a chance of getting a co-ordinated scheme with a heart.'[50]

Spence's plan was largely his speculation upon the University's likely building requirements over the forth-coming years. The library was a fixed point, and 'arts' was allocated the south-east corner of the square. The large square block on the north-east was indeterminate. It was initially labelled 'Convocation Hall', although McEwan Hall already fulfilled that function. The Pollock Trust site, at Bristo Street, was carefully reserved for 'Students' Unions'. However, Spence did demonstrate a flexible

198 Basil Spence's view of his
proposed George Square skyline, seen from the Meadows

HES [Sir Basil Spence Archive:
DP 012580]

layout, permeable in terms of circulation, within which individual buildings might be inserted. It was also far more amenable and susceptible to being built in phases than Holden's monumental blocks.

But when the University sought consent for the first phase of the Medical School, the City's Planning Committee would not consider the application without knowing what the other phases would be like. In July 1955, therefore, Appleton and Charles Stewart accompanied Spence to meet the Planning Committee. While the Principal stressed the urgency of an early commencement to building, the architect, armed with plans, photographs and perspectives, explained how the medical building façades could be humanised with some detailing, such as balconies and, for future phases, colonnades, and the overall height could be reduced. Subsequent phases, which would be subject to individual consents, need not be like Ramsay's prizewinning design, as the massing could be rearranged.

But the discussion went further than just the medical extension, because Spence also demonstrated how this would relate to the square in the context of both its present and future forms, explaining that the buildings on the south and east sides would ultimately have to be demolished in order to achieve the new campus. George Square would not be destroyed, but most of the buildings would be replaced by others of similar scale, but architecturally better, he argued.

The Planning Committee, clearly impressed by Spence's presentation, recommended that consent be given in the following terms:

The foregoing recommendation is made by the committee on the clear understanding, to which Sir Edward Appleton assured the committee that the University were a party, that acceptance of the present proposal is based on the University's intention to proceed, as opportunity offers with the preparation of their scheme for the development of the University in conformity with the broad general lines which were enunciated and illustrated by the Principal and Mr Spence. The various phases and stages of that development would be the subject of detailed consideration by the University and the Corporation from time to time.[51]

This was outline consent for the whole medical extension, and certainly permission for phase one, which meant that building work could begin. But, more than that, it was also tantamount to consent, in principle, for the whole University development along the general lines of Spence's plan. With this, the issue of an alternative proposal with façade retention was seemingly resolved.

It was very bold of Appleton to get Spence to outline the redevelopment of the whole George Square area, when only the proposals for the north side of the square were requested. However, it also had the flavour of an ultimatum, with the latent threat of complete removal to the King's Buildings site, should consent be denied. Spence's perspectives were probably a compelling factor, as they evoked the atmosphere of a campus of modernist buildings with sculptures and water features. A view from the Meadows showed how the skyline could be improved with a series of tower blocks stepping away from the square towards Salisbury Crags in the east.

Sir Edward was now satisfied that all the conditions imposed upon the University had been met, and that the business of obtaining funding and designs for buildings could begin. That the amenity societies, who were seeking preservation of George Square, chose to interpret this outcome differently is an instance of subjectivity clouding judgement. The south and east sides of the square were as good as lost, as Spence had carried the day with his scheme. Everything else was a matter of detail. The preservationists claim to the contrary implies that the full town council was somehow misled by the Lord Provost when it accepted the recommendations of the Planning Committee. Possibly, one or two councillors may have misunderstood the implications, but there was a clear majority of thirty-four to sixteen in favour. Presumably, the apparent compromise of full restoration of the west side of the square was enough to satisfy those previously uncertain. A warrant to begin the foundation work was granted the following month.

Lord Provost, Sir John Dunbar, later said of his predecessor, Sir John G. Banks:

The Lord Provost said that it was a condition of the general approval in principle of the University's proposals for the redevelopment of George Square that the various phases and stages would be the subject of detailed consideration from time to time. He wanted to make it clear that the subject matter of future discussion could only be on matters of detail and not whether the north, east and south sides of the square were to be demolished and redeveloped on general lines indicated in 1955.

To proceed on any other footing would be a gross breach of faith on the part of the Corporation who, by their decision of 1955, clearly gave the University to understand that they were free to proceed with the furthering of their proposals with all which that might involve in the expenditure of time and money.[52]

The first phase of the medical extension received rather more detailed consideration, however, than Spence had

clockwise from above

199 A model of George Square, prepared for Basil Spence about 1956. Ramsay's medical extension stretches across the whole of the north side of the square.

HES [Sir Basil Spence Archive: SC 1117894]

200 A second iteration of Basil Spence's George Square model, probably dating from 1957, when a gap was created to link George Square to the McEwan Hall

HES [Sir Basil Spence Archive: SC 1030942]

201 A model by RMJM of about 1958 showing the first building proposed for George Square under Basil Spence's layout, an arts tower, later built to designs by Robert Matthew as David Hume Tower

HES [Sir Basil Spence Archive: SC 1030943]

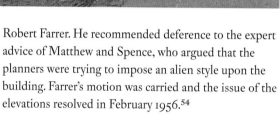

anticipated. His 'humanisation' consisted of giving the elevation to Middle Meadow Walk a skin of artificial rubble stone, in order to relate to both the Royal Infirmary buildings opposite and to west George Square. Here, he also gave the staircase tower convexity. On the south façade, the rubble texture was paired with a central section in smooth ashlar to provide contrast. At ground floor level full-height windows were set behind a group of square columns sheathed in green slate, as the beginning of the proposed colonnade, and the plinth was given an iron railing. But when consent was sought, it was not given. There was no objection to the demolition of no. 15, but the Planning Committee members all had ideas about further detailing, such as ironwork balconies and pilasters.[53] This might have gone on for a long time, but the University appealed against this interference to the City's Dean of Guild,

Robert Farrer. He recommended deference to the expert advice of Matthew and Spence, who argued that the planners were trying to impose an alien style upon the building. Farrer's motion was carried and the issue of the elevations resolved in February 1956.[54]

THE BATTLE FOR GEORGE SQUARE

Having realised the implications of the City's outline consent, the amenity societies renewed their opposition, with the Edinburgh Georgian Society joining the campaign.[55] They called for work on the medical extension to be halted and for a public inquiry to be held, but the Secretary of State, John Maclay, declined to interfere with the University's development, despite the pleas of some apparently influential people, including the Earl of Wemyss, chairman of the Council of the National Trust for Scotland and of the Royal Commission on the Ancient and Historical Monuments of Scotland. They claimed that the redevelopment of George Square, which had now commenced, had not been featured in the public inquiry into the City Development Plan in 1954, therefore they had been given no opportunity to raise objections. However, Holden's proposal had featured in the Abercrombie Plan, and there had been no objection to the creation of an educational / cultural zone. Had the objectors wished to save and preserve George Square, they ought to have objected to the zoning, the principle of reintegration, development on the north side of the square, or all three. They were now campaigning to save merely the façades of the east and south sides. It was unreasonable to expect the government to thwart the University's development for this. But still they persisted.

John Maclay was well aware of the national situation regarding the expansion of university education, of which Edinburgh was only a small, but significant, part. The full effect of the population bulge of the 1940s would impact upon the universities by the mid-1960s, with the forecast of a 50 per cent increase in the student population by 1968, and possibly 70 per cent by the 1970s. Appleton was determined that Edinburgh would play its part by having 12,000 students by the mid-1970s, compared to 3,700 in 1938. The Secretary of State sought the opinion of the chairman of the Historic Buildings Council, who judged the square as a valuable urban layout, as a whole, but the individual buildings of little merit.[56] But George Square was no longer a whole, with the north side already disrupted and its redevelopment generally accepted. The National Trust for Scotland began to distance itself from the issue and the Cockburn Association finally accepted the inevitable. Only the Edinburgh Georgian Society was now pressing for preservation, it seemed.

As specific building projects and the funding became clarified, Spence and Matthew worked on expanding the development scheme and refining the detail. The High School Yards area was incorporated into the scheme as a future development. Indeed, Spence's practice was engaged with the conversion of the old Surgeons' Hall, for natural philosophy, by the end of 1957, and he had a draft scheme for maths / physics on the site of the old surgical hospital, at Drummond Street.

Architects for the George Square development began to be appointed in 1956, with Basil Spence invited to design the main library, although it would be some time before funding was available for that. Robert Matthew, who had launched his own practice in 1956, got the commission for the group of buildings for the arts and social sciences faculties, for which a site was allocated on the south-east of George Square. In the foreseeable future, it was thought that seven blocks, built in three phases, could be realised here. This would provide 300 tutorial rooms, twenty-two lecture rooms and thirteen departmental libraries. By the end of 1958, Matthew had an outline scheme. The first phase would be a fourteen-storey tower, at the south end of east George Square, with an associated lecture theatre block to the east of this, at Windmill Street. The second phase would provide a four-storey tutorial building, with an attached lecture block, on the east side of the square. A 600-seat lecture theatre, for the use of all faculties, and another tutorial block, would be built on the south side of the square, as the third phase. This third phase, together with the proposed library, would complete the new south side of the square. Thus, it was determined that George Square would become the home of arts and social sciences, first-year science, medicine and the main library.

The University launched an appeal for donations for its proposed developments in 1959, and Appleton must have been taken aback at the opposition expressed when he addressed the General Council of the University.[57] There were further calls for a public inquiry, and the Secretary of State, anxious to be rid of the matter, proposed a working party made up of representatives of the University, the City and the amenity societies, to investigate whether there were any practical alternatives to Matthew's arts faculty scheme. The University agreed, so long as they could continue with their plans for phase one: the arts tower. But Charles Stewart's statement to the University Court made the position clear: 'The Principal is extremely anxious that all members of the Court should understand that this commits the University to nothing except joint examination, while at the same time it does allow it to proceed with its new arts building.'[58]

The working group consisted of the University Secretary, Charles Stewart, and his assistant R. Maxwell Young, and John Hardie Glover (Spence's partner), representing the University. The amenity societies were represented by John Kerr, Robert Hurd and A.T. McIndoe (planning consultant to the National Trust for Scotland). T.T. Hewitson, the Town Planning Officer, represented the City. Robert Matthew declined to be involved, since he was satisfied with his design and was working on the details of the tower and its associated lecture block.

Confusion arose, however, as several of the parties, including Scottish Office staff, were under the impression that the arts tower could be built without the destruction of any of the existing buildings in the square, whereas the University's involvement in the working party was on the condition that the tower would not be affected by any outcome. But, while Matthew had positioned the tower outwith the square itself, on the back gardens of nos 47–51, at Windmill Lane, because the City wished to limit the height of the buildings within the square, his design was incompatible with retention of those buildings – the lecture theatre block was to be on the site of nos 40–6 Windmill Street, to the east. The arts faculty group design utilised a podium system linking the buildings at basement level, which entailed excavations requiring the removal of nos 47–51, together with the tenement at nos 26–9 Buccleuch Place.

When Matthew stated that he would never have been associated with the idea that the arts tower could proceed without demolition, the Earl of Wemyss suggested deception, and the Secretary of State had to answer a parliamentary question on the matter. Maclay and Appleton appeared not to have actually realised the incompatibility at the instigation of the working party, but Hurd understood that the University was simply going through the motions.[59] Hurd found himself in a difficult situation of conflicting interests, as he had also accepted the role as conservation architect for the buildings on the west side of the square, following Spence's recommendation. He considered resigning this future commission, but Spence saw no necessity for that.

Hurd and McIndoe did manage to produce an alternative scheme for the arts faculty group. It consisted of façade retention, together with new buildings concentrated on Buccleuch Place, Buccleuch Street, Windmill Street and Crichton Street, with a site for the library beside the old church at Chapel Street. This proposed that the upper floors of the buildings on the south and east sides of the square be converted to tutorial and research rooms, with lecture theatres at ground floor level.[60] It was carefully worked out, but based on the first principle of preservation of façades, rather than on meeting the University's immediate and forthcoming needs. The working party was given two months to create an acceptable plan, but it was wound up after six weeks, on 11 February 1960.[61] In Appleton's statement to the press he claimed that there was a complete lack of agreement, except on the principle that Matthew's scheme was best for the University.[62]

Wemyss accused the Secretary of State of not giving proper consideration to the alternative scheme, but Maclay had sought expert advice on the technical aspects. His advisors calculated that for Matthew to redesign his plans would have taken at least a year, with no guarantee of consent from the City at the end. Hurd's scheme also assumed an immediate commencement on conversion of many buildings, which were all still occupied and in use, whereas Spence and Matthew had calculated the phases of building and the rehousing of departments and occupants during the redevelopment. There were other criticisms too, such as inadequate circulation space and lavatories for the 2,000 students who would use the facilities on a daily basis. There were no car parking spaces either, which Matthew had included at sub-podium level in the third phase. Difficulties also arose over whether the necessary floor loadings could be achieved within the old masonry and timber buildings. The fire authorities, already concerned about safety within the buildings previously converted to student residences and unions, might be difficult to satisfy with further conversions.[63] Essentially, it was all too complicated. The amenity societies were not unhappy with the University's annexation of the square, with its choice of architects, or with modern architecture generally. They were simply arguing for an alternative scheme.

Despite the Secretary of State's ruling, Wemyss continued to demand resiting of the arts tower, but the University now had consent for the necessary demolitions and, had Maclay called in this consent,

the University would have had to replan its buildings and miss the starting date stipulated by the University Grants Committee.[64] This would have been impossible to justify, since the Scottish universities were committed to increasing student numbers and the government was a party to that commitment. Demolition work began in the spring of 1960, with the foundations for the arts faculty buildings commenced in the autumn, and the 'Battle for George Square' was over.[65]

Notwithstanding the prolonged controversy over George Square, Appleton steadily made significant steps toward expansion, reintegration and modernisation, with the stated aim of making the University one of the foremost in Britain. There was now a commitment to take a further 750 students by the mid-1960s, supported by the University Grants Committee grants of £2.4m. But this was not enough to match his ambitions. The appeal for funds, launched in 1959, demonstrated considerable support for the project, and he even donated 1,000 guineas himself to get it started. The brochure for the appeal concentrates on the serious overcrowding of facilities, building works then in hand, and future plans. It also lists a notable array of patrons of the appeal, drawn from the arts, sciences, politics and the aristocracy.[66] No doubt this was aided by Appleton's success in persuading HRH The Duke of Edinburgh to become the Chancellor to the University. Although a largely symbolic and ceremonial role, it gave Prince Philip's royal stamp of approval to the University's endeavours and encouraged support. Even Sir Donald Pollock, who had already endowed a major trust fund for the benefit of the University, while disagreeing its policy, made a further contribution to the appeal fund.

THE PROPOSED UNIVERSITY CHAPEL

In 1954, Edinburgh was the only Scottish university lacking a chapel, although it should be remembered that Robert Adam's original design for Old College did include one, but this was omitted when William Playfair amended the plans to complete the building. Subsequently, Greyfriars Kirk was generally used for University services, or St Giles', when the ceremony required a larger and grander venue, such as the installation in 1953 of HRH The Duke of Edinburgh as University Chancellor. It was only in 1949 that Edinburgh's first University Chaplain, David H.C. Read, was appointed. He proposed that an appropriate building in the redeveloped George Square might be a chapel. Although Basil Spence was unable to find a place for a future chapel within the square, he proposed a site on the corner of Bristo Street and Marshall Street, as indicated by a campanile in his development model of 1956.

The Revd James C. Blackie, successor to Read as chaplain, was keen to pursue the project. In his report to the University Court he asserted: 'There is increasing

204 Bristo Street chapel
proposal scheme by Basil
Spence of 1956

HES [Sir Basil Spence Archive:
SC 1117889]

sympathy towards any movement of a religious
nature in this generation.'[67] The University Court was
sympathetic to the new chapel proposal, as was the
Principal, who was a committed Methodist. However,
while the University Grants Committee was a broadly
Christian organisation, its sympathy could not extend
as far as funding such a building using Treasury money.
Nevertheless, Blackie, with all the fervour of a new
appointee, felt sure that a public appeal for funds would
be successful, and so the Chapel Appeal Committee was
duly constituted, in July 1956. Basil Spence was asked to
produce a sketch scheme for the appeal, together with
cost estimates, and to choose the most suitable site.[68]
He drew up a perspective and a plan, in his inimitable
style, and his quantity surveyor produced an estimate
of £257,000, including demolitions, furnishings and
site layout. The selected site was contentious, and
Pollock was hostile to the very notion of a University
chapel, especially as it required the demolition of the
Barrie Memorial Theatre, the Pollock Memorial Hall
and Seceders' Land. The University Court approved
of Spence's choice of site. It should be said that the
University was anxious to be rid of the Barrie Theatre
and the Pollock Memorial Hall, both of which entailed
an expensive burden of upkeep. Sir Donald Pollock
next insisted that the Memorial Hall already *was* the
University chapel and he would sanction no demolition. Spence had chosen the chapel site because of its
commanding position at the entrance to the University
precinct, where the tower would provide a focal point.
He thought that he might be able to move it slightly to
avoid the Memorial Hall. But it was all to no avail. There

seemed to be no prospect of commencement for at least
six to ten years, so, rather than proceed with the project
on an unsuitable site, the scheme was postponed, and
the funding appeal shelved, in October 1957.[69]

CHAMBERS STREET

Chambers Street was created as part of Edinburgh's
'improvements' of 1867, and laid out by the City's
Superintendent of Works, David Cousin, who dictated
the height of three storeys and, to an extent, the
appearance of the buildings on the north side, which
follow a sort of French Renaissance style, with Mansard
roofs and dormer windows. The University had a policy
of acquiring property in Chambers Street, whenever it
became available. From the late 1940s the University
was involved in three major projects in the street: a new
examination building, Adam House; the Edinburgh
Dental Hospital and School; and the University Staff
Club (now Charles Stewart House).

ADAM HOUSE

The University's first completely new building of the
post-war era, Adam House [fig.205], is named after
Adam Square, which occupied the site until 1867 (the
Adam family of architects had developed the lands
off the Cowgate from the 1720s). The brief was an
interesting one for William Kininmonth as the building
was to be multi-functional, not just for exams. It would
be an asset to the cultural life of the city, hosting
exhibitions, and musical and social events. There was
to be a sprung dance floor in one hall while, in the
basement, a fully equipped theatre/cinema, with seating
for more than 200 people. The City was particularly
welcoming of the University's contribution to the
cultural precinct as it had begun its annual Edinburgh
International Festival in 1947, and was now hoping to
expand this. More arts venues were certainly required.
University events were also to be accommodated,
including student drama and functions, which would be
better served here than in the Barrie Memorial Theatre
and Pollock Hall, both of which would eventually be
demolished. It was also intended to provide a permanent
home for the Torrie Art Collection, received by the
University in 1837, with special niches inserted to display
the bronzes.[70]

The reinforced concrete structure was inserted into
an existing city block and follows its pattern of three
storeys plus attic; however a further three storeys lie
beneath the level of the street. Examination halls are
placed to the rear (north) of the four upper storeys,
with a theatre/cinema in the upper basement and all
the services below this. These rooms could seat 750
examinees, or a total audience of up to 1,400 for other
events. In plan, the oval entrance hall is flanked by

curved stairs and top-lit by a circular light well and cupola. Lifts and cloakrooms flank the corridors leading to the examination halls, which are segregated behind glazed screens and doors and are lit by opaque steel-framed glazed panels to the north. The basement storeys have glass bricks to the north. The examination room in the attic storey, doubling as an art gallery, is top-lit.[71]

While the rear of the building was faced with concrete slabs and glazed panels, the front was sheathed in polished Northumberland stone, and given traditional timber sash and case windows. The stone was chosen for its greyness, and as a substitute for the Craigleith stone of Old College, that quarry having closed. On the front elevation, Kininmonth has carefully maintained the cornice and eaves lines of the buildings that flank it, and thus that of the floor levels. In fact, one of the assumptions of the brief was that the University would ultimately acquire and replace the other buildings in the block, therefore the treatment here was to be one that could be repeated in an acceptable manner to east and west.

From 1955, the building functioned both as examination halls and as a cultural and social venue, as intended, and the University Dramatic Society was centred there for many years. Its increasingly popular use as a Fringe venue, however, has resulted in much wear and tear, with the comings and goings of heavy equipment. In 2015, following the University's merger with Edinburgh College of Art, the building was altered to provide studio space for the recently-formed Edinburgh School of Architecture and Landscape Architecture, with the basement theatre used for lectures. Ostensibly, this is a temporary arrangement since it continues to be let as a venue for the Festival Fringe during the vacation period, and there are plans for new dedicated studios elsewhere.

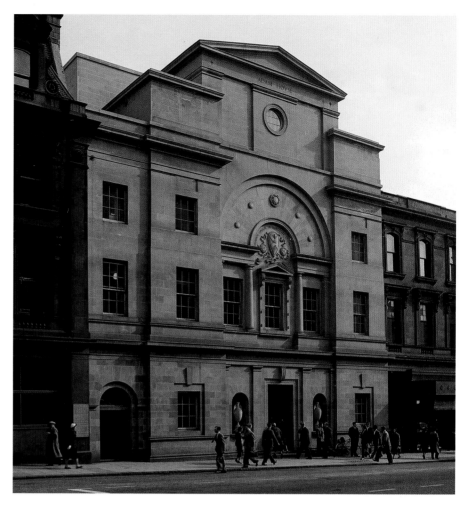

205 Adam House in Chambers Street, designed by William Kininmonth, 1949–54

HES [Tom and Sybil Gray Collection: SC 680325]

FORMER DENTAL HOSPITAL

While Kininmonth was building Adam House at the east end of Chambers Street, he was also undertaking a job at the west end in which the University had an interest. This was the reconstruction of the Edinburgh Dental Hospital and School. Rowand Anderson & Paul & Partners had drafted a scheme to modernise and extend the existing Dental Hospital before the Second World War and it was the subject of a public appeal by the Royal Infirmary, which ran the institution, in 1937. By 1948 funding had been sought by the University from the Department of Education, for the teaching element, while the infirmary was claiming funding for the hospital under the nascent National Health Service. Even so, the financial situation was such that the project was scaled down to a renovation of existing facilities. Reorientation of the entrance was involved and here Kininmonth revised the initial treatment in the light of his Adam House design, as he felt the two buildings represented western and eastern gateways to the street. The Dental Hospital entrance was therefore given similar pilasters to those of Adam House. That building still exists, although it is now in commercial use.[72] In the 1970s the University would commission a new Dental Hospital and School at Crichton Street, by other architects.

206 The former Dental Hospital in Chambers Street, photographed in 1989 before its sale by the NHS

HES [SC 1385123]

CHARLES STEWART HOUSE (FORMER EDINBURGH UNIVERSITY STAFF CLUB)

The two original buildings on the site have a complicated history. The eastern part, formerly nos 9–15, was designed by David Cousin's co-architect John Lessels as a commercial block in the 1870s. There were shop fronts with pilasters and plate glass on the ground floor which no longer exist. Of fairly plain appearance, and built of smooth ashlar, it has ten bays to Chambers Street, and a bay on the chamfered corner to Guthrie Street. A pair of giant pilasters frame the eastern four bays. The upper storeys have elliptical window heads, and dormer windows with arched heads are set into a slated Mansard roof. While the upper window apertures are original, the replacement window frames lack glazing bars.[73]

No. 16 was designed by David Rhind for the Church of Scotland's Education Committee, as a normal school (a training establishment), and then it was acquired by the University in 1914 for the Institute of Mathematics.[74] It is smaller and rather more ornate than its partner, with only three bays to Chambers Street. The basement storeys had a further conversion into a student refectory at the same time as the staff club was created, in 1959. In 1962, the upper storeys were converted into a new home for the women's union by Basil Spence & Partners.[75] The refectory at no.16 continued in use as such until 1970 when the refectory at Potterrow opened, but the building continued to function as an annexe of the Students' Union, and as a Festival venue, known as Chambers Street House, until the 1990s.

In 1956 the University converted nos 9–15 to create the staff club, which opened in 1959, with the work carried out by Basil Spence & Partners. The interiors were completely altered at this time, as was the fenestration of the ground floor, and there was a new single main entrance with service and emergency exit doors to the sides and rear of the building. The club provided a range of social facilities for staff of all faculties and for visiting academics. It closed in 1998 and the building was once again gutted, but photographic records illustrate the Festival Style interiors in 1960; the setting for so much of the University's life during the later 20th century.

The basement storeys had squash courts and various facilities, plus a bar, wine cellar and a caretaker's flat. The ground floor had two lounges and a bar and snack bar, with kitchens to the rear. The first floor contained both waiter-service and self-service dining rooms. A library and reading room, public and private lounges and committee rooms were on the second floor. On the third floor there were billiards and games rooms, as well as a three-bedroomed flat and three bedrooms with en-suite bathrooms, for visiting academics. Plans and interior perspectives were published in the *Edinburgh University Gazette* in May 1957, and the work was complete in 1959. Meanwhile, costs had risen to £100,000, although this now included additional items, such as guest accommodation and the student refectory, of which the University Grants Committee contribution was £65,000.[76]

The staff club facilities were regarded as some of the best in the country at the time. The furnishings and decor received much care and attention, as the

207 The former staff club interior, designed by Basil Spence & Partners in 1956, at Charles Stewart House in Chambers Street, photographed by Henk Snoek, 1960
HES [SC 1044283, SC 1044299]

architects assisted the choices of the advisory panel and provided them with catalogues of furniture and samples of fabrics from the Finmar company, which was Britain's major importer of Scandinavian modern design. The panel included the Professor of Fine Art, David Talbot Rice, and the University Secretary, Charles Stewart, with their wives enlisted to make sure that the interiors were not too masculine, for this was not to be like the stuffy Victorian gentlemen's clubs with which they were all too familiar.[77] All was to be light and airy, and contemporary. Like its near neighbour, Adam House, it perfectly evoked the Festival Style of the era, having Danish copper light shades, curtains and wallpapers with striking patterns, tables and chairs designed by Jacobsen and Aalto, as well as bespoke timber fittings and pine panelling. Some of the original rubble walls were exposed to provide a contrast with the new glazed timber partitions. The *pièce de résistance* was the

concrete flying staircase, with its white steel balustrades. Leonard Rosoman, who was a lecturer at Edinburgh College of Art at the time, was commissioned to paint a large panel for one of the dining rooms.[78] The interiors were featured in the *Architectural Review* in 1960.[79]

The staff club remained at the centre of university life for many years, and much of the University's great post-war expansion was discussed there. Professor Talbot Rice, who disagreed with the redevelopment of George Square, was a mainstay of the staff club project, as was Charles Stewart, who largely directed it. The University's architects, such as William Kininmonth and Hardie Glover, with their wives, were part of the milieu and frequent guests. Sir Edward Appleton and his successors as Principal would meet with their staff and academics from Chambers Street's other institutions, including the Heriot-Watt College during its transition into a university.[80]

208 The former staff club interior, designed by Basil Spence & Partners in 1956, at Charles Stewart House in Chambers Street, photographed by Henk Snoek, 1960
HES [SC 1044284]

Together with Adam House, the University staff club was an important social centre for the Edinburgh Festival, in that era, but gradually lost popularity and support as alternative places for staff to dine and socialise arrived to serve a changing Edinburgh society. It closed in 1998 and the building was converted once again for the University's finance department, incorporating the adjacent building at no. 16 Chambers Street. During conversion the interiors were gutted and reconfigured, with only Spence's staircase, the main staircase and a coffered ceiling of the normal school retained.[81] The fenestration at ground floor level was also redesigned, while the upper pattern of fenestration was retained, but with new window frames fitted.

The building takes its name from Charles H. Stewart, who was University Secretary from 1948 to 1978.

THE PLEASANCE

Originally Bell's Brewery, subsequently part of United Breweries, some of the fabric of the brewery building, at no.46, dates from the 18th century. Following the bankruptcy of United Breweries in 1936, Sir Donald Pollock acquired the property and commissioned Lorimer & Matthew to undertake conversion to a gymnasium, which was then presented to the University. It was in full use by the summer of 1941.

This is a large three-storey edifice of rubble construction with an arched entrance and slate roof, set back from the street behind a courtyard. It is a typical example of Scottish industrial building of the period, now becoming rarer. The north wing appears to be the most ancient part of the structure, the variety of stone types revealing that the masonry was reclaimed from earlier buildings, and the walls are about three feet thick at the base.

The brewery offices, at no. 44, are largely Victorian. They have three storeys and are constructed of rubble, with ashlar dressings, and some structural ironwork. The west elevation, towards the entrance, has a square pend, giving access to the rear of the property. The south elevation, to the courtyard, has canted bay windows.

In 1980, Wheeler & Sproson were commissioned to renovate and enlarge the facilities. This included a large new block to the east. Built of brick, with the roof and upper walls clad in metal sheeting, it has an industrial aesthetic appropriate to the site. A new entrance to the courtyard, from the Pleasance, and a reception block were also constructed. CLWG Architects began a major £5m redevelopment of the complex in 2015 to provide a new societies hub housing a newspaper office, student radio studios, resource centre and film studio as well as the introduction of a lift to improve access.

The Pleasance Complex is a group of buildings currently used for social and cultural events under the auspices of Edinburgh University Students' Association. They all have a complex history before and after being acquired by the University. All of them came to be owned by the Pleasance Trust prior to 1977.

The Pleasance Trust was created in 1913 as a charitable organisation dedicated to the health and wellbeing of the working-class residents of the area, organising educational classes, sports activities and social clubs. It obtained the former Fulton's Brewery property and converted one building to a gymnasium. Sir Donald Pollock probably

209 Plan of the Pleasance
Crown copyright 2017 Ordnance Survey [Licence Number 100021521]

210 Photograph by Francis M. Chrystal of the Campbell Hope and King Brewery buildings in the Pleasance, about 1920
HES [Francis M. Chrystal Collection: SC 1100811]

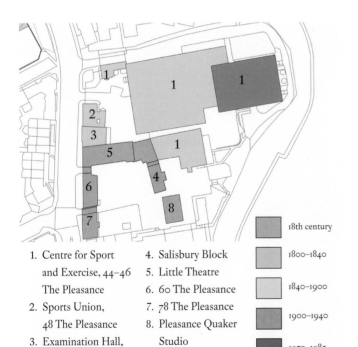

1. Centre for Sport and Exercise, 44–46 The Pleasance
2. Sports Union, 48 The Pleasance
3. Examination Hall, 48A The Pleasance
4. Salisbury Block
5. Little Theatre
6. 60 The Pleasance
7. 78 The Pleasance
8. Pleasance Quaker Studio

18th century
1800–1840
1840–1900
1900–1940
1970–1985

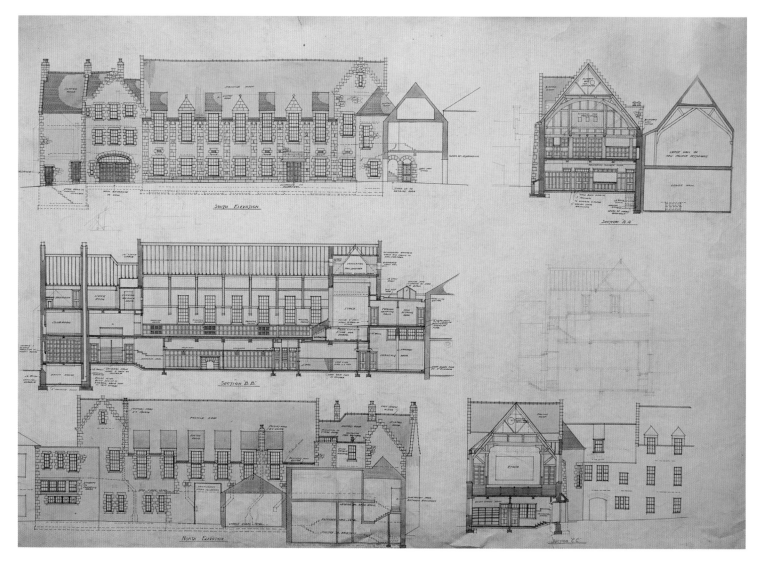

got the idea for his student gymnasium, in another adjacent brewery, from this example. Indeed, the trust's gymnasium was used by the University's Department of Physical Education in its early days. Other buildings were reconstructed in the inter-war years all to designs by James Inch Morrison. The east block, now the Salisbury Building, originally the Welfare Clinic, was built in 1925, and it included an ultraviolet room for the treatment and prevention of tuberculosis and other conditions associated with poverty. Another range, which included the Little Theatre, was added on the north in 1932. Completing the ensemble, in 1937, was the west range towards the street (no.60), with its arched pend leading to the courtyard. Morrison adopted a Scots revival style, borrowing features from the 17th century and from the east coast vernacular. Rubble walls, using the old brewery materials, are twinned with roofs of both pantiles and slates. Crowstep gables are much in evidence, and upper storey windows have wallhead pediments.

The former New College Mission, or Settlement, at nos 48 and 48A, on the north end of the Pleasance

Trust Buildings, preceded the latter as a religious and social project by the Free Church's New College Missionary Society. Their building was designed by Henry Kerr. It comprises two elements. The south block is ecclesiastical, retaining the façade of a former church, with the barest of Gothic detailing in the large traceried upper window while the northern part, of four storeys, displays *fin de siècle* preoccupations. The elliptically arched ground floor windows reveal its vintage. Above this, timbered gables, barge boards and jettied window bays recall contemporary reconstructions at Ramsay Garden and the Lawnmarket in the Old Town, by Patrick Geddes, Henbest Capper, and Sydney Mitchell. It was renovated in 2015 to form multi-use spaces, by CLWG Architects, while exposing the original church roof structure.[82]

The Friends' Meeting House, on the south-east of the complex, was acquired by the trust in 1949. This had been built by the Quakers on part of their burial ground in 1791. A simple rubble structure, with hipped roof, it has some architectural pretensions in the arched windows and the off-centre pedimented classical door

211 Designs of 1930–2 by James Inch Morrison for the addition of the Pleasance Trust Hall, now known as the Little Theatre. The University acquired the Pleasance Trust buildings up to 1977.
University of Edinburgh Estates Collection

acquired Abden House, in Marchhall Crescent, the large garden of which adjoins the Salisbury Green lands. This had been designed in around 1855 by the architect, Thomas Davis, and is essentially a typical Victorian villa with Jacobean style detailing.

Sir Donald Pollock had been busy with his plan for halls of residence at Salisbury Green for some time and it remained an ongoing project, with modifications and additions throughout the 1930s and 1940s. Abden House was actually purchased in 1935, St Leonard's House in 1936, and the purchase of Salisbury Green was not completed until 1942. All of these had sitting tenants at the time and part of the land was a market garden. St Leonard's was occupied by St Trinnean's School, run by Miss C. Fraser Lee, from 1925 until the start of the Second World War, at which point the pupils were evacuated to the countryside and the building was occupied by the Air Raid Protection and Home Guard. Salisbury Green was eventually opened as a student hall for men in 1946, with Sir Donald as informal warden. The following year St Leonard's Hall, as it then became known, opened as a hall for women students. The first students at the Pollock Halls of Residence were few in number and had substantial gardens, with tennis courts, in which to amuse themselves. Pollock's intention for Abden House was that it should become a residence for the Principal.

HALLS OF RESIDENCE PHASE ONE

The architect, William Kininmonth, met with Sir Edward Appleton to discuss development of the land around the old mansion houses in 1948. The new Principal must have been immediately aware of the potential of the site for within weeks the architect was sketching plans for a scheme to house 600 students. The University clearly wanted plans ready for the end of the moratorium on major building projects, in 1955; Kininmonth received the commission in 1950.

Some within the University had questioned the morality of appealing for money for new halls of residence, while at the same time earmarking the existing

212 Aerial view of the site of Pollock Halls in 1951. The large house towards the centre-top of the image is St Leonard's Hall. Salisbury Green House is below the curved field boundary, and Abden House is at the bottom right. The Parkside works of the publisher Thomas Nelson are in the top left.

HES [Aerofilms Collection: SC 1297637]

213 St Leonard's Hall, designed by John Lessels in 1869 for Thomas Nelson Junior, son of the publishing magnate. The house was originaly known as 'Arthursley'.

HES [SC 1470456]

case. It was undertaken by the building partnership of Alexander Paterson (mason) and Thomas Dott (wright).

Changing social conditions after the Second World War meant that the trust's work gradually migrated from the Pleasance. For a time the University leased some of the property for the Department of Psychology, finally acquiring all of the buildings in 1977. The Department of Psychology moved to George Square in 1980.

POLLOCK HALLS
William Nelson, the publisher, had bought the original 18th-century house, Salisbury Green, on Dalkeith Road, in 1860, together with a parcel of land. In 1866, he commissioned the architect John Lessels to make alterations to the previously plain house and dress it up as a Scotch baronial mansion, adding a matching gate lodge. Lessels was called upon again, in 1869, to design an even more extravagant baronial mansion, St Leonard's Hall, for William's brother, Thomas, a little to the north of the first house. Both houses had interior designs by Thomas Bonnar. Then, in 1889, a stable block for the Nelsons was constructed adjacent to the main road. Pollock also

halls in George Square for demolition. But, it was argued, the library was the first fixed point in the plan, as agreed with the City, and without this, there was no plan. Furthermore, those residences in converted buildings were not up to the standard required. Fortunately, the University had the land at Salisbury Green, which Appleton was anxious to fully exploit for new halls. This was not, however, without its tribulations.

Edinburgh had been a non-residential university until the inter-war period when some halls of residence were endowed with the aim of enhancing the corporate life of the University, although the greater part of the student body lived in private lodgings. But, as Appleton stated:

For a University is a place of intellectual roads and bridges: it provides the student with opportunities for contact with other minds and other disciplines. Let me say here that I am thinking here particularly of the contact of student and student – contact which is rendered easy and natural by club facilities, student societies and, above all, by life in a college or other halls of residence. For to my mind students educate one another as much as they are educated by their teachers.[83]

This was a view shared by the University Grants Committee, within which he had close contacts. In a report of 1957 the University Grants Committee advocated halls of residence as an advancement of learning and an effective lengthening of the study day. In addition, the projected post-war expansion made the need for dedicated student accommodation more acute, as there were simply not enough boarding houses in the city to house the student numbers anticipated. Edinburgh was the most cosmopolitan of the British universities, with 20 per cent of students coming from abroad and another 20 per cent from UK countries other than Scotland, at this time. Although it was not a desire for the University to become entirely residential, Appleton wanted every student to be able to spend at least one year in halls of residence.

Inevitably, Pollock objected to the scale, form and ethos of Kininmonth's scheme, which he found 'grandiose' and a gross over-development of the site. In vain, the architect provided twelve different schemes in an attempt to reach a satisfactory solution, but the Principal tirelessly pursued the development he thought was best for the University. Pollock's vision was for minor extensions to the old mansion houses to provide places for a hundred male and a hundred female students, in self-governing halls, and he found numerous sources of complaint. One curious objection was that Kininmonth's outline plan located a large number of male students in close proximity to the existing women's residence. He even commissioned

Frank Mears to draft an alternative scheme, in 1950. Mears was warned that the University would not be associated with this commission, and that it was a private matter between Pollock and himself. The architect admitted that this was not even his ideal scheme but simply what Sir Donald wanted. Between 1949 and 1954 Pollock, through his Pollock Trust Development Committee, managed to avoid finalising any agreement. Further delays could have jeopardised the George Square redevelopment, since demolition of the existing residences was necessary to clear the site for the proposed new main library. However, the City's development plan brought matters to a head.

In the Abercrombie Plan, Salisbury Green was part of a larger area zoned for residential development at 150 persons per acre. The general notion emerged that, since the University's scheme for the site was based on forty to fifty persons per acre, it might be regarded as under-populated. Thus, the City might acquire part of the land for its own housing programme, using powers of compulsory purchase. Pollock was alarmed to hear this. The prospect of local authority housing on, or even close to, Salisbury Green was 'too horrible to contemplate', and his resolve to oppose the Kininmonth scheme was weakened.[84] The University appealed against the zoning density at the public inquiry in 1954, pleading for it to be reduced to fifty persons per acre, with Kininmonth, Charles Stewart and a solicitor representing Pollock attending the hearing.[85] Some accusations of elitism were directed at the University over its apparent cloister of privilege, at a time when there was a desperate need for social housing. Charles Stewart countered this accusation by expressing the ethos of the project in terms of the emerging consensus on meritocracy: 'Since the introduction of grants by local authorities, large numbers of students come from homes which cannot provide the atmosphere of books and culture and it is desirable for people from relatively humble homes to have the opportunity to live completely within academic society.'[86]

The Principal also wrote to the Lord Provost pointing out that HRH The Duke of Edinburgh, Chancellor of the University, was 'very keen to see the halls of residence built'.[87] The University won its case, although it is doubtful that the City had genuinely contemplated acquiring any of the land at Salisbury Green for which the University had plans. Town-planning guidelines did imply that fifty per acre was too low a density for the economical use of building land, but the University was not bound by the recommendation. In later years the University conceded this when it was required to develop the site further. Following the public inquiry, the University resolved to proceed with development as soon as possible.

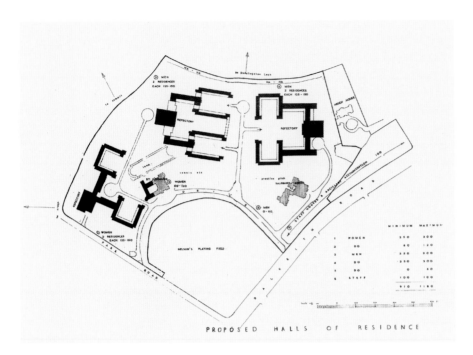

PROPOSED HALLS OF RESIDENCE

214 William Kininmonth's initial layout of the proposed halls of residence at Salisbury Green, 1949

Clive B. Fenton Collection

Salisbury Green, later to be named the Pollock Halls of Residence, was William Kininmonth's largest and longest running commission. At the outset, in 1949, he was asked to provide 600 student places, which would clearly have to be built in several stages. And, although he produced a number of variations on the layout, the essence of the first two phases to be built was contained within his initial scheme.

His recommended solution was for two pairs of halls, with a refectory for each pair. An open-air swimming pool and a theatre might be erected at some stage, if benefactors were willing to assist. Kininmonth preferred reinforced concrete for structures of the scale required.

The layout scheme Kininmonth created was a formal quadrangle arrangement, aligned symmetrically on a north–south axis with a refectory at each end. A bisecting east–west avenue between the two pairs of halls forms a cross-axis. The cross-axis is aligned on the tower of the Romanesque church at Duddingston, while the main axis has a view towards Salisbury Crags, to the north. A model of this design (1953) was produced showing the form and scale of the buildings, with linear three-storey accommodation blocks, with pitched roofs, terminated by stairtowers. These are linked by means of two-storey blocks, containing foyers and common rooms, to the refectories. Interestingly, while the southern refectory has a series of shell vaults, by contrast, the northern one is roofed with a large dome vault. Its grandiosity outraged the Pollock Trust Development Committee. Immediately after the public inquiry, Kininmonth met with Colonel Hardie, Pollock's associate, and, in answer to the criticism of the scheme's overt formality, the architect agreed and bent the north–south axis slightly.[88]

It was hoped to achieve the 600 student places in four phases of development, with the first consisting of one hall, for 150 students, and the southernmost of the two proposed refectories, to seat 300. The second phase would be the second hall on the east side of the quadrangle. With opposition from Pollock silenced, and the principle of development accepted by the City, the next challenge was gaining approval and funding from the University Grants Committee. But the University Grants Committee had misgivings about the scheme. The cost per student was too high, so this would have to be reduced. Grant-aided buildings had to be built in usable stages and the scheme was judged unsuitable for this: a 300-seat refectory to serve 150 students was difficult to justify, as it could not be built in two halves. The residential units of 150 were also considered undesirably large, from a social point of view.

Despite Appleton's great eminence and dignity, he was forced to plead with his friend, the University Grants Committee chairman, Sir Keith Murray, for help. Half of the £42,000 cost of the refectory could be considered part of the second phase, he argued, since the two halls would share it. If necessary, the room size could be reduced, and Kininmonth was asked to examine cost-cutting measures. Murray did not need to be won over to the principle of the project. The higher performance and lower 'wastage' of students at Oxford had already convinced him of the educational benefits. The 'nine-to-five' mentality was the enemy of university education as far as he was concerned.[89] Murray promised to lend his weight to the plan and encouraged Appleton to proceed with the first stage of the development.[90]

Interestingly, the University Court seems to have been determined to maintain a high architectural standard by deciding against some of the cost-cutting proposals. It resolved that the ceiling heights should not be reduced, nor the height of the courtyard arches or refectory. To do so would have spoiled the proportions and affected the quality of the interiors. It also ruled that the architect's chosen angle of roof pitch and its copper cladding should be maintained.[91] Costs over and above the University Grants Committee capital grant of £28,600 would be met from other sources. Sir Donald Pollock accepted the proposal to name the development the Pollock Halls of Residence, in memory of his parents, as he did not wish to be thought vain in having it named after him.

Building work for the first phase, Holland House and the refectory, commenced in the winter of 1956, and it opened in 1960. The second phase, Fraser House, opened four years later.[92] After amendment of the original plans, Fraser House accommodated 215 students, plus seven residential staff and a warden. The increased capacity over that of Holland House, which also necessitated an extension to the kitchen, was achieved by using a smaller building module, incorporating a semi-basement, and with smaller bedrooms, and therefore smaller furniture. Some economies on the form and detailing of the loggias were also made.

SALISBURY GREEN HOTEL, POLLOCK HALLS OF RESIDENCE

The original house probably dates from the early 18th century and is said to have been built for Alexander Scott, an Edinburgh merchant.[93] It would have been a fairly modest single-pile dwelling of three storeys, with a three-bay façade and centrally placed door, the stairs being to the rear of the entrance lobby. Thus there would have been only two rooms on the ground floor. The south gable, unchanged in subsequent alterations, reveals a rubble structure, although it may have been stuccoed originally. A pair of attic level windows here probably indicate servants' accommodation. The Dick family of Prestonfield are said to have bought the house in 1770. A single-storey bowed extension, known as Lady Dick-Cunningham's Drawing Room, probably dates from the Regency period.[94] Also from this period is a gardener's house of three bays, with single-bay pavilions and a hipped roof, bargeboards and exposed refer ends. Executed in ashlar, it has its own entrance gate on Dalkeith Road, where the boundary wall has been cut down to allow light to the windows. It was known for a time as Rosehall Cottage, after 'Rosehall', the house that was demolished to make way for the stable block.

Dick Peddie & McKay carried out alterations in 1947, when it became a hall of residence for men. In 1966 it became a women's residence. Then, in 1977, the architects Gordon, Duncan & Somerville provided a further wing to the east for additional student accommodation, demolishing the remains of Lessels' conservatory in the process. The newer work is of natural stone and has crowstep gables, like the rest of the ensemble, but it is clearly the work of another era. When Salisbury Green was deemed no longer appropriate for student residencies in 2000, Oberlanders Architects carried out further work to convert it into Salisbury Green Hotel.

ST LEONARD'S HALL, POLLOCK HALLS OF RESIDENCE

Originally named Arthursley, as it was in the lea of Arthur's Seat, the new name recalls the medieval St Leonard's Hospital, which had stood a short distance to the north.[95] It was built in 1869–70 for Thomas Nelson Junior, whose brother lived at Salisbury Green. But while the latter house involved conversion of an existing building, this commission allowed John Lessels to create an unfettered *tour de force* of the Scottish baronial style, with its site carefully chosen for maximum picturesque effect against the backdrop of Salisbury Crags.

Working on what was essentially a two-storey structure with attic, attached to a tower of four storeys, the architect was able to maintain a compact plan by locating the kitchens and associated rooms in the basement. The tower has a fairly authentic cap house, with crowstep gables behind a crenellated parapet, like the one at nearby Craigmillar Castle. The rest of the ensemble is far more elaborate than any of the aristocratic houses that it seeks to evoke. Bartizans (corbelled turrets) with conical roofs decorate the machicolated parapets, and oriel windows and crowstepping abound. The portico, to the west, supports a canted bay window, which is then surmounted

215 Salisbury Green Hotel, an 18th-century villa, refronted and enlarged by John Lessels in 1860–7 for William Nelson, son of the publisher, Thomas Nelson
Nick Haynes

216 St Leonard's Hall, designed by John Lessels in 1869 for Thomas Nelson Junior, son of the publishing magnate. The house was originaly known as 'Arthursley'.
Nick Haynes

by a carved balustrade featuring the Nelson coat of arms. The entrance arch has rope mouldings and is flanked at its head by a forbidding pair of carved lions clasping shields, which seem to be emerging from the stonework. Here, the oak doors and side panels have carved grotesque heads.

The prodigious interiors were designed by Thomas Bonnar, who also did the interiors of Salisbury Green, and they reflect Nelson's interest in the Age of Reformation; carved oak furniture in the mannerist style of the 16th century was produced to complete the decorative scheme. Most of the furnishings appear to have been acquired by Sir Donald Pollock together with the house.

The L-shaped entrance hall is grand and lined with oak panelling. It has its own chimneypiece with carved twisting foliate columns and a coat of arms. The decorative ceiling is coffered and has simulated wood graining and star patterns. The piers are emblazoned with pious mottos proclaiming God as the premier architect. The impression of craftsmanship and attention to detail is reinforced by the joinery of the doors and their unique fittings. The carved oak staircase is surprisingly pagan, the lower newel formed by a triton who leads a vigorous procession of birds and beasts to the tune of his conch trumpet.

The library was fitted with bespoke glazed bookcases and a matching chimneypiece; its ceiling was embossed with rose and thistle motifs. The ceiling of each room is unique, although the chivalric and heraldic motifs repeatedly recur in bosses and panels and coffering. The drawing room ceiling has an intricate geometric pattern and here the colourful plaster cornice depicts lizards, birds and foliage in a naturalistic way. But not everything is historicist, as the then modern French windows were installed to provide convenient access to a terrace from which views to Duddingston, Arthur's Seat and Holyrood could be enjoyed. The ceiling of the morning room, which celebrated the Marriage of the Thistle and Rose of 1503, was lost during a subdivision of the room in 1965, but the handsome oak fireplace and the thistle cornice survive. The upper rooms are more tranquil, are well appointed, and have marble fireplaces. Of these, the master bedroom is the grandest, its importance indicated by the coat of arms on the exterior. It has two fireplaces and a thistle and rose patterned cornice.

Between 1925 and 1939 the building housed St Trinnean's School. St Leonard's Hall opened as a residence for women students in 1948, remaining so until it became the administration building for the greatly expanded halls of residence in 1966. It was listed at Category A in 1974. It is currently in use as a hotel.

CONFUCIUS INSTITUTE (ABDEN HOUSE)

Little is known of the designer of Aben House, Thomas Davies, other than that he was a civil engineer associated with the 'Hays of Liverpool', ecclesiastical architects, and that he won the competition to design the layout of the Meadows, in Edinburgh.[96] This rather stern villa, executed in squared rubble, has a vertical emphasis, being raised up on a basement storey. It has an attic storey, and three bays to the principal elevation on the west. The theme is Jacobean, attested to by the tall fluted chimney flues and the curvilinear gables. The dormer heads are also curvilinear, carved with strapwork, and have stone finials of thistle, rose, star and *fleur-de-lis*. There is a single-storey wing on the south, and a service wing, with a coach house and stable, later converted to a garage, attached to the north.

Sir Donald Pollock purchased the house in 1935, with a sitting tenant, possibly intending to live there himself.[97] He later presented it to the University with the intention that it should be the Principal's residence. After renovations, Sir Edward Appleton lived there from 1949 to 1965.[98] Subsequently, it was leased as a function venue until it became the headquarters of the Confucius Institute for Scotland in 2007.

HOLLAND HOUSE AND SOUTH HALL, POLLOCK HALLS OF RESIDENCE

This ensemble constitutes the first two phases of development at the Pollock Halls of Residence. For the plan, the architect employed a quadrangular arrangement, with a pair of C-plan elements placed symmetrically on either side of a north–south axis, while a third such block forms a enclosure on the south of the courtyard. This arrangement came from Kininmonth's original scheme of 1949. The influence is Nordic classicism, indeed the three-storey residential blocks are redolent of the student hostels at Aarhus University in Denmark, with their linear dimensions and pitched roofs. Here, the courtyard elevations are enlivened by loggias on round concrete columns, some with elliptical arches, creating semi-enclosed corridors. Vertical interest is created by the slightly higher square staircase towers that terminate the blocks, guarding the entrances to outer and inner courts. These are surmounted by openwork concrete lanterns, for night lighting. The towers are reminiscent of the campanile of Lansbury Congregational Church, but the real influence is from Sweden, such as the provincial churches of Ragnar Ostberg, and especially his Stockholm City Hall, which also features loggias of arches on round columns.[99]

218 View of Holland House, Pollock Halls, taken in 2001
HES [Crown copyright: SC 794206]

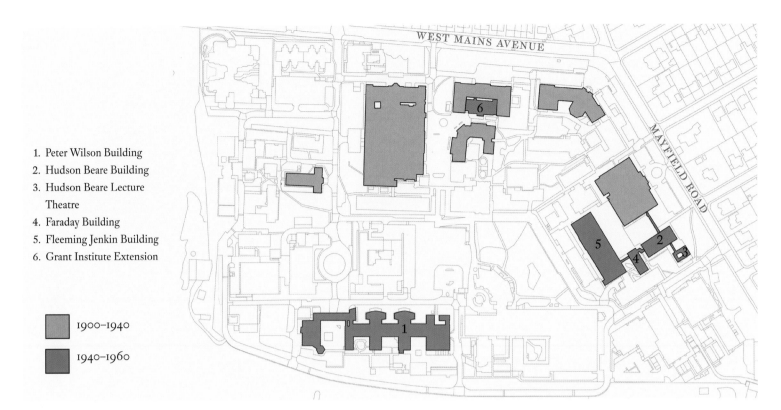

1. Peter Wilson Building
2. Hudson Beare Building
3. Hudson Beare Lecture Theatre
4. Faraday Building
5. Fleeming Jenkin Building
6. Grant Institute Extension

1900–1940

1940–1960

219 Plan showing main developments at King's Buildings 1940–1960

Crown copyright 2017 Ordnance Survey [Licence Number 100021521]

The southernmost block (South Hall) comprises the refectory in the centre, with the kitchen and servery to the rear (south). This is flanked with foyer, common rooms and other facilities, in wings projecting to the north, thus forming an inner garden courtyard. The loggia of the refectory consists of a series of transverse concrete shell vaults carried on slender columns, creating an effect of almost Brunelleschian lightness. Behind this, a wall of full-height glazing lights the dining hall, and the ceiling continues the vault in plaster. Side walls of natural stone rubble provide a contrast of massivity with the transparency of the glazed arcade. From the dining hall, the striking view across the site is to the reddish basalt of Salisbury Crags, the colour of which is emulated in the internal stonework. The use of contrasting facing materials is typical of 1950s style: harled walls, natural rubble, smooth concrete and the copper roofing, which soon turns green. Typical too are the metal flying staircases, with spindly balustrades, to the mezzanine of the refectory. The original furnishings and fittings which include pendant cluster light fittings, wrought iron wall-mounted torcheres, and splay-legged tables and chairs are preserved in photographs.

Holland House and Fraser House, now together renamed simply Holland House, constituted a third of Kininmonth's original scheme for the site, but policy changes over student halls left this as the sole example of its type as a different approach was taken subsequently.

KING'S BUILDINGS 1940–1960

While the University was seemingly entirely engaged in its building programme in the city centre, the Principal was still relentlessly pursuing improvements to science facilities and aiming to establish Edinburgh as a centre for scientific research. Most of this would be at King's Buildings.

The first new post-war building at King's Buildings was for the government's Agricultural Research Council, at the invitation of the University. This was attributable to the expertise of the University's Institute of Animal Genetics. The Agricultural Research Council created the Animal Breeding and Genetics Research Organisation in 1946, basing it at Edinburgh under Professor C.H. Waddington, and appointing him chief geneticist when he took the chair in animal genetics at Edinburgh in 1946. The Animal Breeding and Genetics Research Organisation was initially based in a suburban house, but its Poultry Research Centre required a facility for livestock near to the Institute of Animal Genetics. This was funded by the government's Department of Agriculture, with the aim of improving the nation's poultry breeding.

Consent for the building was granted in 1949, but work did not commence until 1953.[100] A.G. Ingham, who was chief surveyor to the Department of Agriculture, designed the modest low-cost single-storey structure, which was built of bricks and had a harled exterior. Nonetheless, it was symmetrically laid out like a Palladian farm building, oriented to the east, with wings and brachia extending to east and west. The

Poultry Research Centre moved to Roslin in 1980 and the building was later demolished. Reorganisation by the Agricultural Research Council in 1951 led to a separate Animal Breeding Research Organisation, which was also to find a home at King's Buildings in the early 1960s.

During the 1950s, there were a number of extensions to the existing departmental buildings at the science campus. For example, Michael Swann, the Professor of Natural History, was awarded funding for equipment and had an extension added to the Ashworth zoology building in 1959.[101] This project was undertaken by the University's own Department of Works, which was also responsible for a number of buildings, such as animal houses and extensions, of a more or less temporary nature.[102] This led to concerns about the haphazard placement of annexes affecting the siting of new major buildings. Lorimer & Matthew had prepared a development plan for King's Buildings in the 1920s, but no attempt had been made to implement this and the major buildings were simply arranged around the perimeter of the site, with easy access to the main roads. Subsequently, there had been thirty years' worth of huts and temporary units in the interior of the site, and there were also some surviving buildings from West Mains Farm. With major building programmes being planned, William Kininmonth was therefore appointed as planning consultant for the campus in 1958.

Kininmonth had already prepared a plan for King's Buildings in 1950, with the following objectives: developing the site in an orderly way; creating an internal road system; screening the untidy rears of the perimeter buildings; and devising an arrangement for future buildings that would face inwards onto a central open space. He proposed a service road to marshall vehicular traffic around the perimeter, and an internal road to distribute it across the site. The latter drew on the traditions of the great country estates in which vistas terminate on distant features in the landscape. This was a biaxial approach that involved aligning the route from the entrance on West Mains Road with the ancient Liberton Tower, to the south. Bisecting this, an east–west route was aligned with its vista terminating on the Royal Observatory, Blackford Hill, to the west. This is reminiscent of Kininmonth's biaxial scheme for the Pollock Halls of Residence, and may be a predilection acquired when he worked in the office of Sir Edwin Lutyens. The biaxial roads were partly implemented but the architect was perplexed when he was again invited to plan the site and found that the perimeter road was no longer feasible because of encroachment. Nevertheless, a revised scheme was drafted that took into account the growing problem

of car parking, with a car park for each building. Vehicle entrances were to be limited to two, and space was to be left on the south-west to allow for a future road to the south in anticipation of further expansion onto the golf course. The architect recommended that a central area be left free of buildings and that the architectural massing along the southern boundary should be strengthened with future buildings. Here he suggested a trio of taller buildings. The 'hard fact', as he put it, was that there were now only sixteen acres left for buildings, roads and gardens, therefore future buildings would have to be higher, with a smaller footprint. To the east of the central garden, Kininmonth suggested a new common room and refectory; the removal of the existing common room would allow space for the proposed central science library. A site for the proposed examination school was allocated behind zoology and also here would be an additional boiler house, as recommended by the consulting engineers. Car parks and untidy service areas should be screened by planting and he recommended the appointment of the landscape consultant H.F. Clark to advise on this and on the central garden area. The proposals were generally adhered to over the next twenty years.[103]

220 Design for the Peter Wilson Building (agriculture) by Alan Reiach and Ralph Cowan, 1952

HES [Alan Reiach Collection: DP 023987]

opposite

221 Sculptural panel depicting farm animals by Ann Henderson of 1958 on the north side of the Peter Wilson Building

Nick Haynes

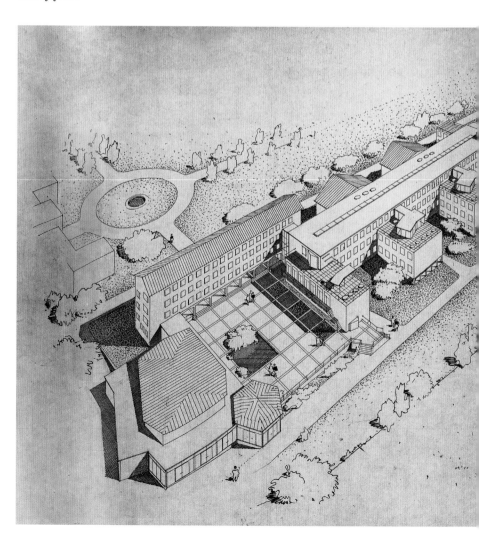

PETER WILSON BUILDING (AGRICULTURE)

In addition to the poultry research building, the government architect Arthur G. Ingham had also produced a draft design for the School of Agriculture project in 1949. This was a joint venture for the Edinburgh and East of Scotland College of Agriculture, along with the University's Department of Agriculture, both of which were to be displaced from north George Square, for the Medical School extension – in 1939 the college had agreed to give up its premises at George Square in return for the University's support for a new building at King's Buildings.[104] Ingham's design proved unsuitable, however, and Alan Reiach, together with Ralph Cowan, were appointed as architects instead, with Ingham advising them. Cowan was Head of Architecture at Edinburgh College of Art from 1955 to 1965, and Reiach lectured there.[105] Although they had their own practices, the two architects occasionally worked together during the late 1940s and early 1950s, for example on a neighbourhood shopping centre at East Kilbride.

The agricultural college was given a site near the southern perimeter, with a direct approach from West Mains Road. The commission was a rather protracted affair, beginning in 1949, but not completed until 1960. The original conception was for a concrete frame structure, but in order to save on reinforcing steel a system of solid brick piers supporting cast in-situ floors was devised. W. T. Marshall, Regius Professor of Engineering, was a consultant. Following delays, mainly because of national shortages of materials, work commenced again in 1954, when steel reinforcing bars were again available, so the construction reverted to concrete frame. Rather than incur further delays by redesigning the whole building, the architects decided to retain the planning and, therefore, appearance of the load-bearing scheme. The architectural press observed that all of this had given the building an eclectic appearance. The planning was, however, commended. The fall in the ground, for instance, had been exploited to create a lower ground floor on the east end where heavy engineering workshops and garages, boiler house and animal accommodation were placed beside a service courtyard.

There were three functional elements: teaching and research; administration; and recreation. The main entrance is through the four-storey administration block. This has an outer leaf of buff brick and a pitched copper roof. The lower floor is an arcade of concrete framing, originally allowing free movement into the south-facing courtyard. The courtyard is flanked by an east range containing common rooms and various conveniences, with the library above. The west range contains a large assembly hall with a canteen and kitchen. It is of irregular plan, but a hexagonal pavilion, the staff dining room, is attached to the south-east corner. The three-storey teaching block is bisected by three transverse blocks, with suites of lecture theatres at the north ends. This block has rendered walls and a flat roof, but the projecting lecture theatres are faced in buff brick and have pitched copper roofs. Interestingly, while the main block appears to terminate the vista of the north–south driveway, the real terminal point, Liberton Tower, is revealed through the arches of the lower floor. These were soon glazed in to defeat the wind, thus creating an additional common room.

Interestingly, the project first appeared in the architectural press in 1952, while it was in abeyance. At that time the cost estimate was £350,000, at 1951 prices. A decade later, it was completed at a cost of almost £575,000.[106]

Eventually, HRH The Duke of Edinburgh, the Chancellor of the University, opened the college in October 1960. The delay between design and construction meant that the building appeared slightly old-fashioned when it opened. However, it can now be seen as another example of the 1950s 'Festival Style' and of the enthusiasm of Scottish architects for Scandinavian architecture and design.[107]

The Peter Wilson Building, as it has been called since 2004 in honour of the Professor of Agriculture and Rural Economy, became the Edinburgh branch of Scotland's Rural Agricultural College in 2012, with the merger of Scottish Agricultural Colleges with Barony College, Elmwood College and Oatridge College, following a rather complicated institutional history.

HUDSON BEARE, FARADAY AND FLEEMING JENKIN (ENGINEERING) BUILDINGS

The other major work of the 1950s at King's Buildings was for the Department of Engineering, including electrical and structural engineering, a group of buildings too substantial to be seen as a simple extension, and with which the faculty's accommodation was greatly enhanced, at a cost of £250,000. A special sub-committee, which included the Principal, Robert Matthew and Basil Spence, met in 1956 to choose the architect for several forthcoming projects and appointed Robert Gardner-Medwin.

With Stephenson, Young & Partners, a Liverpool practice, as associate architects, Gardner-Medwin took a progressive contemporary approach to the commission, and he also took advantage of the fairly unrestricted building plot – this was prior to William Kininmonth's 1961 report on site development. He segregated the functions required by the brief into separate, but linked, buildings or 'units' grouped around a yard: lecture theatre; lecture rooms; staff and library; laboratory and drawing office. The tallest was the five-storey library and staff room unit, with a relatively small footprint. These were grouped to the south of the original Sanderson engineering building, and linked to it by a slender covered corridor. Seemingly wasteful of land, the concept was that the units could be easily adapted and extended when required.

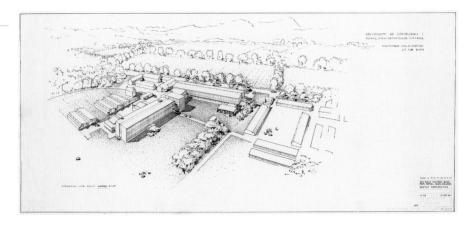

A variety of construction techniques was employed for the various elements: steel frame, in-situ concrete and load-bearing brick. The aluminium window modules used throughout were the unifying factor. The striking Hudson Beare lecture theatre, which expresses its inner form externally, attracted attention in the architectural press and was widely copied.[108] Proudly displaying the board marking of the concrete construction, it rises on its stem from a pool of water, and is accessed by a glazed steel bridge and a metal staircase.

EASTER BUSH 1940–1960

While Reiach and Cowan were amending and redrafting their scheme for the College of Agriculture at King's Buildings, Reiach was already engaged upon drafting schemes, under his own auspices, for one of

222 Alan Reiach's 1956 proposals for a field station at Easter Bush in Midlothian
HES [Alan Reiach Collection: DP 030069]

223 The widely copied lecture theatre forms a distinctive element of the Hudson Beare complex, designed by Robert Gardner-Medwin from 1956. The building has now been painted.
HES [Crown copyright: DP 059103]

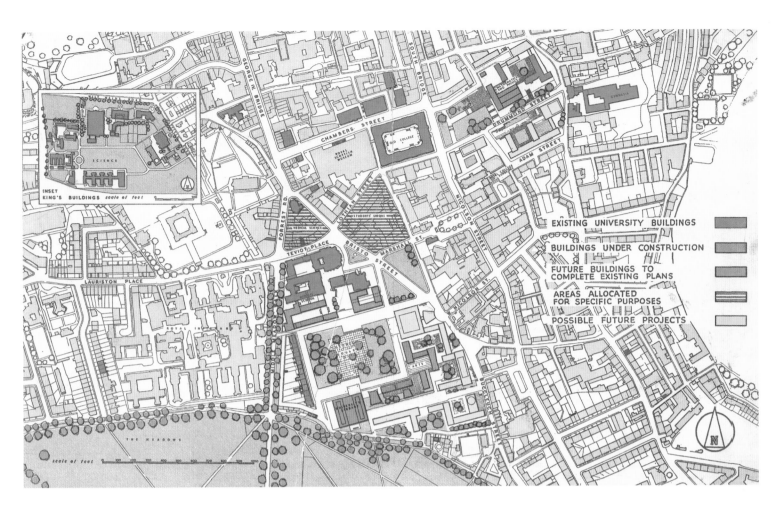

224 Masterplan for the
central development area
by Basil Spence & Partners,
showing the various stages of
planning and construction of
the University estate in 1959
University of Edinburgh Estates
Collection

the University's satellite projects, The Royal (Dick)
Veterinary College had been affiliated to the University
for science faculty degrees since 1934, but in 1951 the
college became part of the University, as the Royal
(Dick) School of Veterinary Studies. The college was
entirely based at Summerhall Square near the city centre
until this time. However, the University Court had purchased a farm and 1,300 acres of agricultural land at the
Easter Bush Estate in 1947, for agricultural research and
practical studies. Land there was allocated for veterinary
science, thus creating a centre for the rural economy.

By 1956, Reiach was working on development plans
for a site next to the estate's home farm, with proposals
for laboratories, as well as student and staff accommodation.[109] Sketch proposals show a number of detached
laboratory buildings and sheds in a simple arrangement,
but linked by covered walkways to create courtyards.
The first approved stage, a laboratory block, was under
way in 1959, and proposals for a second stage were ready
for the University Grants Committee by the following
year.[110] More modern than the College of Agriculture,
the laboratories for the field station were straightforward
examples of contemporary industrial design. The first
phase consisted of research and teaching wings in an
L-plan, on the north and west, later with separate single-
storey blocks for surgery and pathology attached at right
angles to the west wing.[111] The two-storey linear blocks
used a curtain wall treatment, with brick gables and base
courses. The elevations consisted of panels of either
clear or greenish textured opaque glass in white frames.

The north block had a recessed ground floor, with
the upper section cantilevered onto columns to provide
covered car parking. A number of utilitarian sheds for
animals and stores were grouped to the north and south
of the teaching and research buildings, supplementing
the 19th-century vernacular buildings, at this time.
Following completion of the west wing, the design
received the Edinburgh Architectural Association
Centenary Medal in 1964.[112] Reiach was to undertake
further work for the 'Dick Vet' during the 1960s, adding
a further wing to the field station at Easter Bush and
substantial extensions at the Summerhall site.[113]

Chapter Seven

Rapid Expansion 1960–1970

CLIVE B. FENTON

225 The main library and lecture theatre in George Square under construction in June 1966

HES [Sir Basil Spence Archive: SC 1049639]

In terms of both the completion of long-incubated plans and of new architectural commissions, the 1960s was the University's most eventful decade. Of course, this was just a part of a national programme of expansion that had seen the total number of UK students, including postgraduates, rise from 85,421 in 1949–50 to 107,699 in 1960–1. By 1968, the total number of students in higher education was 199,672, a fourfold increase since the start of the Second World War. Every university had to grow to accommodate this massive increase, but concerns arose that there might be a practical limit to the size of any individual university for it still to function as a single corporate entity, rather than a conglomeration of semi-autonomous parts. Thus, many technical colleges were also granted university status and entirely new universities were founded – seven in England and one in Scotland.

Edinburgh had 5,963 student enrolments in 1960, and this had risen to 9,193 by 1968. Capital funding for buildings and sites was allocated by the University Grants Committee according to the number of additional students the University was willing to take. This created a cycle of expansion, since funding for current building projects was dependent upon a commitment to take more students, for whom further space would then be required, and therefore additional accommodation needed. Student residences became as important as academic buildings, not simply for idealistic reasons but because of the lack of space for them in local communities.

In March 1960, the University deemed it judicious to publish a booklet, 'University Development and George Square', in which the planning dialogue over the redevelopment of George Square since the Second World War was carefully rehearsed. This was felt necessary in order to clarify the situation, as a mythology of intrigue had grown around the issue. It came only a year after the launch of an appeal which yielded donations of £256,000 in the first six months, demonstrating considerable public support for the University's endeavours, despite prominent criticism. But it also illustrates that the unprecedented level of funding from the Treasury was nevertheless deficient. Between 1961 and 1963 the University was to spend £2.5m on buildings.

A mission statement emphasises Edinburgh's commitment to national educational policy and the response to the population 'bulge'. A possible increase in UK student numbers by as much as 80 per cent by the 1970s is forecast here and, as Edinburgh was then accounting for 6 per cent of the national university population, that might mean a student body of 12,000 by 1980.

At the time of publication, the only completed major buildings that could be reported were Adam House, an examination building, and the School of

Agriculture at the King's Buildings campus, although the staff club and students' refectory, both at Chambers Street, are listed as significant recent achievements. However, the first phase of the Medical School extension was well under way, and the first phase of the new student halls of residence at Salisbury Green was almost ready, with places for 140 students. Furthermore the City had just granted consent for the demolitions that would enable the commencement of the arts faculty group of buildings at George Square.[1]

Also in the booklet, a photograph of a model shows the first three phases of the arts faculty buildings, which were scheduled to occupy the south-east corner of George Square by 1967. These consisted of a group of four low buildings arranged around a tower, all with distinctive black and white detailing.

Robert Matthew, the University's Professor of Architecture, who had the commission, had started his own private practice after receiving several commissions for power stations and for Turnhouse Airport, as well as a student residence for the University of Aberdeen. In 1956 he went into partnership with Stirrat Johnson-Marshall to form Robert Matthew Johnson-Marshall (RMJM), which was to become one of the largest private practices in Europe by the 1970s. Stirrat Johnson-Marshall, like Matthew, had made his name as a public service architect. He was responsible for the pioneering work on prefabricated school buildings at Hertfordshire County Council in the 1940s and he was appointed chief architect for the Ministry of Education in 1948. Initially, Matthew was to run the Edinburgh branch, while his partner took control of the London office. University work became an important factor in the success of RMJM, including the planning of new campuses at Stirling, York and Bath.

In 1956 Matthew had also established the University's own Department of Architecture. Having found that the School of Architecture at Edinburgh College of Art was not being run in a manner acceptable to him, he resigned from the role of head of school, while retaining the Forbes Chair of Architecture.[2] Another important commission for Matthew, one of great significance to the University, was for the redevelopment of Edinburgh Royal Infirmary, at that time Edinburgh's largest teaching hospital. Its location had determined the siting of the 19th-century Medical School, and consequently the post-war extension onto north George Square that led to the University's post-war development plan.[3]

The first phase of the arts faculty group was to be the fourteen-storey arts tower (Block A), which was placed outwith the building line of the square at the south end of the east side. It was accompanied by a single-storey block of lecture theatres (Block B) to the east, on Windmill Lane. The second phase was to consist of a four-storey linear tutorial building (Block C), adjacent to the tower, on the east side of the square. This was initially allocated to geography, history and political economy. Phase three was to be another linear tutorial building (Block D), at the east end of the south side of the square, ostensibly for psychology, social sciences and phonetics. Immediately to the west of this, a 600-seat lecture theatre, for the use of all faculties, would be the fourth phase. The rest of the south side was allocated to the main library, for which Basil Spence had the commission.

Significantly, the arts faculty group was to be mounted on a podium, with underground links between buildings and a refectory in the basement. The refectory was lit by means of a light well in the podium, where there was a sunken garden court, and there were other such garden courts behind Blocks C and D. The concept behind the linear tutorial buildings was that they could easily be extended to L-plan, then to C-plan, around the sunken courts, where there would be windows to light the basement rooms. Car parking space was also to be provided at sub-podium level beneath Block D.

THE UNIVERSITY COMPREHENSIVE DEVELOPMENT AREA

In 1954, when Basil Spence was commissioned to devise a scheme for George Square and the surrounding streets (the Central Development Area), he was asked to anticipate the University's probable requirements of land and buildings over the coming fifty years, based on Principal Sir Edward Appleton's understanding of the situation at that time. As it was to transpire, these estimates proved

226 A model of the south and east sides of George Square, showing the first three phases of the arts faculty buildings with distinctive black and white detailing

From 'University Development and George Square', March 1960

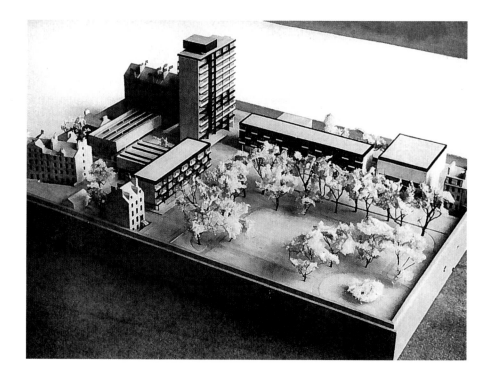

227 The demolition of
Buccleuch Place tenements in
preparation for development
of the arts faculty buildings

quite accurate in terms of capacity of building volume.
However, in 1960 there were indications that the speed
of national university expansion might be faster than
previously thought. In fact, when the University Grants
Committee sought the University's proposals for the
period 1964 to 1968, it warned that national student
numbers might be 35,000 to 40,000 higher than
expected. Edinburgh's share of these additional students
would be around 1,000. Increasing the speed of design
and construction was achievable, given the manpower
and money, but Professor Matthew, the University's
advisor on such matters, realised that the rather slow
process of land acquisition was problematic. He called
a special meeting of the Major Buildings Committee to
outline the issues.[4]

George Square was on the edge of an area known
locally as the South Side, which was occupied by
domestic residences, shops and commercial premises,
and industry. According to the city development plan,
the whole area was 'ripe for development'. Industry

was to be zoned out, meaning that future industrial
development would not be allowed. Most of the
residential property was sub-standard and unlikely to
be rehabilitated. Indeed, it had often been said that
the University was surrounded by slums. The City
had a building programme, with an average of about
1,200 new houses being completed every year, but the
problem was large and city-wide with no end in sight.
As Matthew saw it, University development outside of
George Square was largely dependent upon the City's
rehousing programme and speculative commercial
projects. Developers were likely to take an interest in
derelict industrial and residential properties, resulting
in piecemeal development, with the University having
to compete for sites it required, and with the probability
that its fine new campus would be confronted with the
rears and service areas of future commercial buildings.

From his experience of the rebuilding of London's
blitzed East End, Matthew considered that the solution
was a Comprehensive Development Area. This was a
statutory instrument created by the Town and Country
Planning Act (1947), which allowed local authorities
to acquire property in an area thus designated, using
the powers of Compulsory Purchase Orders to ensure
planned redevelopment according to the local plan.
With this, the City could ensure that redevelopment
followed in an orderly and rational manner, with land set
aside for specific purposes, whether educational, commercial or residential. Crucially, the City would be able
to acquire any land required for the University using its
statutory powers. Appleton must have felt compelled to
agree, as Matthew had already discussed the matter with
the Lord Provost, Sir John Dunbar.

Preparation of a Comprehensive Development Area
would entail a heavy burden of surveys, consultations
and negotiations upon the University's planning
consultant, and Matthew felt that Basil Spence would
be unable to take on this work. Since Spence lived in
London and had recently been appointed president of
the Royal Institute of British Architects, he could not
give it his personal attention. Instead, Percy Johnson-
Marshall was recommended. Percy Johnson-Marshall,
the brother of Matthew's partner, Stirrat, was senior
lecturer in planning in the Department of Architecture
and had worked under Matthew at the London County
Council. Well known in town-planning circles, he
was previously in the Ministry of Town and Country
Planning and Coventry City Architect's Department.
Spence was invited to resign, which he did gracefully in
December 1960, his particular task of creating a masterplan and getting consent for the redevelopment of
George Square being completed.[5] Spence's Edinburgh
office continued to be involved with the University as
architects for a number of its buildings.

Following discussions with the City, Johnson-Marshall's proposed Comprehensive Development Area covered 125 acres, from the Cowgate at the north end, to the Meadows at the south. The western edge was at Meadow Walk, and the City's proposed motorway at the Pleasance / St Leonard's Street would have defined the eastern boundary. The University sector was no larger than Spence's previous layout, and included High School Yards. It was bisected by the south–north route of Nicolson Street and the South Bridge, which was to be flanked by the commercial zone, for shops, cafeterias, cinemas, bars and so on, described as 'the Shopping Centre'. Apart from the University's High School Yards area, the eastern part was for residential development, for which the City would be largely responsible, with the southern part a combination of commercial and private residential building. In certain respects the scheme resembled Frank Mears's proposals of 1930, with its tripartite zoning of the city centre. Johnson-Marshall introduced the segregation of pedestrian and vehicular transport, a major precept of modernist town planning. In order to achieve this and to unify the three zones, it was proposed that the podium, or decking system, that Matthew had devised for the arts faculty group should be used for all the future University buildings and extend across the whole of the Comprehensive Development Area. This would create a sort of megastructure, with pedestrian circulation at first floor level, where there would be an upper level shopping street, and with vehicles and parking and servicing at ground level. This would have made it possible to walk from George Square to High School Yards at upper deck level without encountering any traffic, although numerous pedestrian bridges would have been required. The street layout would be simplified with a one-way gyratory traffic system. It was also recommended that building heights should be kept low in order to allow views from the south to Edinburgh's iconic skyline; and the maximum plot ratio was recommended as 3.5:1.

Wholesale demolition of obsolete buildings would be required, but some buildings of architectural and historical merit were to be retained. Of the non-University buildings, only Playfair's Surgeons' Hall was worthy of preservation, according to Johnson-Marshall. The University had an interesting group of historical buildings, however. This consisted of Old College ('a masterpiece') and the Medical School, McEwan Hall and the Reid School of Music ('fine examples of their period'). These should be given a 'dignified treatment' by the creation of a pedestrian square, 'a great meeting place for students'.

Interestingly, the University Union at Teviot Row was not amongst those considered to be worth keeping, despite having an interesting new extension at the rear

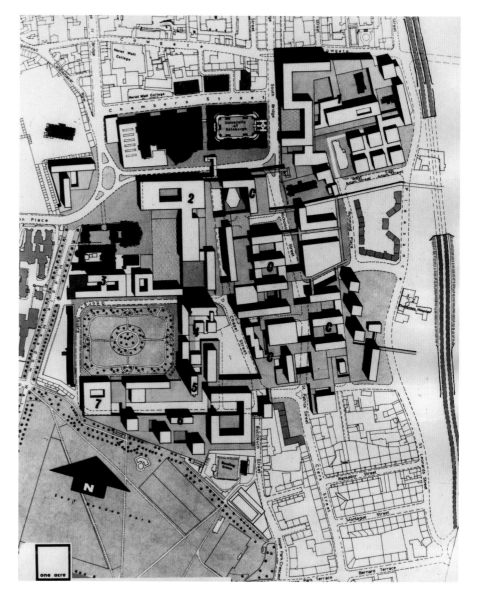

on Charles Street Lane. Executed in 1962, this bold white concrete structure was featured in the architectural press at the time.[6] It was designed by Kininmonth's protégé, Jack McRoberts, and probably inspired by the Italian engineer / architect Pier Luigi Nervi.[7] Concrete columns elevate the structure to the first floor level of the old building to which it is attached. The upper level has a dining room with a gallery around it, and mushroom-headed columns project through the cornice of the exterior, while the lower level is a billiard room. The fenestration consists of three horizontal bands of glazing, without corner supports. The extension was facilitated by transfer of ownership from the University Union to the University Court.[8]

At High School Yards, only Old Surgeons' Hall and the façade of the Old High School were of interest to Johnson-Marshall, while the area between Infirmary Street and Drummond Street would be cleared to create an open square, providing a suitable setting for the façade of Old College.[9]

228 Plan of the University of Edinburgh Comprehensive Development Area, 1962. A motorway was planned to the east of the area, parallel to the Pleasance.
Key:
1. Mathematics and physics
2. Students' union
3. Medical building
4. First year science
5. Arts building
6. Architecture
7. Library
C. Shops, offices and residential
Author's Collection

Johnson-Marshall's proposed new Bristo Square was to be enclosed on the north and east by student amenity buildings on the land donated by Sir Donald Pollock for that purpose – Sir Donald's death, in June 1962, removed the obstacle to demolition of the buildings on the 'island site'. This element of the plan was a reversion to the earlier schemes of Mears and Holden, who proposed a great piazza as a setting for the McEwan Hall, whereas Spence had favoured retention of the ancient street layout between George Square and Potterrow, and had sited his proposed University Chapel here. Johnson-Marshall, however, saw no need for a chapel, so it remained permanently shelved.

A large model, at 1:500 scale, together with plans and perspectives, was produced and, in 1962, the University opened an exhibition at Adam House, with an accompanying booklet, to present the proposals to the public.

The Principal opened the exhibition, declaring that this would be a second New Town – the area involved was actually larger than James Craig's first New Town, which was 110 acres. Edinburgh's town planning committee recommended the scheme and the town council accepted this, in principle, in January 1963.[10] A private development company, Murrayfield Real Estate (later Ravenseft Real Estate) expressed interest, and thus a tripartite standing committee of University, City and business was set up to work on finalising a scheme, the three parties sharing the cost of consultancy fees.[11]

Negotiations with the various relevant parties and preparation of the University / Nicolson Street Comprehensive Development Area proposal were to occupy Johnson-Marshall and his newly formed planning consultancy for the next fifteen years. Much of the stasis of the proposed redevelopment was due to

229 Aerial view of George Square in 1961 showing the completed first phase of Walter Ramsay's medical extensions (now the Chrystal Macmillan Building) on the left of the image, and Robert Matthew's David Hume Tower under construction on the right

The Scotsman Publications Ltd [via www.scran.ac.uk: 000-000-240-526-R]

indecision and counter proposals over the motorway, or relief road, as originally suggested by Abercrombie in 1949, although the connection between this motorway with other routes was never reconciled. At one stage a six-lane spur road from Tollcross to the Pleasance was drafted. However, this was vigorously opposed, as it would bisect the University area. Crucially, the development of the St James Square area as a shopping centre created a rival to Johnson-Marshall's Nicolson Street centre and undermined commercial investment.[12] Although the City still supported it nominally for a few years, the Comprehensive Development Area was not fully ratified and ultimately never achieved statutory force – it was finally determined to be null and void with the reorganisation of local government in 1975.[13] However, during that time the University's building projects were based on the assumption that it would be implemented fully, and therefore Johnson-Marshall's Comprehensive Development Area scheme had a direct influence on their architectural form.

Outwith George Square itself, the University section of Johnson-Marshall's scheme was only partially achieved, but the streets to the west of Potterrow were razed between 1967 and 1971, with only two phases of the Students' Centre completed to replace all of the old buildings.[14] Some twenty years after launching his Comprehensive Development Area proposals, Johnson-Marshall's McEwan Hall piazza was eventually instated as Bristo Square.

CENTRAL AREA 1960–1970
DAVID HUME TOWER AND LECTURE BLOCK

DHT, as it is usually known, is a sleek fourteen-storey tower, of reinforced concrete construction with a cladding of black slate on the east and west, and sandstone on the gables.[15] With its accompanying lecture theatre block, this was the first of the arts faculty group and signalled the redevelopment of George Square. The elevations are well articulated, with recessions on the façade denoting departmental libraries, and the windows are arranged in pairs across seven structural bays. The slabbing continues above the parapet to envelope the plant room, creating a clean roofline. On the south gable, the escape stairs are in a narrow glazed tower.

The original bespoke interior fittings, including doors, cupboards and counters were of high quality, mainly red hardwood and veneered plywood. The stair handrails were of hardwood and glass panels, and fire screens of the same material. The sub-podium refectory is lit by means of a sunken court which acts as a light well.

The two-storey lecture block to the east is linked to the tower at sub-podium level. The lower storey had glazed timber doors and windows to the foyer, and a

fascia of vertical timber slats. The upper storey is blind and has a cladding of York stone. Internally it is divided into three auditoria. The basement houses the kitchen for the refectory.

In 2011–14 Page\Park Architects reconfigured the lower ground floor to provide medium sized teaching rooms, large sized teaching rooms, a teaching studio, a student run retail facility, and a café / kitchen area. New entrances were created at the lower ground and podium levels along with new stairs, lift provision, and landscaping of the podium and courtyard garden.

230 The slate and sandstone cladding of the David Hume Tower in a view from the south-east
Nick Haynes

opposite, clockwise from left:

The Business School
231 Exterior about 1968
HES [Sir Basil Spence Archive: SC 553215]

232 Additional storey by
LDN Architects, 2008–11
Paul Zanre Photography

233 New extension by LDN
Architects, 2008–11
Paul Zanre Photography

234 Interior view of a break-
out area by LDN Architects,
2008–11
Paul Zanre Photography

FORMER ARTS FACULTY GROUP:
50 GEORGE SQUARE (FORMER WILLIAM ROBERTSON BUILDING); BUSINESS SCHOOL (FORMER ADAM FERGUSON BUILDING); LECTURE THEATRE

In Matthew's original design a pair of linear teaching blocks and a large lecture theatre shared the podium with the arts tower. The teaching blocks were intended to be extendible to L-plan and C-plan, if required. The block on the east side of the square (50 George Square) was L-plan by the time of commencement, and had a

lecture theatre in the re-entrant angle. Ultimately clad in sandstone, rather than Matthew's preferred slate slabs, the four-storey blocks have some classical allusions in the engaged concrete columns at podium level. The fenestration consists of horizontal bands of timber-framed windows. Page\Park Architects carried out a major £25m refurbishment and extension project in 2011–14, creating a new circular project room above the existing lecture theatre and adding a further storey at rooftop level.

The large 600-seat George Square Lecture Theatre, cantilevered to front and rear, has a subsidiary entrance

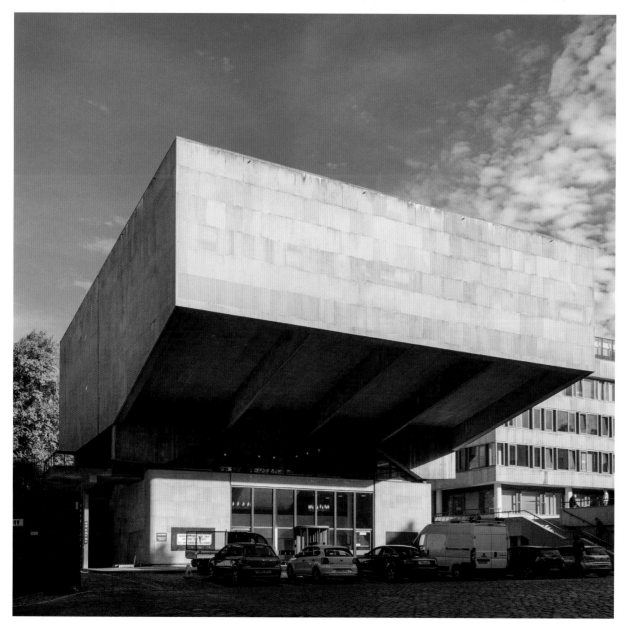

clockwise from bottom left

235 George Square Theatre
HES

236 The café at 50 George Square designed by Page\Park Architects, 2011–14
Andrew Lee

237 The project room in 50 George Square designed by Page\Park Architects, 2011–14
Andrew Lee

238 The lower courtyard between David Hume Tower and 50 George Square designed by Page\Park Architects, 2011–14
Andrew Lee

on Buccleuch Place. Both have advanced revolving doors of glazed hardwood. A horizontal band of glazing on the front elevation lights the landing level. Expressive of its internal form, and clad in York stone, the undersides of the cantilevers reveal the board-marked reinforced concrete structure.

Alterations of 2008–10, designed by LDN Architects as part of a £12m refurbishment project, entailed glazed penthouses to the teaching blocks, which affect the proportions and which take the building height above that originally determined by the City's planners. The 2010 works also included an extension in the form of a glazed box pavilion inserted into the sub-podium garden court of the Adam Ferguson Building.[16]

APPLETON TOWER, CRICHTON STREET

Mounted upon a podium that was intended to encompass the University campus and much of the surrounding area, the tower was named in honour of Sir Edward Appleton, the Principal from 1949 to 1965, who

instigated it as a building for the teaching of first-year science.[17] The project architects were George McNab and John R. Oberlander of Alan Reiach, Eric Hall & Partners. The tower consists of a nine-storey slab block, with a taller glazed stairtower inserted into the south elevation. It is linked to a lecture block, containing five theatres, and a two-storey concourse, on the south, but the ensemble lacks its intended, second phase, i.e. its western entrance / tutorial block on east George Square, where the original houses still remain. The *de-facto* entrance is beneath a canopy on the north. The original fenestration consisted of a grid of windows and spandrel panels, and the cladding was storey-high concrete panels with a blue glass mosaic finish. The lecture theatre block was rusticated by the use of concrete panels with blue river pebbles embedded.

The galleried concourse is top-lit by a glazed roof and served as a crush hall and a linking element, with access to lifts and stairs, and with a gallery giving access to the upper lecture theatres. Most of the upper floors were

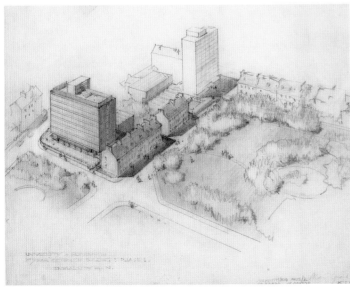

originally in an open-plan arrangement and many had long laboratory benches. The internal arrangements were subsequently altered.

Substantially recast during refurbishment, in 2015–16, the proportions of the original fenestration have been lost. The original mosaic-faced slabs, which were defective, have been replaced with cream-coloured replacement both as spandrel panels and as cladding to the gables. The new fenestration is vertically and horizontally divided by narrow grilles of grey metal. The design team for the recladding consisted of Buro Happold and LDN Architects.

MAIN LIBRARY

This was the hub building of the new George Square campus, according to Basil Spence's scheme of 1954, but it had to await commencement until 1965.[18] Hardie Glover, Andrew Merrylees and John Marshall were the project architects from Sir Basil Spence, Glover & Ferguson. The result was a highly acclaimed library, which was the largest of its type in the UK at the time, at 27,720m². Located in the south-east corner of George Square, and mounted on a podium shared with the arts faculty buildings, it consists of eight storeys in total, including the sub-podium basement and concealed penthouse. Technical services, including a bindery and the vehicle loading bay were in the basement.

Four balconies, wrapped around the entire structure, serve as brise soleil, and are faced with Portland stone. The double-height plate glass entrance front is within a loggia of square concrete columns, which are bisected by beams projecting through the front wall, and across which is slung a concrete fascia. The upper fenestration consists of bands of glazing in aluminium frames. The entrance level is faced with polished black granite, and the side walls of the basement in riven York stone. Meticulous detailing and high-quality materials were the order of the day, in both exterior and interior application.

The concourse is double-height and has a gallery and mezzanine, and square supporting columns of polished concrete. The floor is paved with quartzite slabs, and the wall linings here, and in the suite of rooms to the west, are of teak. The staircase to the mezzanine has hardwood and polished steel handrails. White beech is extensively used for doors and linings on the upper levels. Upper floors have book-stacks in a flexible open-plan arrangement around the vertical circulation core. The landings have glazed hardwood fire screens. The architects designed the desks, which were made by Meredew, as well as the shelving, and carefully chose the other furniture from the catalogues of Arne Jacobsen, Fritz Hansen, Hille and Conran. The library received a Royal Institute of British Architects award in 1968 and a Civic Trust Commendation in 1969.

As part of a phased £37m refurbishment by Lewis & Hickey Architects between 2006 and 2013, the entrance foyer and podium were remodelled, the new Centre for Research Collections was formed on the library's top two floors, a 220 seat café was created on the ground floor, and a mezzanine level was inserted to act as a gallery and exhibition space.[19]

THE MEDICAL EXTENSIONS, PHASE ONE: CHRYSTAL MACMILLAN BUILDING (PATHOLOGY); PHASE TWO: 1 GEORGE SQUARE (NEUROSCIENCE; FORMERLY PHARMACOLOGY)

The medical extension was the starting point for the University's George Square redevelopment plan.[20] Walter Ramsay won the competition, and the commission, to create new medical buildings on the entire north side of the square, in 1951, and he undertook three of four anticipated phases. The first, pathology, was begun in 1956 and completed in 1962. A steel-framed structure, it is essentially a wing, extending south from the

242 The main library in George Square under construction, photographed by Alistair L. Hunter 1967
HES [Sir Basil Spence Archive: SC 1030944]

243 View of the ground floor service desk in the main library, photographed by Henk Snoek, 1968
HES [Sir Basil Spence Archive: SC 1030955]

Rowand Anderson buildings to the north-west corner of
the square. Its cladding, following interventions by Basil
Spence, was a mixture of artificial rubble and artificial
ashlar, with green slate at ground floor level on the south
elevation. The next phase was for pharmacology at the
east end. This is concrete-framed and more modern,
reflecting amendments to the overall design. Consisting
of five bays, forever awaiting completion, it has the fragment of a colonnade of square concrete columns at the
lower level. It has six storeys, with the uppermost blind,
while the first floor has projecting bays. All is clad in York
stone slabs.

Connected by a bridging link, also with projecting
bays, to the first phase is the Hugh Robson Building.
Ostensibly for biochemistry, it was the final new building
within George Square, with the link and courtyard
finished in 1983. The façade detailing was slightly modified after pharmacology, but followed the same principles.
The colonnade is two storeys high to create a loggia, with
its back wall of ribbed concrete panels. The columns here
though are linked to beams projecting through the wall,
in homage to those of the main library on the south side
of the square – Spence's partner, Hardie Glover, advised
on this. The upper façade is also faced in York stone. The
site for a projected fourth phase is still occupied by the
former George Watson's Ladies College.

In 2007–8 the old pathology building underwent
a £10.5m refurbishment for the School of Social and
Political Studies by Davis Duncan Architects. A new
wedge-shaped extension, clad in lead, which houses part
of the undergraduate reading room and a seminar room,
projects westwards along the edge of Middle Meadow
Walk. At the same time the building was renamed to
honour the barrister, suffragist and founder of the
Women's International League for Peace and Freedom,
Chrystal Macmillan, considered to be the University's
first female science graduate in 1906.

ROXBURGH PLACE LEARNING AND TEACHING CENTRE (FORMER PFIZER FOUNDATION AND LISTER INSTITUTE)

In addition to its own teaching and research programmes the University was also enthusiastic in its
support for research and advanced study sponsored
by government agencies and in collaboration with
other institutes, such as the Animal Breeding Research
Organisation and the Medical Research Council. One
such opportunity came in 1958 when Archie Brunton,
an Edinburgh graduate and chief medical officer for
Pfizer Ltd, the pharmaceutical company, contacted
the University with the news that his company wanted
to start a foundation in Edinburgh. The concept was

based on the Ciba Foundation in London. It was to be an international postgraduate medical centre, a place for seminars and symposia, with a club atmosphere. Appleton liked the idea and proposed that the University might convert an existing building and lease it to Pfizer for twenty-five years. A number of buildings were looked at, but none proved suitable, The Royal College of Surgeons, however, came to the rescue. The Royal College of Surgeons intended to rebuild its postgraduate Medical School at Roxburgh Place, to be funded by the Lister Trust, and they had a vacant adjoining site at Hill Square.[21] A collaborative arrangement was made and, in 1960, William Kininmonth of Rowand Anderson, Kininmonth & Paul was asked to prepare a feasibility study.

The architect proposed a reinforced concrete structure in Hill Square for the Pfizer building, costing £100,000. This would be linked to the existing Royal College of Surgeons postgraduate school until that could be replaced with a new school. Thereafter, with a new school erected on Roxburgh Place, there would be a sharing of facilities.[22] The scheme was approved in general although the architect was asked to reduce the cost by 20 per cent.[23] Ian C. Gordon was the project architect.

Consent was granted for the Pfizer building late in 1962 and it was officially opened by HRH The Duke of Edinburgh, the Chancellor of the University, on 2 July 1965, with work on the postgraduate school beginning soon afterwards.[24]

The Pfizer Foundation is a building of four storeys plus basement, which respects the cornice height of the surviving early-19th-century terraced houses of Hill Square, although having a flat roof it fails to reach their ridge height. It occupies the north-east corner and actually consists of two blocks, linked by a slightly lower single-bay element containing entrance and staircase. The eastern block also has an elevation to Richmond Place where it joins the Lister Institute with a two-storey link. The elevations are plain but elegant, and its facing is of pre-cast slabs with an exposed granite aggregate. This provides a good colour match with its Georgian neighbours, and it emulates their cast-iron railings too. The accompanying Lister Institute, on Richmond Place and Roxburgh Place, was completed in December 1967. This is a more severe grey elevation, essentially a six-storey grid of pre-cast window panels. The tall ground floor lacks windows as this zone contains the lecture theatre and the building does not draw attention to the small staff door and the discreet vehicular entrance for hearses.

Plans are in progress for a steel-framed replacement link building, clad with aluminium framed curtain walling and translucent polycarbonate panels, between the two former institutes. The design by Reiach & Hall Architects is intended to repurpose the currently unused buildings as a teaching and learning facility.

On the other side of Richmond Place, the University donated the site for the National Coal Board's Institute of Mining Medicine. Similarly clad in concrete spandrel panels, it was designed by the board's architect, Sydney Greenwood, and completed in 1970. The three buildings helped to create an enclave for postgraduate medical research. Interestingly, the last was to become a student residence when the site reverted to the University.

OLD TOWN 1960–1970
MYLNE'S COURT (PHILIP HENMAN HALL AND EDWARD SALVESEN HALL)

From the beginning of the 1960s there was an increasing interest in conservation within the University, and a desire to be seen as more than just a destroyer of old buildings. As a result of a sequence of events it was able to embark upon a scheme of development with a strong conservation element in the most ancient part of the city. This particularly excited Robert Matthew, and Percy Johnson-Marshall, by virtue

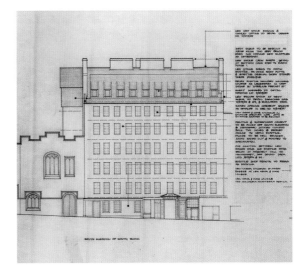

247 Designs by Ian G. Lindsay & Partners for conversion of Mylne's Court to a student residence, 1967
HES [Ian G. Lindsay Collection: SC 842581]

248 Mylne's Court, Lawnmarket, about 1900
HES [SC 421922]

of its connection with Patrick Geddes, whom they regarded as the founder of modern town planning. The Lawnmarket area, between the castle and the Mound, had been the centre of Geddes's activities in the Old Town, where he preached the principle of 'conservative surgery', rather than outright destruction of the historical fabric. It was here too that he instigated Edinburgh's first student hall of residence.[25] For those who venerated Geddes, the place of pilgrimage was the Outlook Tower, an eccentric Baronial edifice that housed a camera obscura, formerly Short's Observatory, which Geddes made into a sort of metaphor for the overview required by planners. This was the location for his museum of town planning, and his centre for civic studies. Geddes had been lauded for his foresight in the creation of student halls by Sir Edward Appleton too, when he opened Lister House as a residence for divinity students in 1954.

NEW COLLEGE, THE MOUND

The most prominent building, in architectural terms, was New College designed by William Henry Playfair for the secessionist Free Church of Scotland, following the Disruption of 1843. When the churches had reunited in 1929, there was no need for a separate college, and the building became the headquarters of the University's faculty of divinity in 1935. Playfair was responsible for some of Edinburgh's most notable 19th-century monuments, and the Tudor-style college, with its pinnacled towers, is an important element of the city's skyline. Its careful composition and its positioning as the terminal point of a north–south vista from the New Town is a masterpiece of urban design.

In the dense urban fabric of the Lawnmarket, there were several other important specimens of Scottish architecture, such as Gladstone's Land, a merchant's house of the 16th century, which had been restored as

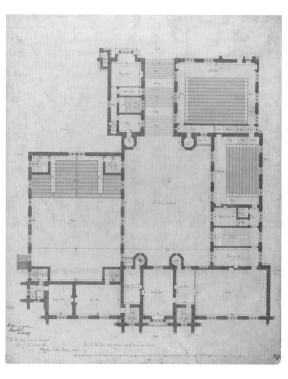

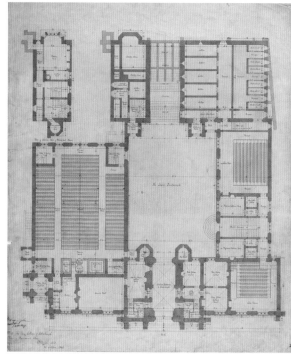

clockwise from top left

Plans of New College by William Henry Playfair, 1846

249 The principal floor
University of Edinburgh [0078855d]

250 The basement floor
University of Edinburgh [0078858d]

251 Longitudinal section looking west
University of Edinburgh [0078854d]

252 North elevation
University of Edinburgh [0078856d]

opposite

253 Detail of north elevation
University of Edinburgh [0078856d]

a museum by the National Trust for Scotland in 1936. There were also Mylne's Court (1690) and James' Court (1703), two imposing residential blocks built around central courtyards, which had served as prototypes for the city's classical tenements of the 18th century.

By 1960, most of the residential properties in the area were below habitable standard, and looked likely to be demolished. New College itself was in desperate need of repair and renovation to improve the obsolete teaching facilities. The former church, which is part of the building, had been converted to a library in 1935, but there was comparatively little accommodation within the seemingly large college, as structure and circulation accounted for 48 per cent of the volume. Estimates for this work ran to £100,000, but since the building was still owned by the Church of Scotland it did not qualify for University Grants Committee funding. The Church therefore agreed to transfer ownership of the building to the University. When Matthew and Johnson-Marshall assessed New College and the surrounding properties, they concluded that there was potential for a redevelopment of great material and symbolic value. Like Geddes, they recommended conservative surgery. Some lesser buildings could be removed to permit extension of New College, while other residential properties could be converted into halls of residence. Funding might be available from such sources as the University Grants Committee, the Historic Buildings Council and the City, while the University would provide what it could from its own funds. Inevitably, Johnson-Marshall thought that the City might consider this as another Comprehensive Development Area and advised buying up property in the area, including the Outlook Tower.[26]

The University demonstrated considerable magnanimity in retaining the services of Ian G. Lindsay & Partners. Lindsay was probably the foremost conservation architect in the country, with the possible exception of Robert Hurd, but he had sought to undermine the George Square redevelopment by attempting to give the

buildings a higher listing status than they already had.[27] Of course, it was useful that Lindsay was an influential member of the Historic Buildings Council. John H. Reid, Lindsay's partner, was put in charge of the project. Ownership of Mylne's Court was split between the City and the Church of Scotland, and both agreed to transfer ownership to the University for the proposed halls of residence reconstruction project. The University Grants Committee favoured the scheme, although without financial commitment, while the City promised £25,000. There was great enthusiasm within the University for this demonstration of its commitment to Edinburgh's architectural heritage, in the wake of the George Square redevelopment.[28] In fact, Mylne's Court was proposed by some as a natural replacement for Masson Hall, which was to be demolished for the main library. But the process was to be a slow one, mainly due to the cost of the work involved.

254 Watercolour of New College quadrangle by Thomas Ross, 1869. The spire of the Highland Tolbooth Church is visible behind the college in the centre of the image.
Capital Collections, Edinburgh [8153]

255 New College library, converted from the church of the college in 1935. A great cycle of stained glass windows was installed to designs by Douglas Strachan between 1911 and 1934.
Nick Haynes

The New College scheme ran into difficulties of the sort experienced with George Square, with opposition both from residents and from critics within the University, over the proposed demolition of Lister House (now Patrick Geddes Hall), the former Ragged School of Dr Guthrie at the top of Ramsay Lane, and the row of old stable buildings between them.[29] On the site of Lister House, Reid proposed a block containing a pair of 100-seat lecture theatres and a pair of large seminar rooms, at both ground and first floor levels, and with a chapel on the upper floor. Immediately to the west, a long seven-storey hostel, on a staggered plan, was to run the length of Ramsay Lane, up to the Outlook Tower, and provide 109 study-bedrooms.[30]

Despite the general approval of the Royal Fine Art Commission of his feasibility study of 1965, Reid was perplexed at the hostility of the Ramsay Garden residents and particularly by 'the University contingent'. The opposition continued unabated until 1975, when both the New College extension and proposed hostel were abandoned in favour of an internal reorganisation of Playfair's building.[31]

Although it was postponed in 1965 in order to concentrate resources on the Pollock Halls, the student residence at Mylne's Court was ultimately successful, although substantial private donations were required to help meet the cost.[32] Foundations had to be underpinned, roofs repaired, all the plumbing and wiring renewed, fire escapes installed, and concrete floors inserted to stiffen the structure, while the partly-demolished east range had to be entirely reconstructed. Work started on the first phase, Philip Henman Hall, in 1966 and the second phase, Edward Salvesen Hall, was completed in 1970, creating 180 student places. Thus a Geddesian vision of a community of scholars in the heart of the Old Town had been achieved.

The rest of the residential project, including James' Court, was ultimately abandoned because the costs were vastly disproportionate to the accommodation that could be provided.[33] The cost per student place was more than double that of Kininmonth's Skarne blocks at Pollock Halls. The University ultimately disposed of the other properties that it had acquired in the area, with the exception of Sempill's Close and Lister House, which were structurally unsound and difficult to sell, and several years were to elapse before their successful rehabilitation.

For Johnson-Marshall and Matthew, however, the scheme was incomplete without the Outlook Tower, which they wanted as a school of civic studies. The symbolic appeal, though, greatly outweighed the practical value of the building, with its narrow turnpike stair. The University did agree to lease the building, however, and a Patrick Geddes Centre, with Johnson-Marshall as

director, was set up in part of the premises, under the auspices of the Department of Urban Design. Material related to Geddes and other urban theorists was deposited there for study, but when the lease expired in 1999, it was not renewed.

ST CECILIA'S HALL

The University's other flagship conservation project of the 1960s did not meet opposition, but it did take eight years to achieve. This was the restoration of St Cecilia's Hall, Scotland's first purpose-built concert hall, and a fine example of Scottish classicism. It was originally built in 1763–5 to designs by the notable architect Robert Mylne for the Edinburgh Musical Society. Interestingly, the designer was the great-grandson of the master mason who built Mylne's Court. Following his grand tour in the 1750s, Mylne became a prominent architect of the neoclassical and picturesque movements after winning the competition to design Blackfriars Bridge, in London. This is his only extant building in Edinburgh.

St Cecilia's has a chequered history. Following the building of the South Bridge, the Cowgate area generally fell into a state of dilapidation. The building was a Baptist chapel by the early 19th century, then part of a Masonic lodge augmented by new premises to the south, in the 1820s, which itself subsequently became a public house (the Bridge Bar). St Cecilia's was a school in the mid-19th century, and the Excelsior Ballroom in the 1940s. When the University acquired the building, in 1959, it was in a state of dereliction and the matters of a suitable use and the money to pay for the work had to

256 The Niddry Street frontage of St Cecilia's Hall photographed in its dilapidated state, 1960
HES [SC 1149965]

be resolved. The City's co-operation in guaranteeing that this would not be affected by proposed road widening of the Cowgate was also necessary.

Happily, the musician and author, Raymond Russell, was enthusiastic about the project and decided to donate his collection of keyboard instruments to the University. And, although he died in 1964, his family carried out his wishes. This made the hall viable as a museum, while reconstruction of the interior created an ideal venue for musical performances once more and thus an extremely useful resource for the faculty of music, and an asset to the musical life of the city. A funding package was eventually assembled, with contributions from the University Grants Committee, the Historic Buildings Council and the Russell family.[34] Ian Lindsay had been appointed at the outset, and he proposed reinstating the original elliptical interior of the auditorium, but he too died soon after work began, in 1966. John Reid took over the job and it was completed in 1968. A new steel-framed east wing with stone base courses and a glazed curtain wall was designed to provide a gallery for the instruments and a conservation workshop. The Freemasons Hall of the 1820s, to which it was conjoined, was incorporated into the scheme.

The west façade, which was the original entrance front, is the only part of the exterior identifiable as the work of Mylne. It is an austere neoclassical composition in polished ashlar, consisting of two storeys and five bays, with the central three advanced. The doorway has a flat cornice borne on consoles, the apertures have plain architraves and the only other decoration is the cill and base courses. Surprisingly, the original imposing Doric order screen in the entrance hall, and the double curved stone staircase have survived, despite the vicissitudes of time. The oval concert hall, reinstated by John Reid, is suitably baroque in form.

In 2013 the University appointed Page\Park Architects to undertake a £6.5m programme of conservation and refurbishment, partly funded by the Heritage Lottery Fund. Key elements of the scheme are: restoration of the original historic frontage of the building and creation of a new signature entrance in the shape of a harpsichord lid to face the Royal Mile; restoration and expansion of the gallery spaces; improvements to the concert hall through the introduction of bespoke tiered seating and staging platforms, reminiscent of the 1763 original, while modernising services; and upgrading the infrastructure to improve access and environmental conditions for the historic instrument collections.

POLLOCK HALLS OF RESIDENCE
(SECOND DEVELOPMENT)

The first pair of new residential halls at Salisbury Green, Holland House and Fraser House, designed in the 1950s, were completed in 1960 and 1964 respectively, providing 355 student places, although the loss of places at George Square had to be taken into account in the overall drive for more student accommodation. Together with the conjoined refectory, these constituted the first two phases of William Kininmonth's layout proposal of 1949, which aimed at a total population of about 1,800. Kininmonth was retained as site consultant and architect for the next phase of residences, but by 1962 the pattern of future development was under review. Now with a new target density of seventy-five persons per acre, he drafted a scheme for four further halls, each to contain 250 beds, together with some staff buildings. But times had changed, and the traditional collegiate halls of residence, with their arrangement of cloistered accommodation connected to refectory and common rooms, was no longer considered desirable by the University Grants Committee. Following a report commissioned from Robert Gardner-Medwin, the preferred type became detached accommodation buildings, containing different types of flatlets, including self-catering.[35] The University Court therefore decided that future development should be of detached accommodation blocks, containing study-bedrooms, to be served by a central catering block, citing Liverpool University as an example. The aim was

now for a population of 2,000 by 1970, with one further development anticipated after this.

To cut costs and construction time, Kininmonth abandoned traditional building methods and proposed instead the Skarne industrialised building system, for which the building company Crudens had the British licence. It had been tried and tested in Sweden during the 1950s, and had proved to be an extremely rapid and economical method of constructing blocks of flats. It reduced building time by 50 per cent over traditional methods, and it required half of the normal workforce.[36] Essentially, the system involved first erecting a concrete core tower, which acted as a stabilising unit and contained lifts, stairs and all the services, including plumbing and venting. With a crane then mounted on top of this, in-situ concrete floors were laid and pre-cast wall units installed. Non-load-bearing external wall panels and prefabricated wall units could then be hoisted into place and attached.[37]

Kininmonth suggested that, with the removal of the two mansions, Salisbury Green and St Leonard's Hall, eight five-storey and four four-storey blocks, a large catering block, and some staff houses could be provided at a cost of about £1.9m, thus providing a further 1,342 student and forty-five staff places. The Pollock Halls Development Committee found this too expensive, and the architects were asked to look at cutting the cost by reducing room sizes, ceiling heights, the number of baths provided, storage and so on. In the meantime a small two-storey warden's house was erected immediately to the north-west of Holland House.[38]

In January 1964, after a variety of permutations had been considered, a scheme was accepted for six accommodation blocks to house 1,006 students, using the Skarne system, at a cost of £914,000. A further phase would involve the catering block, which was also to function as a conference centre, to bring in much-needed revenue during vacation time. Further residential blocks were anticipated in subsequent phases. Tellingly, one proposed layout, of July 1963, shows a total of ten Skarne blocks, which would have entailed the demolition of Salisbury Green and Abden House, as well as March Hall, a privately-owned nursing-home close to Abden. The notion that the Principal's house could be sacrificed demonstrates the urgency of the need to provide student accommodation. As it transpired, the third phase avoided the pre-20th-century buildings.

Salisbury Green was still in use as a student residence, and the others only survived this period because of the costs that would have been entailed by their demolition.

Although the University Grants Committee funding was insufficient to meet the full estimated costs, work started early in 1965 on the first of the six blocks. The residential blocks have an irregular plan of three linked rectangles. Four blocks were of five storeys and two of six storeys, and these were arrayed around the central facility. They were clad in storey-high concrete panels with an exposed aggregate, which were given a reddish tint to relate them to the backdrop of Salisbury Crags. The fenestration is in vertical strips with green spandrel panels. The two-storey John McIntyre Centre, although not using the Skarne system, was clad in similar panels. Progress was certainly rapid, as the first block was ready in October 1966, and three more by the following March, while the other two were approaching completion.[39] This included site works, some demolition of garden buildings and the erection of a boiler house.[40] The demands of the design, however, went beyond the capabilities of Cruden's version of the Skarne system. They necessitated considerable adjustment and modification by the architects and builders. By some careful amendments to the scheme, the accommodation had been increased to 1,020 students in the Skarne blocks, as well as some small flats for academic staff who were prepared to act as wardens. Each floor contained two groups of eighteen study-bedrooms. This was extremely economical of space, as indeed were the apartments of the first Skarne blocks in Sweden, described by journalists as cramped.

In the meantime, students were to share refectory facilities with Holland and Fraser Houses although by this stage a brief had been created for the next phase of development, a catering block to seat 800, which the University Grants Committee asked to be moderated to 600 seats.[63] This was not likely to have been built for several years, if reliant upon the University Grants Committee funding programme. However, fortuitous circumstances led to an earlier delivery. Edinburgh had been selected as the host city for the 1970 Commonwealth Games, formerly the Empire Games. This might be seen as the last major event of Edinburgh's post-war period. The era ushered in by the launch of the International Festival in 1947 was drawing to a close, but the 'Friendly Games' wrung

262 Proposal sketches for the third phase of development at Pollock Halls by Rowand Anderson, Kininmonth & Paul, 1964
University of Edinburgh Estates Collection

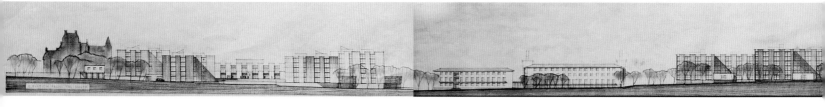

263 Sketch of a study / bedroom in one of the Skarne blocks at Pollock Halls, about 1964

University of Edinburgh Estates Collection

out the last flood of the city's post-war optimism. The British Empire was transformed into a family of nations, while the University had changed from an Imperial to a Commonwealth institution.

Michael Swann agreed to allow the Pollock Halls of Residence to be used as the Games Village, hosting the athletes and their entourages. This was the perfect location, since the City was building a swimming pool adjacent to the site. Furthermore, as a stadium was being built at Meadowbank, to the east, all the journeys between the three locations could easily and quickly be made through Holyrood Park. As catering facilities were felt to be inadequate for the games, influence was brought to bear upon the University Grants Committee to provide early funding for the new refectory in order that it should be ready in time for July 1970. With a budget of £200,000, work on the refectory commenced late in 1968 and, of course, it was ready in time for the Commonwealth Games.[41] The six residential blocks

were named after past University Principals – Brewster; Grant, Lee, Turner, Baird, and Ewing – while the refectory was named the John McIntyre Centre, after the Principal of New College, who had served on the development committee for the Pollock Halls and was the first senior warden there.[42]

A further residential block, with places for 360 students, plus a common room, was erected in two phases, commencing in 1971. This was a three-storey block on a quadrangular plan around a garden court. The load-bearing brick structure used the same fenestration pattern as the Skarne blocks and was given a harled finish. This building, the new Cowan House, was extremely low-cost and when maintenance became a liability it was demolished together with Brewster House, in 2001, to provide a site for a new building, Chancellor's Court, by Oberlanders Architects in 2003. The John McIntyre Centre was transformed in a refurbishment by Lewis Hickey architects, in 2009.

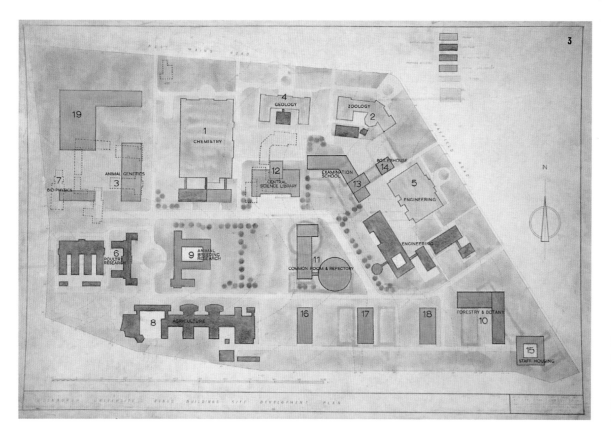

264 Plan and proposed layout
of the King's Buildings site by
William Kininmonth, 1964

University of Edinburgh, Edinburgh
School of Architecture and Landscape
Architecture

KING'S BUILDINGS 1960-1970

In comparison to the complexities involved in creating
the University's city centre precinct, development of
the science campus was fairly straightforward, and
rapid during the 1960s, funding being the only obstacle
to ambition. William Kininmonth remained as site
consultant until 1964, when he retired in favour of the
University's overall planning consultant Percy Johnson-
Marshall, who basically reiterated Kininmonth's
recommendations of 1961, that a radial route around
the perimeter of the site from the gate on West Mains
Road to the entrance on Mayfield Road should be
constructed. This would become a central avenue should
the adjacent golf course, also owned by the University,
eventually be developed. It was accepted that taller
buildings than previously erected (i.e. over two storeys)
would have to be considered.[43] With so many science
buildings now in the pipeline, a scheme for a proposed
student residence at the campus was cancelled. As there
was some concern about the haphazard appearance,
both consultants recommended H.F. Clark to advise
on landscaping and planting. There seemed a need for
a landscaped central amenity space and Clark was a
notable landscape designer who had been a consultant
for the South Bank site for the Festival of Britain and
was appointed senior lecturer in landscape design at
the University's Department of Architecture in 1959. He
devised a low-maintenance scheme to screen some of
the untidier parts. The central landscaped area was only
achieved much later.

In 1960, when Robert Gardner-Medwin's first phase of
extensions to the engineering building were approaching
completion, he received further commissions for the
new botany and forestry buildings, begun in 1963 and
1965 respectively. He was also to continue extending
the engineering complex. Kingham Knight Associates,
now with an Edinburgh office, actually undertook these,
with occasional consultation from the professor. The
second phase began with a large structures laboratory
for civil engineering, and there were further extensions
for that department, one largely funded by the Crudens
Foundation, as well as some for electrical engineering
from 1967. Following the migration of chemical
engineering from Heriot-Watt to the University, Kingham
Knight Associates also designed their large laboratory,
begun in 1968.

In 1960, Michael Laird received commissions for a
new boiler house and a refectory, the first of which did not
commence until 1968, by which time he had the contract
for another amenity building. In addition, a site had been
allocated for the use of the Animal Breeding Research
Organisation in 1959, with Basil Spence & Partners as
designers, which commenced in 1962. Later in the decade
the same practice started designing the physics/maths
building. In 1965 construction began on a building for epigenetics, by RMJM, and on another extension for zoology,
by the Architectural Research Unit. Alan Reiach's final
work at King's Buildings was an extension to the geology
building for experimental petrology, begun in 1967.

ROGER LAND BUILDING
(FORMER ANIMAL BREEDING RESEARCH ORGANISATION BUILDING)

When the Scientific Research Council received funding for a new laboratory facility, the King's Buildings was the obvious location, given the University's pre-eminence in genetics, and the presence of their chief geneticist, Professor C.H. Waddington. Sir Edward Appleton was happy to provide a site for the Animal Breeding Research Organisation building, recommending Basil Spencer & Partners as architects, in 1959.[44] The project team from the firm comprised Hardie Glover, Richard Cassidy and Norman Hunter. An appropriate place was found conveniently close to related departments: the SRC poultry research building, the Institute of Animal Genetics (the Crew Building) and the School of Agriculture. The western part of the campus was becoming quite a centre for animal genetics by this time and there were also a number of low-cost single-storey buildings, including huts and kit buildings, used for animal houses and ancillaries.

Built between 1962 and 1964, the Animal Breeding Research Organisation building was one of the more interesting looking of that time, with its striking external black steel skeleton, contrasting with the brick outer skin – having the stanchions outside the walls was cheaper than fireproofing them internally. Although it follows the earlier two-storey standard for King's Buildings – the taller buildings were soon to come – this one was designed to be extendable upwards.[45] The roof was therefore kept clear of plant, which was a positive factor in its appearance, together with the articulation of the stanchions against the elevations. This approach is a tidier alternative to the extendable-by-wings approach.

The quadrangular plan has a central service yard, with a loading bay where equipment can be concealed – considerable quantities of biological samples would be delivered for testing. The external leaf is facing brick, with mosaics-faced panels to the fascia and spandrels. Steel-framed windows and grey-painted glass panels were set into timber sub-frames. The entrance is through a glazed screen, which is repeated at the rear of the entrance hall, allowing views through the building to a terrace. Some excitement is added at the south-west where the upper storey is supported on pilotis and carried over the single-storey timber conference hall. Its window panes are set between closely spaced timber fins.

The interior consists mainly of small laboratories and offices arranged about a spinal corridor. Commissioned in 1959, it is early enough to still have something of the Festival Style in the internal details, where there are some pine ceilings, fair-faced brick walls, and

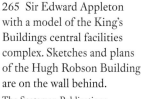

265 Sir Edward Appleton with a model of the King's Buildings central facilities complex. Sketches and plans of the Hugh Robson Building are on the wall behind.

The Scotsman Publications Ltd [via www.scran.ac.uk: 000-000-051-931-R]

exposed timber roof joists. The internal partitions were hardboard-faced, and demountable for flexibility to changing needs.

Originally a government departmental building, it was later inherited by the University and named after Roger Land, a former director of the Animal Breeding Research Organisation.

FORMER WADDINGTON AND WEIR BUILDINGS

A further addition to biological science at the western side of the campus came with the building for the epigenetics research group, designed by RMJM and begun in 1965.[46] It was funded by the Medical Research Council, the Wellcome Trust and the Distillers Company. This is a typical work of the practice, with its emphasis on horizontality and elevations consisting of bands of glazing. A squat tower of four storeys, the plant room on the flat roof appears disproportionately large, but the building was intended to be extendable vertically. It later came to be named after Professor C.H. Waddington, who occupied the top floor for many years. The building was demolished in 2016.

One of Waddington's research staff, G.H. Beale, was also able to add to genetic research facilities at this time, when he received a grant from the Wellcome Trust for a protozoan genetics unit. Located beside the western boundary of the site next to the cluster of genetics buildings, this simple single-storey unit with brick facing was designed by the relatively unknown architect, Cyril McLeod.[47] In the 1990s it was linked with adjacent former genetics annexes to become the science faculty office. Remaining as an administration centre, it is now known as the Weir Building.

ASHWORTH BUILDING EXTENSION (ZOOLOGY)

Science was not the only faculty involved in research. Sir Robert Matthew had set up the Housing Research Unit for postgraduate study, associated with the Department of Architecture. The Housing Research Unit did not merely produce research reports, it also undertook commissions and executed buildings, informed by its research, and there were a number of housing schemes, including those at Kirkcudbright, Prestonpans and Cumbernauld. Much of the unit's methodology was seeking faster, better and cheaper ways to build, by utilising mass production and standardisation. Broadening its field of research, it became the Architecture Research Unit, with a specialism for laboratory design. The director of the unit was Charles Robertson, formerly of Basil Spence & Partners. It was quite appropriate, therefore, that the Department of Zoology should ask the Architecture Research Unit to

address its accommodation needs, especially as speed of construction was a critical factor – there had already been a small laboratory annexe added, in 1960, by the Department of Works.[48]

The response was an extension to the south-east of the Ashworth Building, comprising five storeys, plus basement and penthouse, with Thomas Henney as principal architect. It has a reinforced concrete structure, mainly using pre-cast columns and beams for rapid erection. The front elevation consists entirely of pre-cast concrete panels containing the windows. This rigid system was altered slightly, on the ground floor level, to form a doorway, but there is no grand entrance for, unlike the Ashworth Building, it is deliberately non-hierarchical. The panels have an exposed quartz aggregate which glistens in either sun or rain, thus avoiding the dreary damp staining of many concrete surfaces. The extension is linked to its predecessor with staircases at ground and basement levels.

The basement and penthouses contained the plant and mechanical services, while the ground floor had seminar rooms, technical rooms and workshops, including a glass-blowing room. The other floors had research laboratories and staff offices, and each floor had a central workspace. Funding, provided by the University Grants Committee and the Wellcome Trust, was confirmed by Professor Swann, the future Principal, in February 1964, and the extension was completed in 1966, at a cost of £244,603. Naturally, the construction process was documented and the findings duly published as a research report.[49]

DANIEL RUTHERFORD BUILDING (BOTANY) AND DARWIN BUILDING (FORESTRY AND NATURAL RESOURCES)

Botany and forestry were allocated adjacent sites at the south-east corner of the campus beside the Mayfield Road gate, botany having been based primarily at the Royal Botanic Garden during its transition from the medical to the science faculty. Robert Gardner-Medwin was architect for both, with the anticipation of further related facilities, including a library and glasshouses, as part of a complex for natural sciences, much as he had already done with the group for the engineering departments, discussed previously. As usual, the associate architects were Kingham Knight Associates.

Botany came first, with building consent granted in August 1963.[50] It is a very straightforward construction, on a square plan consisting of two storeys, with the basement storey on the east, and the entrance on the north. The elevations consist of textured concrete spandrel panels and pilasters forming a grid of apertures, which are either glazed or filled with semi-blank panels with clerestory type glazing. These panels define the building's generating module. They were intended to be interchangeable to respond to varying needs over time. Each bay has narrow glazing running the length of the elevation. The same concrete members also form a continuous parapet. The original entrance, on the north, now has a projecting portico formed by a concrete canopy and plate glass doors. To the right of this a diminutive glazed staircase tower also projects. On the west, a glazed bridge on concrete stanchions, which came later, provides an upper level link to the Darwin Library. The building opened in 1965, and was later named after Daniel Rutherford, Professor of Botany at the University during the Scottish Enlightenment.

A start was made in 1965 on the building for forestry and natural resources, which was to be shared with molecular biology, but with only the structural steel completed, there came a sudden enforced halt on building contracts by the University Grants Committee. This left the frame gently rusting for a year until the project could be restarted. But it was completed in 1967 and the Department of Forestry and Natural Resources finally moved from north George Square into the appropriately named Darwin Building.

At ten storeys, it is the tallest building on the campus, disregarding Johnson-Marshall's proposed height restriction, which envisaged the tallest structure as the boiler house chimney. It is another example of the disciplined grid approach.[51] The two lower storeys are largely blind, with only occasional clerestory type windows giving this zone the effect of a plinth. Above it, each bay consists of a window and a concrete spandrel panel. Vertical divisions are giant pilasters formed of textured panels. The façade is recessed slightly at the sixth floor, at the level where accommodation for

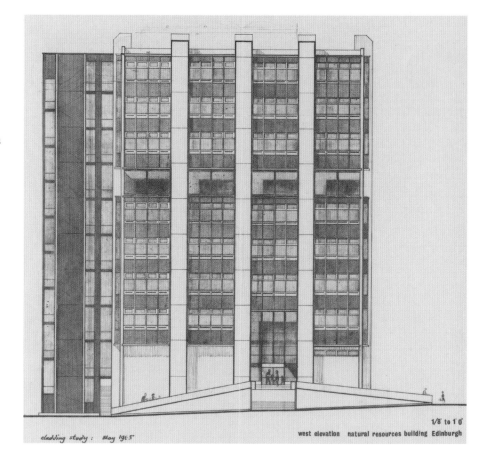

cladding study : May 1965

1/8" to 1'0"
west elevation   natural resources building Edinburgh

molecular biology originally began. Like the Appleton Tower, a glazed stairtower is attached at right angles on the east side. Another similarity is the lack of a formal entrance, as it was anticipated that the lower floors would be linked to other buildings and entered from those. The two-storey Darwin Library block was later to fulfil this role. With its entrance on the west, the external leaf of blockwork is partially rendered, and it

270 Cladding study for the Darwin Building by Robert Gardner-Medwin with Kingham Knight Associates, 1965
University of Edinburgh [0078877d]

271 Photomontage of a proposal for the Darwin Tower by Robert Gardner-Medwin with Kingham Knight Associates, about 1964
University of Edinburgh [0078878d]

272 Darwin Building from the south
Nick Haynes

273 A design for the redevelopment of the Darwin Building by Feilden Clegg Bradley Studios, 2014
Feilden Clegg Bradley Studios

has a projecting parapet of pre-cast slabs. A glazed link at the upper level bridges a side road to connect it to the Daniel Rutherford Building.

In 2014 designs by Feilden Clegg Bradley Studios were published for redeveloping the buildings as part of the strategy for modernising the facilities of the School of Biological Sciences. The re-engineered building will provide state-of-the-art laboratories for more than 350 researchers, an advanced technology hub and space to co-locate and support future growth in three strategic areas of research: epigenetics; infection and global health; and synthetic biology.[52]

ENGINEERING EXTENSIONS, PHASE TWO: ENGINEERING STRUCTURES LABORATORY, JOHN MUIR BUILDING (FORMER CONCRETE LABORATORY)

The first stage of the engineering extensions was completed in 1961 and consisted of what are now named the Hudson Beare Building and Lecture Theatre, the Faraday Building and the Fleeming Jenkin Building. These had been laid out in such a way that further extensions could be added simply, and work was soon in hand for these. The structures laboratory in 1965 was sited to the south-west of the Sanderson Building, creating enclosure to an inner courtyard of the ensemble.

The demand for additional accommodation for the various Departments of Engineering had been anticipated by the architects who had a plan for extensions in phases to the west of the laboratory block (Fleeming Jenkin). For reasons of economy and speed of erection, Kingham Knight Associates utilised the 'Terrapin' patent building system. This came in standard units, of one or two storeys, and employed a timber and steel frame, which were simply unfolded on the site. Windows, doors and plywood panels were then bolted on, and any number of the 200ft² units could be linked together. A number of these were erected during the late 1960s, despite the qualms of the City's planners about their safety – it was claimed that they could withstand winds of up to 72mph. Extensions for the newly renamed Department of Civil Engineering and Building Science (1967 and 1968) and Micro-Electronics (1969) used the system, in a two-storey version.[53] The light-well within the electrical engineering block was also used for extensions.[54]

Apart from the main structures laboratory and the former concrete laboratory (now the John Muir Building) all of the buildings in this stage of the extensions have been demolished. Those to the west of Fleeming Jenkin were replaced by the William Rankine and Alexander Graham Bell Buildings, while chemical engineering made way for the Mary Brück Building.

Chapter Eight

Crisis and Conservation 1970–1985

CLIVE B. FENTON

274 Interior of the former George Watson's
Ladies College, designed by George Washington
Browne in 1910, now the Psychology Department
HES

As the 1960s drew to a close, many began to question the ethos of the nation's post-war reconstruction project, and there was a growing anxiety about the loss of architectural character in the drive for modernisation, improved transport systems and slum clearances. Over-ambitious schemes had resulted in urban sites remaining either empty, or with boarded-up derelict buildings awaiting demolition for years, while protracted discussions about redevelopment took place, and Edinburgh was no exception. A new disease, 'planning blight', was diagnosed, with planners and architects identified as the bearers of infection. A plethora of journal articles and books began to tilt public opinion from modernisation to conservation. In one such book, *The Rape of Britain*, photographs of derelict buildings in Edinburgh's South Side were used to condemn the University's plans.[1] An article in *Country Life*, by one of the University's own fine arts lecturers, was directed specifically against the University's Lawnmarket development plan, and Professor Johnson-Marshall's Comprehensive Development Area scheme was viewed as authoritarian and doctrinaire.[2] Much of the impetus for criticism came from within the University, but there was a growing national appetite for conservation and community involvement in matters of planning and development. The era of deference to experts was clearly passing.

With St Cecilia's Hall and Mylne's Court as successful examples of University rehabilitation, numerous other potential projects were proposed. In 1969, the University published a booklet, 'Conservation and University Expansion', in response to the prevailing mood. The substantial expenditure on conservation by the University is stated as £1.28m, with a further £1.88m committed. There is mention of a change in development policy since 1961, necessitated by the decisions to remove the physics departments to the King's Buildings, and to create new faculties of social science and veterinary studies – the latter was about to build extensions at its Summerhall site, to the south-east of the University central area. The uncertainty about the City's road schemes, and about future commercial development, over which the University had no control, is also explained, and there are descriptions of all the buildings around the University and any known plans for their future. These include tenements in Buccleuch Place, in temporary use by either academic departments or residential tenants, pending redevelopment, and buildings in the Bristo Street area acquired by the City for demolition. Students too joined the clamour, and feasibility studies for further conversions into student flats were demanded throughout the 1970s. Meeting the cost was seldom feasible, though. The conservation lobby even turned its attention to the retention of the surviving buildings on north George Square, including the forestry building of 1912. Their audacious call was disconcerting as it had previously been accepted by all parties that this was earmarked for the medical extensions. Furthermore, tenants of a block of tenements at Lauriston Place succeeded in thwarting its demolition to enable the new Dental Hospital and School, which then had to be allocated a place at Crichton Street, where an extension to the Appleton Tower and a possible gymnasium were already planned.

The economy played havoc with everyone's plans in the 1970s and the inflation of the late 1960s had resulted in escalating building costs. Then came the financial crisis of 1973, causing the Treasury to drastically cut its funding to the University Grants Committee. By 1973, when Sir Michael Swann resigned, the national programme was at a virtual standstill. Universities across the country were unable to proceed with their building plans and were forced to truncate or abandon numerous scheduled works. Industrial unrest and the effects of oil and fuel shortages impacted heavily upon the construction industry.

Under such circumstances it was an onerous business to start on any new buildings after 1974. In some ways it was like a return to the pre-war situation, with universities competing for a share of a very small Treasury allowance, and relatively more reliant upon sponsorship and benefactions.

One medical success story of the late 1970s was the building for reproductive biology at Chalmers Street on the north-west boundary of the infirmary site. Completed in 1979, this was typical of the RMJM style of the period. A five-storey block, with vertical elements suppressed, its elevations consisted of bands of glazing separated by bands of white concrete facings. Taking advantage of the fall in the ground to the south, car parking was created between the structural columns. Significantly, a glazed bridge at third floor level provided access to the infirmary's maternity unit, the Simpson Memorial Pavilion. The building was demolished following the removal of the Royal Infirmary to Little France.

At Edinburgh, some departments expecting new buildings, such as architecture and psychology, had to settle for converted premises instead, while many others remained in ad-hoc accommodation using flats and houses in and around George Square. The survival of the terrace of original houses on the east side of the square was due only to the exigencies of the time, specifically the shelving of further phases of the Appleton Tower group for first-year science. Similarly, stasis on the arts and social sciences building programme reprieved Buccleuch Place.

By 1975 the University had reached a position in which it anticipated no further demolitions, excluding

the outstanding proposals for George Square. The Comprehensive Development Area passed into history and was superseded by a new generation of local plans and designated conservation areas. Percy Johnson-Marshall seemed to engage quite happily with the more conservation-minded and community-orientated atmosphere prevailing at the time and his practice assisted the City in producing the South Side Local Plan in 1975.

There were no longer great hopes of large commercial development at Nicolson Street, and the zoning of the Drummond Street area for housing curtailed University ambitions in that area. Local authority house-building had also fallen away in the recession and a short-term solution was to provide grants to landlords for tenement rehabilitation, to extend the lives of the tenements for about fifteen years. The University had purchased many flats in the area, for decanting tenants and ultimately as sites for new buildings. But the burden of maintenance was high, and with no prospect of development these were transferred to housing associations, such as Edinvar, to take on the rehabilitation. Members of the University were closely involved in the creation of this housing association, ostensibly to rent refurbished flats to staff and students.

John McIntyre, the Dean of Divinity, took the role of Acting Principal until Sir Hugh Robson succeeded Swann in 1974. Robson had previously been Vice-Chancellor of Sheffield University. An alumnus of Edinburgh, and a distinguished medical professor, he was also chairman of the Committee of Vice-Chancellors and Principals. According to Charles Stewart, the University Secretary at the time, all of Robson's wisdom

275 Sketch of the pharmacology building on the north side of George Square by John W. Hart, 1971
University of Edinburgh Estates Collection

276 An aerial view of George Square in 1989 from west to south-west, showing the major developments constructed during the 1960s towering above the surviving Georgian buildings in the square. The large building (top left of the square) is the main library, the smaller building below is the George Square Theatre. Bottom left is the David Hume Tower, the L-shaped building adjacent is the William Robertson Building and the tall structure (bottom right) is the Appleton Tower.
HES [SC 702546]

277 Sketch of the Hugh Robson Building by John W. Hart, 1971
University of Edinburgh Estates Collection

and experience, and all his physical endurance was called upon by the task of ensuring a further phase of the medical extensions should proceed. Stewart believed that the stress and burden of work contributed to Robson's sudden death in 1977.[3] Stewart himself retired that year after thirty years of service during which he was executor of the post-war development plan. By this time it was accepted that the University's current building programme would come to an end with completion of the biochemistry building and the Dental Hospital and School. Of these only the former was achieved.

The next Principal, Sir John Burnett, a botanist and former Professor of Rural Economy at Oxford, did not take up his position until 1979, and remained until 1986. In the interim, Professor Samuel Berrick Saul, and then John McIntyre, carried out the duties of Acting Principal, with Professor Youngson as Acting Vice-Principal. Both Saul and Youngson were economic historians. Known in architectural circles for his book on the building of Edinburgh's New Town, Youngson also served on the Royal Fine Art Commission. This strengthened the conservationist trend within the various building and development committees of the University, and the University Conservation Group was formed in 1975 to take care of the historical properties.[4]

Burnett's tenure saw a government re-assessment of university funding in general, and he had to oversee rigorous economies in running costs. Desperate measures were sought to save money as the University Grants Committee funding for building projects was negligible.

GEORGE SQUARE 1970–1985
THE MEDICAL EXTENSIONS, PHASE THREE: HUGH ROBSON BUILDING (NEW CENTRE FOR INTEGRATIVE PHYSIOLOGY; FORMER BIOCHEMISTRY)

The long-awaited third phase of the medical extensions, for biochemistry, had a difficult gestation. The sub-committee for the project met with the architect, Walter Ramsay, to discuss requirements in November 1970, but by early the next year, lack of a positive response from the University Grants Committee put commencement in doubt. It was nevertheless decided to proceed with the planning. Such was the position when Hugh Robson arrived as Principal in 1974, and he lobbied tirelessly for a positive outcome and searched for funding. The architect was asked to look for savings and the proposed underground car parking was omitted. As it happened, over £600,000 from the Erskine bequest was available for a medical library, so this was incorporated into the scheme. Originally this was anticipated as a separate building, with Hardie Glover, by now a specialist in library design, as architect.

But money was not the only obstacle. The conservationists called for a halt to all further demolition, even the former forestry building and the two reconstructed houses constituting nos 11–14. The University found itself back in a struggle over George Square, but this time about the previously unappreciated north side. Outline consent for demolition for the third phase had been granted in 1972, but as the protests mounted, and the University became sensitive to bad publicity, Johnson-Marshall was instructed to look for alternative sites for biochemistry. None was viable, given the additional costs of replanning and the uncertainty of University Grants Committee approval. With £400,000 already expended on fees, the University sought and received planning permission in July 1976. There was a further debate in the press, a petition, and immediate appeals by the various amenity societies to the Secretary of State to call in the planning consent. Although these buildings had subsequently been given listed status, there was a longstanding agreement that they would be demolished, and numerous outline consents for the medical extensions had been given since 1956 on this basis. The irony of the appeals to save the buildings that had compromised the integrity of the square did not escape the Principal when five Edinburgh constituency MPs demanded that the biochemistry project should be abandoned. Did they not realise that the whole post-war redevelopment had been premised upon the redevelopment of north George Square?[5] In addition, the £2.86m that would be spent on construction gave an

economic imperative to the political situation at a time of recession. Listed Building Consent was given and work commenced in 1977.

Shortly after the death of the Principal it was agreed that the building's name should commemorate his contribution. In use by 1980, the Hugh Robson Building had to wait until 1983 for the link to the first phase to be completed, by which time a fourth phase was an ever-receding hope.[6]

As there were some complexities involved with the structure, mechanical services, and boiler-house provision, the services of engineers Ove Arup & Partners had been engaged specifically to ensure that there were no costly miscalculations, as there had been with phase one. Like pharmacology, this had a concrete frame, and had reinforced concrete structural walls. One of the engineering issues was resolving the structural grids of two buildings within one envelope, since concealed within the building envelope was the Erskine Medical Library, which occupied a portion of the basement, ground and first floors, in between the two light-wells. This was designed separately by Spence, Glover & Ferguson. Apart from the faculty of medicine animal

278 The Hugh Robson Building as remodelled by BDG Architecture + Design, 2004–5
Nick Haynes

279 Detail of the 'concrete corduroy' on the Hugh Robson Building
Nick Haynes

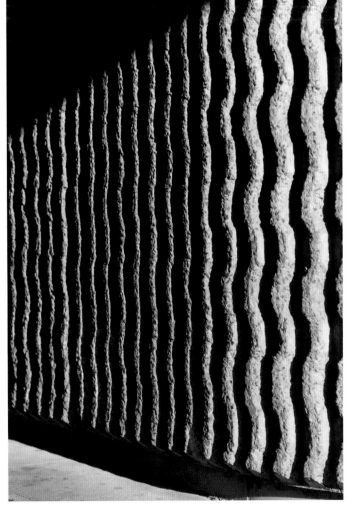

houses, the library and a 300-seat lecture theatre, the rest of the accommodation was laboratories and offices.

The building presents quite a long frontage of eighteen bays on its south elevation, with another six bays on the two-storey link at the west end. Of the six storeys, the upper level of animal houses is blind, while the ground and first floor are set back within the colonnade of square concrete columns, which helps to reduce the apparent bulk. Hardie Glover advised on the façade and surface treatment, as Spence had done for the first phase, and there is considerable enlivening of what might have been a rather austere block, as indicated by Ramsay's prizewinning design of 1951. The walls within the colonnade are clad in chipped ribbed concrete slabs, as a form of rustication, while the upper zone is faced in smooth stone. Beams projecting through the wall engage with the columns, clearly for the sake of continuity with the loggia of the main library on the opposite side of the square. At first floor level, some of the bays project forward, like enclosed balconies hung between the columns, as on the pharmacology block. Here this is continued over the entrance to the landscaped courtyard in the western link, where there is a student common room. At the off-centre entrance, the bays of the first floor also project forward over a portico.

The major £8m refurbishment of the Hugh Robson Building by BDG Architecture & Design in 2004–5 entailed a complete overhaul and modernisation of the building services, and structural interventions to form a seventh storey on top of the existing building for plant areas, freeing up additional educational space on the upper floors. The Erskine Medical Library was removed at this time.

3–7 GEORGE SQUARE (DEPARTMENT OF PSYCHOLOGY; FORMER GEORGE WATSON'S LADIES COLLEGE)

By 1966 the only property on the north side of George Square not owned by the University was George Watson's Ladies College. Of course, the original medical extension scheme was based on the assumption of simple acquisition of all the necessary properties. Discussions in the 1940s implied that the Merchant Company would give up the property when the University needed it. Such had been the case when the Royal Infirmary needed George Watson's Boys' School at Archibald Place for expansion. But negotiations became too protracted in this case. Alternative accommodation was needed for the girls' school and the University hesitated to agree compensation for this at an early stage in the proceedings. Instead the site was scheduled for the fourth phase of the extensions. In 1967 the Merchant Company announced that it was to merge the boys' and girls' schools, thus vacating George

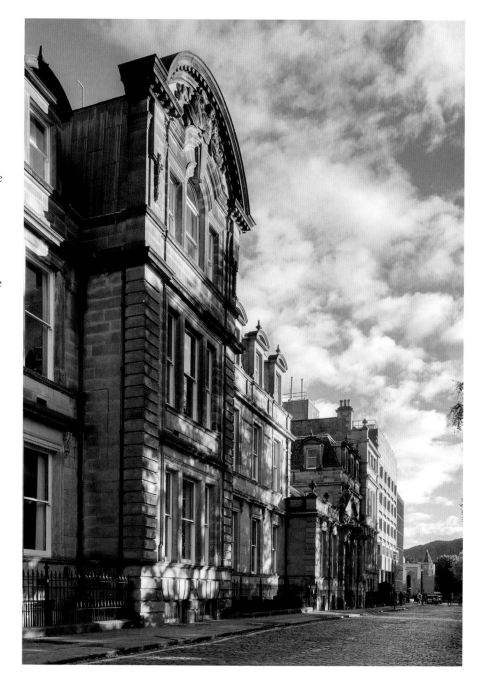

Square by 1974, but still no deal had been struck. The University Grants Committee was not prepared to pay the then asking price for the site, and there would be demolition costs too. An arrangement was eventually concluded in 1973 that involved both money and the transfer of a University playing field to the Merchant Company. By the time the property was finally obtained, there was no prospect of funding the fourth phase of the medical extensions in the foreseeable future, as the University was still trying to commence the third phase. It was decided to allocate the school building for other purposes in the meantime.

The Department of Psychology, based in the Pleasance Little Theatre since 1961, faced both the loss of its proposed Roxburgh Street site through rezoning

280 The Psychology Department (former George Watson's Ladies College), 3–7 George Square. Originally designed by MacGibbon & Ross in 1876, it was extended by Peter Henderson in 1902 and George Washington Browne in 1910–11.
HES

in 1975, and withdrawal of the University Grants Committee funding in 1976.[7] With the Pleasance site under threat, a move seemed nevertheless urgent, so some University Grants Committee 'interchangeability monies' available for conversion costs were assigned for the alteration of the former girls' school, and the services of Spence, Glover & Ferguson were retained for this work. This was all rapidly approved in 1976, and work began late in 1978, being achieved in three phases.[8]

BRISTO SQUARE 1970–85

The City agreed with Johnson-Marshall that Bristo Street should be closed to allow a new square to be created, but instead of widening the street from the Medical School to Old College, as anticipated in the Comprehensive Development Area proposals, the corner at Lothian Street was realigned making it into a curved and banked carriageway. This bypassed South College Street, and it entailed pedestrian communication from Old College to the Student Centre via an underpass and then a ramp up to street level, on the south side. The tunnel is approximately on the site of an ancient gate to the city, Potterrow Port, and was named accordingly. This work, by Lothian Regional Council, which had to be completed first, commenced in October 1978.[9] The City and University had joint responsibility for the cost of Bristo Square – the University's share was to be £468,000.

The purpose of the pedestrian square was to provide a sympathetic setting for the surrounding buildings and to become a meeting place, possibly an amphitheatre, for students, staff and the public generally, although the University decided to retain responsibility, rather than have it adopted by the City. Berrick Saul, the Acting Principal, led a working party to choose the design, for which Percy Johnson-Marshall's own practice had the commission. The design team consisted of Johnson-Marshall with Drew Mackie and Bruce Hare.

Some sketch plans were published in 1979 and, although the Royal Fine Art Commission recommended a modernist design, following consultations, the architects produced a square in a Victorian manner to complement the McEwan Hall. Antique street furniture had been located in a council yard, and Victorian foundry moulds from which to cast bollards to embellish it. The stone and ironwork McEwan lantern that had stood there since 1897 was to be retained at its original position. This scheme was approved, although artificial stone had to be substituted for natural, and a proposed fountain omitted, to reduce costs. The relandscaping of the area commenced in 1980.

The layout of the piazza mediated the fall in the ground from north to south between Lothian Street and George Square with stepped terracing. Raised planters formed partial enclosure, with benches arranged around the internal perimeter – a large bed of shrubbery on the north indicated a plot reserved for a possible extension to the Student Centre, which the revised road layout had reduced to a triangle, but provided screening from traffic. Like the concourse within the Student Centre, it was arranged in the manner of the town squares of Italy and Spain, which are such popular meeting places for the young. While people are less likely to linger outdoors in Edinburgh, the importance of the square for the outflow following graduation ceremonies was quickly appreciated when it was completed in 1983, just in time for the 400th anniversary of the founding of the University of Edinburgh, as the Tounis Colledge. It was proclaimed 'the first new public urban square in central Edinburgh for over a century'.[10] A second phase, to follow completion of the Dental Hospital and School building, was to consist of a tree-lined avenue extending southwards to George Square. This was deferred, and the site between Marshall Street and Crichton Street served as a temporary car park. The dental building was not officially cancelled by the NHS until 1989, but the architects had given up hope long before that. Indeed, that site remained empty until the end of the century. Bristo Square, first proposed by Charles Holden in 1947, can therefore be seen as the final statement of the University's post-war development plan and of the Comprehensive Development Area as proposed in 1962. The square, in the form described, survived only until 2015, when relandscaping began.

POTTERROW STUDENT CENTRE

While the University's redevelopment of the central area was slowing down in the early 1970s, so too was public and private investment in building projects, and Edinburgh, like many cities, had a large number of gap sites where buildings had been cleared in anticipation of some scheme or other. Bristo Street had disappeared entirely, along with Marshall Street, Charles Street, Crichton Street and half of Potterrow and Lothian Street, leaving a gap between the Appleton Tower and Old College. The northern part of this consisted of the sites of buildings restricted in use for student amenities by the terms of Donald Pollock's Trust. The planning consultant's layout for the student amenity site was a series of blocks to be built in phases to form an L-plan as enclosure to the east and north of the new Bristo Square. The McEwan Hall, Reid Music School and the Students' Union would constitute the other sides.

The first appropriate use for Pollock's 'island site' for which funding could be found was a health centre and it was decided that this, together with a refectory, should form the first phase. The architects were Morris & Steedman, appointed in 1960, on the recommendation

of Robert Matthew, who warned them that it might take a very long time to complete the whole of the anticipated Student Centre.[11] Both James Morris and Robert Steedman had been students of Matthew, and their practice made its name designing small modernist houses. By the mid-1960s they were doing larger jobs, such as hotels and offices, and moving into university work with commissions from Strathclyde and Stirling. The architects were less than happy with the 'tenemental' form imposed by Johnson-Marshall, which can be seen in the 'Student Amenity Centre' brochure he produced in 1967, but it was approved by the University and the die had been cast.[12]

In March 1966, Morris & Steedman's design for phase one was approved. As the Lothian Street site was not yet entirely in the hands of the University, the health centre / refectory was placed at north Marshall Street, on the site of the Pollock Memorial Hall. At this time it was assumed that phase two would be on the south side of Marshall Street, and would be a replacement for the gymnasium at the Pleasance, which was under threat of demolition for the Bridges relief road. The City assisted by clearing slums at Bristo Street and building work commenced in October 1968.[13]

During construction, the other buildings on the south side of Lothian Street were demolished. Thus, when it opened in November 1970, the Student Centre stood alone, as if on stilts, in the centre of a building site. And, because it had ultimately to link to the decking system decreed by Johnson-Marshall and future phases, entrance was at first-floor level, necessitating an external stair. This gave it a strange isolated appearance and it was mercilessly lampooned by students, and described as 'unnecessary and expensive' before it had even opened.[14] In truth, it was very necessary because of the growing student body and their need for healthcare and sustenance at reasonable prices. Almost immediately it also became a popular music venue, an important addition to social facilities at the University. The building was described in the architectural press as 'a welcome tool for mass production higher education', having seating for 500 and a serving rate of 1,000 meals per hour.

The Student Centre had a striking façade, with its tripartite arcade at podium level. This was intended to link with subsequent phases to form a covered way along a frontage extending southwards to George Square. But the podium ended abruptly, with a yawning gap between it and the deck at the Appleton Tower. The three upper floors have nine bays, with angular mullions giving an expressionistic effect. At the basement level, a lower colonnade of closely spaced textured columns supports the deck. The whole is clasped between a pair of service towers, clad in ribbed panels, attached to the gables.

The eastern portion of the building is of three storeys, with the lower containing a car park, and most of the south elevation obscured by a skeletal steel fire escape. Towards Potterrow, on the east, basement windows shelter under the colonnade, while there are two galleries fronting horizontal bands of glazing at the upper level. Invisible from outside was the pyramidal cupola, with internal louvres, that lit the galleried refectory. Here, the robust boxy furniture that can be seen in contemporary photographs was especially designed by James Morris.

By the time the health centre/refectory opened in November 1970, plans were well advanced for the next phase, on the adjacent site to the north, at the corner of Potterrow and Lothian Street. This was the Student Amenity Centre, which had originally been anticipated as phase three. It commenced in 1973 and was completed in two years.[15] This contained offices, a bank and a shop, various meeting rooms, and rooms for the Royal Medical Society and a Chaplaincy Centre – ambitions for a full University chapel having been curtailed. Had the whole scheme been completed, this block would have formed the internal corner of the new square.

It is an inward-looking building of two storeys, clad in rendered white panels, enlivened only by the shopfronts and the glazed entrance doors to the corridor, which leads to the central auditorium. The more interesting elevation, with double-height columns and large windows onto the garden courtyard between the two phases, was lost when an extension was added here in the 1990s. It stands out as a landmark by virtue of its black Plexiglas dome, which was devised as an architectural mediation between the domes of Old College and the McEwan Hall. Originally, there was a circular sunken terrace, beneath the dome, intended to evoke a Mediterranean town square, with a fountain and furniture of concrete, and raised beds with luxuriant planting. The galleries on east and west gave access to the various rooms, and there were bars and lounges on two floors, and the lavatories in the basement. The Chaplaincy Centre, on the north, had its own entrance and was arranged over two floors. The tiny contemplative chapel, the full height of the building, and with concealed natural lighting, was entirely plain with roughcast white walls. There have been numerous alterations to the complex including conversion of the refectory into the Management School, in 1991. This necessitated the cafeteria extension, of 2000, and subsequently the levelling of the sunken area to accommodate more traditional seating.

The conservation pressure regarding the properties between Marshall Street and Crichton Street in the early 1970s has already been mentioned. But retention of the condemned tenements would have interfered with ongoing plans, and the University had several proposed

uses for this land: a further phase of the Student Centre, an extension to the Appleton Tower complex for first-year maths / physics and, by 1976, the proposed Dental Hospital and School. Morris & Steedman were appointed architects for all the buildings here, with an expected start in 1980. Although an alternative site for the replacement gymnasium was identified on the east side of Potterrow, the abandonment of the City's road schemes in 1976 meant that the gymnasium at the Pleasance was spared and therefore this land was not needed.

The additional phase of the Student Centre was planned for the site on South Marshall Street, which it would share with the proposed Dental Hospital. The Edinburgh University Student Association wanted a large multi-function concert hall, and as this would not be financed by the University Grants Committee, the Edinburgh University Students' Association enthusiastically began its own fundraising. Ultimately, though, this had to be abandoned due to insufficient money raised by the appeal. The funds raised were instead used for refurbishment of the Teviot Row Union and the site reallocated for the dental building. Morris & Steedman's plan for this was a large block, with two internal light wells, which nevertheless left a space at Crichton Street for the proposed extension to the Appleton Tower.

SUMMERHALL 1970–1985

Having been affiliated since 1935, the Royal (Dick) Veterinary College merged with the University in 1951, becoming the faculty of veterinary studies in 1964. The Veterinary School occupied a building at Summerhall in Edinburgh's South Side and, following the merger, it was able also to take advantage of the facilities at the Easter Bush estate, run as a working farm by the Department of Agriculture. Initially housed in the home farm, it was augmented by the new veterinary field station which opened in 1962. Reiach's tropical veterinary medicine building, located to the south of his previous building, was delayed, but eventually opened by the University Chancellor, HRH The Duke of Edinburgh, in June 1970. It was executed in a similar style to the previous building to complete a C-plan group. The rural nature of the Easter Bush site, and its various existing farm buildings, allowed a number of temporary and ad-hoc small structures, which came and went over the years. The Equine Research and Clinical Research Unit, for instance, completed in 1972, was funded by the unlikely-sounding Horserace Betting Levy Board.

FORMER ROYAL (DICK) SCHOOL OF VETERINARY STUDIES

The college had been at Summerhall since 1916, in a building designed by David McArthy.[16] This was begun in 1913, but not completed until 1923.

When it became feasible to extend the Summerhall premises for the expanding faculty, Reiach was the obvious choice of architect and he was appointed in 1965 to prepare a masterplan. A vacant corner site, formerly occupied by the Hope Park United Free Church, was acquired to increase the footprint but this was insufficient. It was therefore also decided to demolish

the south-eastern pavilion of the McArthy building, at Summerhall Square, in order to permit two new blocks, one for teaching and laboratories and another for clinical and consulting purposes, which was partly grant-aided by the Wellcome Trust.[17]

Consent was granted in 1969, when preliminary work commenced with the courtyard boiler house and chimney. Demolition and erection of the two new blocks started in 1971.[18] The south-east extension, an animal treatment centre, where the public could bring their animals for examination, contained reception and waiting areas, consulting rooms, an x-ray unit, a pharmacy, various staff rooms and animal houses. This was a four-storey building, attached at the upper level to the original building to allow a pend entrance to the courtyard. An external staircase leads to the public entrance at first-floor level, and here, above the entrance, was placed the stone sculpture of a recumbent horse, which had been at the former premises at Clyde Street.[19]

The laboratory block is a seven-storey tower prominently sited on the former church site. Some care was also taken over the siting and treatment of the tower, as can be seen from surviving drawings and perspectives, as it addresses the University's central campus across the Meadows. In that respect the tower follows Basil Spence's proposals of 1954 for a series of

284 Design by Alan Reiach for the laboratory block at the former Royal (Dick) Veterinary College, Summerhall, 1967
HES [Alan Reiach Collection: DP 023985]

towers extending eastwards from George Square to the Salisbury Crags, the others being the Appleton Tower (also by Reiach) and the David Hume Tower.[20]

The extended building was officially reopened in 1973 to mark the 150th anniversary of the foundation of William Dick's original veterinary lecture series. Later the adjacent former Hope Park Congregational Church, by Sutherland and Walker, was acquired and converted to provide a refectory. Much later, in 2004, the decision was made to revert to the former name of the Royal (Dick) School of Veterinary Studies, remove all existing facilities to Easter Bush, and to dispose of the property.

KING'S BUILDINGS 1970–1985

Development at King's Buildings in the 1970s became a test of endurance in the face of mounting obstacles to the ongoing projects. In the summer of 1970 there were problems with completions due to the liquidation of a major contractor. To mitigate the effect the University administration took over the payment of workers and the purchase of materials until new contractors could take over. Nevertheless, this caused delays to the second phase of the maths / physics building and the central facilities complex. Matters worsened with the three-day working week, at the beginning of 1974, imposed by the government to conserve energy, which also affected the supply and delivery of materials; and there was sporadic industrial action to cope with. No further commissions could be contemplated at that time and in the second half of the decade the only ongoing work was on the giant maths / physics building.

In spite of all this there were a number of other completions between 1970 and 1975, such as extensions to the engineering complex for chemical engineering (1971) and electrical engineering (1974); and for zoology and a mammalian genome unit (1975), funded by the Medical Research Council. The last, designed by the Architecture Research Unit, is a simple single-storey brick building, with a basement plant room. Still in existence, as the John Murray Building, its ownership has passed to geosciences. The chemical engineering block, by Gardner-Medwin, was a robust two-storey building in brick and concrete, and a good partner for his earlier structure laboratory, but has now been demolished.

The University also hosted a new guest at West Mains, in the form of the government's Institute of Geological Science (later the British Geological Survey, undertaken by the Department of the Environment's own architect M.J. Mannings. Murchison House, begun in 1971, turned out to be rather an interesting looking building, located on the north-west corner of the campus. While this new arrival was generally welcomed, its site on the western car park caused some consternation as the lack of space for parking had become a major

issue for staff. Relief was provided by the erection of a multi-storey car park. The car park was later removed, while Murchison House was to be inherited by the University when the British Geological Society migrated to the Heriot-Watt campus at Riccarton in 2016.

KING'S BUILDINGS CENTRE (CENTRAL FACILITIES)

Michael Laird had been appointed as architect for both the new refectory and the extension to the boiler house at the science campus as early as 1960. This promise of a commission preceded Laird's most notable works, such as the George Watson's music school (1968) and the Standard Life Assurance building at St Andrew Square (1964), but Robert Matthew clearly knew of his potential when recommending him. Laird was a part-time lecturer in the Department of Architecture and had worked with Matthew on his entry for the Hauptstadt Berlin competition (1957).

Kininmonth's 1961 report on the site had warned of the need to increase boiler capacity in view of the proposed developments. The projected maths / physics building was dependent upon this expansion of services. It was also clear that the pre-war union was overcrowded and lacking in facilities for the ever-increasing population at the campus, projected at 6,000 persons by the time all known future buildings should be complete in the late 1970s. Indeed, the University Grants Committee expressed concerns about this aspect of the campus on a visit to Edinburgh in February 1971. Staff and students had been lobbying for amenities for a number of years – the nearest shop was a quarter of a mile away, and restaurants and cafeterias even further. The University shared this concern, but it had proved difficult to proceed with a suitable scheme, and the University Grants Committee visit came at a time when it was also asking all universities to carry on with expansion in student numbers, but to do so within their existing buildings. There were no surplus buildings at the science campus that could be converted, but work was in hand to ameliorate the situation. Michael Laird's central facilities complex attempted to echo what was being provided at the Potterrow Student Centre, Teviot Row, and at the staff club and Chambers Street union.

The existing boiler house and the union building were adjacent to each other near the centre of the campus, to the south of the geology building. It was logical that both proposed boiler house and refectory should be near these predecessors, but it was something of an imaginative leap when Laird suggested that the two projects be combined to reduce costs. Work commenced on the new boiler house in 1968, with new plant, including an electricity sub-station, installed in a steel frame above the existing boilers. Functions were maintained throughout the operation, and storage tanks were placed to the east. To avoid building a new stack, the old chimney was reduced slightly and given a black coating; a group of steel flues was cleverly attached to this. A screening of curved concrete panel units was used to unify the group and the upper level was mainly glazed. This was quite a striking design and the sculptural qualities of the chimney were admired and much-photographed.

The single-storey refectory was started the following year and completed in 1972.[21] Also with a steel frame, and using the same concrete wall units as the boiler house, it had few windows at the lower level. Instead, a continuous slanting clerestory above the panels lit the dining area. Inside artificial lighting was suspended from an openwork trellis ceiling. The dining area provided facilities for 400 students. To the east of the refectory the architect placed the social facilities block. This was a four-storey concrete-framed structure clad with white wall panels. The lower zone used the same cream-coloured wall units and slanting clerestory, creating a plinth above which the other two storeys rise. Completed in late 1974, it contained a coffee lounge, temporary library, reading room, a bank and shops. The upper floor housed the staff club. To the south of the refectory, a place was reserved for a dedicated science library, but it was the end of the century before this could be provided.[22]

The boiler house and the four-storey building are still intact, but the refectory has been redeveloped for the Noreen and Kenneth Murray Library.

JAMES CLERK MAXWELL BUILDING

The James Clerk Maxwell Building accommodated an exodus of departments from the city centre following the decision, in 1964, to reallocate the physics / maths project to King's Buildings and then to merge this with the Edinburgh Regional Computing Centre.[23] Three out of several proposed phases designed by Spence, Glover & Ferguson were executed by 1978, with Hardie Glover and Coila Clyne as project architects. The building occupies a large site on the south of the campus, the main block having a north–south orientation. This was to be the largest building at the science campus and, indeed, the largest for Spence's Edinburgh office until Glasgow Royal Infirmary. At the east end, a two-storey block (the Edinburgh Regional Computing Centre) serves as a plinth from which the six-storey slab rises. Two wings extend to the south, with a two-storey link between them. The lecture suite, containing three theatres, is in a curved wing to the north, and attached to the main building with a two-storey link.

Development was to be phased over a number of years and intended to provide all the mathematics and physics teaching facilities, except first-year teaching – at

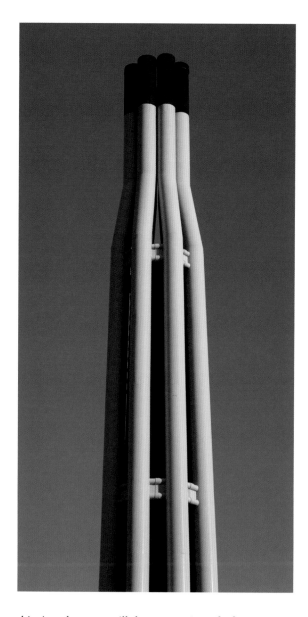

285 King's Buildings boiler house chimney designed by Michael Laird & Partners in 1970, which won a Structural Steel Design Award

Nick Haynes

this time there was still the expectation of a first-year mathematics building at Crichton Street. An E-plan was chosen, similar to that of the School of Agriculture, to enable phasing and to maximise the frontage to the south. Facilities for the Edinburgh Regional Computing Centre were incorporated in a two-storey block on the east and this was the first phase to commence in 1971, although the site preparation and concrete piling began in 1966. In the second phase this was extended, and undertaken together with the first part of the main six-storey laboratory block, and the first of the south wings. The third phase saw completion of the laboratory block, another southern wing for researchers and a separate block containing a suite of three lecture theatres on the north.[24] The building was formally opened in September 1977.

Being considered complete for the foreseeable future, the Departments of Computer Science, Geophysics, Mathematics, Meteorology, Physics and Statistics, as well as the Edinburgh Regional Computing Centre were already in occupation. At this stage an F-plan had been achieved, and the south-east wing of the architects' design postponed.[25] That wing had been intended to house heavy testing laboratories and wave sheds, however, its site was utilised by the Department of Mechanical Engineering for Professor Salter's innovative wave simulation tank. The steel-framed temporary structure that it occupied survived until 2002, when it made way for the Erskine Williamson Building (Centre for Science at Extreme Conditions).

Named after the Scottish physicist, the large James Clerk Maxwell Building dominates the campus, when viewed from the south. It is also a very heavy reinforced concrete structure borne on a raft foundation. The lecture theatre suite, on the north, is arranged on a curved plan facing a landscaped courtyard. The facings are of brick, which the practice now favoured over pre-cast panels because of the negative effect of weathering experienced with the latter, particularly at the genetics and virology buildings at the University of Glasgow. Much care was taken with the elevations in order to manage the huge bulk. In the six-storey block, the brickwork is arranged in panels with a horizontal emphasis, while the lower parts have pilasters articulating the bays vertically. Windows project on the south elevation, relieving the monotony of a sheer façade, and a raised parapet is employed to screen the considerable amount of plant mounted on the rooftop.[26] The interiors are fairly austere, by necessity; for example, the walls are of painted brick to avoid the cost of plastering, but there are some interesting details such as the hardwood handrails on the staircases, which are similar to those in the main library, the timber slatted ceilings in the corridors, and the coffering in the foyer ceiling. The interiors of the lecture theatres appear more lavish, with timber fins lining the walls, for acoustic purposes.[27]

ALRICK BUILDING (ELECTRICAL ENGINEERING)

In 1974 there was an addition to the engineering complex, made possible by a grant in 1971 from the Alrick Trust, which had been set up by an Edinburgh financier. Executed by Kingham Knight Associates this was for the Department of Electrical Engineering and devoted to the industrial application of electronic materials and systems. It was sited on the south-east of the engineering group. Unashamedly industrial, the two-storey, square plan building had horizontal bands of fenestration. Blank panels between the metal-framed windows indicated the flexible interior arrangement. Spandrel panels between floors and at the parapet were of brown tinted pre-cast concrete, while storey-high panels were placed on the corners. Brick makes an appearance on the base courses, in a panel beside the glazed doorway on the east, and as facing on the west link to the adjoining Faraday Building. Designed to be extendable, the Alrick Building had to wait until the 1980s before the second half could be taken up to five storeys on the northern part. This was done using matching panels and glazing units, although the north gable is entirely of brick, while the south gable and a low pitched roof are clad in corrugated metal sheeting. The architect for this work was Thomas Henney.

286 James Clerk Maxwell Building, rooms 5310–12, refurbished to designs by LDN Architects, 2013–14
Paul Zanre Photography

287 West elevation of the James Clerk Maxwell Building, designed by Spence, Glover & Ferguson in 1966, but not built until 1971–7
Nick Haynes

Chapter Nine

A World-Class University 1985 to the Present Day

NICK HAYNES

288 The Informatics Forum
designed by Bennetts Associates, 2005
Paul Zanre Photography

The year 2017 marks the 200th anniversary of work starting on William Henry Playfair's plan to complete Robert Adam's Old College. Although his building remains treasured and repurposed for use at the heart of the modern University, the institution that occupies it has changed beyond all recognition.

Key changes in the size and scope of the University have taken place since 1985, most notably in the mergers with Moray House Institute of Education in 1998 and Edinburgh College of Art in 2011. At the start of the 1985–6 academic year matriculated student numbers at the University of Edinburgh (excluding the Department of Adult and Continuing Education) stood at 8,000. By 1995–6 the figures had doubled to 15,667 total (7,653 women, 8,014 men), and in 2015–16 they stood at 37,510 (22,194 women, 15,288 men, 28 not disclosed). From the late 1990s there have been more female than male students.

The Environmental Association for Universities and Colleges was launched in 1996 with the aim of raising the profile of environmental management and facilitating improvement of environmental performance in member institutions. The University was an early member, and began its commitment to sustainable design at this time. The University's Estates Development Sustainability Strategy now requires new buildings to be assessed for environmental performance under the Building Research Establishment Environmental Assessment Method (BREAM). The method examines the environmental impact of new buildings in a number of areas. These include: management; operational energy; transport; health and well-being; water; materials; land use; site ecological value; and pollution. The University also adopted the Green Guide to Specification of 1996, which first set out a ranking of environmental impacts from A+ (best performance / least impact) to E (worst performance / highest impact). The old High School was the first listed building in the UK to achieve BREAM 'outstanding' accreditation as a result of the refurbishment of the Edinburgh Centre for Carbon Innovation.

In 2009, the year of the Climate Change (Scotland) Act, the University signed the Universities and Colleges Climate Commitment for Scotland and agreed to an ambitious carbon management plan with the Carbon Trust to reduce carbon emissions by 20 per cent within the five-year life of the plan. As part of the plan, all new buildings should be high performance and energy efficient. The University continues to upgrade inefficient buildings and replace inefficient appliances, and power is bought or generated from renewable sources.

In addition to its environmental concerns, the University has increasingly adopted the design philosophy of contextual modernism. Much modern movement architecture in the years immediately after the Second World War had an idealistic, Utopian social programme with an emphasis on function and large-scale, standardised design. Contextual modernism perhaps best describes an approach to architectural design that has developed from the 1980s, rather than a distinctive style or coherent movement. While not looking to historic precedents, contextual modernist buildings are individually designed (rather than off-the-peg), minimalist in their detailing and take account of the scale, height, massing, density, materials and 'grain', or sense of place, of their surroundings. Typically, the design concerns extend into the spaces around the building and its integration into the pedestrian and road network. Often the design process for such buildings is people-centred, engaging with users, the community and other stakeholders, and is favoured by planning departments.

The University of Edinburgh now competes globally for outstanding teachers, researchers and students. The quality of the working environment is recognised as an important factor in attracting the best talent to the University. The University also competes internationally to attract research funding and commercial partnerships. Where quantity was the primary requirement of the 1960s building programme, the emphasis has shifted emphatically to quality in the early 21st century. Another major shift affecting the design of buildings is from subject 'silos' towards a multi-disciplinary and outward-looking approach to teaching and research, with new flexible facilities that actively promote intellectual synergies and collaboration. 'Incubator' facilities to support spin-off commercial activity are now regularly incorporated into new projects.

CENTRAL AREA 1985–PRESENT

Although a number of small in-fill developments, mainly for student accommodation, have taken place in the city centre since 1985, the only major new development for teaching and research is the Potterrow development of the Informatics Forum, Dugald Stewart Building and Bayes Institute. Significant refurbishment projects have been undertaken and are discussed in earlier chapters.

INFORMATICS FORUM, VISITOR CENTRE, DUGALD STEWART BUILDING, DATA TECHNOLOGY INSTITUTE

With the 18th-century tenements of Bristo Street obliterated and only a shabby car park to replace them, for many years the Crichton Street site stood as reminder of the University's over-ambitious and destructive 1960s scheme to extend the George Square campus into Bristo Square. Having secured funding from Scottish Enterprise, the Science Research Investment Fund,

the Wolfson Foundation, a number of benefactors and core University funds, work began finally in 2005 on construction of the first of three phases of a new quadrangular complex of flexible research laboratories, office and teaching spaces. Bennetts Associates designed the scheme in association with Reiach & Hall Architects. The first phase on Crichton Street houses the £42m, 12,000m² Informatics Forum. The second 13,000m² phase on Charles Street comprises Student Support Services, the shop and visitor centre, and the eight-storey Dugald Stewart Building, home to the School of Philosophy, Psychology and Language Sciences, on Charles Street. The final £25.2m phase, started on site in 2015, is the 9,500m² Bayes Institute on Potterrow.

Informatics is an emerging discipline studying multiple aspects of the structure, behaviour, and interactions of natural and engineered computational systems. The design and layout of the forum is intended

289 The atrium of the Informatics Forum
Keith Hunter

to promote cross-disciplinary synergy and collaborations across traditional subject areas such as mathematics, electronics, biology, linguistics and psychology. At the heart of the building is a dramatic full-height atrium.

The building is very large, but takes the form of interlocking blocks of different heights and geometries to break up the bulk and the profile, provide light and views out, and to deal sensitively with the numerous viewpoints into the site. Appropriately for its function, the exterior is expressed in the 'bar code' arrangement of openings, first developed by the Spanish architect Rafael Moneo in his design for Murcia Town Hall of 1991–8. The pedestrian 'street' running through the buildings hints at the alignment of the old Bristo Street that ran from the south-east corner of the site to the north-west.

First Minister, Alex Salmond, opened the Informatics Forum on 3 September 2008. The first two phases of the development won a number of awards, including the Scottish Civic Trust Award 2010, a Royal Institute of British Architects Award 2009, and the prestigious Andrew Doolan Prize for the best building in Scotland in 2008.

KING'S BUILDINGS 1985–PRESENT

The first buildings of the new era, of which the Biospace laboratories (now School of Engineering administration offices in Max Born Crescent) by Kneale & Russell Architects of 1985 and the Ann Walker Building for biological sciences (Thomas Bayes Road) of 1991 by Thomas Henney Architects are examples, were externally barely more distinguished than the temporary sheds that preceded them. The constant development of new sciences and technologies places particular pressure on the University's scientific estate to keep pace. By the 1990s there was a desperate need for modern facilities in a range of subject areas. The first major new building at King's Buildings since the 1970s, the Michael Swann Building of 1993–7, did not bode well for the architectural ambitions of the University, and Campbell & Arnott's Christina Miller Teaching Laboratories extension to the Joseph Black Building (1997–2000) and Parr Partnership's Scottish Microelectronics Centre (1997–2000) similarly lacked a responsiveness to context. However, with the advent of the University's commitment to sustainable design in 1996, a new and more sensitive generation of buildings began to take shape in other parts of the campus. The first of these was the Erskine Williamson Building of 1999–2003 by Hurd Rolland, which explored the possibilities of environmental and contextual design in a colourful and imaginative way. Finances still remained tight, and a much-discussed science and engineering library for the campus, designed by Reiach & Hall Architects, was abandoned in 1999. In order to support the new sustainability agenda, a combined heat and power heating scheme of 2003 replaced the forty-five-year-old steam distribution network to thirty buildings.

More ground-breaking environmental systems were implemented in the 2001–7 Alexander Graham Bell and William Rankine Buildings. In 2009 RMJM Architects

290 Plan showing main developments at King's Buildings 1970–present

Crown copyright 2017 Ordnance Survey [Licence Number 100021521]

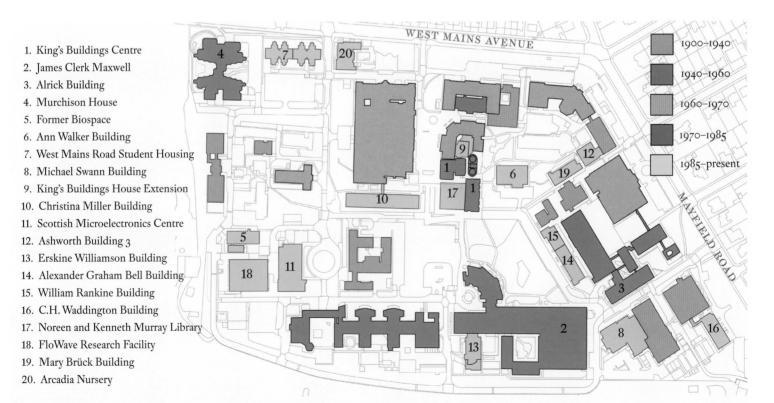

1. King's Buildings Centre
2. James Clerk Maxwell
3. Alrick Building
4. Murchison House
5. Former Biospace
6. Ann Walker Building
7. West Mains Road Student Housing
8. Michael Swann Building
9. King's Buildings House Extension
10. Christina Miller Building
11. Scottish Microelectronics Centre
12. Ashworth Building 3
13. Erskine Williamson Building
14. Alexander Graham Bell Building
15. William Rankine Building
16. C.H. Waddington Building
17. Noreen and Kenneth Murray Library
18. FloWave Research Facility
19. Mary Brück Building
20. Arcadia Nursery

1900–1940
1940–1960
1960–1970
1970–1985
1985–present

drew up a planning framework for the King's Buildings campus. The aims of the framework were to create a flexible long-term strategy for the physical development of the College of Science and Engineering, with a focus on: sustainability; co-location of cognate activities; creation of a coherent structure of routes, links and spaces; creation of space for research, spin-off, commercialisation, support and social functions; promotion of biodiversity.[1] Major considerations of the plan were development of the hierarchy of existing spaces around a 'Green Heart' and restructuring of circulation to make the site more pedestrian – and cycle-friendly. In support of these aims, the University commissioned Ironside Farrah to develop a landscape and public realm strategy, which was endorsed by the City of Edinburgh Council in 2011.

One of the most noticeable changes to the King's Buildings campus for local residents and visitors was the formation of new entrances and streetscape works to improve circulation, connectivity and signage. The scheme was designed by Ironside Farrah and implemented between 2012 and 2014. Further public realm works are underway to designs by HarrisonStevens in the latest attempt to rationalise the campus into urban blocks and integrate it with the surrounding communities and countryside.

At the time of writing, a major six-year project is taking place to consolidate and develop the School of Biological Science's buildings in the south-east corner of the King's Buildings campus to support collaboration and outreach of the various research hubs and laboratories. At the heart of the scheme are a major redevelopment of the Darwin Tower, upgrading of services to the whole campus, and the construction

of five new buildings under a masterplan by Feilden Clegg Bradley Studios in collaboration with Ostick + Williams.[2] In preparation for the project, a number of decant spaces have been created, for example the interim refurbishment of the Roger Land Building by LDN Architects in 2013–14 and the construction behind the Ashworth Building of the temporary pre-fabricated, four-storey Mary Brück Building, designed by McLean Architects. Further major projects are planned for the Nucleus Hub (a mix of new and refurbished buildings housing central teaching facilities, study areas, catering outlets, a gym, retail and a student information centre), geosciences and the School of Engineering.

MICHAEL SWANN BUILDING (BIOLOGICAL SCIENCES)

Funded by the Wellcome Trust, Wolfson Fund and the University's Darwin Trust, this £17m seven-storey wing of the Darwin Building was constructed by Thomas Henney Architects to provide laboratories, research facilities, seminar rooms, offices and a lecture theatre as a centre of excellence for the biological sciences.[3] The positioning failed to recognise the austere and solitary design of the Darwin Tower, which in an uncompromising modernist idiom responded to the ancient towerhouses at Craigmillar and Liberton that crown the neighbouring hills. Externally, the forbidding bulk of the Swann Building is clad with a clinical shiny white rainscreen and articulated by lumpen 'pilasters'. Tiny windows, sized to fit the grid of the rainscreen panels, pepper the lower floors. Only at the fifth floor café does a more generous band of windows offer spectacular views out to the city and surrounding countryside. The

curved stairtower roofs and monopitch penthouse roofs clasp a tall chimney. Internally, the circulation spaces are surprisingly tight and the lift provision inadequate for the number of people accommodated in the building.

The building is named after Professor Michael Swann, under whose leadership as Principal the University established the first Department of Molecular Biology in the UK. The only joyful aspects of this uncompromisingly functional building are two twice life-size sculptures by Eduardo Paolozzi of *Parthenope* and *Egeria*, representing 'the scattered pieces of the jigsaw of understanding, made coherent only by the power of imagination', ranged along the north front. The then Principal, Sir Stewart Sutherland, unveiled the sculptures and opened the building on 12 March 1997.

ERSKINE WILLIAMSON BUILDING (CENTRE FOR SCIENCE IN EXTREME CONDITIONS)

The Erskine Williamson Building marked a new departure for architecture at King's Buildings. Designed by Hurd Rolland Architects, it was the first to actively promote creative and innovative research through the design of core 'thinking' and social spaces in which the staff and students from five different departments (biological sciences, chemistry, engineering, geosciences and physics and astronomy) could meet, exchange ideas and disseminate their work. With user requirements at the heart of its development, it is not just a bland new 'wing', but has its own colourful character and also explores and responds to the context of the site, offering light and airy spaces and views out into the green southern aspect. Energy efficiency too was a key aspect of the design for the first time at King's Buildings.

Three storeys in height, the southern end of the building perches on pilotis, where the sheltered entrance and seminar and social spaces are located. Terracotta rainscreen panels distinguish the centre from its earlier buff-brick neighbours. Louvres shade the glazed cut-away at the south-west corner from excessive solar gain. A further glazed vertical element houses the main stair and lifts, providing access to the more conventional spinal corridor arrangement of offices and optical, cryogenic, chemical and x-ray laboratories. Services are incorporated into the slightly angled roof. The laboratories house researchers in: experiments at high pressures, under magnetic fields and over a wide range of temperatures; extreme conditions technologies; computational materials science.

The Centre for Science at Extreme Conditions was established through an award from the UK Research Councils' Joint Infrastructure Fund in 2000. It is named after Erskine Douglas Williamson, a maths and physics alumnus of the University, who emigrated to join the Geophysical Laboratory at the Carnegie Institution of

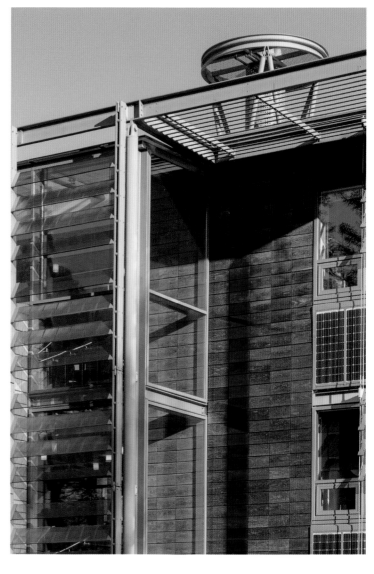

Washington and went on to establish the foundations for the modern studies of planetary interiors. The Adams–Williamson equation saw the beginning of the study of the interior structure of the Earth through seismic velocity measurements.

ALEXANDER GRAHAM BELL AND WILLIAM RANKINE BUILDINGS

Building on the experience of the Erskine Williamson Building, Hurd Rolland were appointed to design two phases of the new quadrangle for the School of Engineering, proposed under the King's Buildings masterplan. The site is that of the old Fleeming Jenkin Building. Both phases were intended to pilot advanced building technology for its educational and research value, notably in the fields of energy efficiency and environmental sustainability.

The first of the two phases, the Alexander Graham Bell Building, houses the Centre for Telecommunications and the Institute for Digital Communications along with part of the Institute for

Infrastructure and Environment. It was pioneering for the University in its use of sustainable and low-energy technologies. One such technology was Serraglaze, a patent light-bending film sandwiched between plates of glass, which redirects incoming light towards the ceiling, bouncing it deeper into the rooms. As the film slightly obscures views, it is restricted to the two upper glazed louvres of each floor. Externally, the four-storey rectangular-plan building is clad in terracotta rainscreen panels. Five rooftop stacks handle the passive ventilation system. Internally the planning is conventional, with rooms opening off spine corridors and offices to the south-west and laboratories to the north-east.

The William Rankine Building forms a linear extension of the Alexander Graham Bell Building and the second phase of the development. It was the first building constructed under the University's sustainable design policy. Also intended as a demonstration building, the William Rankine Building is pioneering in its use of sustainable design features such as the first photovoltaic system integrated into the façade of a

clockwise from top left

295 Erskine Williamson Building designed by Hurd Rolland, 1999–2003
Paul Zanre Photography

296 Detail of the William Rankine Building showing the terracotta rainscreen, photovoltaic panels, ventilation stack, brise soleil, and Serraglaze louvres
Nick Haynes

297 Alexander Graham Bell Building in 2004, before the linear addition of the William Rankine Building to the left
Paul Zanre Photography

building in Scotland. Like the Alexander Graham Bell Building, the William Rankine Building is clad in light grey terracotta rainscreen panels, employs Serraglaze louvres to distribute light into the interior, and uses a natural ventilation system. Computer thermal modelling was used to calculate the optimum plan form, depth, storey height and elevational configuration. The highly efficient passive ventilation concrete slab ceilings with high thermal mass allow heat absorption during the day. Sun pipes bring natural daylight into the centre of the building. Spine corridors access the laboratories on the north-east side and the prep rooms, small laboratories and offices on the south-east side.

C.H. WADDINGTON BUILDING
(CENTRE FOR SYSTEMS BIOLOGY)

Following the refurbishment of the adjacent Daniel Rutherford Building by Holmes Partnership (now Holmes Miller), the University commissioned the firm to build a new £4.6m home for systems biology in 2006. The brief required the provision of over 1600m² of floor space for bespoke laboratories with associated ancillary spaces and equipment rooms, as well as meeting rooms, offices and other support spaces. A spine corridor runs through the building dividing two zones: offices to the east and laboratories to the west. Communal spaces including meeting rooms, a seminar room and a common room are located on the ground floor. Containment Level 2 laboratory accommodation incorporating dry lab write-up and ancillary spaces and offices are located on the floors above. A key element of the brief was linkage with the Rutherford Building, encouraging communication between the two facilities and their staff.

The modular design of the three-storey building is expressed in the grid of windows along the east elevation. Floor to ceiling windows allow ample natural light and views into the gardens for the offices on the east side of the building. Initial plans for a rooftop greenhouse have not been carried out.

The building is named for Conrad Hal Waddington, former Professor of Animal Genetics, who is widely regarded as laying the foundations for the modern discipline of systems biology, epigenetics and evolutionary developmental biology. A second phase extension, part of the enabling works for the refurbishment of the Darwin Tower, is in progress. The design by Feilden Clegg Bradley continues the height, rhythm and alignment of the phase one building, but adopts a new and distinctive grammar of glazed vertical panels over a recessed ground floor. The extension is intended to house plant science research teams, who require specialist plant-growing facilities to allow study of plants through all stages of their development.

right

298 C.H. Waddington Building designed by Holmes Partnership, 2006
Andrew Lee

299 Noreen and Kenneth Murray Library by Austin Smith:Lord LLP, 2011–12
Nick Haynes

Following pages
300 Tank room of the FloWave Ocean Energy Research Facility designed by Bennetts Associates, 2011–14
Jane Barlow

NOREEN AND KENNETH MURRAY LIBRARY

The £5m Noreen and Kenneth Murray Library, designed by Austin Smith:Lord LLP Architects, was built on the site of the old Robertson Library to support flexible study and innovative teaching and research. It comprises 1,950m² of teaching and study spaces over four storeys. The library itself is designed to hold the University's principal printed book collections in biology, chemistry, engineering, geosciences, mathematics, physics and statistics as well as the Edinburgh Mathematical Society's book collection. King's Buildings Café is on the ground floor.

In consultation with user groups Austin-Smith:Lord developed a four-storey, nine-square grid plan with

a two-storey 'Podium Hub' on the lower levels with a café, soft study and meeting areas for discussion and debate. On the higher levels there is a series of quieter and acoustically separated study spaces, and a second floor roof terrace with views facing to the south and west. Key features of the new building included: low energy design; barrier-free access; future adaptability; a Building Research Establishment Assessment Method 'excellent' rating, the first achieved by the University; use of recycled newspaper and timber insulation; external walls designed with a 'breathing', moisture diffusive construction; free heating using surplus hot water from the adjacent CHP building; natural ventilation – when windows in the south elevation open, windows at the top of the stairs also open, to draw air through the library and up the stairwells; provision of a high level of daylighting to all library spaces but use of timber louvres and blinds to control glare; Scottish-sourced European larch timber cladding and western red cedar louvres; a sedum moss carpet laid over all the roof area, which provides an increased mix of biodiversity in the area as well as slowing down the rainwater run off from the roof.[4]

The building is named in honour of the pioneering biologists, Sir Kenneth Murray, Biogen Professor of Molecular Biology, and his wife Noreen, Professor of Molecular Genetics. The couple established the Darwin Trust in 1983 and donated the royalty earnings from their hepatitis B vaccine towards the advancement of research and education in natural science.

FLOWAVE OCEAN ENERGY RESEARCH FACILITY

Designed by Bennetts Associates Architects, the low-key exterior of the FloWave Ocean Energy Research Facility belies a spectacular internal tank room in which the wave and current conditions found around the UK and most European coastlines can be replicated at 1/20th scale. Marine research engineers and developers of renewable energy technology can test scale models of devices or arrays safely on shore and refine them before deploying full-sized versions to the real marine environment. Physical modelling enables developers to validate layouts, micro-siting and energy yield predictions without the costs and risks of ocean testing. The facility builds on the experience gained from earlier test tanks, the 'wide tank' of 1977 and the 'curved tank' of 2002, which were constructed by the Edinburgh University Wave Energy Group and located in the Hudson Beare Building.

The £9.2m capital outlay on the FloWave Building and the wave and current generation equipment was grant-funded by the Engineering and Physical Sciences Research Council and loan-funded by the University.

FloWave, a subsidiary company of the University, operates the facility and works closely with the Institute for Energy Systems within the School of Engineering.

Externally the elevations are clad in vertical profiled metal panels over a rendered base course. Windows to the offices, meeting rooms and workshop are all grouped on the west side of the building, facing the views. The entrance, marked by a canopy, is on the south side of the building towards Nicholas Kemmer Road.

At the heart of the building is a 30m-diameter concrete basin in which the 25m-diameter wave and current tank is located. The tank contains 2.4 million litres of water and is divided into upper and lower volumes of water by a 1m-thick movable floor.[5] There are 168 absorbing wave makers surrounding the upper 2m volume. Twenty-eight flow-drive units in the lower volume drive currents across the upper volume. The tank is capable of simulating waves up to 28m high, currents in excess of 28 knots, and a sea area of approximately 2km². An overhead crane can lift devices of up to 5 tonnes into the tank. The circular construction of the tank ensures that it is non-directional: waves and currents can act in any combination and in any relative direction across the upper volume 25m in diameter and 2m deep. Complex wave and current conditions for normal, challenging and extreme conditions can easily be simulated and repeated time after time, allowing devices and control algorithms to be iteratively adjusted to find optimal performance settings.

ARCADIA NURSERY

The £2.5m Arcadia Nursery, by Malcolm Fraser Architects, brings together two nurseries from other sites in the city, and caters for 113 children from nine months to five-years-old. It is designed around the concept of 'free play', commonly defined as behaviour that is freely chosen, personally directed and intrinsically motivated. The benefits of free play are identified as support for the development of social skills and collaboration, stimulation of physical activity, and the encouragement of creativity, imagination and problem solving.

A key element of the one-and-a-half storey nursery design is its setting, utilising the existing trees and mature planting between the Joseph Black Building and West Mains Road in three secure zones as outdoor play space (play equipment), an activity zone (water features, rope bridge, log ladders etc.) and meadow (for interaction with wild flowers, birds and insects).[6]

The nursery building's eye-catching golden copper alloy roof and bright, free-flowing, interconnected spaces are also designed to stimulate imagination and creativity. Three large classrooms, two with mezzanines for different activities, are ranged along the east of the building and open directly onto a covered terrace, which in turn provides access to the gardens. The offices are incorporated in the attic space at the southern end of the building. Each of the major classroom spaces is articulated in the angular roofscape above.

The building is pioneering for non-residential buildings in Scotland in its use of cross laminated timber,

301 The eye-catching copper alloy roof and wall-cladding of Arcadia Nursery designed by Malcolm Fraser Architects, 2015

Nick Haynes

302 Murchison House, designed by the Architects Division of the Property Services Agency, 1971–7

Nick Haynes

an engineered timber product, which has relatively low environmental impact, is renewable, has both strength and low weight, and is manufactured off-site for fast construction of walls and floors.[7] In this case, the low weight was a determining factor, allowing the building to be raised off the ground on piles to minimise disruption to the root structure of the existing mature trees. The construction also enabled the building to achieve a Building Research Establishment Assessment Method rating of 'excellent'.

MURCHISON HOUSE (FORMER INSTITUTE OF GEOLOGICAL SCIENCE / BRITISH GEOLOGICAL SURVEY BUILDING)

In 1967 the Natural Environment Council agreed a lease of the north-east corner of the King's Buildings campus for the construction of a new building to house the functions of the Institute of Geological Science, formerly dispersed over several offices across Edinburgh and in England.[8] Proximity to emerging scientific disciplines in marine geology and North Sea oil exploration was key to the decision to locate the research and related commercial services of the institute in Edinburgh.

The Architects Division of the Property Services Agency was responsible for the innovative design of the H-plan structure. Mike Mannings was the superintending architect on the project, but the ministry architect of the Royal Botanic Garden glasshouses, Allan Pendreigh, was probably the lead designer.

Two staggered modular blocks of pale buff brick are linked by a central cross-corridor running from north to south. Each block has horizontal banks of (replacement) metal-frame glazing units running the length of each floor level. Full height stairtowers with angular glazed roofs clasp each block to the east and west. The structural design and plan form of Murchison House, including the octagonal supporting columns throughout, evoke naturally occurring geological formations, particularly those of basalt rock and crystalline forms. The horizontal bands of bellying windows, with units jutting out at seemingly irregular angles, are suggestive of rock strata. The design philosophy and unusual composition of Murchison House is indicative of some of the more innovative designs for office buildings of the period, which were exploring new ways to arrange working areas in flexible modules, using irregular and stepped plan forms and connecting buildings with their landscape.

Murchison House is named after the eminent Scottish geologist and explorer, Sir Roderick Murchison, who was appointed Director-General of the Geological Survey of Great Britain in 1855 and established the first chair of geology and mineralogy in Scotland at Edinburgh in 1871. The University acquired the building on the relocation of the British Geological Survey to the Lyell Centre at the Riccarton campus of Heriot-Watt University. Reiach & Hall Architects are fitting out part of the building as office space and a business incubator hub for Edinburgh Research and Innovation, the commercialisation arm of the University.

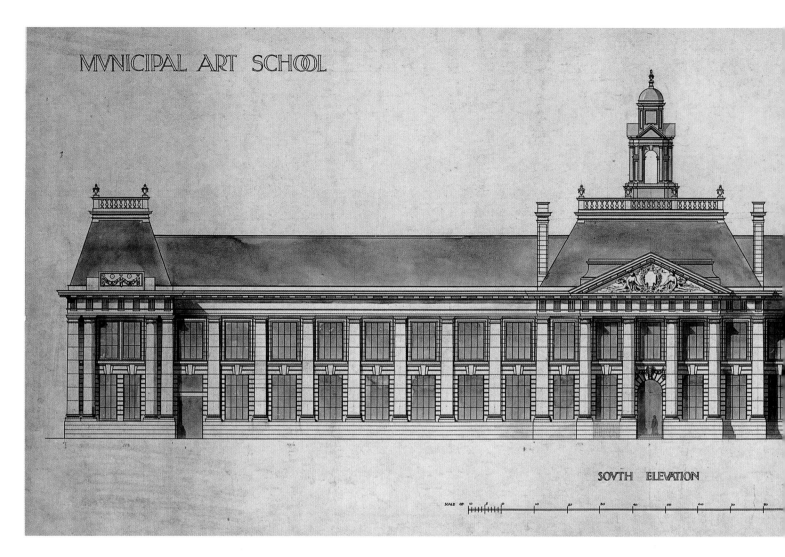

MVNICIPAL ART SCHOOL

SOVTH ELEVATION

SCALE OF

EDINBURGH COLLEGE OF ART 1985 TO THE PRESENT

Edinburgh College of Art merged with the University to form a new school within the College of Arts, Humanities and Social Science on 1 April 2011. At the time of the merger with the University, Edinburgh College of Art owned four buildings, all on the campus bounded by Lauriston Place, Lady Lawson Street, West Port and Keir Street: the main building; the Architecture Building; the Hunter Building; and Evolution House.

The College of Art has a very long and distinguished history in its own right, dating back to 1760, when the Board of Trustees for Fisheries, Manufactures and Improvements in Scotland established the Trustees Drawing Academy of Edinburgh. The aim of the academy, originally based in rooms in Picardy Place, was to train designers for the manufacturing, particularly textile, industries. From 1826 the classes were held at the Royal Institution buildings (now the Royal Scottish Academy) on the Mound. As the 19th century progressed, the focus of the Academy shifted from the applied arts to the fine arts, and it gained a reputation for excellence in painting and design.

In 1858 the academy became affiliated to the Science and Art Department in London as the Government School of Art for the City of Edinburgh. Under the 'South Kensington system' the department promoted science, technology and design. In 1907, as responsibilities for technical education devolved from London, the Academy amalgamated with the Life School of the Royal Scottish Academy, the Art Department of Heriot-Watt College and Rowand Anderson's School of Applied Art to form the Edinburgh Municipal Art School (later Edinburgh College of Art) under the Scottish Education Department.[9] The main building was constructed at this time using donations matched by government funds totalling £60,000.[10]

The College of Art thrived in the new building. The list of distinguished alumni, too long to set out here, reads like a 'Who's Who' of artistic and cultural activity in Scotland in the 20th century, and continues to this day. By the mid-1950s the main building was crowded and the facilities for architecture, sculpture and town planning students were poor. Under the government's £100m technical-college building programme, derived from the White Paper on technical education of 1956,

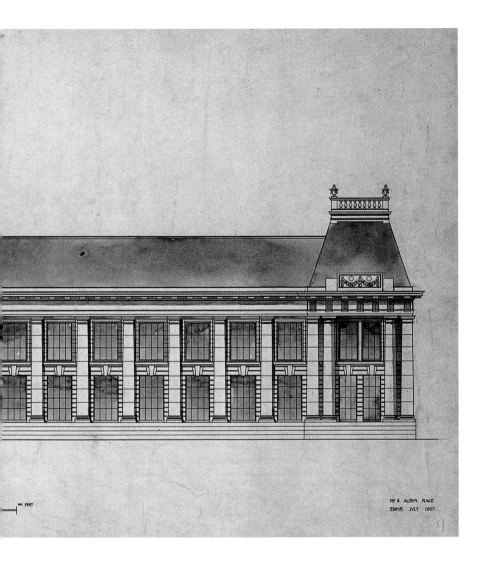

the college was allocated money to build a new School of Architecture and for adaptations to the existing main building.[11] The Head of the Architecture School, Ralph Cowan, proposed specialist studios for architectural design and new accommodation for town planning, along with dining and common room facilities. These were duly constructed on the site of several tenements at the dog-leg corner of Keir Street.

The main building continued to serve the School of Art, but specialist facilities for artists other than painters were lacking, and improvements were needed for communal services, such as the library and dining room. Although further extension was planned in 1968, it was not until 1971 that further ranges of Keir Street tenements and Lauriston Place houses were demolished to construct the L-plan Hunter Building and form the courtyard. The college acquired other buildings in the Grassmarket during the 1980s, but these were sold when it purchased Evolution House in 2006.

In 2016 the University purchased the former fire station on the corner of Lauriston Place with a view to forming an arts and cultural hub, enhancing the college estate and completing the ownership around the courtyard. The City Architect, Robert Morham, designed the Central Fire Station in Renaissance style in 1897.[12]

MAIN BUILDING

The *Building News* reported the construction of the main building in its edition of 31 May 1907:

At the last Dean of Guild Court, plans were passed for the new Municipal Art Schools at the Cattle Market, Lauriston. Mr J. M. Dick Peddie is the architect, and it is estimated that the buildings will cost £40,800. The site of the school is the north part of the market, and the building will be in the form of a parallelogram, measuring 370 feet by 126 feet. There will be an access from Lauriston Street and another from Lady Lawson Street. There will be two internal courts, separated by the centre clock, which will contain the main staircase, and all the buildings surrounding these courts will be two stories high, excepting the west wing, which will be one story high. Over the main entrance there will be on the first floor a hall 60 feet by 30 feet. The building will be treated in the simplest manner possible. The hewn work will be of red stone, and the rest of the wall surfaces of rubble from Hailes Quarry.[13]

The description of the building remains largely true to this day, with the exception that a last minute donation of £10,000 by Andrew Grant of Pitcorthie, merchant banker and Liberal MP for Leith Burghs, and match-funding by the government took the available budget to £60,000. This allowed for a significantly higher level of ornamentation in the design, particularly for

the entrance front and the public spaces of the interior including the entrance hall, main imperial staircase and sculpture court. The building provided studios and classrooms for architecture, painting and sculpture, and an exhibition room, library, lecture hall and dining room. The basement allowed for stained glass, printing and etching classrooms. Generations of artists have enjoyed the use of the great north-facing painting and drawing studios and the spectacular top-lit exhibition space of the arcaded and galleried sculpture court, which was inspired by the École Nationale Supérieure des Beaux-Arts in Paris as a home for the college's magnificent antique cast collection including friezes from the Parthenon. The corresponding court was roofed over in 1925. It originally housed a small glass pavilion for plein-air painting and an access through from the front of the building for horses and other large subjects.

Notable features of the exterior are the corner pavilion roofs, which reflect the influence of the French Beaux Arts school of design. Dick Peddie intended the building to make its mark on the skyline and in views from the castle. The full story of the design is told in Dawn McDowell's essay for volume XIII of *Architectural Heritage*.[14] LDN Architects are currently supervising a major scheme of repairs and upgrading of services.

NORTH-EAST STUDIO BUILDING (FORMERLY ARCHITECTURE BUILDING)

Peter Womersley and Tom Ridley drew up proposals to extend the College of Art with an expressed concrete structure and walls that were intended to be decorated by the students using a special sandblasting tool and technique developed in Norway, called Naturbeton.[15] However, it was Ralph Cowan, Head of Architecture at the college, who eventually designed the modernist structure that was built against the eastern end of the

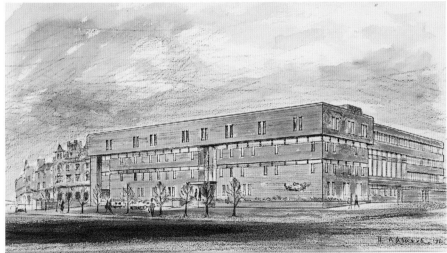

main building.[16] The ground floor now houses the famous College of Art student institution, the Wee Red Bar. Key features of the building are the stepped rows of pod-like architecture studios ranged across the north elevation, each with a projecting bay window facing Edinburgh Castle.

HUNTER BUILDING

The four-storey Hunter Building, completed 1977, was designed by Sir Anthony Wheeler of Wheeler & Sproson Architects in 1971. It is aligned in an L-plan along Keir Street and Lauriston Place, creating the boundary to a large central courtyard for the college campus behind. Like Edinburgh Castle on the hill behind, the Hunter Building presents a powerful fortress-like mass of masonry peppered with slot windows towards the sunny south and noisy Lauriston Place. The fiery red skin of masonry over the reinforced concrete structure was chosen to match the Locharbriggs sandstone ashlar of the main building and the neighbouring former Central Fire Brigade Station.[17]

The two-block Lauriston Place range contains the window-less main lecture theatre and studios that shun direct south light and solar gain, lit instead by the slots and high narrow strips of glazing. Staircases divide the eastern lecture theatre block from the western studio block and the north range of studios. At all levels the studios, workshops and offices open off corridor spines. The elevations facing the courtyard and Keir Street are amply lit with bands of black-framed windows running the length of the building. Originally the studios, workshops and research units housed students of interior design, fashion, stained glass, engraving, silversmithing, weaving, and tapestry amongst other subjects.[18] A large dining room and kitchen occupied the entire ground floor of the north range, and the library was located on the ground floor of the western block of the Lauriston Place range. The blockwork interiors are robust and functional, rather than beautiful.

EVOLUTION HOUSE

In 2000 AMA (New Town) Ltd commissioned Reiach & Hall Architects to design a speculative office development on the plot at the corner of Lady Lawson Street and West Port, left vacant by the demolition of the Chalmer's Territorial United Free Church in the 1970s. The College of Art purchased the strategically important building in 2006 and returned to Reiach & Hall to space-plan and fit out the building with studios for graphics, illustration, interior design, furniture product design departments and Edinburgh's Art, Space and Nature post-graduate course, an open-learning library and learning zone, administrative and executive offices, board room suite and café. Services, stairs, access and

emergency lighting also required alteration for the new uses. First Minister, Alex Salmond, opened the £20.5m building on 19 June 2008.

MORAY HOUSE SCHOOL OF EDUCATION AND THE HOLYROOD CAMPUS

Moray House School of Education, within the University's College of Humanities and Social Science, has its origins in three former independent colleges of education: Moray House College of Education, Callendar Park College of Education and Dunfermline College of Physical Education. Callendar Park merged into Moray House in 1981. Moray House and Dunfermline colleges then merged as the Moray House Institute of Education in 1987. On 1 August 1998 the institute merged with the University to become the faculty of education. Under the restructuring of the University in 2002, the faculty became Moray House School of Education.

Moray House College of Education began life as the Free Church of Scotland's Normal and Sessional School in 1843. It was a product of the great 'Disruption' of the same year, when a schism in the Church of Scotland over the spiritual independence of the Church and the rights of wealthy patrons to install ministers against

the will of the local presbytery led to the formation of the Free Church of Scotland. With more than a third of the ministers now outside the established Church of Scotland, there was an urgent need to establish teacher training to provide Sabbath schools. Initially, the exiled Free Church teacher trainers from the established Church's 'normal school' (after the 'norms', or rules, of teaching) set up temporary accommodation in the Whitefield Chapel in Carrubber's Close off the High Street and then in Rose Street.[19] Finally the trustees of the Free Church purchased Moray House in October 1846, and work began on converting it into a permanent home for the normal school. It opened to some thirty or forty students on 13 September 1848 under the first Rector, James Fulton. Although co-educational and non-residential, the majority of Free Church's Normal and Sessional School students were men.

The government took an increasing interest in the funding and regulation of teacher training. However, it was the Education (Scotland) Act of 1872 that really transformed teacher training. The 1872 Act made elementary education between the ages of five and thirteen compulsory and transferred the management of burgh and parish schools to state-funded school boards. Suddenly there was a need for more training facilities to cope with the demand for teachers. Moray House

308 An engraving by James B. Allen of a drawing by T.H. Shepherd of Old Moray House, about 1830. Distinctive features include the great obelisk gatepiers, tall chimneys and street balcony incorporating 'planta genista' motifs, possibly emblematic of the rock-binding properties of the plant and reflecting the Countess of Home's favourite piece of jewellery: a 'peascod' pendant given to her by the 3rd Earl of Bedford.

HES [DP 095269]

opened a new training department in the old garden ground of the house in 1878.

In 1905 four Provincial Committees were established by the government to take over the rôle of the churches in training the teachers of Scotland. The Edinburgh Committee inherited a rag-tag of buildings around the city, including properties in Johnston Terrace, Chambers Street and the Canongate. The dispersed nature of the sites, the increasing numbers of students, and the new requirements of teacher training made consolidation into one site with new premises a high priority. The largest site was at Moray House, but even that was insufficient without the acquisition of the old Moray Free Church, which fronted Holyrood Road and had been designed by the Rogue Gothic architect, Frederick T. Pilkington, in 1862. A new training college building, Paterson's Land, was designed by the Scotch (later Scottish) Education Department's consulting architect, Alan K. Robertson, and opened in 1913.[20] Robertson also designed halls of residence for the college at Suffolk Road in 1914–25.[21] His assistant, Frank Wood, took on the role following Robertson's death in 1925, designing both the demonstration school in 1928–31 and the nursery in 1932.

The baby boom after the Second World War instigated the next peak in demand for teacher training. The National and Provincial Committees were abolished in 1959, and each college operated under its own board of governors, responsible to the Secretary of State for Scotland. Once again more accommodation was needed, and a long programme of building and refurbishment began in and around Moray House. For most of the 1950s and 1960s the firm of Gordon & Dey acted as college architects, designing the sports pavilion (1952),

St John's Land reconstruction (1955), Dalhousie Land (1960–3), the physical education block (St Leonard's Land, 1968–70), Moray House refurbishment (1969–72), Charteris Land (1964–9), Simon Laurie House reconstruction (1968), and St Mary's Land and Chessel's Land (1980). From conservative beginnings in the 1950s, the firm moved towards ever more abstract and bunker-like Brutalist structures into the 1980s, such as the recently demolished Weir's, St Mary's and Chessel's Lands.

Over-capacity in the teacher training system in the 1970s led to consolidation in the 1980s. Smaller higher educational institutions, such as Moray House, struggled both financially and with a legacy of dilapidated buildings from the boom years of the 1950s and 1960s. The Cramond campus of Dunfermline College of Physical Education was sold in 2001 following the merger with the University and enlarged physical education facilities provided on Holyrood Road. The University has continued to invest in the Holyrood campus, refurbishing and extending existing buildings, and commissioning new postgraduate accommodation, O'Shea Hall.

OLD MORAY HOUSE

The original builder, or rebuilder, of old Moray House was Mary Sutton, daughter of Theodosia Harington and Edward Sutton, 5th Baron Dudley.[22] Mary was the second wife of Alexander Home, a courtier who had played a significant role in James VI's triumphal return to Edinburgh in 1617. It seems that following her husband's death Mary 're-edified, constructed and builded [...] ane great ludging with gardens' in the then aristocratic suburb of the Canongate.[23] Her daughter, Margaret Home, married Lord Doune in 1627, and became the Countess of Moray on her husband's accession as 4th Earl of Moray in 1638. The couple and James, 2nd Earl of Home, also had rooms in the house. Along with her sister Anne (who married the powerful aristocrat and politician John Maitland, later 1st Duke of Lauderdale), Margaret inherited the Canongate house from her mother in 1644. By agreement between the sisters, Margaret took on the building, which then remained in the Moray family until 1845, when the North British Railway Company acquired the house.[24] The following year the Free Church of Scotland bought the building for use as a 'normal school', and it has been in educational use ever since.

Although it remained in the Moray family ownership, a number of notable tenants and guests occupied the house at various points. Oliver Cromwell lodged in the house and held levées there on his visits to Edinburgh in 1648 and the autumn of 1650. On 19 May 1650, the Marquess of Argyll famously broke away from his son's wedding celebrations to watch from the balcony of Moray House as the Royalist captain general James Graham, 1st Marquess of Montrose, passed by on his way

309 Plan of Holyrood and Moray House campus

Crown copyright 2017 Ordnance Survey [Licence Number 100021521]

1. Old Moray House
2. Porter's Lodge
3. Old Moray House Summerhouse
4. Old Moray House Gateway
5. St John's Land
6. Simon Laurie House
7. Paterson's Land
8. Thomson's Land
9. Former Nursery
10. Dalhousie Land
11. Charteris Land
12. St Leonard's Land
13. Old Kirk Postgraduate Centre
14. Holyrood South
15. Holyrood North

17th century
18th century
1800–1940
1900–1940
1940–1960
1960–1970
1970–1985
1985–present

to the Tolbooth prison before his execution two days later. James Ogilvy, 4th Earl of Findlater and 1st Earl of Seafield, the Lord Chancellor of Scotland and a leading proponent of the Articles and Acts of Union in 1705–7, leased the house in the early 18th century. Traditionally the Union with England Act, by which the Scottish Parliament enacted the 1706 Treaty of Union, is said to have been signed in the Moray House summerhouse to avoid the protesting mob outside Parliament House. There is no evidence for the location of the passing of this controversial Act, but it is quite possible that discussions and negotiations took place at Moray House away from the tumult surrounding the Parliament House. John Campbell, 2nd Duke of Argyll, leased the house from about 1730 until 1739, at times reserving it for the exclusive use of General George Wade, the 'Commander in Chief of His Majesty's forces, castles, forts and barracks in North Britain'. Later tenants included the British Linen Company, which occupied and extended the building from 1752 as a counting house and linen warehouse, and the Cowan family, who managed it from 1793 as a tea and paper warehouse.[25]

From the mention in a charter of 1653 that Mary 're-edified' the house, it seems likely that there was an existing structure on the site.[26] The 1632 testament of James VI's principal master mason and probable designer of Heriot's Hospital, William Wallace, records a debt of £100 owed to him by the Countess of Home,

which suggests at least some involvement by him at Moray House, if not a greater design role in its reconstruction into a two-storey, quadrangular-plan house in the 1620s and early 1630s.[27] Winton House in East Lothian is another building associated with Wallace, also in flamboyant Anglo-Flemish style and containing exuberant plasterwork. Work continued at Moray House, notably on the Canongate 'Balcony Room', into the 1630s, possibly to designs by John Mylne, and over the subsequent years a great many alterations, additions and demolitions have taken place to accommodate the various later uses of the building.[28]

The oldest surviving parts are the block facing the Canongate and the block facing west behind the gateway. Sir William Bruce, a gentleman-architect and 'effective founder of classical architecture in Scotland', designed stables and a gate for Charles Stuart, 6th Earl of Moray, and Anne Campbell (daughter of Archibald, 9th Earl of Argyll, and widow of Richard, 4th Earl of Lauderdale) in 1703, and probably designed and supervised a major internal refurbishment and decorative scheme in 1706–10.[29] The new house, a rectangular-plan wing, was added to the south in 1755. William Burn designed a new cornice for the Balcony Room in 1837.[30] Significant alterations were made to the old house during 1848 and 1849, and further classroom blocks were constructed in the garden in 1856 for the Normal and Sessional School and by John Watherston & Sons in 1876 for the Moray

clockwise from left

310 Old Moray House, Canongate
Nick Haynes

311 Plasterwork ceiling of the Balcony Room, rebuilt in 17th-century style following a fire in 1736
Nick Haynes

312 'A Sacrifice to Apollo' by Roderick Chalmers and James Norie after an engraving by François Perrier, part of the painted decorative scheme in the Cromwell Room of Old Moray House
Nick Haynes

313 The Cromwell Room,
Old Moray House

Nick Haynes

Salisbury Crags. An extraordinarily sophisticated decorative scheme, comprising painted neoclassical Roman scenes by Roderick Chalmers and James Norie (relating to the Emperor Constantine in cream and brown 'grisaille' imitation stone) and symmetrical wainscot panelling by James Macfarlane, lines the walls.[34] Although now painted chocolate brown, the panelling was probably marbled or painted a pale grey in its first state. It has been established that the room was decorated, probably to designs by Sir William Bruce in about 1710. The overall design of the room may have been based on that of the 'room of the masks' in the Golden House of Nero in Rome, and a number of Renaissance sources for the paintings have been identified.[35] To those in the know the theme of the paintings was likely to provide a subtle sign of Jacobite sympathies: the first Christian Emperor Constantine battling his brother-in-law Maxentius to gain his throne mirrored the struggles of the Stuart pretenders. A serious fire in November 1736 caused considerable damage to both the Cromwell and Balcony Rooms. Signs of the fire can be seen in the repainting of damaged areas in the Cromwell Room. The signs are not visible in the Balcony Room, as this seems to have been largely destroyed and completely rebuilt from 1737, including the plasterwork ceiling in the style of its predecessor.[36]

The gardens of Moray House were some of the most opulent of the numerous mansions that lined the Canongate in the 17th century:

On the south side of the Canongate, not far from the public Cross, are the gardens along with the house of the Earl of Moray, of such elegance and cultivated with such industry that they easily rival the gardens of warmer regions, indeed almost of England herself. And here you will be able to see the power of human art and industry in supplying the defects of nature herself: hardly anyone would believe that in cold regions such horticultural beauty could be achieved.
(David Buchanan, about 1654)[37]

Gordon of Rothiemay's 1647 plan of the Canongate [fig.5] shows the distinctive obelisk gatepiers and the enclosed gardens divided into four distinct zones of three parterres and an orchard.[38] Notable early features of the garden included a fountain, an ancient thorn tree, known as Queen Mary's Thorn, which stood just to the south-east of the house, and 'Queen Mary's Bower', an arbour made from the twisted branches of fruit trees. The surviving garden gateway (in a new position) is possibly the one designed by Sir William Bruce in 1703, using an existing elaborate strapwork pediment, relocated from elsewhere in the garden.[39] Even with the advent of the Industrial Revolution and the rapid encroachment of the area by breweries, tanneries, works

House Training College. Another large-scale reconfiguration and renovation by Gordon & Dey Architects occurred in 1969–72 to convert the building for use as the Music Department of Moray House College.[31]

Certainly the least-altered part of the building, and that most associated with the Countess of Home, is the mannerist Anglo-Flemish style west wing with its tall offset chimneys, projecting staircase and grand stone balcony. Mary Home's initials, surmounted by a coronet, are to be found in the middle window pediment of the south gable of the house, facing the garden. The 'lions of Home and Dudley' once adorned the corresponding window overlooking the Canongate.[32]

Much of the original interior of the building has been reconfigured on several occasions, but three key spaces retain magnificent early decorative features. The western turnpike staircase has a turned oak newel post that supports the centre of a plasterwork saucer-domed ceiling, decorated with emblems of the home nations. On the first floor, at the top of the staircase to the south, is the Cromwell Room (former 'grein chalmer' or green room, later the dining room) and to the north, overlooking the Canongate, is the Balcony Room ('the new rowme that hes the balconie nixt the streit', later the drawing room).[33] Both have splendid vaulted decorative plasterwork ceilings of early-17th-century type.

Originally a balcony also adorned the Cromwell Room, from which there were views to the garden and

and factories from the mid-18th century, the Moray House gardens remained a tranquil horticultural oasis into the mid-19th century. The acquisition of the house and garden by the Free Church in 1847 started the gradual erosion of the garden ground as the Normal and Sessional School expanded. A tarmac playground, provided for the new demonstration school in 1931 and converted into a car park for the college in 1968, seemed to mark the end of the garden for good. However, in preparation for the 150th anniversary of the college in 1998, plans to revive part of the space as a garden were put forward. The sundial with the Latin inscription *Nosce Te* ('Know Thyself') was installed at this time. Eventually in 2015–16, as part of the Holyrood North scheme, all the car parking was removed and the area between Old Moray House and Paterson's Land relandscaped, partly with hard surfacing and partly with lawns and planted beds, to designs by HarrisonStevens Landscape Architects.

PATERSON'S LAND

With due ceremony, the Lord Provost of Edinburgh, Sir William S. Brown, laid the foundation stone of the new training college buildings in South Back of Canongate (Holyrood Road) on 21 October 1911.[40] Alan Keith Robertson was the architect for the £65,000 building.

THOMSON'S LAND (FORMER DEMONSTRATION SCHOOL)

The demonstration school was intended to allow students to practise in conditions as close to the real world of teaching as possible. Designed in a very pared down classical style on a long, narrow site between Paterson's Land and Old Moray House by Frank Wood in 1928, the building was opened by the Principal of the University, Sir Thomas Holland, on 27 May 1931.[41]

OLD NURSERY SCHOOL BUILDING

Moray House nursery was founded in 1908 at the Gilmore Place home of a college lecturer, Margaret Drummond. However, it was not until 1932 that Frank Wood constructed a purpose-built demonstration nursery at Moray House College, using Montessori principles to guide the design. Lewis and Hickey Architects converted the nursery in 1997–9 to be the School of Education's reception area and Moray House College archive.

DALHOUSIE LAND

The earliest of the extensions to the newly-formed (1959) Moray House College, Dalhousie Land, designed as an arts education facility by Gordon & Dey Architects in 1960, looks back to Scandinavian Modern and the Festival Style popularised by the architects of the Festival of Britain on London's South Bank in 1951. Todd Jamieson Partnership (now part of Lewis &

Hickey Architects) refurbished and converted the main building, removing the swimming pool, to form a new library. Cochrane Mcgregor Architects added a discreet extension on the east side in 1999–2001 to house the library stock from Cramond.

ST LEONARD'S LAND

At the core of the block now known as St Leonard's Land is the physical education block, designed as a specialist teaching centre by Gordon & Dey Architects in 1967. It was a sculptural Brutalist structure, the finned exterior of which can still be seen, now painted blue, within the 1999 extension. In that year Faulkner Browns Architects won a competition staged by the University to design a new Sports Science Department and improve the forbidding, fortress-like, appearance of the existing building. The new building wrapped around the existing block in a U-plan, completely concealing it from Holyrood Road with a lighter and more welcoming

314 Paterson's Land, Holyrood Road, designed by Alan Keith Robertson in 1910 as the training college for Moray House, photographed by Francis M. Chrystal, about 1930
HES [Francis M. Chrystal Collection: SC 1098182]

315 'The Maze', 'Growth and Development' and 'Assimilation of Knowledge' – three (of four) remaining sculptural panels at Charteris Land, designed by David 'Dusty' Miller to illustrate key concepts of learning. The concrete was cast into polystyrene moulds in a single twenty-nine hour operation.
Nick Haynes

Browne, Wemyss-place, are the architects. The plan of the body of the church is T-shaped, the extremity of the long arm being octagonal; and against the angled sides being set circular stairs leading to the galleries, and a porch and vestibule which form the principal entrance. The nave is covered in one span with a hammer-beam roof, and is ceiled with a narrow boarding at the level of the collars. Behind the pulpit, completing the cruciform plan of the church, are an organ and choir gallery, and under a vestry and lavatories. The church will be seated for 875 people, exclusive of the choir, 535 being accommodated in the area, and 340 in the gallery. The estimated cost is £4,000, consequently there are no purely decorative features. The walls will be built of square snecked rubble, with scabbled stone dressings, and the roof covered with plain red tiles. Messrs Wm. Beattie and Sons are the principal contractors, and Mr. T. Bryning acts as clerk of the works.[42]

As *Building News* described, the new building was certainly without frills. In 1944 the National Committee for the Training of Teachers acquired the building and converted it for use by the music and educational handwork departments in 1949.[43] With wartime austerity continuing, the first-floor stage was constructed from the timbers of old desks. The church hall was demolished in 1979, and Moray House Building Services occupied the Old Kirk itself until the merger with the University in 1998. At the time of writing the building is undergoing a further reconfiguration as a postgraduate centre to designs by Consarc Design Group of Belfast.

316 St Leonard's Land showing Faulkner Browns' 1999 frontage to the old physical education block on Holyrood Road
Keith Hunter

317 St John Street Church (now Old Kirk Postgraduate Centre) designed by Robert Rowand Anderson, 1880
University of Edinburgh [0078884d]

frontage. The project combined a new sports science teaching and research facility with an eight-court sports hall, 25m swimming pool, laboratories, seminar rooms, teaching accommodation, academic and administrative offices.

OLD KIRK POSTGRADUATE CENTRE (FORMER ST JOHN STREET CHURCH)

By 1880, Robert Rowand Anderson's practice was highly successful, and he was at work on major projects including the University's Medical School and Glasgow Central Station when he was given the commission for the St John Street Church, which was one of the first projects undertaken with his new partner George Washington Browne:

Operations have just been commenced for the erection of a church at the north-west angle of South-Back of Canongate and St. John-street. Messrs. Anderson and

HOLYROOD SOUTH AND NORTH, O'SHEA HALL AND OUTREACH CENTRE

Holyrood South (2011–14), designed by Richard Murphy Architects for the corner site of Holyrood Road and Viewcraig Gardens, has a separate architectural treatment to the Holyrood North site opposite. Here the 248-bed student residence is clad in white, smooth-faced, clay brick, punctured by serried ranks of projecting windows. Conviviality is encouraged by the more informal and colourful design of the internal courtyard, which provides the main access to the six-person apartments via two suspended spiral staircases and open deck balconies.

The size and ambition of the Holyrood North development is such that it constitutes the creation of a new quarter within the Old Town. The brief provided for a variety of accommodation for international postgraduates and mature undergraduates, including a 476-bedroom 'collegiate' hall of residence (O'Shea Hall), a 250-seat café / restaurant, and an Outreach Centre for continued education, community learning, conferences and events. The University owns the site, while Balfour Beatty Investments is responsible for the design, build and maintenance of the buildings at both Holyrood North and South over a fifty-year concession.

Taking the scale, massing and traditional development pattern of the Canongate as the starting point,
as recommended in John Hope's 2007 masterplan for the area, the design team for Holyrood North, Oberlanders, JM Architects and HarrisonStevens Landscape Architects, have created an attractive contemporary campus that works with the grain of the city. There is movement and variety in the pre-fabricated, brick-clad elevations facing Holyrood Road. Narrow pedestrian routes between the long, linear buildings reflect the traditional closes, wynds, vennels and courts off the Canongate, and the eclectic mix of heights and materials invite exploration. The landscaping takes inspiration from the volcanic landscape of Arthur's Seat and Salisbury Crags. An innovative feature of O'Shea Hall is the large top-lit communal kitchen, which has been designed to allow over 400 residents to cook, eat and meet.

POLLOCK HALLS 1985–PRESENT

After the construction of Cowan House in the early 1970s, no new building took place at Pollock Halls until the bland Masson House by McLaren, Murdoch & Hamilton Architects in 1993–4. Substantial refurbishments of the existing buildings were also required at this time, such as Parr Partnership's alterations to the refectory in 1992–3 and Hurd Rolland's scheme for Fraser House in 1995. In about 2000 Oberlanders Architects produced an overall masterplan for the Pollock Halls

clockwise from top left

318 Holyrood South Hall of Residence by Richard Murphy Architects, 2011. The design of the projecting windows subtly references the projecting MSP pods of Enrique Miralles' nearby Scottish Parliament building.
Nick Haynes

319 A view through the garden of Holyrood North complex by Oberlanders Architects 2011–16
Chris Humphreys

320 The communal kitchen in the Holyrood North Hall of Residence
Chris Humphreys

321 Chancellor's Court, Pollock Halls, designed by Oberlanders Architects, 2000–3. The double court-yard layout forms a variation on William Kininmonth's original 1948 proposals for the site.

Paul Zanre Photography

site, and subsequently developed several of the major projects including Chancellor's Court, John Burnett House and the refurbishment of Salisbury Green House as a hotel.

CHANCELLOR'S COURT

Work began in July 2001 on Chancellor's Court, a large £21m residential courtyard development on the site of the old Cowan and Brewster Houses in the northernmost sector of the Pollock Halls campus.[44] The design by Oberlanders Architects sought to define the northern edge of the campus in a sensitive location, where it meets Holyrood Park, enhance the setting of St Leonard's Hall, and create a sheltered south-facing semi-enclosed double courtyard garden. The first phase of the 526-bedroom complex was delivered in 2002, with the remaining phases handed over in the following year.

Taking a cue from their Baronial neighbours, but expressed in contemporary dark copper and glass cladding, are the protruding stair and pantry towers, which define the extent of the building and serve to break up the horizontal massing of the elevations and roofline. The limited palette of materials carefully articulates the various elements of design: local brick at the ground and lower ground floors; off-white render and boarded timber panels to the windows of the main floors; boarded timber and metal to the recessed top

floor. Internally, the building is based on clusters of fifteen en-suite bedrooms sharing the communal stairs and pantry spaces.

JOHN BURNETT HOUSE

Oberlanders were also responsible for the design of John Burnett House in 2007–9, a five-storey block containing 118 rooms for 145 residents on the site of the old warden's house. By using the existing layout of Baird and Lee Houses, the new L-plan block creates a semi-enclosed courtyard garden to the north-east.

MCEWAN HALL GATES

As part of the 2015–17 scheme to redevelop Bristo Square and refurbish the McEwan Hall, the old gates between the McEwan Hall and the Reid Concert Hall were removed. Initially the gates were to be sold, but after a campaign by alumni, students and staff, the gates were retrieved from the auctioneers and relocated to the Dalkeith Road entrance of Pollock Halls.

The gates were originally installed adjacent to the new McEwan Hall in about 1896, possibly by Thomas Hadden & Co.. Their purpose was to control access to the Reid music classroom and the Medical School from Bristo Square, which had been opened up by the town council's removal of tenements on the south side of Bristo Street.

WESTERN GENERAL HOSPITAL

The University's responsibilities for buildings at the Western General Hospital are complex: in some cases the buildings are owned outright by the University; in other instances the University has use of buildings, or parts of buildings, owned by other parties and pays for rent, services and/or maintenance. The land is all leased from NHS Lothian. Only the significant buildings in predominantly University use are considered here.

Teaching of medical students through the newly introduced 'hospital experience' programme began in 1933, and from that point the University had an increasing involvement in the site. After the War and the hospital's incorporation into the National Health Service in 1948, the Western built up a number of specialisms, including heart disease, oncology, infectious diseases, gastrointestinal medicine, radiotherapy and neurosurgery. The University's current responsibilities for buildings relate mainly to research into these specialisms, and are the structures mostly grouped on the eastern edge of the site.

WELLCOME TRUST CLINICAL RESEARCH FACILITY (CLINICAL RESEARCH BUILDING)

The Wellcome Trust Clinical Research Facility, designed by Boswell, Mitchell & Johnston Architects in 1998, supports the epidemiology and statistics, genetics and imaging/image analysis, and mass spectrometry cores (support for research in humans, their tissue, or data in compliance with regulatory and legislative governance frameworks) as well as the education programme, information technology and research support services.

The three-storey, square-plan building, clad in blue rainscreen panels with a shallow piended roof and deep overhanging eaves, incorporates study bedrooms, day study areas, intensive study rooms, consultation rooms, managed and calibrated equipment rooms, offices and space for clinical sample processing and storage. The south-west corner is a glazed cut-away. HM The Queen opened the facility on 6 July 2001.

MEDICAL RESEARCH COUNCIL INSTITUTE OF GENETICS AND MOLECULAR MEDICINE (IGMM) COMPLEX

The Medical Research Council Institute of Genetics and Molecular Medicine was formed in 2007 by the University in partnership with the Medical Research Council and Cancer Research UK from three existing centres and units: the Medical Research Council Human Genetics Unit, the Centre for Genomic and Experimental Medicine and the Edinburgh Cancer Research Centre. The four existing buildings (north, centre, west and south) were linked together by the construction of a new systems medicine building (east) in 2012–15.

IGMM NORTH (CENTRE FOR GENOMIC AND EXPERIMENTAL MEDICINE; MOLECULAR MEDICINE CENTRE)

One of a very few postmodern buildings undertaken for the University, the Centre for Genomic and Experimental Medicine was designed by Boswell, Mitchell & Johnston in 1996. Postmodern was a style that reacted against the minimal formalism of the International Style with humour and eclectic ornamentation, often derived from historical styles, particularly classicism. It had its origins in the 1950s, but still thrived in the dot-com era of the late 1990s. Here the six-storey, rectangular-plan building loosely evokes the form of a Roman temple with its corniced podium of reconstituted stone, blue rainscreen pilasters, deep eaves cornice and pediment. It contains wet laboratory facilities along with ancillary laboratory support accommodation, meeting and seminar spaces.

IGMM WEST (HUMAN GENETICS)

The Medical Research Council Effects of Radiation Unit leased space in the existing hospital buildings from its inception in 1956. The first purpose-built laboratories opened in 1968 in the small three-storey, rectangular-plan centre to the rear of what is now IGMM Centre. This design by Alan Reiach, Eric Hall & Partners, a neat quadruple-decker sandwich comprising reinforced concrete spandrels and strip windows, was to influence the aesthetic of its larger eastern neighbour.

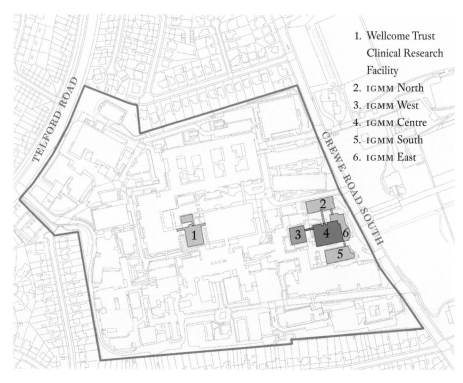

1. Wellcome Trust Clinical Research Facility
2. IGMM North
3. IGMM West
4. IGMM Centre
5. IGMM South
6. IGMM East

322 Plan of Western General Hospital
Crown copyright 2017 Ordnance Survey [Licence Number 100021521]

323 The east and systems medicine block of the Institute of Genetics and Molecular Medicine, Western General Hospital, designed by Oberlanders Architects, 2012–15
Keith Hunter

IGMM SOUTH (EDINBURGH CANCER RESEARCH CENTRE)

The Imperial Cancer Research Fund Medical Oncology Unit, a centre for basic, translational and clinical cancer research, was established at the Western in close partnership with Cancer Research UK and Lothian Health Board (now NHS Lothian) in 1980. The initial mission of the centre in the 1980s was the development of more successful drug therapies for all forms of cancer and looking for new ways of reducing the side-effects of anti-cancer drugs. Under the leadership of Professor John F. Smyth, the director, the unit acquired a small research lab in 1981, then accommodation within the MRC building. In 1997 fundraising for a £7m purpose-built centre began. BDG McColl Architects provided the designs, which include a blue-glazed facetted tower with brise soleil facing Crew Road South and a double mono-pitched roof at different levels.

IGMM EAST (SYSTEMS MEDICINE)

The Wellcome Trust and Wolfson Foundation, the Medical Research Council and the University jointly funded the £14m east and entrance building. Oberlanders Architects designed the building to link the three partner centres and units (the Human Genetics Unit, the Centre for Genomic and Experimental Medicine and the Edinburgh Cancer Research Centre) physically and intellectually. Apart from providing a single entrance to the complex from Crew Road South, the new building was intended to resolve issues of levels and access to the existing buildings and supply a central social / interaction space, dry lab computational research space for computational biologists and bioinformaticians and office and meeting / lecture room facilities.

The restricted site that wraps around the east and north sides of the Genetics Unit allowed for a relatively shallow building that would act as a welcoming show front to the complex behind. Although the site was L-plan in shape, the architects have introduced a number of angular features to provide interest and dynamism to the street elevation, such as the two-storey curved and finned glass wall floating on pilotis and the deep aluminium aerofoil terrace canopy. Peterson grey facing brick is the main cladding material, with vertical timber cladding picking out the curved form of the ground floor lecture theatre.

Essentially the five-storey building has a single aspect facing east, which provides for three upper levels of open-plan flexible research space with spectacular views out to Fettes College and across the city. The lecture theatre and reception are at the level 1 ground floor and the café at level 2 above. An atrium provides light through the heart of the structure. The building is based on the principle of a sealed envelope to avoid problems of noise from Crew Road South and pollution from existing ventilation systems on the site.

IGMM CENTRE (HUMAN GENETICS UNIT)

By 1968 the University had established a Department of Human Genetics, and new shared facilities were needed for computer analysis of blood samples, cytology and cytogenetics facilities, and ancillary laboratories, offices, seminar rooms, a library and common room.

In 1969 additional land was purchased from the Fettes Trust for construction of a much bigger new home for the unit. The Medical Research Council returned to Alan Reiach, Eric Hall & Partners as architects for the second phase of their centre. Before the construction of the new entrance building in 2012–14 the main entrance was from the north on the second level (of three). Internally, the facilities were grouped in areas: large rooms, such as the computer room, common room and seminar room in the central core; laboratories on the west to facilitate services from the existing hospital; and offices to the east for the views of the city. Solar gain proved problematic in these offices. Unplastered concrete block walls and black-painted concrete ceilings formed the internal finishes.

The new building was opened by HRH The Duke of Edinburgh in 1974. Boswell Mitchell Johnston Architects carried out a phased refurbishment between 2001 and 2005 to update the wet and dry lab spaces, offices, meeting and seminar rooms, imaging suites and other facilities.

EASTER BUSH
CAMPUS 1985–PRESENT

Until 2011 the Royal (Dick) School of Veterinary Studies continued to occupy two sites: Summerhall at Newington in the city centre; and the Easter Bush Estate (and several surrounding farms) in Midlothian. The Easter Bush site contained the Alan Reiach-designed Veterinary Field Station and Centre for Veterinary Medicine and a number of small ad-hoc and temporary structures in a rolling farmland setting at the foot of the Pentland Hills. There had been relatively little investment in the buildings since their construction, the planning of the site was haphazard, and there were very few facilities for students and staff. The site retained the character of an outpost field station rather than a core campus.

From 2000 the University has had a stake in the nearby Edinburgh Technopole, a 51-hectare commercial science and business park based around the 18th-century Bush House. The first major new building at Easter Bush since the 1960s, the Hospital for Small Animals, was added in 1999 [fig.325]. Three years later the University purchased the nearby Langhill Farm in order to provide improved livestock facilities for the estate's 220 dairy cows. The new Equine and Large Animals Hospital opened in 2003. At this time the University was considering two options for an increased intake of 180 undergraduate students (from about 100) to pre-clinical veterinary teaching: to move the pre-clinical element to a central site alongside the Medical School at Little France; or to consolidate the Veterinary School at Easter Bush.

Following a feasibility study, options appraisal and production of a business case, the University Court gave formal approval in May 2005 to a scheme to quit Summerhall and consolidate all the veterinary teaching facilities alongside a collaborative Biosciences Research Centre on the one site at Easter Bush. The maintenance costs of Summerhall were high, but more critically it was a constrained 1-hectare site with little scope for expansion, redevelopment or collaborative use and no possibility of integrating teaching and research with practice. Reiach & Hall Architects and Derek Carter Associates, Landscape Architects, drew up a development framework for the University's two committed projects at Easter Bush, the Veterinary School itself and the Riddell-Swan Veterinary Oncology Unit, along with block plans for potential future development.

By 2008 further consolidations and collaborative partnerships for veterinary research had taken place. In April 2007 the Neuropathogenesis Unit of the Institute for Animal Health merged with the Roslin Institute. In turn this combined organisation became a part of the Royal (Dick) School of Veterinary Studies in April

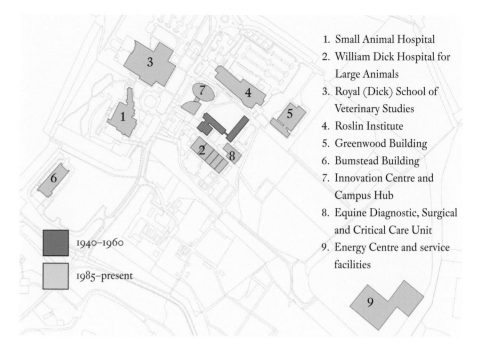

1. Small Animal Hospital
2. William Dick Hospital for Large Animals
3. Royal (Dick) School of Veterinary Studies
4. Roslin Institute
5. Greenwood Building
6. Bumstead Building
7. Innovation Centre and Campus Hub
8. Equine Diagnostic, Surgical and Critical Care Unit
9. Energy Centre and service facilities

1940–1960

1985–present

324 Plan of main developments at Easter Bush campus

Crown copyright 2017 Ordnance Survey [Licence Number 100021521]

of the following year. The Roslin Institute had been established in 1993 as a wholly owned independent institute of the Biotechnology Research Council, but its origins lay ultimately in the Institute of Animal Genetics founded at the University in 1919.[45] Another important development in veterinary science was the formation in April 2008 of the Easter Bush Research Consortium, comprising the University (including its new Roslin Institute), the animal science researchers of the Scottish Agricultural College, and the Moredun Institute. The new consortium was intended to create one of the largest concentrations of experts in animal life sciences in the world and bring together a wide range of expertise from different disciplines, with a view to fostering new ideas and streamlining research in effective disease controls and treatments, food safety, animal welfare and sustainable management of farm animals, with a focus on animal and human health.

A key element of the Easter Bush Research Consortium proposal was co-location of researchers on the Easter Bush campus to exploit the synergies between the various partners. Clearly the outpost status of the site was about to change and a revised framework was needed to guide the transformation into a major academic and business campus with associated facilities and commercial space for bioscience companies. Reiach & Hall and Derek Carter Associates were re-engaged to revise the 2004 framework to include new projects, broader strategic issues and further essential infrastructure requirements, including upgraded public transport provision, open space and landscaping, parking, footpaths, cycle routes, support facilities and service infrastructure (power, drainage etc.).[46] An Easter Bush Strategic Project Board was established under the University Estates Committee, and ultimately the University Court. Each new project now has its own project board and user group.

Oberlanders Architects began a comprehensive masterplanning exercise for the Easter Bush Estate in 2008.[47] The masterplan sets out a vision for the campus, including a two-part layout on either side of the existing Bush Farm Road, perimeter roads to remove traffic from the heart of the campus, and principles for design and materials. The southern segment of the layout contains a wedge-shaped park with pockets of public space between the buildings and two Sustainable Urban Drainage Systems ponds. The larger teaching and research buildings are concentrated around Bush Farm Road, while the lower clinical buildings are located further south.

The first priority building was a research facility to house the Roslin Institute, which was constructed in tandem with the Veterinary School and completed in 2011. The second phase of development included the Avian Research Unit and Facility. At the time of writing phases 3 (Roslin Innovation Centre and Campus Hub), 4A (Equine Diagnostic, Surgical and Critical Care Unit), 4B (Large Animal Research and Imaging Facility) and 5 (Energy Centre and Campus Infrastruture) are under construction or nearing completion. A further three phases are at the design stage: a pathology extension to the Royal (Dick) School of Veterinary Studies; a childcare nursery; and the Hospital for Small Animals project. In 2016 Page\Park Architects produced a campus appraisal, which provides complementary analysis in support of the masterplan, and Oberlanders and Wardell Armstrong Engineering & Environmental Consultancy developed an Easter Bush Public Realm Strategy.[48]

HOSPITAL FOR SMALL ANIMALS AND RIDDELL-SWAN VETERINARY ONCOLOGY AND IMAGING CENTRE

When it opened in May 1999, the Small Animal Hospital, designed by Forum Architects of Newmarket, was the largest of its kind in the UK and the best equipped in Europe with eight consulting rooms, four specialist treatment rooms, three general wards, four operating theatres, kennels, tutorial rooms and offices.[49] It also provided a dedicated ward for exotic animals and a wildlife ward, which made it unique among hospitals run by the UK's six Veterinary Schools.

A significant donation by Minnie Riddell-Swan in memory of her husband, John, an alumnus of the Dick Vet, enabled the construction in 2007–9 of a £3m extension by BMJ Architects to focus on state-of-the-art diagnosis and treatment of animal cancer. The Riddell-Swan Veterinary Cancer Centre contains Scotland's only Varian therapeutic linear accelerator for radiotherapy, CT and MRI scanners, and the UK's only Positron Emission Tomography for functional imaging of cancer.

In 2015 the University appointed Oberlanders Architects to conduct a comprehensive review of the existing Hospital for Small Animals and to prepare a capability assessment for future development options.

The bronze statue of an Afghan hound, which stands outside the hospital, commemorates Olive Smith, former head nurse at the old hospital in Summerhall, who drowned in 1997 trying to rescue a friend's dog after it fell into the burn at the Hermitage of Braid. The sculptor Mathew Lane Sanderson depicted the dog at full sprint on one side, and revealed its skeleton on the other side.

325 Small Animals Hospital and Riddell-Swan Veterinary Oncology and Imaging Centre, Easter Bush
Nick Haynes

326 John Rhind's 1883 statue of William Dick presides over the entrance hall of the Royal (Dick) School of Veterinary Studies designed by BDG Architecture + Design, 2005–11
Paul Zanre Photography

327 Exterior of the Royal (Dick) School of Veterinary Studies
Paul Zanre Photography

328 The 'study landscape' in the Royal (Dick) School of Veterinary Studies
Nick Haynes

329 The Roslin Institute designed by HDR Architecture, 2008–11
Chris Humphreys

ROYAL (DICK) SCHOOL OF VETERINARY STUDIES

The decision to consolidate all the Royal (Dick) School of Veterinary Studies teaching at Easter Bush generated the requirement for a flagship building on the campus to accommodate more than 1,000 students and staff. BDG Architecture + Design were selected to design the £44m, 11,000m² building. At the core of the complex three-storey design is the 'lecture theatre pod' containing two lecture theatres with multi-media technology. A dramatic top-lit atrium wraps around the lecture theatres linking the main spaces and providing a bright and spacious environment for student and staff interaction. Off the atrium at various levels are the library and study landscape (multi-media learning centre for self-directed study), study area, restaurant, flexible seminar rooms, offices, a post mortem suite and anatomy dissection area, as well as teaching and

research laboratories. Sophisticated acoustic modelling and design were undertaken to ensure that the spaces function without excessive noise.

Externally the building has a complicated geometric profile with each element defined by a simple palette of natural sandstone, white render, light grey cladding and dark grey window panels. The entrance, picked out in white render with pilotis and strip glazing is suggestive of the great 'machine for living' in the suburbs of Paris, the Villa Savoye by Le Corbusier of 1931.

The design incorporates a number of sustainable and environmental measures including an oversailing sedum roof for insulation and reduced visual impact on views from the Pentland Hills, harvesting and reuse of rainwater, reuse of top soil excavated for the building's foundations and hard landscaping, and a Sustainable Urban Drainage System. Cop Crag sandstone was used to help integrate the building into the rural Midlothian landscape. The new building obtained a Building Research Establishment Assessment Method 'very good' rating.

Jim Jordan, a specialist glass expert, conserved the panels of stained glass from the staircase at Summerhall for rehanging in the entrance foyer of the new building. John Rhind's 1883 statue of William Dick, which had been moved to Easter Bush after conservation by Christa Gerdwilker of Croma in 2000, was also installed in the foyer and keeps a watchful eye over the school.[50]

HRH The Princess Royal performed the official opening of the building on 27 September 2011.[51]

ROSLIN INSTITUTE

Following formation of the Easter Bush Research Consortium in April 2008, work began in earnest on development of a new building to co-locate the partners' 500 researchers. The Biotechnical and Biological Sciences Research Council contributed £37m towards

the £60.5m costs. The site on the south side of Bush Farm Road, opposite the teaching building, was selected on the basis of a number of criteria, including campus integration, orientation to the path of the sun, views, site presence, infrastructure investment, parking location and expansion capability.

In tribute to the old Roslin Institute's most famous creation, Dolly the Sheep, HDR Architecture's design takes inspiration from the shape of a pair of chromosomes, with coloured panels representing the DNA 'fins' which link the two parallel ranges of office and research laboratories together.[52] After extensive user consultation with the four organisations of the Easter Bush Research Consortium, the architects identified the determining factors for the arrangement of the building as: co-location and integration of all parties in the same office space; separation of laboratory and the laboratory office space whilst maintaining visual connectivity between them; potential of the central space to concentrate social interaction along circulation routes; ability of the office element to provide visual impact and identity.[53]

The laboratory block is articulated by solid walls punctuated by tall, narrow windows, which light the lab support spaces. By contrast, the light transparent form of the office range is expressed by large panels of flush glazing, interspersed with perforated metal (behind which are openable vents). User anecdote suggests that, in spite of the natural ventilation, window blinds, external sunshades, skylights and special glass coating, the great arc of glazing facing south-west generates excessive heat in the large open plan offices on sunny days.[54] The glazed zone between the two ranges contains the main horizontal and vertical circulation spaces and connects the primary social areas of the café, the lecture theatre and the library on the ground floor. The coloured fins catch the eye and provide vibrancy and visual stimulation in the shared space. Efficient space planning, break-out areas and transparency through the building promote openness and interaction, and territorial ownership of research space is discouraged through shared lab vestibules. The large café is carefully sited to encourage collaboration and provide access and views to the campus green. The offices above the café share this aspect.

330 The office range of the Roslin Institute designed by HDR Architecture, 2008–11. The building was inspired by the form of a pair of chromosomes.
Chris Humphreys

331 Design for the Easter Bush Innovation Centre and Campus Hub by Atkins Global, 2013–17
Atkins Global

332 Detail of the Easter Bush Innovation Centre and Campus Hub
Nick Haynes

GREENWOOD AND BUMSTEAD BUILDINGS

The Greenwood Building is the first of two buildings designed by Oberlanders Architects to house the National Avian Research Facility. The new buildings were required to replace the facilities on the old Roslin Institute campus at Bush House. The Greenwood Building is used for conventional avian research. It is essentially a simple agricultural shed block fronted by a facilities range containing smaller poultry rooms, laboratories, office, showers and other ancillary accommodation with the north-west entrance accentuated by green metal cladding.[55] The building is named in honour of Alan Greenwood, who laid the foundations of avian research at the University in the 1920s and founded the first Poultry Research Centre in 1947.

The second and larger of the two National Avian Research Facility buildings is the Bumstead Building.[56] The steel-framed design is a single monolithic block with few openings, expressive of function, treated with simple form, finish and detailing. The facility is named after Nat Bumstead, who had a major role in establishing worldwide research on the genome of the chicken.

INNOVATION CENTRE AND CAMPUS HUB

The brief for the Innovation Centre and Campus Hub required the provision of a landmark building to 'bring together the clinical teaching, research and enterprise activities into a vibrant, interactive core at the heart of the innovation and research campus of Easter Bush'.[57] The building contains shared facilities, such as the shop, gym, coffee kiosk, student advice centre, a multi-faith room, meeting rooms, changing and shower rooms and also the Centre of Comparative Pathology, the International Centre for Livestock Improvement, an outreach centre for the wider community, commercial 'incubator' research laboratories and offices, and support facilities. Principal funders apart from the University are the Scottish Government and the Biotechnology and Biological Sciences Research Council.[58]

Designed by Atkins Global, the building occupies the site of the main block of the original field station, and stands at the entrance to the wedge of land allocated for garden space in the masterplan. A glazed atrium links the two distinctive blocks of the building and provides a visual gateway through the complex to the garden. The northern block is oval in plan and the glazed upper floors overhang the ground floor. The southern block has a quadrant plan and is clad in panels of sandstone and 'living wall'. The glass is treated with a decorative geometric leaf pattern or 'manifestation' that is symbolic of the building's purpose to grow knowledge and businesses.

EQUINE DIAGNOSTIC, SURGICAL AND CRITICAL CARE UNIT AND LARGE ANIMAL RESEARCH & IMAGING CENTRE

Located next to the existing equine hospital, the new £3.7m, 1,100m² equine diagnostic facility is intended to focus on the health, welfare and rehabilitation of racehorses. It is formed from four interconnected parts: a diagnostics and triage area; two surgery theatres and a standing surgery suite; a six-box critical care unit; and a support hub for teaching, client counselling, clinician facilities and offices. The design by Sheppard Robson Architects incorporates a strong angular roofline and profiled sheet metal cladding and timber panels, reflecting the form and materials of traditional agricultural barns in a contemporary manner.

The £25m Large Animal Research and Imaging Centre, also designed by Sheppard Robson, will support the study of the biology of large animals with all the resources of a human hospital. Imaging facilities will include PET, MRI, ultrasound and CT scanning. Again, the design is intended to reflect the form and materials of traditional barns, but expressed in a subtle contemporary fashion. The single-storey building has a saw-tooth roof that articulates the various internal functions:

it rises from the ends, where the staff accommodation is located, towards the centre, where the height requirements for the servicing plant for the laboratories are greatest. Natural ventilation to the animal holding areas and photovoltaic panels on the south faces of the roof will contribute to the low carbon energy requirements of the building.

ENERGY CENTRE AND SERVICE FACILITIES

As part of the University's carbon reduction drive, a new Combined Heat and Power energy centre is being constructed alongside a number of other service buildings.[59] The gas-fired system uses fuel efficiently to produce electricity and heat at the same time. Atkins Global's proposal for the £12m Energy Centre incorporates the flexibility to increase the plant, or the building itself, at a later stage. The design adopts a traditional steading cluster layout around a service yard and low, vernacular-style sheds clad in profiled metal sheeting in earthy colour tones and timber-boarded links.

ROYAL INFIRMARY OF EDINBURGH, LITTLE FRANCE

In November 1994 the Secretary of State for Scotland, Ian Lang, approved the outline case for removal of the Royal Infirmary of Edinburgh from its site in Lauriston Place to a new purpose-built campus, also incorporating the Simpson Memorial Maternity Pavilion, the Princess Margaret Rose Orthopaedic Hospital and the City Hospital, at Little France on the outskirts of the city. Little France takes its name from the entourage brought to Scotland from France by Mary, Queen of Scots, who settled nearby at Craigmillar Castle. A significant element of the proposal was the relocation of the University's Medical School and construction of a research institute at the same site. The scheme started in earnest in 1998, when the then Secretary of State for Scotland, Donald Dewar, agreed the detailed scheme for the hospital to be funded under the controversial Private Finance Initiative, and the whole Little France site was purchased. The University took long leases on the sites from the Royal Infirmary of Edinburgh NHS Trust and opted to fund the construction of the Medical School and research institute by means of external borrowing and fundraising.[60] The new hospital opened to its first patients in January 2002, and the Medical School began teaching in the Chancellor's Building later that year. The Queen's Medical Research Institute completed phase one of the Little France development in 2005.

Following the opening of the new Royal Infirmary and Chancellor's Building, Scottish Enterprise, the University, NHS Lothian and the City of Edinburgh Council began to develop complementary proposals for a major international bioscience hub of clinical

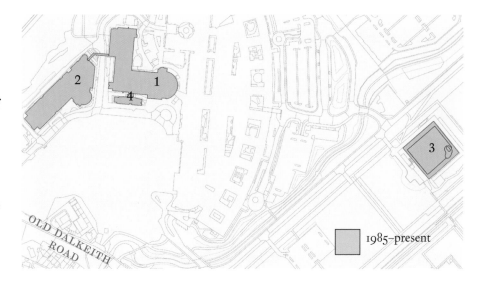

medical research and commercial development to rival San Francisco's Mission Bay, Singapore's Biopolis and Stockholm's Novum Biocity. Keppie Design, the architects for the infirmary and Chancellor's Building, drew up a masterplan for the new hub in 2004, taking account of the Queen's Medical Research Institute, which was then under construction. In 2006 the Scottish Executive announced funding of £24m towards the first building of the new cluster, the University's Scottish Centre for Regenerative Medicine. The following year the partners rebranded the centre for biomedical research as Edinburgh BioQuarter, and Scottish Enterprise appointed a US property company, Alexandria Real Estate Equities, as the development partner for the 55-acre site adjacent to the infirmary and University buildings.[61]

In 2009 Scottish Enterprise purchased further land to the south-east, and the area achieved Enterprise Area status in 2011. Alan Murray Architects drew up a new Edinburgh BioQuarter masterplan in the same year, which was adopted in 2014. The masterplan includes mixed-use proposals for a hotel, restaurants, leisure facilities, residential accommodation and streetscape improvements in addition to life science developments. The first commercial facility, opened in 2014, was a speculative (BioIncubator) laboratory and office development known as 'Nine', designed by Oberlanders Architects. Work began in March 2015 on construction of a new building for the Royal Hospital for Sick Children and the University's Department of Clinical Neurosciences to the design of HLM Architects.

CHANCELLOR'S BUILDING

The official opening of the new Medical School building took place on 12 August 2002, when it was named in honour of the University Chancellor, HRH The Duke of Edinburgh. Designed by Keppie Design in 1998 alongside the new Royal Infirmary of Edinburgh, the

333 Plan of Little France campus
1. Chancellor's Building
2. Queen's Medical Research Institute
3. Scottish Centre for Regenerative Medicine
4. Anne Rowling Regenerative Neurology Clinic
Crown copyright 2017 Ordnance Survey [Licence Number 100021521]

334 The clinical white cladding and disjointed geometric volumes of the Chancellor's Building, home of the University of Edinburgh Medical School since 2002
Nick Haynes

335 Queen's Medical Research Institute designed by BMJ Architects, 2001–5
Keith Hunter

14,000m² building took four years to complete.[62] The accommodation included two auditoria, seven seminar rooms, student microlabs and video conference capabilities, five dry laboratories, a library and a clinical teaching resource centre.

The building is arranged in an L-plan with a lecture theatre drum at the end of the eastern range, answering the drum at the entrance to the adjacent Royal Infirmary building. The detailing and materials are also similar, with clinical flush white rainscreen panels, buff sandstone feature panels and grey profiled metal roof.

QUEEN'S MEDICAL RESEARCH INSTITUTE

Following the removal of the Medical School and Royal Infirmary of Edinburgh to Little France in 2002, three important medical research centres remained in the city: cardiovascular research; inflammation research; and reproductive medicine. As planned in the 1990s, and in order to encourage a 'bench to bedside' approach to medical research, the University determined to locate a dedicated building adjacent to the Chancellor's Building and Edinburgh Royal Infirmary at Little France. BMJ Architects designed the new £43m Queen's Medical Research Institute both to house the three centres and to promote collaboration and cross-fertilisation of ideas between them. Funding came from the Scottish Higher Education Funding Council Research Infrastructure Fund, Wellcome Trust, British Heart Foundation, Wolfson Foundation, Medical Research Council and the American Kresge Foundation amongst other benefactions.

Three storeys of laboratories, now housing more than 650 researchers, are arranged in a rectangular plan with a further wedge containing the communal spaces, café, restaurant and main lecture theatre at the north-eastern end. Internally, the building is planned with three vertical blocks separated by atria containing stairs and circulation spaces. Smaller offices, meeting rooms and ancillary spaces line a corridor spine, with large thirty-person laboratories facing outwards on both sides of the building. Following the award of £7m in European Union funding at a relatively late stage in the design process, the University introduced a requirement for an imaging centre to be incorporated at a later stage in the basement.

The Chancellor of the University, HRH The Duke of Edinburgh, opened the institute on 7 August 2006. Completion and fitting out of the £20m Clinical Research Imaging Centre in the basement with a 3-T magnetic resonance imaging scanner, a 64-multidetector

computerised tomography (CT) / positron emission tomography scanner, and a state-of-the-art 320-slice CT scanner followed in 2008–10 in partnership with NHS Lothian Health Board.[63]

SCOTTISH CENTRE FOR REGENERATIVE MEDICINE

In 2006 the Scottish Executive announced funding of £24m towards a £59m Scottish Centre for Regenerative Medicine, the first large-scale, purpose-built facility of its kind in the UK for the development of new treatments for human diseases including cancer, heart disease, diabetes and also degenerative diseases such as multiple sclerosis, Parkinson's disease and liver failure.[64] The brief provided for state-of-the-art research facilities, manufacturing capacity and commercialisation facilities with an aim of bringing together world-leading basic stem cell research with established clinical excellence in a 'bench-to-bedside' approach to therapeutic medicine.

According to architects Sheppard Robson, the rooms are arranged like a 'pebble in a pond', with smaller, darker spaces, such as the cell culture rooms, positioned in the centre of the building while laboratory spaces are positioned in the middle and write-up spaces are located next to the outer walls, allowing for natural ventilation and lighting.[65] The 8,700m² building's cantilevered structure is clad in clear and opaque curtain walling and features vertical aluminium fins to minimise solar gain. The building's sustainable features include ground source heat pumps, rainwater harvesting, photovoltaics and chilled beams (a type of low-energy heating, ventilation and air conditioning system designed to heat or cool large buildings).[66]

HRH The Princess Royal, Chancellor of the University, opened the new building on 28 May 2012. A new Institute for Regeneration and Repair will be built on the adjacent site to provide space for an interdisciplinary research environment, integrating chemists alongside biologists and clinical researchers to address key challenges in the translation and commercialisation of regenerative therapies.

ANNE ROWLING REGENERATIVE NEUROLOGY CLINIC

Designed by Keppie Architects in a competition of 2010, the clinic undertakes research into a number of degenerative neurological conditions, including multiple sclerosis and motor neurone disease. It is named in memory of J.K. Rowling's mother, Anne, who died from complications resulting from multiple sclerosis at the age of forty-five. The Harry Potter author contributed £10m, the University's largest ever individual donation, for the new purpose-built facility. The Chancellor of the University, HRH The Princess Royal, opened the clinic on 8 October 2013.

The project involved the construction of a single-storey extension linked to the Chancellor's Building and alterations within the existing building to accommodate staff / office areas. The long, single-storey, 450m² extension provides a suite of consultation and examination rooms, along with patient-orientated relaxation and interaction areas around a central atrium, which allows the building to be flooded with natural daylight throughout. The intention was to form a comfortable, positive and protective environment for patients and modern and flexible working conditions for clinicians and researchers.

339 Anne Rowling Regenerative Neurology Clinic designed by Keppie Architects in 2010–12. The clinic was funded by J.K. Rowling in memory of her mother.
Keppie Design

Looking Forward

This book has described the development of the University's estate over 400 years from its modest beginnings in the Earl of Arran's townhouse to more than 350 core buildings, comprising 864,000m² of floor space, spread across five major campuses. Since 2014, there has been a hugely ambitious programme of works and strategic acquisitions led by Principal Timothy O'Shea and Director of Estates, Gary Jebb. This has begun to transform the estate in numerous ways with the aim of 'creating a world-class estate for a world-class University'. A new strategic long-term plan and integrated vision for the estate guides the investment of more than £150m per annum. The aspiration is to make an open, inclusive, attractive and flexible estate that is both functional and inspiring for University staff and students and also welcoming to the wider community.

At the time of writing, major refurbishment or new-build projects in progress or about to be completed include: the Law School in Old College; the McEwan Hall and Bristo Square; the Bayes Institute on Potterrow; Appleton Tower; Buccleuch Place and Meadow Lane student accommodation; St Cecilia's Hall; the main building at Edinburgh College of Art; the Pleasance complex; stonework repairs to New College; Old Kirk, Holyrood Road; Darwin Tower and Murchison House, King's Buildings; and the Innovation Centre and Campus Hub and the new Large Animal Research and Imaging Centre at Easter Bush.

In addition to these substantial projects, planning and preparatory work for future enhancement continues across the estate, including advanced schemes for an extended student centre in Charles Street, a major geosciences centre at King's Buildings, and an Institute of Regeneration and Repair and a new Usher Institute at Little France.

The recent purchase of two key historical buildings in Lauriston Place, the old Surgical Hospital and the former Central Fire Station, opens up new possibilities for a fundamental reorientation of the University's activities in the central area, creating a chain of interdisciplinary centres from Holyrood Road via High School Yards, Old College and George Square to Quartermile and Lauriston, complementing the topography and the traditional east-west development and connectivity pattern of the city's historic core.

It is impossible to know how future generations will look back on the University's current architectural activity, but it seems likely that the sheer scale and quality of the work, both in augmenting and refurbishing the historic estate and in creating a legacy of innovative contemporary buildings, will mark this as a new golden age.

340 The former Central Fire Station, designed by Robert Morham in 1897. It is proposed as a culture and arts hub to expand the existing Edinburgh College of Art complex.
Nick Haynes

341 The old Surgical Hospital in Lauriston Place, designed in Scots baronial style by David Bryce in 1870, and opened in 1879. Bennetts Associates have now been appointed to transform the building, giving it a long-term future at the heart of the University's estate.
Bennetts Associates

Principals & Chancellors

PRINCIPALS OF THE UNIVERSITY

1586 Robert Rollock (previously Regent)

1599 Henry Charteris

1620 Patrick Sands

1622 Robert Boyd

1623 John Adamson

1653 Robert Leighton

1662 William Colvill

1675 Andrew Cant

1685 Alexander Monro

1690 Gilbert Rule

1703 William Carstares

1716 William Wishart (primus)

1730 William Hamilton

1732 James Smith

1736 William Wishart (secundus)

1754 John Gowdie

1762 William Robertson

1793 George Baird

1840 John Lee

1859 Sir David Brewster

1868 Sir Alexander Grant, Bt

1885 Sir William Muir

1903 Sir William Turner

1916 Sir James Ewing

1929 Sir Thomas Holland

1944 Sir John Fraser, Bt

1949 Sir Edward Appleton

1965 Sir Michael Swann

1974 Sir Hugh Robson

1979 Sir John Burnett

1987 Sir David Smith

1994 Sir Stewart Sutherland

2002 Sir Timothy O'Shea

CHANCELLORS OF THE UNIVERSITY

1859–1868 Henry Brougham,
  1st Baron Brougham and Vaux

1868–1891 John Inglis, Lord Glencorse

1891–1930 Arthur Balfour, 1st Earl of Balfour

1930–1937 Sir James Matthew Barrie, Bt

1937–1946 John Buchan, 1st Baron Tweedsmuir

1946–1952 Victor Hope, 2nd Marquess of Linlithgow

1953–2010 HRH The Duke of Edinburgh

2011–present HRH The Princess Royal

Acknowledgements

The authors would particularly like to thank Michelle Andersson (HES); Mary Bownes (EU); Clare Campbell; Richard Emerson; Paul Fleming (EU); Philip Graham (EU); Gary Jebb (EU); Chloe Kippen (EU); Hugh Langmuir; Ranald MacInnes (HES); Richard Mann (EU); Elly McCrone (HES) and Michael Pearce.

Numerous other people have contributed to the research and production of this book, for which the authors are extremely grateful: Keith Adam; Tom Addyman; Denise Anderson (EU); Stephen Astley (Soane Museum); Alan Barkess (NGS); Francesca Baseby (EU); Graham Bell (EU); Mark Blaxter (EU); George Boag (EU); Iain Gordon Brown; Malcolm Brown (EU); Grant Buttars (EU); Ines Castellano (NMS); Julia Chambers; Peter Clapham (ECA); Brenda Connoboy (ECA); Scott Docking (EU); Isla Duncan (EU); Althea Dundas-Bekker; Stuart Eydmann; Alistair Fair (EU); Chris Fleet (NLS); Andrew Fleming; Jill Forrest (EU); Andrew G. Fraser; Serena Fredrick (EU); Catriona Gourlay (NGS); Norman Gray; Thomas Gübitz; Paul Harding; John Hart (EU); Anna Hawkins (EU); Eilidh Henderson (Page\Park); Carsten Hermann (HES); Charles Hill (EU); Chris Humphreys; Keith Hunter; Richard Hunter (ECA); Stephen Jackson (NMS); Sarah Jeffcott (NGS); Andrew Kerr; Vikki Kerr (ECA); Daniel Killeen; Andrew Lee; John Lowrey (EU); Jacky MacBeath (EU); Malcolm MacCallum (EU); Gordon MacDougall (EU); Dawn McDowell (HES); Joseph Marshall (EU); Debbie Mays; Jenny Nex (EU); Trine Nordkvelle (NGS); Howard Parsons-Hewes (EU); Duncan Peet (HES); Susan Pettigrew (EU); Vincenzo Piscioneri; Steven Poliri (EU); Lesley Richmond; Joe Rock; Callum Robertson (EU); Norman Rodger (EU); Alistair Rowan; Marion Rozowski; Justine Sambrook (RIBA); Neale Smith; Jo Spiller (EU); Vanessa Stephen; Helen Stocks (EU); David Taylor; Stephen Willis (EU); and Paul Zanre.

ABBREVIATIONS

ECA	Edinburgh City Archives
EU	University of Edinburgh
HES	Historic Environment Scotland
NLS	National Library of Scotland
NGS	National Galleries of Scotland
NMS	National Museums Scotland
RIBA	Royal Institute of British Architects

Bibliography

ADAM 1764
Robert Adam, *The Ruins of the Palace of the Emperor Diocletian at Spalatro in Dalmatia*, London, 1764

ADAM 1899
Robert Adam (ed.), *Edinburgh Records: the Burgh Accounts*, 2 vols, Edinburgh, 1899

ADAM BROTHERS 1773–1822
Robert and James Adam, *The Works in Architecture of Robert and James Adam*, London, 1773–1822

ADDYMAN 2011
Addyman Archaeology, Old College Quadrangle, *University of Edinburgh, Data Structure Report for Archaeological Excavations: June–October 2010*, Edinburgh, 2011

ANDERSON, LYNCH AND PHILLIPSON 2003
Robert D. Anderson, Michael Lynch, Nicholas Phillipson (eds), *The University of Edinburgh: An Illustrated History*, Edinburgh, 2003

ARNOT 1779
Hugo Arnot, *The History of Edinburgh*, Edinburgh and London, 1779

BATH 2003
Michael Bath, *Renaissance Decorative Painting in Scotland*, Edinburgh, 2003

BATH 2010
Michael Bath, 'Andrew Bairhum, Giovanni Ferrerio and the "Lighter Style of Painting"', in *Journal of the Northern Renaissance*, issue 2, 2010

BEARD 1978
Geoffrey Beard, *The Work of Robert Adam*, Edinburgh, 1978

BERTRAM 2012
Geoffrey Bertram, *The Etchings of John Clerk of Eldin*, Taunton, 2012

BIRSE 1983
Ronald M. Birse, *Engineering at Edinburgh University: A Short History 1673–1983*, Edinburgh, 1983

BIRSE 1994
Ronald M. Birse, *Science at the University of Edinburgh, 1583–1993: An Illustrated History to Mark the Centenary of the Faculty of Science and Engineering 1893–1993*, Edinburgh, 1994

BOLTON 1922
Arthur Thomas Bolton, *The Architecture of Robert and James Adam, 1758–1794*, 2 vols, London, 1922

BOWER 1817
Alexander Bower, *The History of the University of Edinburgh*, 2 vols, Edinburgh, 1817

BOWER 1822
Alexander Bower, *The Edinburgh Student's Guide: or, an Account of the Classes of the University, Arranged Under the Four Faculties, etc.*, Edinburgh, 1822

BROWN 1891
Peter Hume Brown (ed.), *Early Travellers in Scotland*, Edinburgh, 1891

BROWN 1989
Iain Gordon Brown, *Building for Books: the Architectural Evolution of the Advocates' Library, 1689–1925*, Aberdeen, 1989

BROWN 1992
Iain Gordon Brown, 'Robert Adam's Drawings: Edinburgh's Loss, London's Gain', in *Book of the Old Edinburgh Club*, New Series, vol.2, Edinburgh, 1992

BROWN 1993
Iain Gordon Brown, *Monumental Reputation: Robert Adam and the Emperor's Palace*, Edinburgh, 1993

BROWN 1997
Iain Gordon Brown, 'Surpassing Expectations: An East Anglian Visitor's Report of 1790', in *Book of the Old Edinburgh Club*, New Series, vol.4, 1997

BRYDEN 1990
D. J. Bryden, 'The Edinburgh Observatory 1736–1811: A Story of Failure', in *Annals of Science*, vol.47, issue 5, London, 1990

BUCHAN 2003
James Buchan, *Capital of the Mind – How Edinburgh Changed the World*, Edinburgh, 2003

CALAMY 1829
Edmund Calamy, *An Historical Account of My Own Life, with Some Reflections on the Times I Have Lived In (1671–1731)*, 2 vols, London, 1829

CAMPBELL, GLENDINNING AND THOMAS 2012
Louise Campbell, Miles Glendinning, Jane Thomas (eds), *Basil Spence: Buildings & Projects*, London, 2012

COCKBURN 1856
Henry Cockburn, *Memorials of His Time*, Edinburgh, 1856

CONNOLLY 2003
David Connolly (ed.), *South Bridge / Cowgate: Edinburgh – Historical and Analytical Assessment of the Fire-Damaged Buildings*, Edinburgh, 2003

CRAUFURD 1808
Thomas Craufurd, *History of the University from 1580 to 1646*, Edinburgh, 1808

CRUFT AND FRASER 1995
Kitty Cruft, Andrew Fraser (eds), *James Craig 1744–1795: 'Ingenious Architect of the New Town of Edinburgh'*, Edinburgh, 1995

CUTHBERTSON 1890
David Cuthbertson, *College Echoes: sketches and scenes of university life at Edinburgh*, Edinburgh, 1890

CUTHBERTSON 1910
David Cuthbertson, *The Edinburgh University Library: an account of its origin with a description of its rarer books and manuscripts*, Edinburgh, 1910

DALZEL 1862
Andrew Dalzel, *History of the University from its Foundation*, 2 vols, Edinburgh, 1862

DEFOE 1727
Daniel Defoe, *A Tour Thro' the Whole Island of Great Britain, Divided into Circuits or Journies*, vol.3, London, 1727

DIBDIN 1838
Thomas Frognall Dibdin, *Bibliographical, Antiquarian and Picturesque Tour of the Northern Counties and Scotland*, 2 vols, London, 1838

DONALDSON 1983
Gordon Donaldson (ed.), *Four Centuries: Edinburgh University Life, 1583–1983*, Edinburgh, 1983

DUNBAR 1999
John G. Dunbar, *Scottish Royal Palaces: The Architecture of the Royal Residences during the Late Medieval and Early Renaissance Periods*, East Linton, 1999

EE
Helen Armet, Robert Kerr Hannay, James David Marwick, Marguerite Wood, *Extracts from the Records of the Burgh of Edinburgh 1589–1718*, 14 vols, Edinburgh, various dates 1869–1927

EMERSON 2004
Roger L. Emerson, 'The Founding of the Edinburgh Medical School', in *Journal of the History of Medicine and Allied Sciences*, vol.52, no.2, Oxford, April 2004

EMERSON 2008
Roger L. Emerson, *Academic Patronage in the Scottish Enlightenment: Glasgow, Edinburgh & St Andrews*, Edinburgh, 2008

FARINGTON 1978
Kenneth Garlick, Angus D. Macintyre, Kathryn Cave (eds), *The Diary of Joseph Farington*, 17 vols, New Haven, 1978–98

FINLAYSON 1980
Charles P. Finlayson, *Clement Litill and his library: the origins of Edinburgh University Library*, Edinburgh, 1980

FLEMING 1962
John Fleming, *Robert Adam and his Circle*, London, 1962

FRASER 1986
Andrew G. Fraser, *Walking Tours of University Buildings*, Edinburgh, 1986

FRASER 1989
Andrew G. Fraser, *The Building of Old College – Adam, Playfair & The University of Edinburgh*, Edinburgh, 1989

FRASER 1994
Andrew G. Fraser, 'Edinburgh University new buildings: the Medical School and McEwan Hall', 1994 [typescript: HES National Record for the Historic Environment, shelf no.D.8.41.UNI.P]

GIFFORD 1989
John Gifford, *William Adam, 1689–1748: A Life and Times of Scotland's Universal Architect*, Edinburgh, 1989

GIFFORD, MCWILLIAM, WALKER AND WILSON 1991
John Gifford, Colin McWilliam, David M. Walker, Christopher Wilson, *Buildings of Scotland: Edinburgh*, Harmondsworth and New York, 1991 (1984 edition reprinted and revised)

GLENDINNING, MACKECHNIE AND ORAM 2004
Miles Glendinning, Aonghus MacKechnie, Richard Oram, *The Architecture of Scottish Government from Kingship to Parliamentary Democracy*, Dundee, 2004

GOW 1984
Ian Gow, 'William Henry Playfair', in *Scottish Pioneers of the Greek Revival*, Edinburgh, 1984

GOW 1990
Ian Gow, 'Playfair: A Northern Athenian', in *RIBA Journal*, London, May 1990

GRAHAM 1860
John Murray Graham, 'A Notice of the Life and Works of William Henry Playfair, Architect', in *Transactions of the Architectural Institute of Scotland*, Edinburgh 1860

GRAHAM 2009
Roderick Graham, *Arbiter of Elegance: A Biography of Robert Adam*, Edinburgh, 2009

GRANT 1884
A. Grant, *The Story of the University of Edinburgh*, 2 vols, London, 1884

GRAVES 1912
Frank Pierrepont Graves, *Peter Ramus and the Educational Reformation of the Sixteenth Century*, New York, 1912

GREEN 2010
Thomas Green, 'The Court of The Commissaries of Edinburgh: Consistorial Law and Litigation, 1559 – 1576', PhD Thesis, University of Edinburgh, 2010

GRIER AND BOWNES 2014
Jean Grier, Mary Bownes, *Private Giving, Public Good: The Impact of Philanthropy at the University of Edinburgh*, Edinburgh, 2014

GUILD AND LAW 1982
Jean R. Guild, Alexander Law (eds), *Edinburgh University Library 1580–1980 – A Collection of Historical Essays*, Edinburgh 1982

GUNN 1849
William M. Gunn (ed.), *Selected Works of Robert Rollock, Principal of the University of Edinburgh*, 2 vols, Edinburgh, 1849

HANNAY 1916
Robert Kerr Hannay, 'Visitation of the College of Edinburgh in 1690', in *The Book of the Old Edinburgh Club*, vol.8, Edinburgh, 1916

HARDING 2013
Paul Harding, 'John Mylne IV (1611–1667): Great Artisan, Grave Senator', in *Architectural Heritage*, vol.xxiii, Edinburgh, 2013

HARRISON 1884
J. Harrison, *Oure Tounis Colledge: Sketches of the History of the Old College of Edinburgh*, Edinburgh, 1884

HERMANS AND NELISSEN 1994
Jos M.M. Hermans, Marc Nelissen (eds), *Charters of Foundation and Early Documents of the Universities of the Coimbra Group*, Groningen, 1994

HORN 1957
David Bayne Horn, 'Principal William Robertson, D.D., Historian', in *University of Edinburgh Journal*, no.18, Edinburgh, 1957

HORN 1966A
David Bayne Horn, 'The Anatomy Classrooms in the present Old College, 1725–1880', in *University of Edinburgh Journal*, no.22, Edinburgh, 1966

HORN 1966B
David Bayne Horn, 'The Origins of the University of Edinburgh', parts 1 and 2, in *University of Edinburgh Journal*, no.22, Edinburgh, 1966

HORN 1967
David Bayne Horn, *A Short History of the University of Edinburgh*, Edinburgh, 1967

HORN 1969A
David Bayne Horn, first draft of chapters 1–4 from a projected 'Long History of the University of Edinburgh', unpublished manuscript in the University of Edinburgh Centre for Research Collections, ref. GB 237 Coll-26 (left unfinished on Horn's death in 1969)

HORN 1969B
David Bayne Horn, first draft of sections 1–2 from a projected *History of the Buildings of the University of Edinburgh*, unpublished manuscript in the University of Edinburgh Centre for Research Collections, ref. GB 237 Coll-26 (left unfinished on Horn's death in 1969)

HUGHES 1926
T. Harold Hughes, 'Great Scottish Architects of the Past: William Henry Playfair', in *Quarterly of the Royal Incorporation of Architects in Scotland*, vols 17 and 18, Edinburgh, 1926

JOHNSON AND ROSENBURG 2010
Jim Johnson, Lou Rosenburg, *Renewing Old Edinburgh: the Enduring Legacy of Patrick Geddes*, Edinburgh, 2010

JONES AND MCKINSTRY 2009
David Jones, Sam McKinstry (eds), *Essays in Scots and English Architectural History: a Festschrift in Honour of John Frew*, Donington, 2009

LEE 1839
J. Lee, *The University of Edinburgh from its Foundation in 1583 to the Year 1839: a Historical Sketch*, Edinburgh, 1839

LONG AND THOMAS 2007
Philip Long, Jane Thomas (eds), *Basil Spence Architect*, Edinburgh, 2007

LORD HIGH TREASURER ACCOUNTS 1877–1978
Thomas Dickson, C.T. McInnes, James Balfour Paul (eds), *Accounts of the Lord High Treasurer of Scotland*, 13 vols, Edinburgh, 1877–1978

LOWREY 2001
John Lowrey, 'From Caesarea to Athens: Greek Revival Edinburgh and the Question of Scottish Identity within the Unionist State', in *Journal of*

the Society of Architectural Historians, vol.60, no.2, Berkeley, June 2001

LOWTHER 1894
Christopher Lowther, *Our Journall into Scotland Anno Domini 1629, 5th of November*, Edinburgh, 1894

LYNCH 1981
Michael Lynch, *Edinburgh and the Reformation*, Edinburgh, 1981

LYNCH 1982
Michael Lynch, 'The origins of Edinburgh's "toun college": a revision article', in *Innes Review*, no.33, Edinburgh, 1982

LYON 1873
David Murray Lyon, *History of the Lodge of Edinburgh (Mary's Chapel) no.1, Embracing an Account of the Rise and Progress of Freemasonry in Scotland*, Edinburgh, 1873

MACDONALD, LYNCH AND COWAN 1994
A. A. MacDonald, Michael Lynch, I.B. Cowan (eds), *The Renaissance in Scotland: Studies in Literature, Religion, History and Culture offered to John Durkan*, Leyden, 1994

MACINNES 1993
Ranald MacInnes, 'Robert Adam's Public Buildings', in *Architectural Heritage*, vol.4, Edinburgh, 1993

MCKINSTRY 1991
Sam McKinstry, *Rowand Anderson – 'The Premier Architect of Scotland'*, Edinburgh, 1991

MCWILLIAM 1957
Colin McWilliam, 'Modern Athenian', in *Scotland's Magazine*, vol.53, no.8, Edinburgh, August 1957

MAHON 1930
Reginald Mahon, *The Tragedy of Kirk o'Field*, Cambridge, 1930

MAITLAND 1753
William Maitland, *History of Edinburgh from its Foundation to the Present Time in Nine Books*, Edinburgh, 1753

MALCOLM AND HUNTER 1948
Charles A. Malcolm, J. Norman W. Hunter, *Moray House: A Brief Sketch of Its History*, Edinburgh, 1948

MARWICK 1871
James D. Marwick (ed.), *Charters and documents relating to the Collegiate Church and Hospital of the Holy Trinity, and the Trinity Hospital, Edinburgh*, Edinburgh, 1871

MARWICK 1891
James D. Marwick, *History of the Church of Holy Trinity and Hospital*, Edinburgh, 1891

MAYS 1997
Deborah Mays (ed.), *The Architecture of Scottish Cities*, Edinburgh, 1997

MILLAR 1827
James Millar (ed.), *Encyclopaedia Edinensis*, 6 vols, Edinburgh, 1816

MILNE 2013
Hugh M. Milne (ed.), *Boswell's Edinburgh Journals 1767–1786*, Edinburgh, 2013 (first edition 2001)

MONTEITH 1834
R. Monteith, *Collection of Epitaphs and Monumental Inscriptions, Chiefly in Scotland*, Glasgow, 1834

MORGAN 1937
Alexander Morgan (ed.), *University of Edinburgh: Charters, Statutes and Acts of the Town Council and the Senatus 1583–1858*, Edinburgh, 1937

NAMIER AND BROOKE 1985
Lewis Namier, John Brooke, *The History of Parliament: The House of Commons, 1754–1790*, London, 1964 (reprinted 1985)

NAUDÉ 1627
Gabriel P. Naudé, *Advis pour dresser une bibliothèque*, Paris, 1627

NICHOLS 1828
John Nichols, *The Progresses, Processions, and Magnificent Festivities of King James the First, His Royal Consort, Family and Court*, vol.3, London, 1828

NICOLL 1836
John Nicoll, *A Diary of Public Transactions and Other Occurrences, Chiefly in Scotland, from January 1650 to June 1667*, Edinburgh, 1836

PARLIAMENTS OF SCOTLAND 1814–44
Archibald Anderson, Cosmo Innes, Thomas Thomson (eds), *The Acts of the Parliaments of Scotland*, 12 vols, London, 1814–44

PENNANT 1772
Thomas Pennant (ed. Charles W. J. Withers), *A Tour in Scotland and Voyages to the Hebrides in 1772*, Edinburgh (1998 edition)

PLAYFAIR 1822
James George Playfair (ed.), *The Works of John Playfair Esq.*, 4 vols, Edinburgh, 1822

POLLEN 1901
John Hungerford Pollen, *Papal Negotiations with Mary Queen of Scots during her Reign in Scotland, 1561–1567*, Edinburgh, 1901

PRESTON AND OLIVER 1829
William Preston, George Oliver, *Illustrations of Masonry*, London, 1829

PRIVY COUNCIL
Peter Hume Brown, John Hill Burton, Robert Kerr Hannay, David Masson, Henry Paton (eds), *Register of the Privy Council of Scotland 1569–1578*, series 1, 14 vols, Edinburgh, 1877–98

PRIVY SEAL
Matthew Livingstone, David Hay Fleming, James Beveridge, Gordon Donaldson (eds), *Register of the Privy Seal of Scotland*, 8 vols, Edinburgh, 1908–82

ROBERTSON 1768
William Robertson, *Memorial Relating to the University of Edinburgh*, Edinburgh, 1768

ROCK, HILLMAN AND BUNCH 2011
Joe Rock, Martin Hillman, Antonia J. Bunch, 'The Temple of Harmony: A New Architectural History of St Cecilia's Hall, Edinburgh', in *Architectural Heritage*, vol.20, Edinburgh, 2011

ROWAN 1974
Alistair Rowan, 'After the Adelphi: Forgotten Years in the Adam Brothers' Practice', in *Journal of the Royal Society of Arts*, vol. 122, no. 5218, September 1974

ROWAN 1985
Alistair Rowan, *Designs for Castles and Country Villas by Robert & James Adam*, London, 1985

ROWAN 2003
Alistair Rowan, *'Bob the Roman': Heroic Antiquity & the Architecture of Robert Adam*, London, 2003

ROWAN 2004
Alistair Rowan, 'Robert Adam's ideas for the North Bridge in Edinburgh', in *Architectural Heritage*, vol.15, issue 1, Edinburgh, 2004

ROWAN 2007
Alistair Rowan, *Vaulting Ambition: the Adam Brothers, Contractors to the Metropolis in the Reign of George III*, London, 2007

SANDERSON 1982
Margaret H.B. Sanderson, 'Robert Adam's Last Visit to Scotland, 1791', in *Architectural History*, vol.25, London, 1982

SANDERSON 1992
Margaret H.B. Sanderson, *Robert Adam and Scotland – Portrait of an Architect*, Edinburgh, 1992

SMELLIE 1800
William Smellie, *Literary and characteristical lives of John Gregory MD, Henry Home, Lord Kames. David Hume, Esq. and Adam Smith LLD: To which are*

added A dissertation on public spirit; and three essays, Edinburgh, 1800

SPEC 1845
Various authors, *History of the Speculative Society of Edinburgh*, Edinburgh, 1845

SPEC 1905
Various authors, *The History of the Speculative Society, 1764–1904*, Edinburgh, 1905

STEWART 1973
Charles H. Stewart, *The Past Hundred Years: the Buildings of the University of Edinburgh*, Edinburgh, 1973

STEWART 2012
Margaret Stewart, *The Edinburgh College of Art Cast Collection and Architecture*, Edinburgh, 2012

TAIT 1978
A.A. Tait, 'The Sale of Robert Adam's Drawings', in *Burlington Magazine*, London, July 1978

TAIT 1993
A.A. Tait, *Robert Adam: Drawings & Imagination*, Cambridge, 1993

TAIT 1996
A.A. Tait, *Robert Adam – The Creative Mind: from sketch to the finished drawing*, London, 1996

TAIT 2004
A.A. Tait, 'Adam, Robert (1728–1792)', in *Oxford Dictionary of National Biography*, Oxford, 2004; online edn, October 2009 [http://www.oxforddnb.com/view/article/105, accessed 30 May 2015]

TOMASZEWSKI 1968
Wiktor Tomaszewski (ed.), *The University of Edinburgh and Poland*, Edinburgh, 1968

TURNER 1933
Arthur Logan Turner (ed.), *History of the University of Edinburgh, 1883–1933*, Edinburgh, 1933

WATSON 1929
Charles Brodie Boog Watson (ed.), *Roll of Edinburgh burgesses and guild-brethren, 1406–1700*, Edinburgh, 1929

WATT 1946
Hugh Watt, *New College Edinburgh*, Edinburgh and London, 1946

WOMERSLEY AND CRAWFORD 2010
Tara Womersley, Dorothy H. Crawford, *Bodysnatchers to Lifesavers: Three Centuries of Medicine in Edinburgh*, Edinburgh, 2010

YOUNGSON 1966
A.J. Youngson, *The Making of Classical Edinburgh*, Edinburgh, 1966

Notes and References

ABBREVIATIONS

EE: Extracts from the Records of the Burgh of Edinburgh

HES: Historic Environment Scotland

NLS: National Library of Scotland

NRS: National Records of Scotland

ECA: Edinburgh City Archives

ECA/TCM: Edinburgh City Archives, Town Council Minutes

ECA/DOGC: Edinburgh City Archives, Dean of Guild Court

ECA/CC: Edinburgh City Archives, College Commissioners

ECA/CCM: Edinburgh City Archives, College Commissioners' Minutes

ECA/CCR: Edinburgh City Archives, College Commissioners' Records

ECA/CTA: Edinburgh City Archives, College Treasurers' Accounts

EU: Edinburgh University

EU/CRC: Edinburgh University, Centre for Research Collections

EUA: Edinburgh University Archives

EUL: Edinburgh University Library

CHAPTER ONE
PAGES 11–31

1. Hermans and Nelisson 1994, p.43. The original vellum charter is on permanent loan to the University (ref. EUA/GD4) from ECA (ref. ECA/SL1 Charter 65). A zoomable image of the charter can be accessed via the University's image database: http://images.is.ed.ac.uk. A transcription of the full Latin text is in Morgan 1937, pp.12–16.

2. Milne 2013, p.106.

3. See Grant 1884; Robert Hannay in Turner 1933; Horn 1966b and 1967; James Kirk in Guild and Law 1982; Lynch 1982; and Michael Lynch in Anderson, Lynch and Phillipson 2003 for some of the controversy surrounding the establishment of the University.

4. Privy Seal, vol.iv, p.555 and pp.581–2, no.3144, 5 February 1556.

5. Ibid., no.3268, 8 June 1556.

6. See Kirk in Guild and Law 1982, p.16 and note 96. See also Finlayson 1980, p.9 for more on Henryson and his circle.

7. Green 2010, p.22.

8. Adam 1899, vol.i, p.177.

9. Horn 1966b, pp.218–24.

10. Graves 1912, pp.47–8.

11. Horn 1966b, p.223.

12. Pollen 1901, p.416 (appendix 1 containing extracts from the letterbook of Ferrerio; letter of 2 May 1555 to Robert Reed [Reid]).

13. Privy Council, vol.ii, pp.528–9.

14. Ibid., vol.iii, pp.472–4.

15. Lynch 1981.

16. EE (1557–71), vol.iv, p.146.

17. Privy Seal, vol.v, part 1, p.242, no.965 (23 January 1562, Pennycuik's grant from the queen).

18. EE (1557–71), vol.iv, p.182 and p.184.

19. EE (1573–89), vol.v, p.103. Also Marwick 1871, p.74 and Kirk in Guild and Law 1982, p.22. Robert Pont, the Provost of Trinity College, was the father of the noted cartographer, Timothy Pont. William Littil was one of the masters of the hospital, EE (1573–89), vol.v, p.63.

20. EE (1573–89), vol.v, p.136.

21. Craufurd 1808, p.26 and p.70.

22. Marwick 1891, p.4.

23. Ibid., p.30.

24. Ibid., pp.128–30 and p.130, note 2.

25. EE (1589–1603), vol.vi, pp.352–3.

26. The name 'Litill' has at least seven variant spellings in contemporary documents. This variant was used by Litill himself on his marriage contract. See Finlayson 1980, p.1, note 1.

27. See Finlayson 1980 and Kirk and Finlayson in Guild and Law 1982 for the career and collection of Clement Litill and more on William Litill.

28. NRS, Edinburgh Commissaries, ii, f.365v.

29. Finlayson 1980, p.23.

30. EE (1573–89), vol.v, p.350.

31. EE (1573–89), vol.5, p.563.

32. Gunn 1849, pp.lxii–lxv.

33. George Scott, *Memoires of Sir James Melvil of Hal-hill*, London, 1683, p.78.

34. Grant 1884, vol.i, p.170.

35. Mahon 1930, pp.7–8.

36. Fraser 1989, p.47, n.9 makes the plausible suggestion that the Darnley murder scene sketch was made from the upper storeys of Hamilton Lodging.

37. Craufurd 1808, p.150. See also EE (1665–80), vol.xi, pp.80–1, where the winning of stones from the 'quarrell of the

colledge' was granted as an incentive to the builders of student chambers.

38. Addyman 2011, p.140.

39. Ibid., p.141.

40. Craufurd 1808, pp.21–2.

41. EE (1573–89), vol.v, p.302.

42. Craufurd 1808, p.41 and EE (1573–89), vol.v, pp.141–2.

43. Craufurd 1808, p.31.

44. Ibid., p.21 describes this lane as leading from the Cowgate to the Potterrow Port. See also Mahon 1930, p.7 for discussion of the lane.

45. Lord High Treasurer Accounts, vol.10, pp.xxiii–xxiv. The description of Arran as a mighty prince is from Parliaments of Scotland, vol.2, pp.603–4.

46. Mahon 1930, p.7, n.1.

47. Addyman 2011, p.30, pp.35–42, pp.63–7, and p.142.

48. Lord High Treasurer Accounts, vol.10, p.211.

49. Addyman 2011, p.72.

50. Craufurd 1808, p.150 refers to the 'north jamb'. Mahon 1930, p.17 calculates the dimensions of the house.

51. Ibid., p.129.

52. Addyman 2011, pp.66–7 and p.142.

53. Ibid., p.39.

54. Craufurd 1808, pp.23–4.

55. EE (1589–1603), vol.vi, p.8.

56. Craufurd 1808, p.151.

57. See Bath 2003, pp.272–4 and Bath 2010, p.8 for analysis of the decorative scheme at Kinneil.

58. Lord High Treasurer Accounts, vol.10, pp.90–1 and p.109. The footings and entrance jambs of the southern turnpike stair appear to be those identified during the 2010 excavation of Old College Quad.

59. Horn 1967, p.12.

60. EE (1642–65), vol.ix, pp.135–6.

61. Morgan 1937, pp.103–4.

62. Defoe 1724, p.42.

63. Mahon 1930, p.10.

64. EE (1642–55), vol.ix, p.140 and Craufurd 1808, p.99.

65. EE (1642–55), vol.ix, p.145.

66. For discussion of this issue, see Mahon 1930, pp.12–17 and Horn 1969b, section 1, pp.8–10.

67. EE (1655–65), vol.x, p.351, p.352, p.373 and p.379.

68. EE (1573–89), vol.v, p.571.

69. Lynch 1981, p.284, p.303, p.308, p.370 and p.372.

70. ECA/TCM, 3 January 1583. Sclater had previous experience of building projects from his involvement with the proposed hospital of 1568, see EE (1557–71), vol.iv, pp.247–8.

71. EE (1573–89), vol.v, p.311.

72. Nichols 1828, p.309.

73. Nicoll 1836, pp.307–17.

74. This quarto volume is now in the British Museum.

75. Craufurd 1808, pp.81–2.

76. Ibid., p.87.

77. Ibid., p.166.

78. Addyman 2011, p.103 and pp.111–15.

79. Craufurd 1808, p.79.

80. EE (1604–26), vol. vii, p.135 and note 2. ECA City Treasurer's Accounts, 1615–16, pp.377–96.

81. Craufurd 1808, p.150 and EE (1604–26), vol.vii, p.138 and note 1.

82. The delay is noted by Craufurd 1808, p.80 and appears to be confirmed by the substantial drop in expenditure in 1616–17. See also EE (1604–26), vol. vii, p.138 and note 1.

83. EE (1604–26), vol.vii, p.155.

84. Naudé 1627.

85. See Addyman 2011, p.111 for the walling materials and ECA/TCM, 25 July 1753, for the slates and pitch of the roof.

86. EE (1642–55), vol.ix, p.6.

87. EE (1655–65), vol.x, p.148.

88. Addyman 2011, p.128 and p.143.

89. Monteith 1834, pp.67–8.

90. Lowther 1894, pp.36–7.

91. EE (1655–65), vol.x, p.56.

92. See Addyman 2011, p.115, pp.142–3 and p.144.

93. EE (1626–41), vol.viii, p.17.

94. EE (1626–41), vol.viii, p.16 and Guild and Law 1982, p.46. Drummond bequeathed his whole library to the University on his death in 1649.

95. EE (1681–9), vol.xii, p.198.

96. One of the architectural elements found in the archaeological investigation of 2010 appears to be a fragment of one

97. ECA/TCM, 27 February 1755.

98. ECA/TCM, 30 July 1755, vol.ii, 1755; and ECA/McLeod bundles C0008A, bundle 8, letter dated 23 July 1755 from George Stuart to Baillie George Lind.

99. ECA/TCM, 25 July 1753. For the complicated history of the Adam family properties off the Cowgate, see section 8.2 by William Kay in Connolly 2003, pp.68–82.

100. ECA, ref. C0011/31, letter from William Robertson to the Lord Provost concerning the library, 11 May 1774.

101. ECA/TCM, 8 May 1751; 31 July 1751; and 17 October 1753.

102. ECA, estimate of repairs by J. Herriot, November 1775.

103. Craufurd 1808, p.92. See also EE (1604–26), vol.vii, p.225.

104. Bryden 1990, pp.446–7.

105. EE (1626–41), vol.viii, pp.4–5.

106. EE (1604–26), vol.vii, p.51 and pp.283–94, appendix vi.

107. EE (1626–41), vol.viii, p.140.

108. Scots Magazine, April 1790, pp.163–4 and Craufurd 1808, p.152. Johnston appears to have been the executor of the will of Jossie's father, a merchant in the City of London who left 1,000 merks to Heriot's Hospital, see EE (1626–41), vol.viii, p.52 and also Monteith 1834, p.68, for the carved inscription to Robert Johnston.

109. Craufurd 1808, p.150.

110. EE (1642–55), vol.ix, p.85 and pp.135–6.

111. Nicoll 1836, pp.170–1.

112. EE (1642–55), vol.ix, p.253.

113. Scots Magazine, April 1790, p.163.

114. Ibid., pp.163–4.

115. ECA/TCM, 29 August 1705 and 18 December 1706 (payment to wright).

116. EE (1626–41), vol.viii, p.210.

117. Grant 1884, vol.i, p.206.

118. Addyman 2011, pp.32–3.

119. Craufurd 1808, p.151 and Addyman 2011, pp.36–7.

120. Craufurd 1808, p.153.

121. EE (1642–55), vol.ix, p.202 and EE (1655–65), vol.x, pp.34–5.

122. Nicoll 1836, p.35.

123. EE (1642–55), vol.ix, p.19 and p.23.

124. EE (1655–65), vol.x, pp.22–3 and p.34.

125. ECA/CTA, vol.i, 1647.

126. ECA/TCM, 13 May 1670, identifies John Hamilton as the mason for the new chambers. See also EE (1665–80), vol.xi, pp.80–1 and p.95.

127. Quoted in Brown 1891, p.281.

128. Guild and Law 1982, p.49.

129. EE (1642–55), vol.ix, p.6.

130. For donors, see: ECA/CTA, vol.i, accounts of John Jossie in building of the new library, 1643; Craufurd 1808, p.153; and EE (1642–55), vol.ix, pp.58–9. Mylne inscribed Hamilton as a fellow and master of the masons' lodge of Edinburgh no.1 (Mary's Chapel) in 1640, see Lyon 1873, p.80.

131. ECA/CTA, vol.i.

132. See Glendinning, MacKechnie and Oram 2004, pp.114–16 for the Parliament House roof and Harding 2013, pp.27–8 for the Tron Kirk roof.

133. Dalzel 1862, vol.2, p.128.

134. EE (1642–55), vol.ix, p.22.

135. EE (1642–55), vol.ix, p.152.

136. EE (1642–55), vol.ix, p.216.

137. ECA/TCM, 9 January 1764; 19 June 1764; 15 January 1766; and 9 April 1766.

138. ECA/TCM, 9 April 1766.

139. ECA/CTA, vol.ii, 1766–7.

140. Fraser 1989, p.44.

141. Addyman 2011, p.73.

142. Calamy 1829, vol.ii, p.175.

143. Maitland 1753, p.375.

144. Bower 1817, vol.2, p.252.

145. ECA/TCM, 16 December 1767 and 23 December 1767 and EU/CRC, Senatus minutes, March 1768.

146. ECA/TCM, 23 December 1767. Unfortunately the plan is not now traceable.

147. Robertson 1768 and Caledonian Mercury, 12 and 15 February 1768, p.1.

148. Robertson 1768, pp.4–5.

149. Robertson 1768, p.5. The subjects included: 'Divinity, Church History, the Law of Nature and of Nations, Civil Law, Scotch Law, Anatomy, Theory of Physic, Practice of Physic, Chymistry, Botany and Materia Medica [pharmacology], Midwifery, Mathematics, Civil History and Roman Antiquities, Moral Philosophy, Natural History, Natural Philosophy, Logic and Metaphysics, Rhetoric and Belles Lettres, the Hebrew, Greek, and Latin Languages'.

150. Robertson 1768. p.10.

151. See Fraser 1989, p.92 for the various failed proposals of the 1770s.

152. ECA/TCM, 20 October 1725.

153. ECA, McLeod bundles, letter from the two Monros to the Lord Provost and town council, 5 September 1758.

154. ECA, McLeod bundles, vol.vi, p.12 (18), letter from Monro secundus to the Lord Provost and Town Council, 1764, and ECA/TCM, 4 July 1764.

155. ECA, McLeod bundles, (92), letter from Monro secundus to the Lord Provost and Town Council seeking additional funding, 11 December 1764.

156. This accounts for the two flooring levels discovered during the 2010 excavations of Old College Quad. See Addyman 2011, p.144.

157. Caledonian Mercury, 8 September 1764, p.2. ECA/CC, 1/1, petition by Dr Monro [secundus] to the Lord Provost, magistrates and council of the City of Edinburgh, 4 December 1784.

158. Horn 1966a, pp.68–9.

159. ECA/CCM, 10 June 1793, p.75.

160. Spec 1905, p.2.

161. Spec 1845, p.17.

162. ECA/TCM, 4 January 1769.

163. Spec 1905, p.6.

164. ECA/TCM, 7 June 1775.

165. Spec 1905, p.18. and ECA/CCM, trunk 2 and vol.2, p94.

166. ECA/TCM, 11 November 1724.

167. ECA/CTA, vol.ii, 1781–2.

CHAPTER TWO
PAGES 33–55

1. Dalzel 1862, vol.1, p.94.

2. See Tait 2004 for the eighteenth- and nineteenth-century reception of Adam's works.

3. Lowrey 2001, p.149 and pp.136–57

4. See Ranald MacInnes in Mays 1997, pp.78–86.

5. NLS, ref. MS 19992, Paterson–Adam Correspondence, 30 October 1790.

6. Adam Brothers 1773–8, p.2

7. See Tait 1993.

8. Adam Brothers 1773, p.1, n.1

9. London Metropolitan Archives, ref. CLC/B/227/MS03070/11 (letter from Robert Adam to Innes & Clerk, 5 July 1755).

10. Tait 1993.

11. Nick Haynes in Jones and McKinstry 2009, p.28.

12. 1785 Act, p.3. This multipurpose Act included provisions for creation of The Mound and draining of the Meadows to the south of George Square.

13. 1785 Act, p.21 and ECM/TCM, vol.106, 6 July 1785, p.286.

14. Scots Magazine, 2 December 1785, p.628.

15. An Act for Widening Several Streets in the City of Edinburgh. An act for making a Road from Saint Bernard's Street, in the Town of Leith, to the Foot of Leith Walk, in the County of Edinburgh; and for widening and enlarging certain Streets in the city of Edinburgh, and the Avenues leading to the same; and for amending Two several Acts passed, relative to the said City, in the Twenty-fifth and Twenty-sixth years of his present Majesty's Reign, 1787.

16. See Ian D. Grant in Cruft and Fraser 1995, pp.13–15.

17. Caledonian Mercury, 6 February 1768, p.3.

18. MacInnes 1993, pp.10–11 and Rowan 2004, pp.34–9.

19. Caledonian Mercury, 7 October 1790, p.3.

20. Fraser 1989, pp.56–8.

21. Brown 1775, p.11.

22. EU/CRC, ref. EUA INI/GOV/SEN/COR (Draft Bill for a lottery, probably 1777–8. The draft contains a list of trustees, including Sir Gilbert Elliot, who acquired his title as 4th Baronet of Minto in 1777, and John Dalrymple, Lord Provost, who occupied the office between 1777 and 1778.)

23. p.668 from 'Proposals for erecting a BRIDGE across the COWGATE, and for establishing an effectual Fund for the support of the POOR of Edinburgh, humbly submitted to the Public. By a Citizen' in Scots Magazine, appendix, 1784, pp.665–8

24. Scots Magazine, 2 December 1785, p.628.

25. Fraser 1989, p.55.

26. NLS, ref. MS 20500, letter from Robert Adam addressed to 'the Rt Honble James Hunter Blair Lord Provost', 14 July 1785. The first page mentions Robert's endeavours to make the designs 'agreeable to the information I had from your Lop [Lordship] in London'.

27. NLS, ref. MS 20500, letter from Robert Adam at the Adelphi in London addressed to 'the Rt Honble The Lord Provost of Edinburgh', 25 June 1785.

28. NLS, MS 20500, letter from Robert Adam addressed to 'the Rt Honble James Hunter Blair Lord Provost', 14 July 1785.

29. NLS, ref. MS 20500, estimate of prices for building a bridge across the Cowgate, 17 June 1785.

30. NLS, ref. MS 20500/20, copy account from Robert Adam addressed to 'the Rt Hon. & Hon. Trustees of the South Bridge &c at Edinburgh', 12 July 1785.

31. The triumphal arch returns to the theme of one of Robert's earliest commissions in the city, a temporary timber arch constructed for the masonic ceremony at the laying of the foundation stone for the Royal Exchange in the High Street in 1753. The design is illustrated in Fraser 1989, p.71 and pp.356–7 and described in Preston and Oliver 1829, pp.216–24.

32. ECA, South Bridge Trustees minute book, 27 September 1785 (authorisation for payment of £18.8s.6d. to John Buego, presumably for the engraved plan and section later published in the Universal Scots Almanack of 1787).

33. Cruft and Fraser 1995, pp.120–8.

34. NLS, ref. MS 20500, copy letter from Robert Adam to the Lord Provost, 30 December 1785.

35. NLS, ref. MS 20500/10 and ECA, South Bridge Trustees minute book, trunk 2, bundle 6, item 3, copy of Lord Provost's letter, 6 February 1786.

36. NLS, ref. MS 20500, 13 November 1789, copy of papers sent to Henry Dundas and objections to the claim of Messrs Adam.

37. Caledonian Mercury, 3 October 1789, p.3.

38. HES, ref. H2/ADR(P), transcripts of two letters from Robert Adam to Thomas Kennedy of Dunure from the originals in the possession of Lt Col. J.K. MacFarlan, letter of 3 October 1789.

39. HES, ref. H2/ADR(P), transcripts of two letters from Robert Adam to Thomas Kennedy of Dunure from the originals in the possession of Lt Col. J.K. MacFarlan, letter of 20 October 1789.

40. Blair Adam Muniments, ref. 4/221.

41. HES, collections ref. EDD220/1 (elevation and section, signed 'Robt Morrison, Edinr, 15th Oct 1789'). Morrison was a former draughtsman of the Adam brothers in London. See Fraser 1989, pp.133–4, for discussion of this drawing.

42. ECA, College trustees minute book 1 (1789–1801), p.1 and Caledonian Mercury, 7 November 1789, p.1.

43. ECA, College trustees minute book 1 (1789–1801), pp.3–4.

44. Fraser 1989, pp.96–9.

45. Scots Magazine, November 1789, p.527.

46. Sir John Soane's Museum, ref. Adam 28/34 (principal storey plan). The plans of the basement and attic are missing from the set. The mention of duplicates suggests that both the London and Edinburgh offices of Robert Adam held copies of the University presentation drawings. The client also held a set.

47. The complicated history of the Adam office drawings (including re-ordering and some inaccurate labelling) between the death of Robert Adam and their arrival in Sir John Soane's Museum is set out in Tait 1978, pp.451–4; Rowan 1985, pp.10–13; Fraser 1989; and Brown 1992, pp.23–33.

48. In May 1815 Robert Reid had 'a Copy of Mr. Adams original plan distinguishing the portion of the buildings which had been erected agreeable to that plan...'. (ECA/CCM, trunk 2, vol.2, p.241). In 1816, when the competition to complete the University was advertised, the town clerk held a copy of Mr Adam's plans. These plans might have been the original client drawings, or possibly later copies. These drawings are no longer traceable in ECA. William Adam also wrote to Sir John Marjoribanks offering his services to complete the College building in 1816 on the basis of his late brother's plans 'in his possession' (ECA/CC, 2/6, draft minute of the trustees of the College, 12 September 1816, p.2). This set of plans, presumably one of the office copies, is likely to be the one now lodged at the Sir John Soane's Museum. Hugh Cairncross's son, George, also had possession of 'plans that could be depended on as exact copies of Mr Adam's [which had inabled him to commence the building of the Great Hall/Chapel block in 1815] and thereby obtain the first grant...' (ECA/CCM, trunk 2, vol.2, pp.86–7).

49. ECA/CC, 9/41, shelf 23L, trunk 2, box 1

50. Scots Magazine, 2 December 1785, p.629.

51. Scots Magazine, 2 December 1785, p.628 (open letter to Henry Dundas) and November 1789, p.525 (student numbers quoted in the description of the foundation stone ceremony).

52. Horn 1767, pp.79–82.

53. Certainly there were no contemporary examples in the UK on which Adam could draw, although he had experience of designs to complete the Great Court at King's College, Cambridge in 1784–7.

54. ECA/CC, 9/41, shelf 23L, trunk 2, box 1.

55. Sanderson 1982, p.44.

56. ECA, College trustees minute book 1 (1789–1801), p.14, 15 January 1790; p.16, 22 January 1790; p.29, 30 June 1790; and p.38, 26 November 1790. Although the family had moved to 25 George Square in 1776, it appears that the family retained their tenement in College Wynd. The College trustees purchased the tenement from Walter Scott Senior.

57. Dalzel 1862, vol.1, p.85.

58. NLS, ref. MS 19992, Paterson–Adam Correspondence, 23 March 1791.

59. Scots Magazine, November 1789, p.527.

60. ECA/TCM, 16 June 1784.

61. Horn 1969, p.4 and Scots Magazine 1785.

62. EU/CRC, ref. INI/GOV/SEN, Senatus minutes, 19 October 1789.

63. ECA, contract and agreement between Robert Adam Esq. and James Crichton, 1790.

64. ECA, College trustees minute book 1 (1789–1801), p.24, 6 April 1790.

65. Scots Magazine, December 17989, p.615.

66. Dalzel 1862, vol.1, p.81, letter to Sir Robert Liston, February 1890.

67. Ibid., p.90, letter to Sir Robert Liston, 19 November 1791.

68. ECA, College trustees minutes, vol.1, 6 April 1790, p.23.

69. NLS, refs MS 20500 and MS 19992, Paterson–Adam Correspondence, 4 April 1791.

70. Caledonian Mercury, 25 April 1791, p.3 (Calcutta) and 7 May 1791, p.3 (Russia).

71. NLS, ref. MS 19992, Paterson–Adam Correspondence, 7 April 1791.

72. Sanderson 1982, p.40.

73. ECA, College trustees minutes, vol.1, 2 July 1791, p.50.

74. ECA, College trustees minutes, vol.1, 6 April 1790, p.29.

75. ECA, College trustees minutes, vol.1, 16 April 1792, pp.62–3.

76. ECA, College trustees minutes, vol.1, 13 November 1792, p.68.

77. ECA, College trustees minutes, vol.1, p.7.

78. Ibid.

79. Cockburn 1856, pp.6–7.

80. Scots Magazine, November 1789, pp.521–8. At least two versions of Allan's engraving were made, see Fraser 1989, p.1.

81. Caledonian Mercury, 26 October 1789, p.3. For the precedent of a triumphal arch designed by Robert Adam for a similar Masonic ceremony at the foundation of the Royal Exchange, see Preston and Oliver 1829, pp.216–23. The provision of a triumphal arch for the foundation stone ceremonies of public buildings was a Masonic tradition.

82. ECA/TCM, 18 November 1789.

83. Scots Magazine, November 1789, pp.527–8.

84. Ibid., pp.523–7.

85. Dalzel 1862, vol.1, p.81.

86. NLS, refs MS 20500 and MS 19992, Paterson–Adam Correspondence, 15 February 1790; Scots Magazine, April 1790, p.163; and ECA, College trustees minutes, vol.1, 28 July 1790, p.32.

87. NLS, ref. MS 19992, Paterson–Adam Correspondence, April 1790.

88. ECA, ref. C0013, masonry price agreement between Robert Adam and James Crichton, 21 November 1789.

89. ECA, College trustees minutes, vol.1, 10 September 1793, p.78.

90. ECA, College trustees minutes, vol.1, 28 July 1790, p.32.

91. NLS, ref. MS 19992, Paterson–Adam Correspondence, 30 October 1790; 23 November 1790; and 22 and 23 March 1791.

92. NLS, ref. MS 19992, Paterson–Adam Correspondence, 22 and 23 March and 7 April 1791.

93. Edinburgh Evening Courant, 24 March 1792.

94. NLS, ref. MS 19992, Paterson–Adam Correspondence, 8 February 1790.

95. Ibid., 1 February 1790. See also Brown 1989, pp.62–4, for discussion of Adam's town planning of a West Bridge Street on the line of Forrester's Wynd.

96. NLS, ref. MS 19992, Paterson–Adam Correspondence, 1 February 1790.

97. Caledonian Mercury, 21 October 1790, p.3 and 19 March 1791, p.3 and NLS, ref. MS 19992, Paterson–Adam Correspondence, 19 and 23 March 1791. The letter of 19 March indicates that John Clerk of Eldin provided advice to Paterson on the technical issues of manipulating such a large stone, but Clerk's advice proved to be impractical on the ground.

98. NLS, ref. MS 19992, Paterson–Adam Correspondence, 4 April 1791.

99. ECA, College trustees minutes, vol.1, 15 December 1791, p.56.

100. Sanderson 1982, p.44.

101. ECA, College trustees minutes, vol.1, 9 April 1792, pp.58–9.

102. ECA, College trustees minutes, vol.1, 9 April 1792, pp.59–60.

103. ECA, College trustees minutes, vol.1, 9 April 1792, p.59. Hamilton Lodging is described as 'the ruinous buildings which run from north to south and stand in the way of proceeding with several new Classes adjoining the north west corner ...'

104. ECA, College trustees minutes, vol.1, 10 June 1793, p.75.

105. ECA, College trustees minutes, vol.1, 6 December 1793, p.80.

106. ECA, College trustees minutes, vol.1, 6 December 1793, p.81.

107. ECA, College trustees minutes, vol.1, 3 August 1795, p.85.

108. ECA/CC, letter from William Adam to the trustees, 23 December 1818.

CHAPTER THREE
PAGES 57–85

1. EU/CRC, ref. DA.3, Petition to Henry Dundas, 1799.

2. Ibid., p.2.

3. ECA/CC, 1/7, draft representation and petition of the University of Edinburgh to the Right Honble the Lords of the Treasury, 1810, appendix A.

4. Joseph Frank, *Reise nach Paris, London und einem grossen Theile des übrigen Englands und Schottlands*, Vienna, 1805, pp.216–7.

5. ECA/CC, 1/5, copy memorial of the Royal Burghs of Scotland, 1809, p.7.

6. Bower 1822, p.138.

7. Cockburn 1856, p.27.

8. ECA/CC, 1/5, copy memorial of the Royal Burghs of Scotland, 1809, p.10.

9. ECA/CC, 1/2, copy representation to Mr Dundas respecting the University of Edinburgh, 24 June 1799.

10. ECA, ref. MacLeod bundles U0013/0102, letter from the Lord Advocate regarding a warrant for £5,000.

11. *Scots Magazine*, February 1805, pp.86–7, 'Scheme for completing the New College of Edinburgh', which suggested a lottery could raise between £75,000 and £150,000 for the project.

12. EA/CC, trunk 1, 1/3, estimates for building and finishing the University of Edinburgh, 17 December 1808.

13. See NRS, ref. RHP6525/15, 'Elevation of the fronts towards the Parliament Square', signed 'Robt. Reid, Archt, Edinbh, 1803'.

14. The Barons of the Court of Exchequer in 1810 were: Robert Dundas of Arniston (Chief Baron), Fletcher Norton, George Buchan Hepburn, John Stuart and James Clerk of Penicuik.

15. ECA/CC, trunk 2, 1/2, estimate by Robert Reid, architect, of the expense of completing the new university buildings agreeably to the reduced plans, Edinburgh, January 1810 and trunk 1, 1/8, estimates for building and finishing the University of Edinburgh, 23 January 1811.

16. ECA/CC, trunk 2, p.24, printed 'Reports &c. relative to the Completion of the College Buildings', November 1816. A memorandum of August 1816 from Robert Reid, printed in the 'Reports', notes that the original plans and other papers had been 'mislaid' by the Treasury and that he had been obliged to provide copies.

17. ECA/TCM, 26 August 1812.

18. Crichton resubmitted plans dated 1812 to the competition of 1816.

19. *Scots Magazine*, October 1813, pp.752–3, letter signed 'Edinburgh, 7th Oct. 1813. J.A'.

20. ECA/TCM, 31 March 1813.

21. EU/CRC, Senatus minutes, 1 April 1813.

22. *Caledonian Mercury*, 29 June 1815, p.4, attributed the success of the application to Parliament largely to William Dundas and Sir John Marjoribanks, the Lord Provost. In 1817, the commissioners also attributed the securing of government grants as 'very much owing to Mr Dundas', see ECA/CCM, trunk 2, vol.2, p.90, 21 June 1817.

23. For the record of the debate in the House of Commons see *Hansard*, first series, vol.31, 21 June 1815, cols 915–16.

24. ECA/CC, trunk 2, p.24, printed 'Reports &c. relative to the Completion of the College Buildings', November 1816 and ECA/CCM, trunk 2, vol.2, pp.240–3.

25. David Stevenson, *A Life of Robert Stevenson, Civil Engineer*, London and New York, 1878, pp.95–100. See also, ECA/CCM, trunk 2, vol.2, pp.149–50, 12 December 1818, showing payment of £10 10s to Robert Stevenson for his observations when the grant for the College was before a Committee of the House of Commons.

26. ECA/CC, 2/7, p.2, draft minute of the trustees of the College, 3 October 1816. Horner had hoped to attend the Commissioners' meeting of 3 October 1816, but ill health prevented him, and he sent a letter instead, again promoting the views of the professors as paramount.

27. ECA/CC, trunk 1, 2/6, p.2, draft minute of the College trustees, 12 September 1816.

28. ECA/CC, trunk 2, *Reports &c. Relative to the Completion of the College Buildings*, Edinburgh, November 1816, p.3.

29. ECA/CC, 2/6, pp.3–4, draft minute of the College trustees, 12 September 1816.

30. *Caledonian Mercury*, 8 August 1815, p.3 (demolitions) and Millar 1827, vol.1, p.76 (image of the College at the time of John Sadler's balloon ascent). *The Scots Magazine*, November 1815, p.869, describes Sadler's balloon voyage.

31. ECA/CC, trunk 2, pp.24–7, printed 'Reports &c. relative to the Completion of the College Buildings', November 1816. Eventually, in October 1816, Reid updated his 1810 plans to take account of the professors' new requirements, as printed and circulated to the competition architects.

32. ECA/CC, 2/6, pp.2–3, draft minute of the College trustees, 12 September 1816.

33. New chairs since Robert Adam's last set of published plans in 1791 included: Medical Jurisprudence and Police (1807); Clinical Surgery (1803); and Military Surgery (1806). According to Bower 1822, pp.188–9, some 1,280 students matriculated in 1791–2 and 2,097 students matriculated for the session 1815–16.

34. *Caledonian Mercury*, 3 August 1803, p.1.

35. Daniel Robertson and his brother, Alexander, entered into partnership with William Adam in 1800. See William Whyte, 'Robertson, Daniel (*c*.1770–1849)', *Oxford Dictionary of National Biography*, Oxford University Press, April 2016 [http://www.oxforddnb.com/view/article/109384, accessed 9 June 2016].

36. ECA/CC, 2/2, letters from George Harrison, Secretary to the Treasury, to the Lord Provost of Edinburgh, 28 June 1816 and 23 August 1816 and ECA/CC, 2/3, letter from the College Commissioners to the Earl of Liverpool, First Lord of the Treasury, 6 July 1816.

37. ECA/CC, 2/3, letter from the College Commissioners to the Earl of Liverpool, First Lord of the Treasury, 6 July 1816.

38. ECA/CC, 2/6, p.3, 12 September 1816. Arthur Bolton, Adam's great champion in the early twentieth century, was extremely critical of the decision to omit the cross-range and of Playfair's handling of the resulting single courtyard, see Bolton 1922, vol.2, pp.242–7.

39. Fraser 1989, p.167.

40. ECA/CC, trunk 2, box 1, *Report of Mr. Playfair*, 1816, pp.3–4.

41. ECA/CC, 2/9, p.3, 25 October 1816. Seventy-six copies of the report were printed, one of which is held in ECA/CC, trunk 2, printed 'Reports &c. relative to the Completion of the College Buildings', November 1816.

42. ECA/CCM, trunk 2, vol.2, p.38, 4 December 1816.

43. ECA/CCM, trunk 2, vol.2, p.38, 4 December 1816.

44. Ian Spence, 'Playfair, William (1759–1823)', *Oxford Dictionary of National Biography*, Oxford, 2004 [http://www.oxforddnb.com/view/article/22370, accessed 11 March 2016].

45. NLS, ref. Adv.MS.33.5.25, James Playfair's 'Journal of Architecture'.

46. Playfair's address is recorded as 9 Howland Street from 1783 to 1785 and 13 Russell Place from 1787 to 1793, see Algernon Graves, *The Royal Academy of Arts: a Complete Dictionary of Contributors and their Work from its Foundation in 1769 to 1904*, 8 vols, London, 1905, vol.6, p.162.

47. The Playfair brothers appear to have had several property interests in London. James Playfair certainly owned, and possibly built, nos 14 and 13 Russell Place, and leased properties in Howland Street and Howland Mews West at various times.

48. London Metropolitan Archives, Fitzroy Chapel, Register of Baptisms and Churchings, ref. P90/SAV/001 (the entry for 28th August 1790 records 'William Henry, S: of James & Rachael Playfair, Born 15th July 1790'). However, various sources provide differing information about Playfair's date of birth, the name of his mother, and the number of his siblings. His self-designed memorial in Dean Cemetery, Edinburgh, records his birth date as 28 August 1790. A number of obituaries noted a birth date of July 1789 (e.g. *Edinburgh Evening Courant*, 21 March 1857, p.2), and Playfair himself recorded his birthday in his diary for 7 July 1817: 'My Birth day – 27 years of age' (EU/CRC, ref. MS Dc.3.73, p.3). Several sources record James Playfair's wife as Jessie Graham, but the death registers of South Leith Parish (NRS, Old Parish Registers, South Leith Parish, Calton Burial Records, ref. OPR Deaths 692/02/0330 0173) and Mrs Playfair's Will & Testament (NRS, ref. Prob 11/1687/87) confirm that her maiden name was Rachel Barclay.

49. Farington 1978, vol.1, p.180, 18 April 1794. The name of the son and the circumstances of his death are not known. A John Playfair is recorded in the Westminster burial records for 15 October 1792, the only recorded death of anyone with the surname 'Playfair' in the early years of the 1790s according to the websites www.ancestry.com and www.findmypast.com.

50. See Farington 1978, vol.1, p.189, p.204, pp.212–13, p.262.

51. Sir John Soane's Museum, ref.1895, *A catalogue of the genuine and valuable collection of drawings, designs in architecture; ... by the late ingenious Mr. Playfair, dec*, 10 January 1795. Soane and the diarist Joseph Farington helped Rachel Playfair dispose of some of the drawings.

52. James George studied under James Cririe at the Royal High School from 1797 to 1800 (ECA, ref., library subscription book, p.377). The household is described in Playfair 1822, vol.1, p.xxii.

53. Farington 1978, vol.4, p.1335. It is not clear what happened to Rachel Playfair after William Henry left for Scotland, but the rent books for the Hamlet of Hammersmith record a Mrs Playfair renting a house in Chiswick between 1803 and 1805 (London Metropolitan Archives, Hamlet of Hammersmith Parish land tax records 1805, ref. MR/PLT/4860–2).

54. Farington 1978, vol.4, p.1545.

55. ECA, ref. SL137/15/3 (Royal High School, library subscription book, 1779–1806), p.409.

56. EU/CRC, ref. EUA INI/ADS/STA/2 (matriculation album, 1804–10).

57. McWilliam 1957, pp.20–1.

58. An unsigned and undated early 19th-century sepia pen and wash drawing of the portico, possibly in Playfair's hand, is in the collections of the Royal Institute of British Architects in London, ref. PA28/6(5).

59. See Lowrey 2001.

60. University of Cambridge, Department of Manuscripts and University Archives, ref. MS Add.6305 (William Henry Playfair: Memoranda, 1811). The Cambridge memoranda contains a journal of an excursion from Edinburgh to Arran and back, 1–9 May 1811, which suggests that Playfair was established in Edinburgh by this date.

61. See vol.3, p368 in H.J.C. Grierson (ed.), *Letters of Sir Walter Scott*, 8 vols, London, 1932–7.

62. Dictionary of Scottish Architects [www.scottisharchitects.org, search 'William Stark']. David M. Walker, 'Stark, William (1770–1813)', rev. *Oxford Dictionary of National Biography*, Oxford University Press, 2004 [http://www.oxforddnb.com/view/article/38005, accessed 28 April 2016]. Outstanding payments for the Cornwall Asylum are identified in William Stark's testament in the NRS, ref. CC8/8/142, f.315. Brown 1989, pp.80–112, details the complicated design and construction arrangements for the Signet and Advocates' Libraries.

63. For the Bell Rock crane sketches see University of Cambridge, Department of Manuscripts and University Archives, ref. MS Add.6305, folios 47v and 45 (William Henry Playfair: Memoranda, 1811). For other student drawings by Playfair see the Royal Incorporation of Architects in Scotland Collection, held by HES.

64. Gow 1984, p.45.

65. EU/CRC, ref. COLL-1675 (Playfair, letterbook, vol.4, 1830–3), p.387.

66. NLS, ref. K.R.16.f.5(1), Thomas Nisbet, *Catalogue of the Valuable Library of the Late W.H. Playfair Esq. Architect, sale on Saturday 28 November 1857*, lots 431 and 439.

67. EU/CRC, ref. COLL-1675 (Playfair, letterbook, vol.4, 1830–3), pp.386–7 and 400–1. For the Gosford drawings see Christie's sale no.11567, South Kensington, 17 June 2015, lot 97. The author is grateful to Richard Emerson for pointing out this reference.

68. HES, National Record of the Historic Environment, Royal Incorporation of Architects in Scotland Collection, ref. AYD70/33–40 (plans and elevations of Dalquharran Castle, identified as student drawings, but probably early

career drawings). EU/CRC, ref. DC.3.73 (Playfair, Abstract of a Journal, 1817–22), no page number [13].

69. See the Dictionary of Scottish Architects for a full list of works by Playfair (www.scottisharchitects.org.uk, search 'Playfair').

70. See Chapter Seven for a history of this building within the University estate.

71. NRS, ref. SC70/4/51 (Edinburgh Sheriff Court Wills, William Henry Playfair, 1857). EU/CRC, Senatus minutes: 27 October 1858; 6 November 1858; 25 February 1860; and 19 July 1860. The drawings were catalogued by James Hamilton, Playfair's former clerk, and stored in the attics of the Upper Library before removal to the strong room of the new Main Library in 1967.

72. EU/CRC: ref. COLL-13 (architectural drawings); ref. DC.3.73 (Playfair, Abstract of a Journal, 1817–22); and ref. COLL-1675 (letterbooks, vols 4 and 7, 1830–3 and 1840–5). The project correspondence of the College Commissioners from 1816 to 1836 includes a number of letters to and from Playfair and a series of his progress reports, ECA/CCM, trunk 2, vols 2 and 3, copy letters and miscellaneous papers. Correspondence with Andrew Rutherfurd and his family is held in the NLS, ref. MS 9704.

73. EU/CRC, ref. COLL-13/24 (drawing for roofing of the Museum).

74. EU/CRC, ref. DC.3.73 (Playfair, Abstract of a Journal, 1817–22), p.11.

75. *The Builder*, 10 June 1882, p.717.

76. Gow 1984, p.52. Playfair always lived in the New Town, moving on numerous occasions in the 1820s, but settling at Great Stuart Street from 1830. He lived at: 2 Albany Row (10 Albany Street) (ECA, 27 April 1816, letter); 79 Queen Street (Post Office Directory 1820–21); 17 Abercromby Place (PO Directory 1821–2); 17 Northumberland Street with Dr Playfair (PO Directories 1822–4); 43 Heriot Row (PO Directory 1824–5); 63 Great King Street (PO Directory 1828–9); 11 Great Stuart Street (PO Directory 1830–1); and 17 Great Stuart Street (PO Directories 1831–57).

77. Charles McKean, 'Playfair, William Henry (1790–1857)', *Oxford Dictionary of National Biography*, Oxford, 2004 [http://www.oxforddnb.com/view/article/22371, accessed 5 Aug 2016].

78. *Perthshire Courier*, 4 December 1817, p.2. As a result of Playfair's actions, the fire did not spread and the damage was relatively minor.

79. See John Rickman (ed.), *Life of Thomas Telford, Civil Engineer*, London, 1838, p.661.

80. NRS, ref. SC70/4/51 (Edinburgh Sheriff Court Wills, William Henry Playfair, 1857).

81. Rules and list of members of The Athenaeum, 1842.

82. ECA/CCM, trunk 2, vol.2, pp.42–50, record of a meeting on 25 January 1817 and a copy of 'Report of Committee as to conducting & superintending the Work', dated 15 January 1817.

83. ECA/CCM, trunk 2, vol.2, pp.50–3. Playfair initially recommended Robert Brown, assistant to Robert Reid at the Exchequer building and Advocates' Library (now Signet Library), but Brown declined on the grounds of being too busy with other projects. The Commissioners rejected Playfair's second nomination, John Thin, because he was inexperienced in large building projects. Playfair eventually employed Thin as a draughtsman in the 1820s.

84. ECA/CCM, trunk 2, vol.2, pp.59–3, record a meeting on 25 January 1817 and a copy of 'Report to the Honourable Committee for College Buildings by W.H. Playfair'.

85. EU/CRC, ref. DC.3.73, p.6, Playfair, Abstract of a Journal, 1817–22. ECA/CCM, trunk 2, vol.2, pp.67–8.

86. EU/CRC, ref. DC.3.73, p.1, Playfair, Abstract of a Journal, 1817–22. ECA/CCM, trunk 2, vol.2, p.92.

87. EU/CRC, ref. DC.3.73, p.2, Playfair, Abstract of a Journal, 1817–22.

88. ECA/CCM, trunk 2, vol.2, pp.87–8 and pp.96–8.

89. ECA/CCM, trunk 2, vol.2, pp.96–7.

90. Laurence Jameson, *Biographical Memoir of the Late Professor Jameson*, Edinburgh 1854, p.32.

91. ECA/CC, box 1, pp.14–17, papers relating to the adoption of a plan for the College, 1810–16 and William Henry Playfair, Report Respecting the Mode of Completing the New Buildings for the College of Edinburgh, 1816.

92. ECA/CCM, trunk 2, vol.2, pp.217–20, 24 November 1819 and 20 January 1820.

93. EU/CRC, ref. DC.3.73, p.5, Playfair, Abstract of a Journal, 1817–22, 25 October 1817.

94. Fireproof was defined as 'construction in which incombustible materials only are employed', *Building News*, vol.7, 5 July 1861, p.557.

95. ECA/CCM, trunk 2, vol.2, pp.101–2.

96. ECA/CCM, trunk 2, vol.2, p.193.

97. ECA/CCM, trunk 2, vol.2, p.382.

98. EU/CRC, ref. DC.3.73, p.6 and p.8, Playfair, Abstract of a Journal, 1817–22, 20 November and 4 December 1817 and EU/CRC, ref. COLL-13/158. Also, ECA/CC, trunk 1, general correspondence

including a letter from Playfair in London to Carlyle Bell in Edinburgh dated 12 February 1817.

99. ECA/CCM, trunk 2, vol.2, p.177.

100. ECA/CCM, trunk 2, vol.2, p.92.

101. EU/CRC, ref. COLL-13/24.

102. Lowrey 2001, pp.136–57.

103. ECA/CCM, trunk 2, vol.2, pp.229–33, 28 June 1820.

104. C.R. Cockerell, *Diary*, August 1822, quoted in John Harris, 'C.R. Cockerell's "Ichnographica Domestica"', in *Architectural History*, vol.14, London 1971, p.15.

105. ECA/CCM, trunk 2, vol.2, p.139.

106. ECA/CCM, trunk 2, vol.2, p.146.

107. ECA/CCM, trunk 2, vol.2, pp.235–6 and ECA/CC, trunk 3, box 4, various estimates and bills by William Trotter. Of all the furniture, only one display case is now traceable in the collection of the National Museums of Scotland (see Fraser 1989, p.208).

108. ECA/CCM, trunk 2, vol.2, p.228.

109. ECA/CCM, trunk 2, vol.2, p.410, copy letter of 14 July 1824 from the commissioners to Playfair, attributing damage to the Natural History collection to his delay of over a year in fitting up the rooms over the entrance arch as additional space for the museum.

110. See vol.I, p.42 in Francis Darwin (ed.), *The Life and Letters of Charles Darwin, including an Autobiographical Chapter*, 3 vols, London, 1887.

111. Grant 1884, vol.I, p.354.

112. Logan 1933, p.306.

113. HES, National Record of the Historic Environment, ref. IGL W612/31–43 (Ian G. Lindsay plans for the Student Art Centre, 1969–72). *Glasgow Herald*, 20 October 1970, p.10.

114. ECA/CCM, trunk 2, vol.2, p.102.

115. ECA/CCM, trunk 2, vol.2, p.159 and p.194.

116. ECA/CCM, trunk 2, vol.2, p.194 and p.226.

117. ECA/CCM, trunk 2, vol.2, p.226.

118. ECA/CCM, trunk 2, vol.2, p.294.

119. EU/CRC, ref. COLL-13/287.

120. ECA/CCM, trunk 2, vol.2, p.238.

121. ECA/CCM, trunk 2, vol.2, p.384.

122. ECA/CCM, trunk 2, vol.2, p.195.

123. The author is grateful to Andrew Kerr for information drawn from his Valedictory Address to the Speculative Society of 18 March 2009.

124. ECA/CCM, trunk 2, vol.2, p.148 and p.152.

125. ECA/CCM, trunk 2, vol.2, pp.384–5, W.H. Playfair, Report to the Commissioners, 11 September 1820.

The total excluded the clerk, the super-intendent and architect's fees, the plate glass for the museum and the money for purchasing the houses to the west of the College. Playfair reminded the commissioners that his original estimate was £99,000.

126. ECA/CCM, trunk 2, vol.2, p.291. The materials of the old 1642 Building and chemistry buildings, minus any carved stones, were purchased by the contractors for the east range, Henderson & Currer, for £200.

127. ECA/CCM, trunk 2, vol.2, pp. 262–3.

128. EU/CRC, ref. coll-13/347, W.H. Playfair, Southern Elevation of the Northern Buildings, 19 April 1821.

129. ECA/CCM, trunk 2, vol.2, p.291.

130. ECA/CCM, trunk 2, vol.2, p.392.

131. ECA/CCM, trunk 2, vol.2, p.454.

132. ECA/CCM, trunk 2, vol.2, p.466.

133. ECA/CCM, trunk 2, vol.2, pp.316–24, 'report by a Committee of the Commissioners … shewing the State of the Work and the necessity of a further grant to complete the Buildings', 15 January 1823.

134. ECA/CCM, trunk 2, vol.2, p.339.

135. ECA/CCM, trunk 2, vol.2, p.390.

136. ECA/CCM, trunk 2, vol.2, p.420 and pp.427–8.

137. ECA/CCM, trunk 2, vol.2, pp.508–17.

138. ECA/CCM, trunk 2, vol.2, p.394, report by Playfair to the College Commissioners, 21 February 1824.

139. ECA/CCM, trunk 2, vol.2, p.393.

140. Dibdin 1838, vol.2, p.585.

141. Brown 1989, p.91.

142. ECA/CCM, trunk 2, vol.2, p.356, 18 July 1823. Playfair moved his office to the room intended for the Divinity Hall in the east range, which was not then in use by the professor.

143. ECA/CCM, trunk 2, vol.2, p.508.

144. ECA/CCM, trunk 2, vol.2, p.525.

145. ECA/CCM, trunk 2, vol.2, p.538, 22 August 1827.

146. ECA/CCM, trunk 2, vol.2, p.524, 30 June 1827.

147. EU/CRC, ref. coll-13/428.

148. ECA/CCM, trunk 2, vol.3, p.31, 19 September 1828.

149. Fraser 1989, p.276, n.27.

150. ECA/CCM, trunk 2, vol.3, p.249.

151. ECA/CCM, trunk 2, vol.3, pp.1–7.

152. Dibdin 1838, vol.2, p.586.

153. ECA/CCM, trunk 2, vol.3, pp.202–3.

154. The Scotsman, 23 April 1887, p.9.

155. Edinburgh Evening News, 5 August 1886, p.4.

156. Edinburgh Evening News, 10 February 1887, p.3.

157. St James's Gazette, 14 November 1888, p.6.

158. EU/CRC, ref. EUA INI/GOV/SEN/MIN/1/8, Senatus minutes, vol.8, pp.194–5, 26 March 1887.

159. The Builder, 18 August 1888, p.116.

160. 'A torch racer', Mapping the Practice and Profession of Sculpture in Britain and Ireland 1851–1951, University of Glasgow History of Art and HATII, online database 2011 [http://sculpture.gla.ac.uk/view/object.php?id=msib6_1212415051, accessed 21 Sep 2016].

161. The Scotsman, 23 April 1887, p.9 and The Builder, 18 August 1888, p.116.

162. Edinburgh Evening Courant, 30 October 1866, p.2.

163. The Builder, 8 January 1887, vol.52, p.77 and Edinburgh University Calendar, 1901–2, p.840.

164. Fraser 1989, pp.292–3.

165. EU/CRC, ref. PJM/PJMA/EUD/B/12.1.

166. HES, National Record of the Historic Environment, refs: IGL E69; W612/1–69; W654/1; W664/1; W809/1; and W894/1–3.

CHAPTER FOUR
PAGES 87–111

1. Edinburgh University Calendar 1900–1, p.28

2. Edinburgh Evening Courant, 11 May 1858, p.2.

3. Grant 1884, vol.2, p.1.

4. EU/CRC, ref. EUA INI/GOV/SEN/MIN/1/8, Senatus minutes, vol.8, p.209, 6 May 1857.

5. Universities (Scotland) Act 1858, London, 2 August 1858.

6. House of Commons Papers, Return of the Sums Annually voted by Parliament and chargeable on Consolidated Fund to Universities of Scotland, Royal Observatory and Royal Botanic Garden in Edinburgh, 1879–89.

7. Turner 1933, pp.xix-xx.

8. Edinburgh University Property Arrangement Act 1861, London, 6 August 1861.

9. Grant 1884, vol.2, p.136.

10. Report of the General Committee of the Association for the Better Endowment of the University of Edinburgh, to be laid before the annual general meeting of the Association on Friday the 30th of November 1866 [via www.archive.org].

11. Turner 1933, p.45.

12. Sophia Jex-Blake, Medical Women: Two Essays, Edinburgh and London, 1872.

13. Birse 1994, p.88.

14. Robert Anderson in Anderson, Lynch and Phillipson 2003, p.142.

15. Turner 1933, p.351.

16. Roy M. Pinkerton in Donaldson 1983, p.119.

17. Grant 1884, vol.2, p.487.

18. This section draws on information contained in Johnson and Rosenburg 2010, pp.39–46.

19. Helen Meller, 'Geddes, Sir Patrick (1854–1932)', in Oxford Dictionary of National Biography, Oxford, 2004; online edn, January 2008 [http://www.oxforddnb.com/view/article/33361, accessed 2 November 2016].

20. Johnson and Rosenburg, p.24.

21. Geddes taught extramural courses at the Edinburgh Summer Meeting 1886, see Johnson and Rosenburg, 2010, p.71.

22. Edinburgh University Calendar 1889–90, Appendix, p.18.

23. Edinburgh Evening News, 23 June 1887, p.3.

24. Edinburgh Evening News, 23 June 1887, p.3.

25. Edinburgh Evening Courant, 30 October 1866, p.2.

26. Edinburgh University Calendar 1882–3, appendix, p.31.

27. EU/CRC, Senatus minutes, vol.9, 24 November 1866, p.222.

28. Records of the Tercentenary Festival of the University of Edinburgh, Celebrated in April 1884, Edinburgh, 1885.

29. Donald Wintersgill, 'Bell, Robert Fitzroy (1859–1908)', in Oxford Dictionary of National Biography, Oxford, October 2009 [http://www.oxforddnb.com/view/article/100753, accessed 8 Oct 2016].

30. Edinburgh University Calendar 1890–1, appendix, p.20.

31. Building News, 25 July 1879, p.108 and C.M. Usher, The Story of Edinburgh University Athletic Club, Edinburgh, 1966, pp.4–5. The field was taken over by the Royal High School in 1897.

32. The Student, pp.44–6. Edinburgh Evening News, 29 October 1898, p.4. The pavilion was altered in 1912 and enlarged subsequently.

33. HES, National Record of the Historic Environment, ref. LOR/E/106/1/1 (plan of a boathouse by R.S. Lorimer, Architect, March '97).

34. Mentioned in EU/CRC, ref. EUA INI/COM/B2/6/1, University of Edinburgh Buildings Extension Scheme,

1874 (proof copy of booklet in scrapbook), p.7. See also Grant 1884, vol.2, p.208.

35. Edinburgh University Calendar 1869–70, p.270 and EU/CRC, ref. EUA/INI/CON/B2/1/1 (vi), letter from Peter Bell, Clerk to the Managers of the Royal Infirmary to Professor John Wilson, dated 1 November 1869.

36. Caledonian Mercury, 2 March 1807, p.3.

37. The Scotsman, 14 April 1862, p.6.

38. Christopher D.S. Field, Arnold Myers, Donaldson's Apparatus: Exhibition of mid 19th-century Acoustical Equipment, Edinburgh, 1997

39. The Scotsman, 14 April 1862, p.6.

40. EU/CRC, ref. EUA INI/GOV/SEN/MIN/1/8, Senatus minutes, vol.8, p.142, 20 March 1857. An existing lease of the ground was also acquired for £45.

41. EU/CRC, ref. EUA INI/GOV/SEN/MIN/1/8, Senatus minutes, vol.8, p.144, 6 May 1857.

42. Dictionary of Scottish Architects [www.scottisharchitects.org.uk, architect search 'Cousin'].

43. The Builder, vol.45, 10 June 1882, p.717.

44. ECA/TCM, vol.273, p.358, 26 January 1858.

45. EU/CRC, ref.Dc.2.58, letter from David Cousin to D.R. Hay, Secretary of the Aesthetic Club, 22 April 1853.

46. ECA/TCM, vol.273, pp.357–8, 26 January 1858.

47. Royal Scottish Academy catalogue, p.694.

48. The Builder, vol.45, 10 June 1882, p.717.

49. ECA/TCM, vol.273, p.365, 26 January 1858. The cuts are not detailed, other than as mason work at £240 and wright work at £30, but presumably related mainly to the omission of the elaborate cornice on the south side of the building, which was later reinstated as part of the scheme.

50. ECA/TCM, vol.273, pp.366–7, 26 January 1858 and EU/CRC, ref. EUA INI/GOV/SEN/MIN/1/8, Senatus minutes, vol.8, pp.175–8, 28 November 1857.

51. The Scotsman, 17 February 1858, p.3; Caledonian Mercury, 3 February, p.2 and 8 February 1858, p.2; and ECA/TCM, vol.274, p.69, 10 March 1858.

52. EU/CRC, ref. EUA INI/GOV/SEN/MIN/1/8, Senatus minutes, vol.8, pp.194–5, 2 February 1858.

53. ECA/TCM, vol.274, pp.281–4, 30 November 1858.

54. Edinburgh Evening Courant, 11 May 1858, p.2.

55. *The Scotsman*, 14 April 1862, p.6.

56. *The Scotsman*, 9 December 1869, p.2.

57. *The Scotsman*, 21 February 1862, p.4.

58. HES, National Record of the Historic Environment, ref. IGL W770/1 (plans, sections and elevations showing organ installation).

59. See p.212, note 26 in Fiona McLachlan, *Architectural Colour in the Professional Palette*, London, 2012.

60. *Edinburgh Evening News*, 23 June 1887, p.3.

61. ECA/DOGC, ref. Lawnmarket, 8 June 1893.

62. Robert Hurd converted the building back into private flats in 1947–50. HES, National Record of the Historic Environment, Hurd Rolland Collection, ref. bag 157 57/2.

63. ECA/DOGC, ref. Lawnmarket: 9 October 1890; 17 November 1892; 18 April 1895; and 2 May 1895.

64. ECA/DOGC, ref. St Giles Street, 2 May 1895.

65. ECA/DOGC, ref. Castlehill: 9 February 1893; May 1893; and June 1894.

66. *The Builder*, 19 August 1893, pp.140–1.

67. *The Builder*, 4 June 1892, p.432.

68. Johnson and Rosenburg 2010, pp.74–7.

69. Grant 1884, vol.2, p.208.

70. EU/CRC, ref. EUA/INI/COM/B2/1/1 (xxiii), report of the sub-committee (College Extension Site Committee of the Senatus), signed by Professors Norman Macpherson and William Turner and dated 23 November 1871.

71. EU/CRC, ref. EUA INI/COM/B2/1/3, minute book 1 of the acting sub-committee for the University Buildings Extension Scheme, 1874–82, p.13 and p.20.

72. Ibid., pp.39–40.

73. Ibid., p.8.

74. EU/CRC, ref. EUA INI/COM/B2/6/1, University Buildings Extension Scheme, 1874 (proof copy of booklet in scrapbook).

75. EU/CRC, ref. EUA INI/COM/B2/1/3, minute book 1 of the acting sub-committee for the University Buildings Extension Scheme, 1874–82, p.63.

76. Ibid., p.48 and pp.59–60.

77. Ibid., p.62.

78. Ibid., pp.69–70.

79. Ibid., p.75.

80. EU/CRC, ref. EUA/INI/COM/B2/1/3 (viii), *Edinburgh University Extension: Notes of Plans submitted by R Anderson, Architect* (printed booklet), 30 December 1874, pp.1–2.

81. EU/CRC, ref. EUA INI/COM/B2/1/3, minute book 1 of the acting sub-committee for the University Buildings Extension Scheme, 1874–82, pp.174–5 (insert).

82. *The Student*, 1876, p.10.

83. EU/CRC, ref. EUA INI/COM/B2/1/3, minute book 1 of the acting sub-committee for the University Buildings Extension Scheme, 1874–82, p.179.

84. Ibid., p.180.

85. Ibid., pp.246–7.

86. Ibid., p.221.

87. Ibid., pp.260–1.

88. *The Scotsman*, 10 July 1880, p.3.

89. EU/CRC, ref. EUA INI/COM/B2/1/3, minute book 1 of the acting sub-committee for the University Buildings Extension Scheme, 1874–82, p.191.

90. HES, National Record of the Historic Environment, ref. EDD393/1–7.

91. EU/CRC, ref. EUA INI/COM/B2/6/1, scrapbook and tender invitation letter dated 30 June 1879 signed by Robert Rowand Anderson.

92. EU/CRC, ref. RRA/2.3/117, design for electric street. The lamp as built differs considerably in design from the drawing held by the University.

93. Gifford, McWilliam, Walker and Wilson 1991, p.246.

94. EU/CRC, ref. EUA/INI/COM/B2/1/3 (viii), *Edinburgh University Extension: Notes of Plans submitted by R Anderson*, Architect (printed booklet), 30 December 1874, p.3.

95. EU/CRC, ref. COLL-1167 (Patrick Geddes Collection, Centre Catalogue 1998, vol.I, A.7: The Palin Drawings and photographs made for the decoration of the interior of the McEwan Hall).

96. *The Student*, McEwan Hall Special Edition, 1897, pp.25–9. Reginald Whitworth, 'Organ in the McEwan Hall, Edinburgh', in *The Organ*, vol.XIII, 1934, p.223.

97. *The Scotsman*, 4 December 1897, p.9.

98. *Edinburgh Evening News*, 3 March 1884, p.2. Edinburgh University Calendar 1891–2, appendix x, p.21. Iain Catto (ed.), *'No Spirits and Precious Few Women': Edinburgh University Union 1889–1989*, Edinburgh, 1989.

99. Edinburgh University Calendar 1878–9, appendix ix, p.97. Edinburgh University Calendar 1882–3, appendix ix, p.34. ECA/DOGC warrant, 12 May 1881 (3–4 Park Street, alterations for the Students' Club).

100. *The Scotsman*, 28 June 1884, p.7.

101. *Dundee Evening Telegraph*, 18 February 1887, p.2.

102. *The Scotsman*, 28 June 1884, p.7.

103. Robert Fitzroy Bell and James Avon Clyde (eds), *The New Amphion*, Edinburgh, 1886, pp.ix–x.

104. *Dundee Evening Telegraph*, 11 May 1887, p.2.

105. *Edinburgh Evening News*, 8 December 1887, p.2. and *The Scotsman*, 5 March 1888, p.6.

106. *The Builder*, vol.56, 20 April 1889, p.294.

107. *The Scotsman*, 21 October 1889, p.8.

108. *The Scotsman*, 14 January 1903, p.10.

109. HES, National Record of the Historic Environment, ref. SMW 1880/53/2/1–4.

110. Iain Catto (ed.), *'No Spirits and Precious Few Women': Edinburgh University Union 1889–1989*, Edinburgh, 1989, p.17.

CHAPTER FIVE
PAGES 113–139

1. ECA/DOGC, George Square, June 1912.

2. Clive B. Fenton, 'George Square 1876–1976' in *Book of the Old Edinburgh Club*, New Series, vol.5, Edinburgh, 2002, p.40.

3. Cowan provided £30,000, with £10,000 from the Carnegie Trust. 'Extension of Buildings – Principal developments since 1924' (document of 1929). EUA, box 140 VE (misc.).

4. ECA/DOGC, 33–7 George Square, 24 June 1927.

5. ECA/DOGC, 52–3 George Square, 25 September 1919; and 51–4 George Square, 8 July and 17 June 1927.

6. Edinburgh University Calendar, 1901–2, p.3. and U. Maclean, 'The History of the Usher Institute', in R. Bhopal and J. Last (eds), *Public Health: past present and future: celebrating academic public health in Edinburgh 1902–2002*, Norwich, 2004, pp.49–69.

7. Dictionary of Scottish Architects (www.scottisharchitects.org.uk, search 'Thomas Leadbetter').

8. *The Scotsman*, 12 June 1902, p.4.

9. ECA/DOGC, Warrender Park Road, 28 September 1899. 'The John Usher Institute of Public Health', in *British Medical Journal*, 28 June 1902, p.1610.

10. 'New Buildings and Alterations' minute book of the Faculty of Medicine, 24 February 1920 p.67–8.

11. John Hughes Bennet is best remembered for first describing leukaemia. An alumnus of the University of Edinburgh, he was an innovator in the field of experimental physiology. He was Professor of Physiology and Clinical Medicine at the University, from 1848 to 1874, and Pathologist at Edinburgh Royal Infirmary, from 1843 to 1874. His daughter, Mrs Cox, paid for the new laboratory in memory of her father, see *British Medical Journal*, 27 July 190, pp.229–30.

12. ECA/DOGC, Park Place, 27 September 1919.

13. Sir David Percival Delbreck Wilkie was an Edinburgh alumnus, later Professor of Clinical Surgery, then Professor of Systematic Surgery, member of the Medical Research Council, and member of the British Empire Cancer Campaign. Known for his philanthropy, he was also the Director of the Edinburgh Medical Mission and patron of the Kirk o' Field College. From 1935 he served on the Edinburgh University Court. The University and Kirk o' Field College were among the benefactors of his will [Royal College of Surgeons. Plarr's Lives of the Fellows Online].

14. EUA, DRT 95/002 box 140 VE (misc. post First World War), statements regarding present and prospective needs, 1919.

15. Professor William Oliver, an Edinburgh engineering alumnus, was head of the Department of the Organisation of Industry and Commerce, and also an entrepreneur.

16. Often described as the Indian Students' Union, the Edinburgh University Indian Association had leased the premises since 1907.

17. EUA DRT 95/002 box 140 VE, Medical Buildings Extension Scheme, statement by the University Court for the information of the Development Commission, 1939.

18. EUA DRT 95/002 box 140 VE, Medical Buildings Extension Committee, minutes of first meeting on 5 December 1939. The special committee consisted of Professors Oliver, Hudson Beare (Engineering), Sydney Smith (Forensic Medicine) and Ivan Daly (Physiology).

19. HES, National Record of the Historic Environment, Dick Peddie & McKay Collection, DPM 1940/71/1–7, 1940.

20. EUL, Special Collections, Rowand Anderson Collection, University Drawings, nos 150–4.

21. EUL, Special Collections, Rowand Anderson Collection, University Drawings, nos 170–4.

22. ECA/DOGC, High School Yards 'Alterations to Old Surgeons' Hall', 6/11/57.

23. Dictionary of Scottish Architects (www.scottisharchitects.org.uk).

24. EUL, Special Collections, Rowand Anderson Collection, University Drawings, nos 150–64, Engineering Department.

25. James Cordiner (Works Dept), 1949 'Erect store and laboratory'. Thomas Henney (Architects) 'Alterations', 1980.

26. HES, National Record of the Historic Environment, EDD 414/2, engraved view of Edinburgh High School, by J. and H.S. Storer, Chapel St Pentonville, 1 June 1819.

27. EUL Special Collections, DRT 95/002 box 20, note of Principal's meeting on 28 January 1918.

28. University of Edinburgh Appeal (£500,000 for Applied Chemistry, Natural History and Geology).

29. EUA DRT 95/002 (part 1 list D) box 20 'Faculty of Science': report of subcommittee on site for new Department of Zoology, 11 January 1924; letter from Professor Ashworth outlining the disadvantages of King's Buildings for Zoology; and a copy of a note of the Principal's meeting with Heads of Chemistry, Natural History, Zoology and Geology, 18 January 1924.

30. The Animal Breeding Research Department, 1920 was the first of its kind in Britain, and not fully integrated into the University until 1928. See Birse 1994, p.111.

31. HES, Aerofilms Collection SC 01315439.

32. ECA/DOGC warrants, West Mains Road: boilerhouse, August 1928; New Engineering Building, 25 October 1929; and Geology Building, 6 December 1929.

33. EUA, DRT 95/002, box 28 'Faculty of Science': letter from Sir Alexander Grant to Sir Alfred Ewing, 18 March 1929, with cheque for £25,000 and the promise of a similar amount in twelve months; and a memo from Lorimer & Matthew to Professor Hudson Beare with an estimate of £54,000, excluding road making and architect's fees.

34. Birse 1994, p.87. Student numbers at Edinburgh were 4,437 in 1930–1, and 3,895 in 1935–6.

35. EUA, DRT 95/007 pt.1: King's Buildings Common Room/Union, letter from John Somerville (Secretary of Edinburgh University Union) to the University Court on the condition of the timber huts; and a report to Sir Thomas Holland on the need for a new building and a proposed plan.

36. Alexander Carrick is often credited with the sculptural work here, but this seems extremely unlikely, on stylistic grounds.

37. Grants included £74,000 from John D. Rockefeller's International Board for Education and £18,000 from the Carnegie Trust.

38. ECA/DOGC, West Mains Road, Zoology, petition of 1 June 1927, warrant of 1 July 1927.

39. The extension was jointly funded by the University Grants Committee and the Wellcome Trust.

40. Report, 'An Extension to the Department of Zoology Laboratories. University of Edinburgh, Architecture Research Unit', April 1968.

41. The initial annexes for Animal Genetics consisted of: a sheep building, provided by the Empire Marketing Board, to the south-west; a brick poultry house, to the north-west; a large pig building; and a goat house, provided by the Department of Agriculture, to the north. There were also a number of sheds, as well as paddocks, in place by 1931. *University of Edinburgh Journal* vol. 4, 1930–1, pp.35–7.

42. ECA/DOGC, Mayfield Road, New Department of Engineering, 25 October 1929.

43. ECA/DOGC, Mayfield Road, New Engineering Building, 7 March 1968 and 30 May 1958.

44. Kingham Knight Associates was a Liverpool based practice with a branch office in Edinburgh. In *Concrete Quarterly*, no. 47, Oct–Dec 1960, however, Gardner-Medwin's associates are given as Stephenson, Young & Partners. William Knight was in the latter practice before setting up in partnership with Norman F. Kingham, so it is likely that Knight was the project architect here.

45. *Architectural Design*, January 1962, p.19. 'Form follows function in the new lecture theatre, Edinburgh University', in *Concrete Quarterly*, no.47, pp.2–4.

46. ECA/DOGC, West Mains Road, Geology, 25 October 1929.

47. ECA/DOGC, West Mains Rd, Student Union King's Buildings, 11 August and 27 August 1927.

48. *University of Edinburgh Journal*, vol.10, 1939–40, p.27.

CHAPTER SIX
PAGES 141–177

1. *University of Edinburgh Journal* vol.10, 1939–40, p.III.

2. *University of Edinburgh Journal* vol.10, summer 1940, 1939–40, p.162.

3. *University of Edinburgh Journal* vol.11, summer 1941, 1940–2, p.69.

4. Sir Walter Moberly, *The Crisis in the University*, London, 1949. Moberly was the first post-war chairman of the University Grants Committee.

5. *University of Edinburgh Journal*, summer 1938, p.129 and autumn 1938, p.213.

6. HES, National Record of the Historic Environment, the Lorimer & Matthew Collection, hold drawings for the conversion at 46 the Pleasance, dated 1938 and 1939.

7. James L. Clyde, later Lord Clyde, became Lord Advocate in 1951, and was a Unionist MP from 1950 to 1954.

8. The Future of Edinburgh. Report of the Advisory Committee on City Development, 1943 by J.L. Clyde KC, Sir Thomas B. Whitson LLD and Sir J. Donald Pollock (Bart).

9. Exhibition 'Rebuilding Edinburgh' by the Edinburgh Architectural Association, July–August 1943. Patrick Geddes is frequently cited by Robert Hurd and lectures were given by Frank Mears and the conservation architect, Ian G. Lindsay.

10. EUA, DRT 95/002 box 141 VE, memorandum on behalf of the University of Edinburgh in reply to a letter of 12 May 1943 from the advisory committee on City development, 19 July 1943.

11. Other buildings of historical interest in the area included Lady Yester's Church (1805) and the Protester Meeting House (1821), in Infirmary Street, both of which are now statutorily listed.

12. When the City began building houses at Dumbiedykes, in the 1950s, it was decided that the schools would still be required for a number of years, until they could be replaced with new buildings.

13. John Falconer WS was a town councillor from 1932, a member of the University Court from 1937, and Lord Provost from 1944 to 1947.

14. EUA, DRT 95/002 box 141 VE, William Oliver 'memorandum on the University Extension and Consolidation Scheme', January 1944.

15. EUA, DRT 95/002 box 141 VE, correspondence between the Secretary and Pollock regarding alternative developments and regarding the University Court meeting of 20 November 1944 where Pollock begged for a stay-of-execution for George Square.

16. ECA, minutes of the Lord Provost's Special Committee, 7 February 1945.

17. The area of land that would be built upon, according to Oliver's plan, really only exceeded that of Macartney's by 27,000 sq. ft. The garden of George Square amounted to 350,000 sq. ft, the open ground in the alternative scheme amounted to 209,000 sq. ft.

18. EUA, DRT 95/002 box 141 VE, Professor Oliver's analysis of the alternative scheme.

19. EUA, DRT 95/002 box 135 VE: 'Pollock Trust': correspondence between Pollock and Sydney Smith, January 1948; University Court signed minutes vol.XIX; and Pollock's statement to the University Court that it was necessary to acquire his permission for any usage or development at the 'island site'.

20. EUA, DRT 95/002 box 135 VE, University Court signed minutes vol.XIX. In March 1946 Pollock insisted that the building was not unsafe. In October 1946, glass 'tell-tales' attached to the building by Oliver appeared to prove otherwise.

21. ECA, Lord Provost's committee meetings. At a special sub-committee on Post-War Development, 7 February 1945, Patrick Abercrombie was proposed as the ideal consultant.

22. EUA, DRT 95/002 box 142 VE, correspondence from Abercrombie to Fraser with recommendations, January 1946, and from Fraser to Holden requesting help, February 1946.

23. *The Scotsman*, 26 July 1946, 'University Precinct', with reference to a meeting at the City Chambers on 17 July 1946.

24. EUA, DRT 95/002 box 142 VE, correspondence between Holden and the University Secretary.

25. ECA, minutes of the Lord Provost's Special Committee, 29 May 1947. Professors Gray, Sydney Smith and Oliver, together with the University Secretary, Mr Jardine Brown, accompanied Holden to the meeting.

26. (Edinburgh) *Evening Dispatch*, 26 July 1946.

27. (Edinburgh) *Evening Dispatch*, 29 May 1947.

28. *The Scotsman*, 3 June 1947.

29. EUA, DRT 95/002 box 142 VE, letter from Holden to the Post-War Development Committee, 31 May 1947.

30. Ibid., transcript of Pollock's speech, 18 July 1947.

31. Ibid., Holden's response to the objections of 18 July 1947.

32. As part of his city bypass proposals, Abercrombie suggested a dual carriageway extending through St Leonard's Street and the Pleasance, before bisecting the Old Town at Blackfriars Street and then in a tunnel through Calton Hill. One of its interchanges would have been adjacent to High School Yards. See Patrick Abercrombie and Derek Plumstead, *A Civic Survey and Plan for Edinburgh*, London, 1949, plate XXIII.

33. NRS, SRO DD32/84, letter from the Edinburgh Georgian Society to the Secretary of State, 3 September 1955.

34. Patrick Abercrombie and Derek Plumstead, *A Civic Survey and Plan for Edinburgh*, London, 1949, pp.71–2 and plate XLIV.

35. Sir Lancelot Keay was Liverpool's City Architect at this time, previously Liverpool's Director of Housing. He was President of the Royal Institute of British Architects from 1946 to 1948.

36. EUA, DRT 95/002 box 143 VE, minutes of the Post-War Development Committee, 3 December 1948. Keay proposed Farquarson & McMorran, or Keppie, Henderson & Gleave as suitable candidates.

37. EUA, DRT 95/002 box 143 VE, minutes of the Post-War Development Committee, 10 February 1949. The committee met to consider architects for a competition by invitation. As well as Keay's nominees the work of the following architects was considered: Leslie Graham Thomson; William Kininmonth; John Needham; and Louis Soissons. The architect J.R. McKay questioned the legality of a competition since he had already provided a design for the Pathology Building in 1939, but it was held that this had now elapsed and his account was settled.

38. EUA, DRT 95/002 box 143 VE, letter from the Town Clerk to the University Secretary and minutes of a special meeting of the University Court, 12 January 1949. ECA, minutes of the Planning Committee, letter from the University Secretary, 26 January 1949.

39. EUA, DRT 95/002 box 143 VE, re-statement of the City's conditions for development of north George Square.

40. ECA, minutes of the Planning Committee, 3 February 1949.

41. Sir Edward Appleton, 'The University and the Community', speech at the Conference of University Lecturers and Vice-Chancellors, Cambridge, July 1955. Manuscript in EUA, box 151 VE.

42. Appleton was initially approached by the Lord Provost, Sir Andrew Murray, as prospective Principal, soon after the death of Sir John Fraser. However, after visiting Edinburgh he felt that the administration involved would preclude him undertaking any scientific research. He also thought that Abden House, which had been offered as a residence, was 'a slum'. But the University persisted and, following the appointment of the extremely able Charles Stewart, as Secretary, and a promise to refurbish Abden House, Sir Edward accepted the position. This information was supplied to Appleton's biographer by Lady

Appleton. See Ronald Clark, *Sir Edward Appleton*, Oxford, 1971.

43. EUA, DRT 95/002 box 143, the Post-War Development Committee memo of alternative developments.

44. EUA, DRT 95/002 box 143, extract from the minutes of the University Court, 19 December 1949.

45. ECA/DOGC, warrants for the Examination Halls: 6 April 1951; 18 May 1951; and 8 June 1951.

46. Representations were made by the Saltire Society, the Cockburn Association, the Old Edinburgh Club, the Royal Commission on the Ancient and Historical Monuments of Scotland, and a deputation of George Square residents, led by the architect, Robert Hurd.

47. EUA, DRT 95/002 box 144 VE, letter from the Town Clerk to the University, 7 February 1951.

48. A.G.R. Mackenzie's assessment in *Architect and Building News*, 9 February 1951. Messrs P. Neville Taylor and J. Holt and A.J.M. Tolhurst were awarded second and third prize respectively.

49. Building Industries, February 1951.

50. Basil Spence, quoted in *Architect and Building News*, 11 August 1955.

51. ECA, minutes of the Planning Committee, 13 July 1955.

52. Quoted in the brochure *University Development and George Square*, 1960.

53. ECA, minutes of the Planning Committee, 27 July 1955.

54. ECA, minutes of the Planning Committee, 22 February 1956. ECA/DOGC, warrant, 20 April 1956. An interim warrant for excavations and operations up to basement floor level was granted on 5 August 1955.

55. The Edinburgh Georgian Society was founded by Eleanor Robertson, the wife of Giles Robertson, Watson Gordon Professor of Fine Art at the University of Edinburgh.

56. NRS, Scottish Office file DD32/84, 'advice on the architecture of George Square'.

57. *The Scotsman*, 28 November 1959, review of General Council meeting.

58. University Court signed minutes, letter from Charles Stewart, 14 December 1959.

59. Secretary of State, draft parliamentary statement, 8 December 1959 (copy). Letter from Hurd to the National Trust for Scotland, doubting the sincerity of the University, 25 January 1960, HES, National Record of the Historic Environment, Hurd Rolland Archive, HR 14/8.

60. NRS, Secretary of State file DD12/2724, the alternative scheme.

61. Glendinning Collection, Robert Matthew University file, minutes and reports of the George Square Working Group (7/1/60 – 11/2/60).

62. *The Scotsman*, 14 March 1960, Appleton's press statement.

63. NRS, Scottish Office file DD 32/84, 'advice on the architecture of George Square'.

64. NRS, Secretary of State's file HH 041/01836, correspondence between John Maclay and the Earl of Wemyss.

65. ECA/DOGC, warrants for the demolitions at 47–51 George Square, 26–29 Buccleuch Place and 40–56 Windmill Place were granted on 25 March 1960. Detailed plans for the Arts Tower, at Windmill Lane, were submitted on 10 March 1960, with a letter of approval on 28 March 1960. Consent for excavations and foundations at 47–51 George Square was granted on 16 September 1960.

66. University of Edinburgh Appeal, April 1959.

67. Chaplain's Report, minutes of the University Court, vol. XXII, June 1956.

68. When Charles and Marie Stewart were invited to dine with Basil and Joan Spence in November 1956, the architect was extremely excited about the Chapel project, and never gave up hope of eventually having it built. Marie Stewart interviewed by Clive B. Fenton.

69. EUA, DRT 95/007 (microfilm), Chapel Appeal Committee 1956–7. Spence attended meetings of the committee on the 10 October and 30 October 1957, with his Edinburgh partner, Hardie Glover, who would have been responsible for executing the building, attending the latter meeting. Glover also attended a meeting of the Pollock Trust Development Committee on 26 February 1957. Pollock did not attend any of these meetings but, according to a memorandum written by Appleton, they met privately to discuss the matter.

70. The bequest of Sir James Erskine of Torrie was made in 1824. It consists of paintings, bronzes and marbles. The collection was received by the University after the death of Sir James's brother, in 1836, and was loaned to the Royal Institution. The bulk of the collection was brought back to the University in 1954, and it was felt that Adam House might be an appropriate place to display it. However, there were doubts about security and of the authenticity of some of the works. See Duncan Macmillan, *The Torrie Collection* (exhibition catalogue), Edinburgh, 1983.

71. Rowand Anderson Partnership Archive, Adam House file, drawings EN/28.

72. The rear part of the building was actually a converted tenement that survived from Brown Square, which had preceded the creation of Chambers Street. The 1937 scheme entailed the replacement of this part, while the 1927 building at the front was to be internally reorganised. The older building to the rear survived until the 1990s when it was demolished to make way for the new Sheriff Court. Consent for the post-war scheme was sought in 1948, and in 1952 there was a deviation to amend the entrance design. Rowan Anderson Partnership Archive, Job BS 'Dental Hospital'.

73. An engraving of Chambers Street, about 1880, in *Grant's Old and New Edinburgh*, shows this building in its original form.

74. ECA/DOGC, Chambers Street, Church of Scotland Education Committee, 1878.

75. ECA/DOGC, 16 Chambers Street, 29 October 1962.

76. EUA, DRT 95/007, minutes of the Major Buildings Committee, 23 September 1958.

77. John 'Archie' Dewar, furniture specialist with Basil Spence & Partners, interviewed by Clive B. Fenton.

78. Leonard Rosoman was known as a war artist and for his work at the South Bank, for the 1951 Festival of Britain. He taught at Edinburgh College of Art from 1948 to 1956.

79. *Architectural Review*, May 1960, pp.333–6.

80. Information from Marie Stewart.

81. Mistaken address and attribution to William Kininmonth, and wrong date of 1967 for staff club in HES listing text. Also there is a mistake about the fire in the building.

82. City of Edinburgh Council, 15/01930/LBC (Listed Building Application), April 2015.

83. Edward Appleton, *Science and the Nation: The BBC Reith Lectures for 1956*, Edinburgh, 1957.

84. EUA, DRT 95/002 box 153, 'Pollock Trust', letter from Pollock to Appleton, 16 May 1953.

85. After an initial approach from the University, the city had proposed rezoning at 75 persons per acre, but this would have theoretically allowed the city to acquire 5 acres of the site for housing 7000 at 140 per acre.

86. EUA, DRT 95/002 pt.1 box 147, precognition of Charles H. Stewart, *Report of Public Local Inquiry March-April 1954*, vol.VI.

87. EUA, DRT 95/002 pt. 1, box 147, letter from Appleton to the Lord Provost, January 1954.

88. EUA, DRT 95/007 box 28, Halls of Residence – Salisbury Green 1943–54, letter from Kininmonth to Colonel Hardie, 19 June 1954.

89. University Grants Committee, Report of the Sub-Committee on Halls of Residence, London, 1957.

90. EUA, DRT 95/002 box 135, Appleton's intimation to this effect is recorded in the minutes of the Pollock Trust Development Committee, 4 June 1954.

91. EUA, University Court minutes, vol. XXII, May 1956.

92. ECA/DOGC warrants Dalkeith Road/Salisbury Green: 2 September 1956 (interim); 26 October 1956; and 7 December 1956. Phase two warrants dated 6 July 1962 and 8 February 1963.

93. Joyce M. Wallace, *Historic Houses of Edinburgh*, Edinburgh, 1987.

94. Sir Daniel Wilson, *William Nelson. A Memoir*, Edinburgh, 1889. Wilson claims that the Salisbury Green was bought in 1770 as a dwelling, possibly a dower house, for Lady Dick-Cunningham.

95. The change of name may have been inspired by George Forrest's *An Account of the History and Antiquities of St Leonard's, its Chapel and Hospital* published in London in 1865. The ruins of St Leonard's having been destroyed in 1854.

96. Information from the Dictionary of Scottish Architects (www.scottisharchitects.org.uk), which also states that the design of Abden House was exhibited at the Royal Scottish Academy in 1855.

97. EUA, box 138 VE, Pollock Trust Properties. Abden was leased to the American Consulate and occupied by a Mr Nasmith, who intended to vacate in November 1946 (memo of 4 June 1954).

98. Appleton was unimpressed with the condition of the house when he visited Edinburgh in 1948, prior to his appointment as Principal. William Kininmonth was personally charged with renovating the property. Kininmonth's drawings for this are in the Ian G. Lindsay Collection, HES, National Record of the Historic Environment, IGL 1940/1/1, DP 142067.

99. Stockholm City Hall (1923), by Ragnar Ostberg, was much admired by British architects of Kininmonth's generation.

100. ECA/DOGC warrant: West Mains Road, Agriculture Research Council, 18 March 1949.

101. ECA/DOGC warrant: West Mains Road, laboratory block, University Department of Works, 18 December 1959.

102. ECA/DOGC warrants were granted for West Mains Road: 8 August 1947, Animal Research Department; 16 November 1955, laboratory; 6 September 1957, Animal House; 30 May 1958, Chemistry Extension; and 25 July 1958, one-storey building.

103. 'King's Building Site Development. Report on Redevelopment and Service', Rowand Anderson, Kininmonth & Paul, consulting engineers, Steensen, Varming & Mulcahey, January 1961.

104. The Agricultural College had received consent for a new building designed by T.P. Marwick, on the site of nos 14 and 15, in 1913, but this was shelved because of the First World War. ECA/DOGC, George Square, 12 June 1913. The agreement to give up the George Square site was to allow the University's Medical Extension Building, designed by J.R. McKay, which was shelved in 1940 because of the Second World War.

105. Reiach had some experience of King's Buildings, having worked for Lorimer & Matthew in the 1930s. Subsequently, he undertook a number of commissions for the University, in his own right. Cowan's career was primarily academic and he became Professor and Head of Architecture and Town Planning. His architectural works are few, but include the Architecture Building at Edinburgh College of Art (1962).

106. *Architectural Design*, 6 June 1952, pp.169–70 and *The Architects' Journal*, 26 July 1961, pp.126–7. George A. Macnab and (Alexander Thomas) and Lawrie Nisbet are credited as architectural staff in *The Architects' Journal*.

107. *Building Scotland: A Cautionary Guide* by Alan Reiach and Robert Hurd was published in 1943, by the Saltire Society, as a sort of primer for post-war reconstruction, with a foreword by Thomas Johnston, Secretary of State for Scotland. A second edition, in 1944, was expanded to include more housing and public works.

108. *Architectural Design*, January 1962, p.19. *The Builder*, 20 January 1961, p.100–4.

109. G.A. Macnab is credited as partner in charge, with J.R. Oberlander as senior architect, *Architectural Design*, January 1962, p.40.

110. *The Builder*, 1 April 1960, p.654.

111. *Concrete Quarterly* 61, April–June 1964, p.16.

112. *The Builder*, 26 June 1964, p.1373.

113. HES, National Record of the Historic Environment, Alan Reiach Collection, has drawings for proposed developments dating from 1956 to 1964. A partial photographic survey of Reiach's buildings was carried out by the Royal Commission on the Ancient and Historic Monuments of Scotland, prior to demolition in 2011.

CHAPTER SEVEN
PAGES 179–205

1. ECA/DOGC warrants: 25 March 1960, demolitions at 47–51 George Square, 26–9 Buccleuch Place and 40–56 Windmill Lane; 16 September 1960, excavations and foundations at 47–51 George Square; 29 December 1961, Windmill Lane, erect first section of new Arts Faculty Buildings, interim warrant of 29 December 1961, final warrant of 16 September 1962. Detailed plans for the latter were submitted on 10 March 1960.

2. The Forbes Chair of Architecture was ratified in 1948, when an agreement was reached between the University and Edinburgh College of Art that the Professor should occupy the then vacant headship of the School of Architecture and that architecture students should take academic courses at the University, in accordance with ordinances of the Royal Institute of British Architects. R. Gordon Brown was the first Forbes Professor of Architecture; however his tenure proved unsuccessful, with a high failure rate amongst students for the new MA degree and he resigned from the post in 1950. In May 1952, Appleton wrote to Robert Matthew inviting him to apply for the chair. Matthew tendered his resignation from Edinburgh College of Art in September 1954, and the arrangement between Edinburgh College of Art and the University was terminated in December 1956. EUA, DRT 95/002 pt. 1 'Architecture' file, special committee on the future of Architecture. EUL Special Collections, Robert Matthew Papers MS 2533 'Personal'.

3. Matthew was appointed consultant to the Edinburgh Research Institute in 1956, and by 1960 had a scheme for the gradual replacement of all its buildings on the existing, and adjacent sites. Only a small portion of this was achieved, and the subsequent decision to remove the infirmary to a new suburban site at Little France led to the ultimate redundancy of the Medical School at Teviot Place and George Square.

4. EUA, DRT 95/007, minutes of a special meeting of the Major Buildings Committee, 5 December 1960.

5. EUA, DRT 98/005 box 1: letters from Charles Stewart to Basil Spence, 22 December 1960 and 4 January 1961 and from Spence to Stewart,

30 December 1960; and minutes of the University Development Committee, 13 January 1961. Johnson-Marshall was appointed on 13 January 1961.

6. *Concrete Quarterly* 61, April–June 1964, pp.14–16.

7. Information from Alex McIver (Rowand, Anderson, Kininmonth & Paul) interviewed by Clive B. Fenton. ECA/DOGC warrant of 26 January 1962.

8. Kininmonth had been asked to design an extension, on the site of the fives court, as early as 1948 and proposed a stone building to match the original Union. After the property was transferred to the University, McRoberts designed a cheaper, and faster, alternative.

9. University of Edinburgh Comprehensive Development Area Report, June 1962, by Percy Johnson-Marshall.

10. University of Edinburgh Comprehensive Development Area, June 1962 (second edition, 1964).

11. In Johnson-Marshall's initial report, of 1962, two companies, Messrs Cotton & Clore and Murrayfield Real Estate, were cited as participants, but by 1963 the former appears to have withdrawn.

12. 'CDA Plans Hang Fire', in *University of Edinburgh Bulletin*, vol.8, no.1, October 1971, pp.1–5.

13. The redevelopment of St James Square for commercial purposes undermined the University Comprehensive Development Area, as both the private developer and the city saw this as a more immediate possibility, given the level of indecision about Edinburgh's proposed new roads schemes through the South Side, and the difficulties about providing alternative accommodation for both businesses and residents.

14. ECA/DOGC warrants for demolition: 29 September 1967, nos 35–49 Potterrow and nos 7–21 Bristo Street; 13 September 1968, no. 15 Potterrow; 5 December 1969, nos 2–12 Lothian Street; and 12 November 1971, nos 1–6 Bristo Street and nos 14–56 Lothian Street.

15. *Architectural Design*, January 1962, p.35; *Concrete Quarterly*, April–June 1964, pp.14–16; *Architectural Review*, June 1968, p.440; Miles Glendinning (ed.) *Rebuilding Scotland: The Postwar Vision 1945–75*, Edinburgh, 1997, pp.165–7; and Miles Glendinning, Ranald MacInnes and Aonghus MacKechnie, *History of Scottish Architecture from the Renaissance to the Present Day*, Edinburgh, 1996, p.447.

16. *Architects' Journal*, vol.234, issue 19, 12 August 2011, pp.36–40.

17. *Architects' Journal*, November 1967, p.1169; *Concrete Quarterly*, April–June

1964; and *Architectural Design*, January 1962, p.40.

18. J.H. Glover, *Edinburgh University Library*, Edinburgh, 1968; P. Willis, *A New Architecture in Scotland*, Edinburgh, 1977, pp.12–13; *Architectural Review*, June 1968, p.440; and *Architects' Journal*, June 1968, pp.1391–404.

19. *Architects' Journal*, 23 August 2013.

20. *Architect and Building News*, 9 February 1951, pp.165–7 and Clive B. Fenton, 'A Century of Change in George Square, 1876–1976' in *Book of the Old Edinburgh Club*, New Series, vol.5, Edinburgh 2002, pp.35–81.

21. The Royal College of Surgeons acquired the redundant Pleasance Church at Roxburgh Place and the adjacent church hall at Hill Square and had these demolished in 1940.

22. Rowand Anderson, Kininmonth & Paul 'Report on Pfizer Foundation and Post-graduate School of Medicine', 16 November 1960. Rowand Anderson Partnership Archive.

23. EUA, DRT 95/002 pt.2, Pfizer Foundation file.

24. ECA/DOGC warrants: 16 November 1962, Hill Square; and 30 April 1965, 5 Roxburgh Place.

25. Geddes's University Hall, at 2 Mound Place, was opened in 1887. By 1896, 120 residents were living in self-governing halls, in a variety of buildings in the Old Town, under the auspices of the Town and Gown Association.

26. In a lecture given to the Town and Gown Association in 1960, Matthew expressed his hope that the University would be associated with bringing the Outlook Tower 'back to life' as a centre for discussion on 'the urgent town planning problems of today', published in the *University of Edinburgh Journal*, 1961/2.

27. David M. Walker, 'Listing in Scotland: Origins, Survey and Resurvey', in *Transactions of the Ancient Monuments Society*, vol.38, 1994.

28. EUA, DRT 95/007 box 56, bundle no.2: record of Ian Lindsay's appointment; estimates of accommodation and costs; report of negotiations with Edinburgh Corporation over acquisition; and minutes of the Major Buildings Committee, 9 June 1961. It was agreed that the University would provide £70,000, while anticipating £56,000 from the Historic Buildings Council.

29. The Ragged School was only acquired by the University in 1972. It was given listed status in 1972 and sold in 1982.

30. Ian Lindsay & Partners, 'New College: Report on the accommodation requirements 1966. University of Edinburgh

Mound/Lawnmarket Development Area 1970' (appeal brochure).

31. Residents included what Reid referred to as 'the University contingent'. He wrote to the factorial secretary R. Maxwell Young expressing his frustration and pleading for the Principal to put a stop to their activities, letter of 16 May 1969 in EUA, DRT 95/007 box 30.

32. Philip Henman offered £100,000 towards the restoration of the north wing as a residence for postgraduate students.

33. Schemes to rehabilitate Sempill's Close, for five flats, and another 71 undergraduate places at nos 3 and 7 James Court, were initially approved in 1969, EUA, DRT 95/007 pt.1 box 30, Halls of Residence.

34. The University Grants Committee provided £23,000; the Historic Buildings Council £17,000; and the University and Russell family £41,000. EUA, DRT 95/007, minutes of the Major Buildings Committee, 12 January 1965.

35. R. Gardner-Medwin, 'Halls of Residence Report', London, 1961.

36. 'A Visit to Sweden and Denmark', in *Concrete Quarterly*, October–December, 1959.

37. Alex McIver (formerly of Rowand Anderson, Kininmonth & Paul), interviewed by Clive B. Fenton in October 2000.

38. ECA/DOGC warrants: 8 February 1963 and 12 March 1963, Dalkeith Road, Warden's House. This is a three-bedroomed house, in brick, with a flat roof, by Rowand Anderson, Kininmonth & Paul. The drawings are dated May 1961.

39. ECA/DOGC warrants: 18 November 1964, Dalkeith Road, 3rd development preliminary works; and 29 January 1965, accommodation for students.

40. ECA/DOGC warrants: 12 February 1965, Dalkeith Road, demolish buildings; 6 August 1965, demolish buildings; and 1 October 1965, erect boilerhouse.

41. ECA/DOGC warrant: 11 October 1968, Dalkeith Road.

42. Professor John McIntyre, Professor of Divinity, Principal of New College (1968–74), and Acting Principal of the University (1973–4 and 1979).

43. 'King's Buildings Site Development. A Report on Redevelopment and Services', Rowand Anderson, Kininmonth & Paul, January 1961. 'King's Buildings Site. Interim report by the Planning Consultant', Percy Johnson-Marshall, 23 April 1964.

44. *Architect and Building News*, 6 October 1965, pp.625–9.

45. Information from Richard Cassidy and Archie Dewar (ex-Basil Spence &

Partners), interviewed by Clive B. Fenton, 8 June and 25 January 2005, respectively.

46. ECA/DOGC warrant: 4 December 1964, West Mains Road.

47. ECA/DOGC warrant: 26 February 1965, West Mains Road.

48. ECA/DOGC warrant: 18 December 1959, 'laboratory block', West Mains Road. Containing research rooms and laboratories, this simple structure with timber walls and a felt roof is now the John Murray Building, and has acquired a further extension.

49. The Architectural Research Unit, 'An Extension to the Department of Zoology Laboratories, University of Edinburgh. Report and Assessment', April 1968.

50. ECA/DOGC warrant: 16 August 1963, Mayfield Road.

51. 'King's Buildings Site. Interim report by the Planning Consultant', Percy Johnson-Marshall, 23 April 1964.

52. *Architects' Journal*, 6 May 2014.

53. ECA/DOGC warrants: 12 May 1967, Mayfield Road (Civil Engineering – wind tunnel and building physics laboratories); 25 October (Civil Engineering Concrete Laboratory); and 21 May 1969 (Micro-electronics).

54. ECA/DOGC, application of 24 June 1967, Mayfield Road.

CHAPTER EIGHT
PAGES 207–219

1. Colin Amery and Dan Cruickshank, *The Rape of Britain*, London, 1975, p.60.

2. Alistair Rowan, 'A Cuckoo in the Nest', in *Country Life*, 25 December 1969, pp.1702–4.

3. Unpublished manuscript by Charles H. Stewart, 'A Short History of the University of Edinburgh (1889–1979)', by courtesy of the late Marie Stewart.

4. The University Conservation Group was a sub-committee of the Central Area Development Committee. The original convenor was Professor Blackie. After Blackie's death in 1976, Alistair Rowan took over. Other committee members were Professor Barbier; D. Bowman; Andrew Fraser; M.S. Higgs; Professor Michaelson; and Percy Johnson-Marshall.

5. University of Edinburgh Bulletin, 9 December 1976.

6. ECA, DOGC, certificate of completion, 10–14 George Square, phase three of the Medical School, 10 June 1983.

7. The University Grants Committee made a commitment of £249,000, in 1971. Outline consent for the site at the corner of Roxburgh Street and East Adam Street, owned by the city, had been given, and Spence, Glover & Ferguson

were appointed. In 1973 the Merchant Company put the price at £1.5m, but the University Grants Committee would only provide £400,000. Later this sum increased to £480,000, but not until 1981. Part of the final cost was met by the transfer of the Craiglockhart Playing Field from the University to the Merchant Company.

8. ECA, DOGC warrants: 'George Watson's Building', 25 June 1976; 14 June 1978; 9 September 1977; 23 September 1977; 14 July 1978; 5 January 1979 (phase 2); and 4 January 1980 (phase 2 A)

9. Edinburgh University Bulletin, supplement, October 1978.

10. Edinburgh University Bulletin no.6, 1979.

11. James Morris interviewed by Clive B. Fenton in August 1998.

12. University of Edinburgh Student Amenity Centre 1967 (brochure prepared by Percy Johnson-Marshall).

13. ECA/DOGCs warrants: 29 September 1967, 7–21 Bristo Street 'demolish'; and 16 February 1968, erect Health Centre etc.

14. *The Student*, 30 October 1969, p.7.

15. ECA/DOGC warrants: 12 November 1971, 1–6 Bristo Street 'demolish'; and 3 April 1972, erect Student Amenity Centre.

16. C.H. Stewart, *The Past Hundred Years: The Buildings of the University of Edinburgh*, Edinburgh, 1973, p.35.

17. The Hope Park United Free Church (1867), by Peddie & Kinnear, was demolished in 1949.

18. ECA/DOGC warrants: 25 April 1969; and 17 February 1971 for Summerhall.

19. The sculpture, about 1830, was carved by A. Wallace. This was removed to the Easter Bush Veterinary Centre in 2003.

20. A perspective, dated 1967, is preserved in the Alan Reiach Collection at HES, National Record of the Historic Environment, AR25/3.

21. ECA/DOGC warrants: West Mains Road, 30 August 1968, erect boiler house; and 26 September 1969, refectory.

22. In 1999 consent was granted for a Science and Engineering Library to designs by Reiach & Hall (City of Edinburgh Council, planning application 99/00775). However, this was not built.

23. ECA/DOGC warrants: West Mains Road, 28 October 1966; 25 June 1971; 7 January 1972; 2 May 1973; 15 April 1977; 3 June 1977; and 1 July 1977. HES, National Record of the Historic Environment, Spence, Glover & Ferguson Collection, SGF 1960/14/38–68.

24. ECA/DOGC warrants: West Mains Road, 28 October 1966 (maths/physics form piling); 25 June 1971 (Regional

Computing Centre), 7 January 1972 (extend Physics Block); 2 May 1973 (physics extend); 15 April 1977 (erect Physics / Maths Building); 3 June 1977 (extend Physics / Maths building); and 1 July 1977 (alter Physics / Maths Building).

25. HES, National Record of the Historic Environment, Spence, Glover & Ferguson Collection, SGF 1960 / 14 / 12 / 8, drawing dated December 1971. Interestingly, the architects continued to work on designs for the building's 'block N' until September 1978.

26. An additional south wing, the Erskine Williamson Building (The Centre for Science at Extreme Conditions), designed by Hurd Rolland, was added in 2004, although in a different style and with an orange cladding.

27. Additional information from Coila Clyne and Archie Dewar, of Sir Basil Spence, Glover & Ferguson.

CHAPTER NINE
PAGES 221–256

1. RMJM Architects, *King's Buildings Planning Framework*, February 2009, p.6.

2. *Perspective* (Journal of the Royal Society of Ulster Architects), October 2016, pp.14–15.

3. *Royal Incorporation of Architects in Scotland: Review of Scottish Architecture* 1996, p134 and *Architects' Journal*, 6 March 1997, p.12.

4. See Austin-Smith:Lord Architects website: www.austinsmithlord.com / projects / noreen-and-kenneth-murray-library.

5. Information from FloWave TT website: www.flowavett.co.uk / the-facility / test.

6. *Architecture Today*, vol.285, May 2015, pp.22–7.

7. *Architecture Today*, vol.285, May 2015, p.24.

8. Information from HES listed building description.

9. For an institutional history of the College see Scott J. Lawrie, 'The Edinburgh College of Art (1904–1969): A Study in Institutional History', MPhil Dissertation, Heriot-Watt University, 1996.

10. Dawn Caswell McDowell, 'Drawings on the Past: The Edinburgh College of Art' in *Architectural Heritage*, vol.13, pp.132–3.

11. *Hansard*, House of Commons Debate 29 May 1963, vol.678, cc138–41W.

12. Dictionary of Scottish Architects (www.scottisharchitects.org.uk, search 'Central Fire Station').

13. *Building News*, 31 May 1907 p.753.

14. Dawn Caswell McDowell, 'Drawings on the Past: The Edinburgh College of Art' in *Architectural Heritage*, vol.13, pp.128–39.

15. Ravindra Dhir and Thomas Dyer (eds), *Concrete in the Service of Mankind: Concrete for environment enhancement and protection*, London, 1996, p.210.

16. *The Builder*, 11 November 1960, p.908; 28 April 1961, p.803; and 11 May 1962, p.974.

17. *Architects' Journal*, 4 January 1978, p.2.

18. HES, National Record of the Historic Environment, refs: WHS 27 / 1–3, 27 / 25–33 (drawings); WHS 27 / 34 (display board (1974); WHS 27 / 10–24 and 57 / 9 / 1–2 (photos); and DC 90470 (photo of perspective drawing).

19. William Bain, 'The Historical Perspective' in *Moray House and Professional Education* (ed. Gordon Kirk), Edinburgh, 1985, p.2.

20. *The Scotsman*, 16 October 1913, p.10

21. These were sold in the 1990s and do not form part of the legacy estate.

22. Michael Pearce, 'Moray House Edinburgh inventory 1631–46' [via www.academia.edu]; Joe Rock, 'Decorated room at Moray House' [via www.sites.google.com / site / joerocksresearch-pages]; and Paul Harding, 'Tracing the Path of the Mylne Family's Jupiter', unpublished conference paper [Scottish Renaissance Studies: A New Platform, Perth, 26–7 October 2013].

23. RCAHMS, *Edinburgh Inventory*, Edinburgh, 1951, p.175.

24. Malcolm and Hunter 1948, pp.15–16.

25. University of Edinburgh website, information compiled by Hugh Perfect, Honorary Archivist, Moray House Archive, and David Starsmeare, 2002–3 [www.ed.ac.uk / education / about-us / maps-estates-history / estates / history].

26. RCAHMS, *Edinburgh Inventory*, Edinburgh, 1951, p.175.

27. NRS, ref. CC8 / 8 / 56, testament of Williame Wallace, 1632. Michael Pearce's PhD thesis, 'Vanished Comforts', Dundee, 2015, Fig.9.2, sets out a possible arrangement of the 1st-floor rooms.

28. The construction date of the Balcony Room is likely to be about 1635–8. Pages added to the Inventory after 1631, but before 1638, describe the Balcony Room as 'new'. Paul Harding (see note 22 above) suggests plausibly at pp.22–4 that the street balcony is the work of John Mylne.

29. Joe Rock, 'Decorated room at Moray House' (see notes above). The quotation about Bruce is from Howard Colvin, *A Biographical Dictionary of British Architects* 1600–1840, London, 1978 edition, p.153.

30. Joe Rock, *Decorated room at Moray House* (see notes above).

31. HES, National Record of the Historic Environment, ref. EDD / 40 / 11–19 (copies of plans and sections of Moray House by Gordon & Dey Architects).

32. David MacGibbon and Thomas Ross, *The Castellated and Domestic Architecture of Scotland*, vol.2, Edinburgh, 1892, p.536.

33. Terms in quotation marks derived from the 1631–46 Inventory.

34. See Joe Rock's Research Pages for much of the detail relating to the decoration of the Cromwell Room.

35. See Joe Rock's Research Pages for further details. The principal sources for the decorative paintings are: Francois Perrier, *Icones et Segmenta Illustrium e Marmore Tabularum Que Romae adhuc extan*, Rome, 1645; the *Triumph of Bacchus and Ariadne* (1597–1608) by Annibale Carracci for the Palazzo Farnese in Rome; and Titian's *Worship of Venus* (1516–18), etched by Andrea Podestà.

36. Information courtesy of Joe Rock.

37. NLS, ref. ADV.MS.31.6.19, David Buchanan, *A Description of the Province of Edinburgh*, about 1654 (translation by Ian C. Cunningham from the original Latin via NLS website: [http:// maps.nls.uk / atlas / blaeu / browse / page / 157].

38. National Register of Archives, Moray Papers, ref. NRAS 217, box 5, no.5 (the 1631–46 Inventory). The orchard included several plum trees, cherry trees and a great apple tree. The inventory further mentions two summer houses or 'banketing houses', a mount, a bowling green, a bowling alley and a fountain. Information courtesy of Michael Pearce.

39. Joe Rock's Research Pages quote a letter regarding a garden gate from Sir William Bruce to the Earl of Moray of 17 September 1703.

40. *The Scotsman*, 21 October 1911, p.11.

41. *The Scotsman*, 26 May 1931, p.13.

42. *Building News*, 15 April 1881, p.434. The original drawings for the building are housed in the University of Edinburgh CRC, ref. GB / 237 / Coll-31 / EC.109.

43. Malcolm and Hunter 1948, p.23.

44. University of Edinburgh Annual Review 2003–4.

45. The complicated genesis of the Roslin Institute is set out at www.roslin.ed.ac.uk / about-roslin / history-of-the-institute.

46. Reiach & Hall Architects, Derek Carter Associates Landscape Architects, Easter Bush Framework, May 2008.

47. Oberlanders Architects, *Easter Bush Campus Masterplan*, 2012.

48. Page\Park Architects, The University of Edinburgh – Easter Bush Campus Appraisal, 2016. Oberlanders Architects, Wardell Armstrong, Easter Bush Public Realm Strategy, 2016.

49. *Edit* (alumni magazine), summer 1999, p.6.

50. *Dick Vet News*, spring 2000, pp.1–6.

51. *Dick Vet News*, winter 2011, p.5.

52. Information via www.worldarchitecturenews.com.

53. HDR Architects, Easter Bush Research Centre: Design Statement, May 2008.

54. *Architects' Journal*, 21 February 2011.

55. Oberlanders Architects, Roslin Phase 2a – Easter Bush Campus: Planning Application Design Statement, May 2012.

56. Oberlanders Architects, Roslin Phase 2b – Easter Bush Campus: Planning Application Design Statement, October 2012.

57. Atkins Glabal, Centre Building, Easter Bush Campus – Design and Access Statement, February 2014, p.2.

58. *Dick Vet News*, summer 2014, p.32.

59. Atkins Global, Planning Statement, 2014.

60. Royal Infirmary of Edinburgh NHS Trust, *The New Royal Infirmary of Edinburgh: Full Business Case*, Edinburgh, July 1997, p.6.

61. University of Edinburgh Annual Review 2006–7, p.23. *Financial Times*, 9 May 2007 [via www.ft.com].

62. 'Medicine for the Millennium' in University of Edinburgh Annual Report 1997–8.

63. Judy Ozkan, 'Centres of Excellence: Queen's Medical Research Institute, Edinburgh, Scotland' in *Circulation: European Perspectives in Cardiology*, (Journal of the American Heart Association) 15 April 2008, pp.85–7. HRH The Duke of Edinburgh opened the Imaging Centre on 29 October 2010.

64. University of Edinburgh Annual Review 2006–7, p.21 and *Architects' Journal*, 16 February 2012.

65. Luke Therman, associate at Sheppard Robson, quoted in *Urban Realm*, via www.urbanrealm.com / buildings / 664 / Scottish_Centre_for_Regenerative_Medicine.html.

66. *Architects' Journal*, 16 February 2012.

Index